Handbuilding Techniques

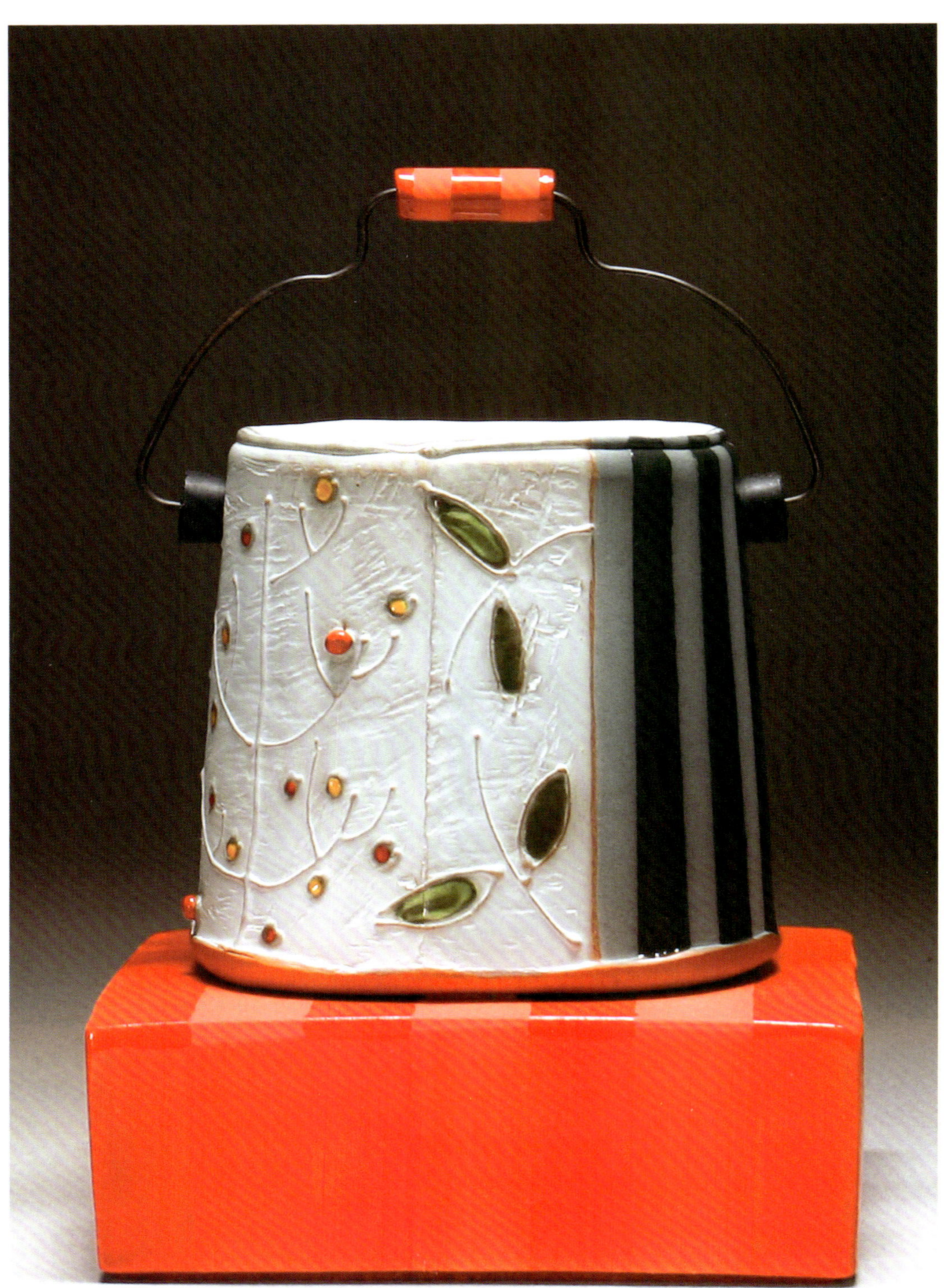

Ceramic
Arts
Handbook
Series

Handbuilding Techniques

Edited by Bill Jones
The American Ceramic Society
600 N. Cleveland Ave., Suite 210
Westerville, Ohio 43082
www.CeramicArtsDaily.org

The American Ceramic Society
600 N. Cleveland Ave., Suite 210
Westerville, OH 43082

ISBN: 978-1-57498-347-0 (Paperback)

ISBN: 978-1-57498-582-5 (PDF)

Publisher: Charles Spahr, Executive Director, The American Ceramic Society

Managing Director: Sherman Hall

Editor: Bill Jones

Graphic Production: Pamela S. Woodworth

Series Design: Melissa Bury

Cover Image: Slump-molded and handbuilt vase, porcelain, underglaze and glaze, fired in oxidation to cone 6, by Brenda Quinn.

Frontispiece: Floral and striped pail, handbuilt earthenware, slip-trailed patterns, terra sigillata, underglaze, glaze, wire, rubber, by Liz Zlot Summerfield.

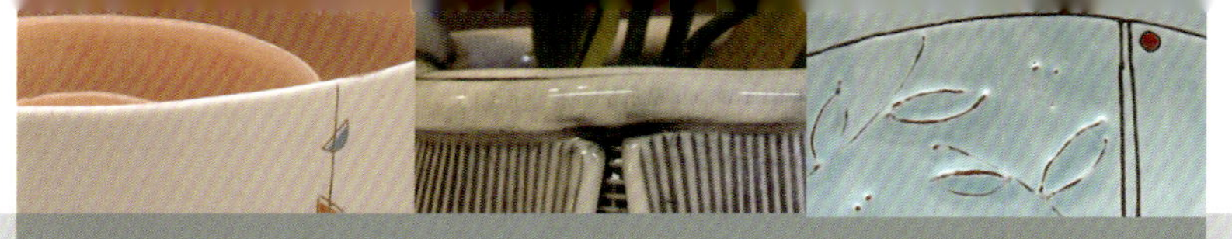

Table of Contents

1 Pinch & Coil Techniques

Pinched Coil Pitcher 1
Emily Schroeder Willis

Pinched Coil Vase 6
Cheryl Malone

Pinched Teapot 9
Ron Korczynski

Flat Coil Large Jars 13
Karen Terpstra

2 Plates & Platters

Footed Slab Plates 17
Liz Zlot Summerfield

Molded Plates 20
Amanda Wilton-Green

Plate Ring Supports 22
Russell Fouts

Adding Volume to a Rim 27
Mark Cole

3 Slab Construction

From Drawing to Clay 31
Liz Zlot Summerfield

Soft Slab Pitcher 36
Elizabeth Kendall

Building with Tarpaper 41
Jonathan Kaplan

Using Bisque-Molded Slabs 47
Nancy Zoller

Soft Slab Teapot 51
Margaret Bohls

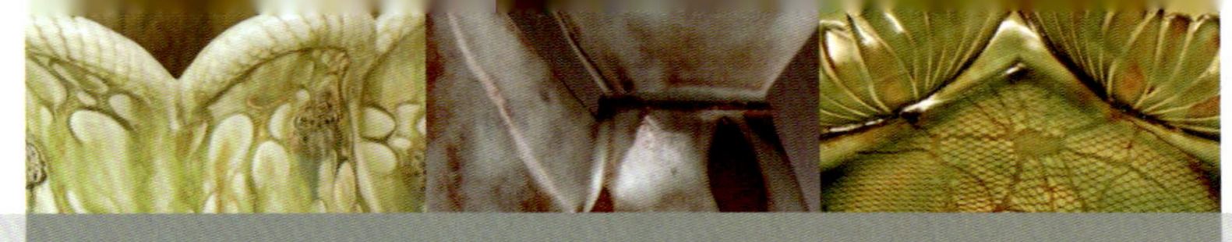

4 Using Templates

Form Templates for Accuracy and Strength 57
Jay Jensen

Tart Tin Nesting Bowls 60
Annie Chrietzberg

Creating Hexagonal Forms 65
Don Hall

Cups and Handles 68
Annie Chrietzberg

5 Using Molds

Kaleidoscope Covered Jars 75
Deborah Schwartzkopf

Vase with Slumped Sides 80
Brenda Quinn

Clover Dish with Slumped Bottom 84
Joe Singewald

Adding Volume to a Form 89
Ben Carter

Recycled Plastic Molds 92
WangLing Chou

Wood Block Molded Dish 95
Tom Quest

Handbuilding with Sprigs 99
Kate Maury

Shaping and Shaving 103
Shoko Teruyama

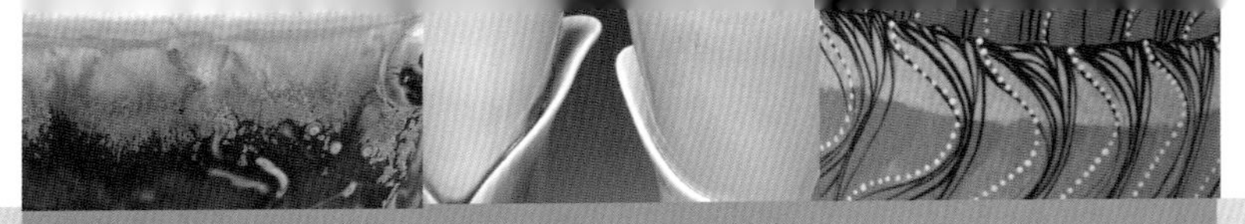

6 Advanced Techniques

Belly-Bottomed Dishes 107
Birdie Boone

Scalloped Flower Vase 112
Allison McGowan Hermans

Large Nesting Bowls 117
Courtney Murphy

Textured Flower Vase 121
Marion Peters Angelica

Calla Lily Wine Stems 126
Marion Peters Angelica

Utensil Handles 131
Kristin Pavelka

Preface

During the many years I was editor of *Pottery Making Illustrated*, we surveyed our readers on a regular basis, and one of the things that stood out in every survey was that handbuilding was by far one of the most sought after forming methods for our readers. Why is handbuilding so popular? Simple—it's suitable for any skill level, it requires minimal tools and resources, and the range of what one can create is up to one's own imagination.

Whether you're teaching, a recreational potter, or a full-time professional, you'll find there's no barrier to tackling any of the projects in this book. From a simple molded plate to a challenging soft slab teapot, every step-by-step project provides a way to be uniquely creative while honing your skills.

As for an investment in tools, you really don't need much to get started. The essential tools are as simple as a bag of clay, your hands and a work surface. When you look at what potters have used over the past 20,000 years, you'll soon realize that your most important resource is your desire to create.

Finally, the range of what you can create is limited only by your imagination. You can combine techniques for slabs, coils, molds, and textures to serve your creative needs; or select random tips to enhance your current handbuilding style. Some of the artists in this book spend their entire time making a wide range of forms and shapes using just a single technique.

Although I was trained in the Japanese wheel-throwing tradition, I've always enjoyed the pace and variety handbuilding has to offer. While the wheel provides a way to quickly and efficiently produce multiple round forms, handbuilding allows me to slow down and enjoy the whole clay experience in a much more relaxing way. In addition, I enjoy the ability to add textures and decoration at every step of the forming process from soft slab to leather hard.

Joe Singewald (see page 84) states "Every clay maker's artistic journey unfolds like a 'Choose Your Own Adventure' book. Decisions made along the way determine our creative path and personal work. Every studio we enter and all of the potters we meet have an impact on who we are as artists and what we create. The greatest part of this self-chosen adventure is the fact that our quest is never complete."

Through this book, I hope you'll discover many adventures of your own as you travel your creative path.

Bill Jones

PINCHED COIL PITCHER

by Emily Schroeder Willis

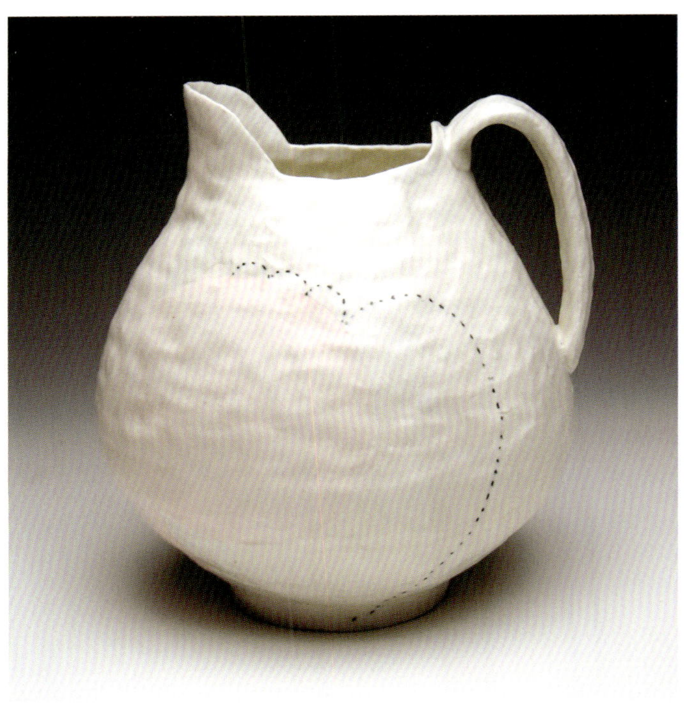

Drawing is a critical aspect of the ceramic process. The ceramic artist Greg Payce once said to me, "If you can't draw it, you can't make it." As someone who builds pots primarily by pinching clay, I see how important and true this statement is.

In many ways, making pots is drawing three dimensionally—creating a handle, a spout, or a profile of a pot, is like creating a line in space. Drawing on paper trains your eye to see more thoughtfully and be more critical of your work. I found that after sketching things like spouts and handles repeatedly, I saw a significant difference in the ease with which I could create them. The simple gesture of putting pencil on paper several times to get a form right made an immense impact, solidifying how my hands needed to move to create that element in my work when it was time to actually build it in clay. The other reason I now see the importance of sketching is that my hands and fingertips need to be in tune with the physical and/or mental image I'm creating. I use very few tools to shape my work. My fingers and my lap are my biggest tools and I sometimes even use the slack of my apron in my lap to help shape larger slabs that I'm pinching into a form. So, I always start with a drawing of the form, and I always have that image present when I'm making objects.

Process

I prefer to work with porcelain, finding the smoothness excellent for capturing each mark my fingertips impress into the clay. I love the fresh bright palette I achieve through glazing when I use porcelain.

To begin the form, I pinch out a small curved disk to use as the bottom to create a foot. To pinch a curved disk, start with a round ball of clay about the size of a plum, pushing your thumb into the middle of it, leaving about half of an inch of clay between your thumb and the outer wall (figure 1). Then, create the proper thickness by pressing a thumb

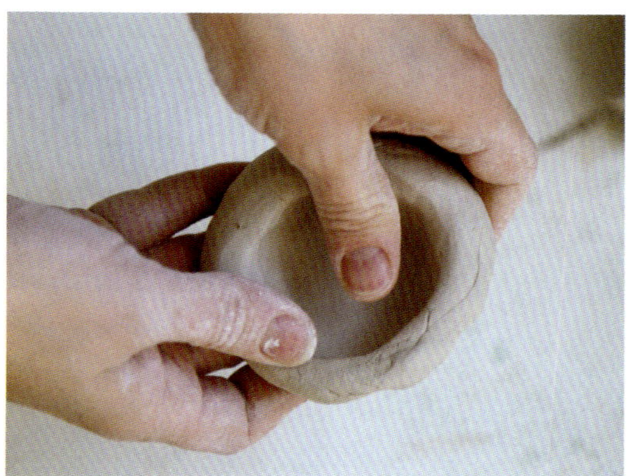

1. Press your thumb into the plum-sized ball of clay and rotate the ball as you thin the walls.

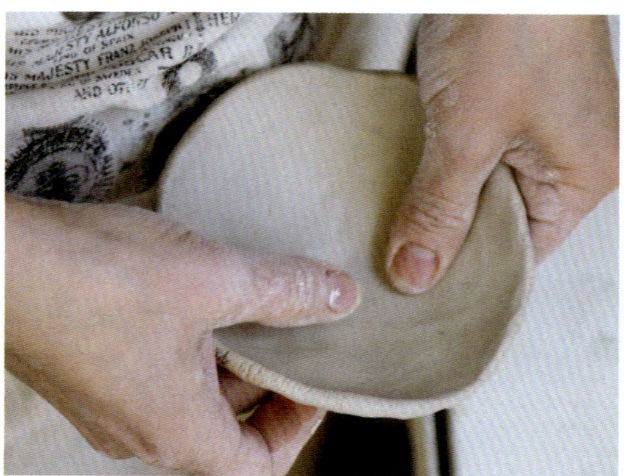

PROCESS PHOTOS: DARCY DEMMEL

2. Slowly work your thumbs to the outer edges of the pinch pot, until each are uniform in thickness.

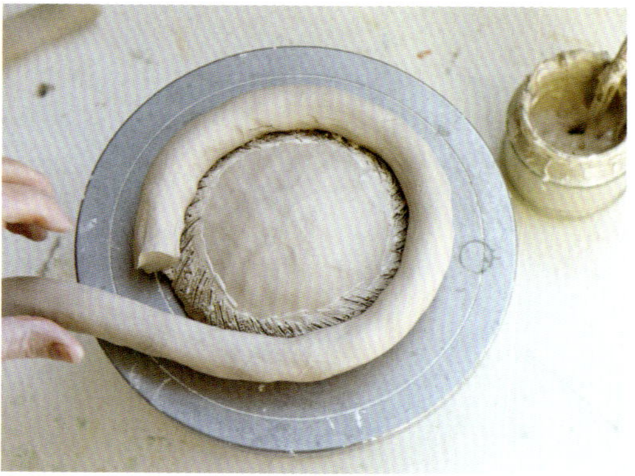

3. Lay a coil on top of the inverted pinch pot after scoring the attachment area and adding slip.

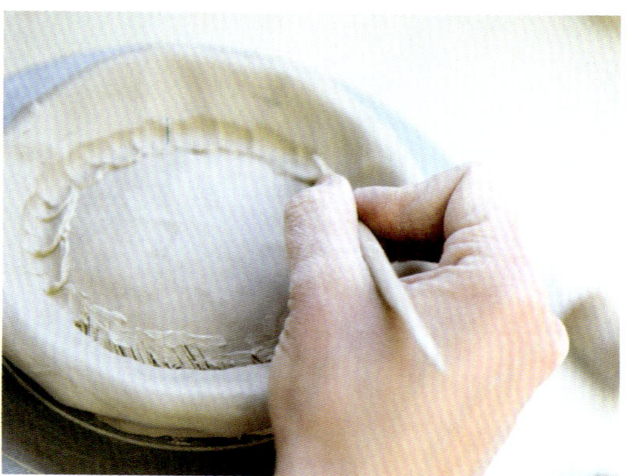

4. Cut the coil at an angle, join, then use a wooden modeling tool to connect the coil along the seam.

into the clay, proceeding to rotate the ball in small, ½-inch, counterclockwise increments, slowly working to the outside edges until each area is uniform in thickness (figure 2).

Creating Coils

I add thick coils to help shape and add height to the work. To make coils nice and round, start shaping the coil while wedging the clay. Begin wedging and slowly shift from wedging to rolling the clay into a 3-inch thick log shape. From there, pick up the log, squeezing and twisting it into a slightly thinner log, roughly 2 inches in diameter, which also helps to compress the clay further. Make sure it's uniform in thickness, then slowly start to roll out the coil, using your entire hand, held flat, rather than just your palms.

Gently but firmly apply even pressure onto the surface of the coil, keeping your hands as flat as possible, yet relaxed, gliding them over the surface, starting in the middle and working your way out to the ends. If at any time the coil starts to become uneven, simply pick it up, reshape it, and squeeze it into shape. Be careful not to let your coils get too thin—coils should always be thicker than the wall thickness you want on your work. This is the biggest misconception in creating coils. Some clay will be removed in the processes of attaching the coil and creating height. So, to achieve a wall that's ¼ inch thick and roughly 1½ inches high, use a coil that is approximately 1 inch thick.

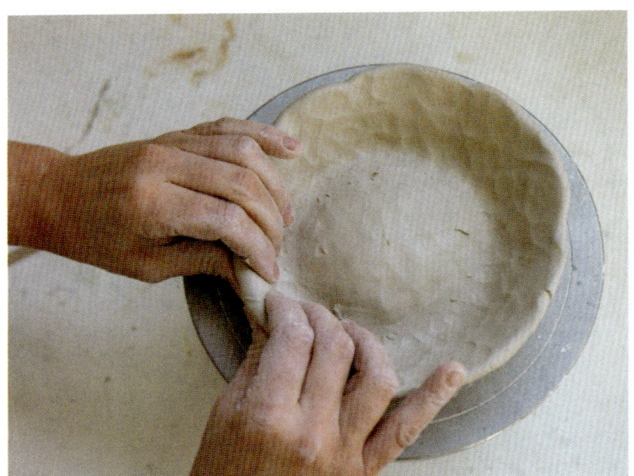

5. With thumbs on the exterior and index fingers inside, pinch the coil up to thin the walls and add height.

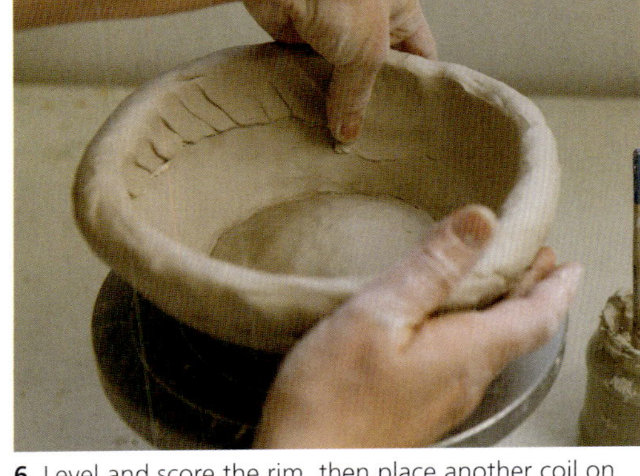

6. Level and score the rim, then place another coil on and join it using a crisscross motion with your thumb.

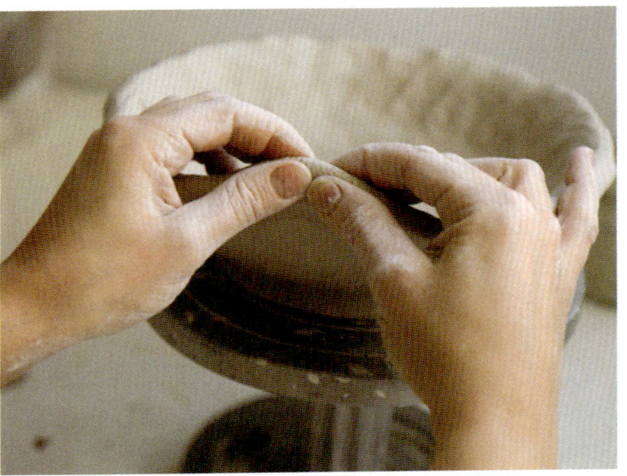

7. After joining the coil, use thumbs and index fingers to pinch the coil up, turning the pot as you work.

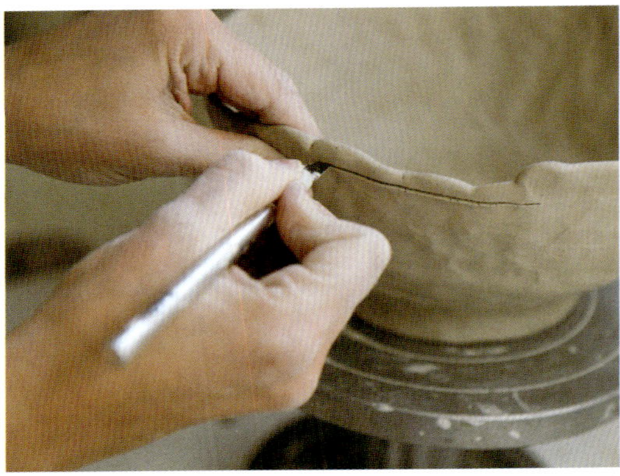

8. Trim the top edge of the pot before you add each coil to remove the driest clay and to keep the walls even.

Building the Form

Place the pinched base onto a banding wheel. Heavily score the base (I use a tool made from needles stuck into a wine cork), put a layer of slip on top of the base, and rescore the slip-coated area. Take a coil, lay it on top of the slip (figure 3) and cut each end at a 45° angle, pushing the ends together and smoothing them over. Then use a round- or straight-edged wooden modeling tool to attach the clay on the interior of the vessel (figure 4), slowly rotating the vessel with one hand and using your other hand as your working hand. Using an X, or crisscross, motion with your left thumb, push the clay down, starting at the top right, pushing down to the bottom left, and then lifting your thumb and pushing from the top left down to the bottom right (see figure 6). Repeat this motion around the entire vessel. Once the coil is properly attached, redefine the interior space with the wooden modeling tool.

Next, work on attaching the coil to the exterior using the same X motion on the exterior. After the coil is fully attached, flip the piece over and push out the bottom, which usually loses some of its shape when attaching the coil on the inside. Lastly, pinch the coil into its final shape so it fits the profile you want. I set my work on a taller banding wheel so I can see the profile of the vessel more easily. Place your hands in front of you with both thumbs on the exterior of the vessel and both index fingers on the interior of the vessel. You'll use both your thumbs and index fingers together to dictate the shape of the wall (figure 7). Pinch up, almost creating a subtle vertical or diagonal spine shape on the vessel every 4 inches around the cir-

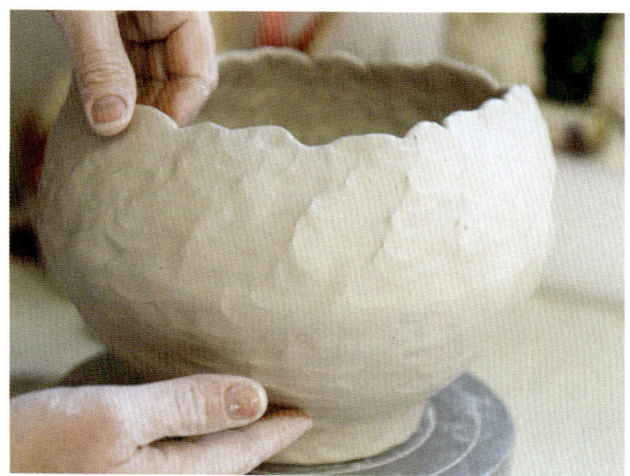

9. To taper the pot in, press your thumbs in against your fingers as you pinch the coil into shape.

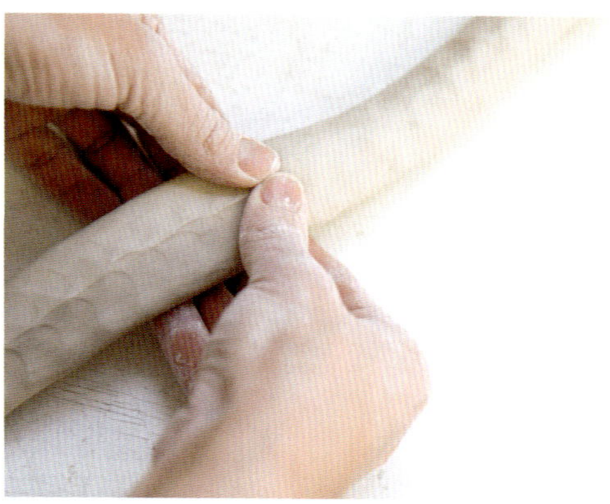

10. Create a handle by rolling out a coil, then pinch up along the length to flatten and create a spine.

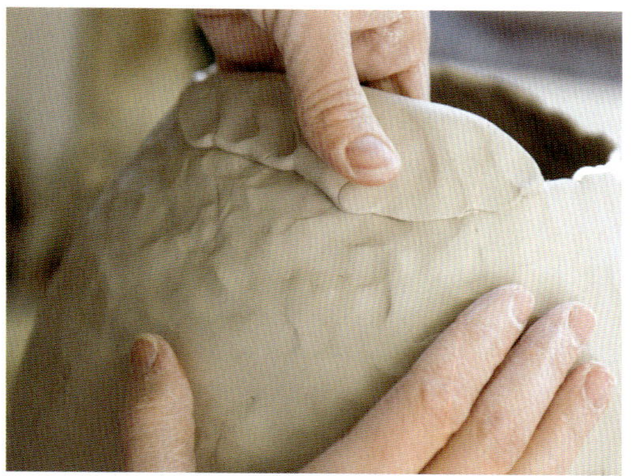

11. Create a spout by first rolling out a short, tapered coil, then score the rim of the pot, and add the coil.

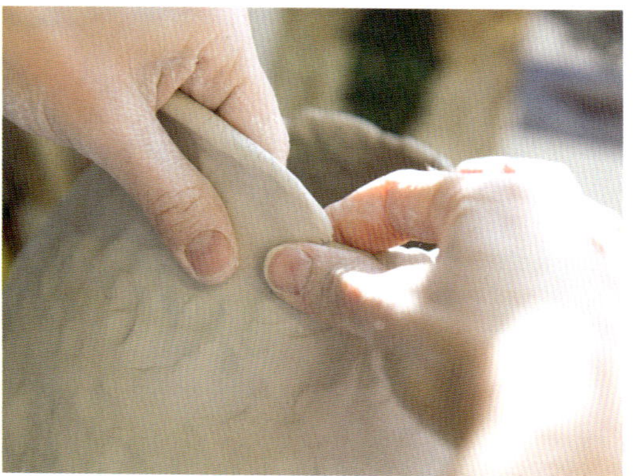

12. Gently shape an arch to the lip as you pinch the coil up to create the spout.

cumference, which you can later smooth over with your fingers. If you want the shape to roll outward, use more pressure on both index fingers and almost roll your thumbs backwards to create an arc in the form. If you want the form to curve in, your thumbs become more dominant and push the clay over both index fingers (see figure 9).

Adding Layers, Creating Form

The most important element in making pinched work is patience. It takes several days to create larger forms, so it's best to work on multiple pieces at once. To add another coil of clay, the work must be sufficiently dry, but slightly softer than leather hard. This can take anywhere from three hours to a whole day depending on the humidity/temperature/sunlight/air circulation in your work space. If you try adding a coil too early, it will be difficult to control the shape because the bottom can't support the weight and the pressure of the new coil. If you wait too long, the clay will be too dry to manipulate into shape. Make sure that everything is as close to the same level of dampness before adding more coils.

Before adding on more coils, trim off a thin layer of clay, leveling off the pot (figure 8). This removes the area that is usually drier than the rest of the vessel, creating a slightly more malleable area to add a coil to. Additionally, it allows the vessel's height to increase at the same rate all around. Add a layer of slip on the exposed edge and score it with a serrated rib. I use a serrated rib rather than the cork needle tool because the coil's edge is thin, and the serrated rib creates a finer scored area. Placing the coil on top, continue to attach the coil as in the first layer using the X motion with

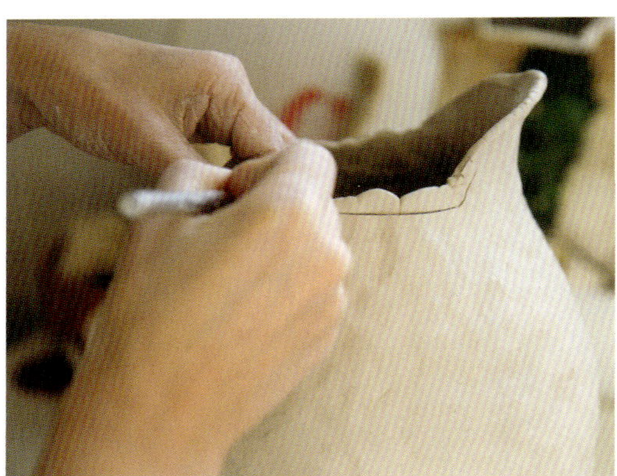

13. After shaping the spout, cut the lip down to the desired height and shape with an X-Acto knife.

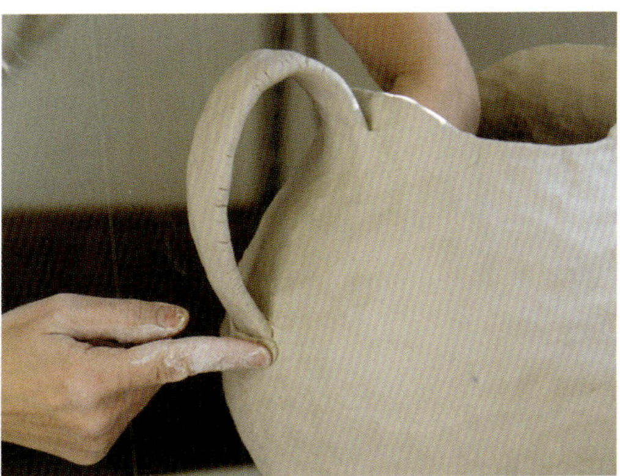

14. Cut the handle to length, thicken the ends, score and slip the attachment points, then attach.

your thumb (figure 6), then pinching up to gain height. When you are ready to add another coil, level the pot again using an X-Acto knife (figure 8) and then repeat the process.

Once the base of the vessel has been established, I find it easier to shape a vessel that is going to flare out by attaching the exterior of the added coil first, that way, while I'm smoothing out the interior coil, I can begin to push the shape out. As long as I work with soft clay, I don't have problems with cracking. If I want the vessel to curve in, I attach the added coil on the interior first and pinch up while applying more pressure with my thumbs on the exterior (figure 9). By smoothing out the exterior coil, I can begin to push the vessel in and not worry about ruining what I have just shaped. To dramatically bring something in, I really compress the clay as I'm pinching, almost as if I'm trying to squeeze it together. I find that if I overcompensate on flaring or constricting the form, it usually ends up spot on.

Making a Handle

Making a handle is very similar to making a coil. The thickness of the coil depends on the size of the object it will be attached to. Cups and pitchers require handles of different thicknesses. For a tall or medium-sized pitcher, make the coil about 1 inch in diameter. Start at the bottom of the coil and pinch up, creating a spine up the middle of the coil (figure 10). Then, place the coil between your thumb and forefinger, flattening out the coil a bit more. Cut the ends of the coil at a 45° angle, tapping the ends to thicken them, making them easier to attach later. Hold the handle up to the vessel, checking the proportions and cutting it down to size. Then, bend it into the desired curve and lay it on the table to dry sufficiently so you can attach it later without ruining the shape.

Creating a Spout

To create a spout, roll out a short coil that is tapered on each end. Score and slip the area where it will be attached and place the coil on the slipped area (figure 11). When attaching the coil, gently shape an arch into the rim and lip immediately (figure 12). Using a knife, cut the lip down to the desired height (figure 13), and shape and smooth it over with your fingers, creating a gradual and soft curve.

Finishing Up

Attach the handle by first placing a ruler across the top of the pitcher so that one edge bisects the spout and rests on the opposite rim. Mark the rim of the pitcher where the handle should be attached, then score and slip the top and bottom attachment points. Attach the top part of the handle first, then, making sure that the arc of the handle and its length are appropriate, recut the bottom of the handle and proceed to attach it (figure 14). Let the piece dry under plastic and slowly open the plastic up over a series of days until it's completely dry.

PINCHED COIL VASES

by Cheryl Malone

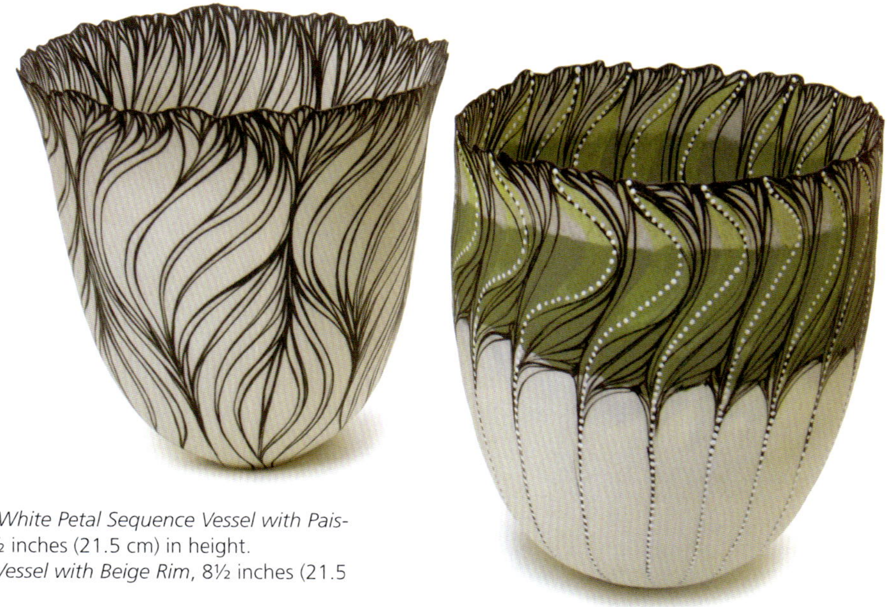

Left: *Black and White Petal Sequence Vessel with Paisley Centre II*, 8½ inches (21.5 cm) in height.
Right: *Foliated Vessel with Beige Rim*, 8½ inches (21.5 cm) in height.

Along with the exquisite diversity of the natural environment in which I live in South Africa, the analogies found between the coil-forming process and the growth patterns of plants continues to be my most important source of inspiration. Although I did not initially follow Fibonacci rhythms and phyllotaxies and logarithmic spirals, they all inform my work and the appreciation of the end result.

Deliberate Forming

The working process begins by continuously rotating and pinching while opening out a wedged 200-gram porcelain ball that fits into your palm. Be sure that the base remains thick enough to anchor the pinched form (figure 1). After pressing the pinched pot down on to a banding wheel, use a metal kidney rib to open out the form further and smooth the outside (figure 2). Additional coils are added and simultaneously pinched and folded onto the inside surface of the vessel (figure 3). Using the left hand to pinch the coil up and the right hand to fold it down, attach the coil to the exterior wall surface (figure 4). The wall surfaces are again smoothed and the vessel is pinched upwards with the thumb and forefinger using both hands simultaneously until the vessel gains height (figure 5) and the coil becomes integrated (figure 6). My intention here is to achieve an even wall thickness throughout the form and to unify the coils making up the piece. Again, use the metal kidney rib to smooth out the form. The more the walls are stretched and smoothed, the more translucent the final vessel will be. Each coiled layer should dry sufficiently (not quite to leather hard) but still be slightly plastic before the next coiling cycle begins. This allows the vessel to be strong enough to hold each successive layer.

I often work on two or more pieces simultaneously (figure 7). I choose to work on a form from

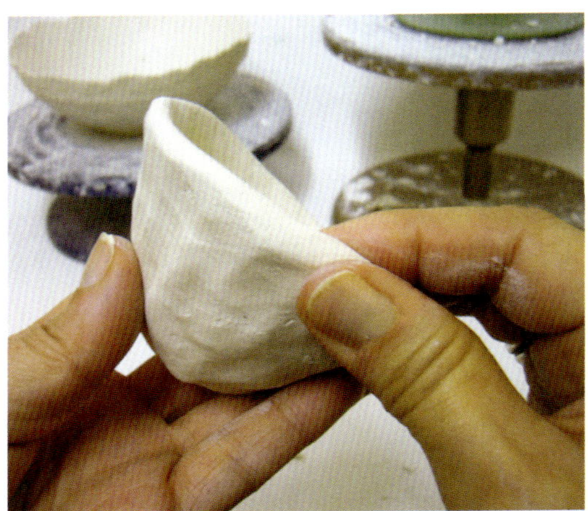

1. Begin by pinching a small pot from a ball of clay, rotating it while pinching to keep the walls even.

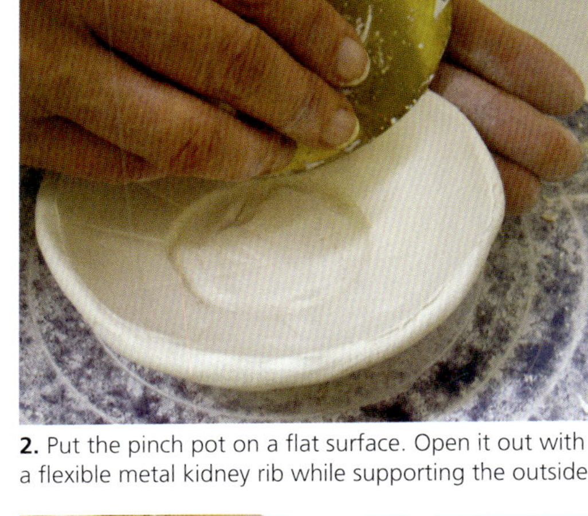

2. Put the pinch pot on a flat surface. Open it out with a flexible metal kidney rib while supporting the outside.

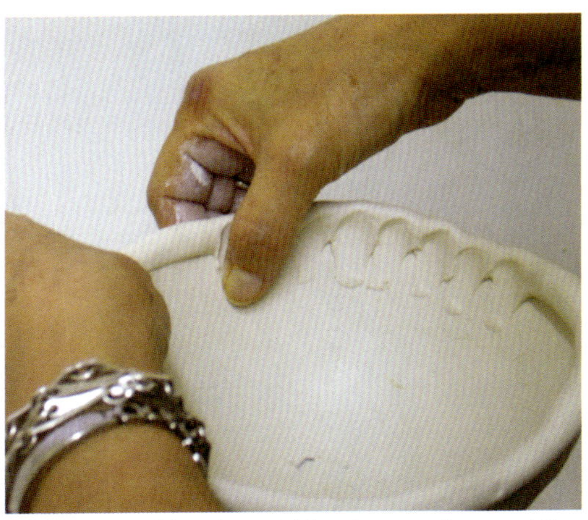

3. After smoothing the outside, place a coil around the rim then pinch and fold it to the inner wall.

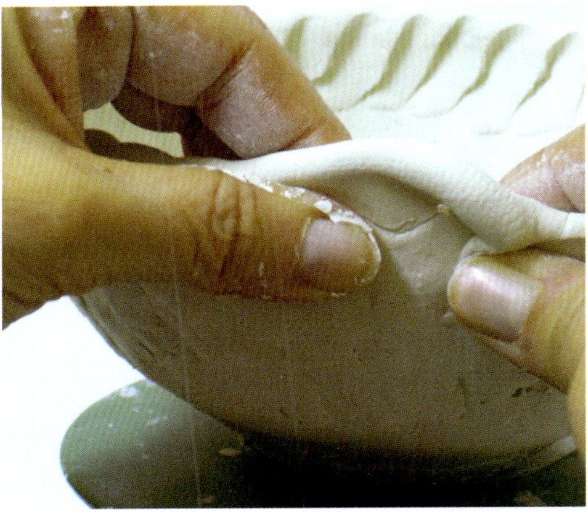

4. Use the left hand to pinch the coil up and the right hand to fold it down to the exterior wall surface.

my Petal Sequence Vessel series while also working on one from the Foliated Vessel series. Although each series is quite different, an interesting dialog and subtle resonance evolves between the vessels by working in this way, which would otherwise not occur.

Incorporating Colored Layers

The stratified colored layers (figures 7 and 8), are made visible by wedging dry measures of oxides (or commercial body stains) into the porcelain clay body prior to coiling. The color of the green band is achieved by adding a quarter teaspoon of chrome oxide and half a teaspoon of tin oxide to 400 grams of porcelain body. Wearing gloves and a mask, the two are wedged until fully integrated and plastic (makes about 4–5 coils). For the rim, 1/8 teaspoon of black iron oxide is wedged into 200 grams of porcelain body (makes 3 coils) The colored coils are added to the vessel and incorporated just like the previous porcelain coils were added. Keeping layers visible and separate takes practice and patience (figure 9). To remove unwanted smudges or fingerprints of colored clay from the white areas of the vessel, use a sharp metal kidney rib to scrape the colored clay off of the surface, then use the same rib or a rubber rib to smooth the surface. After the last coil is added,

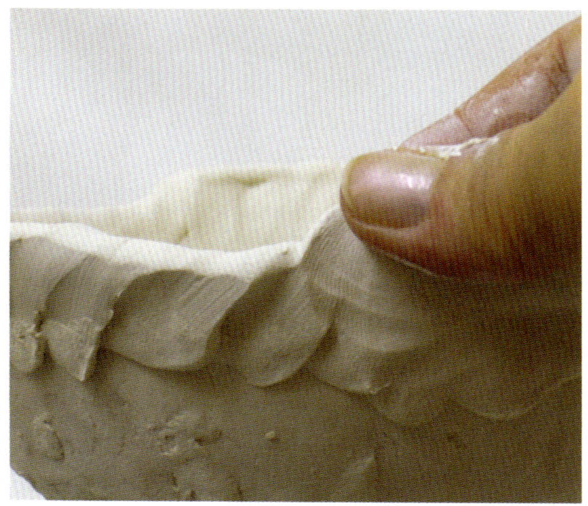

5. Pinch the coiled rim upward between your thumb and fingers to raise the height of the pot.

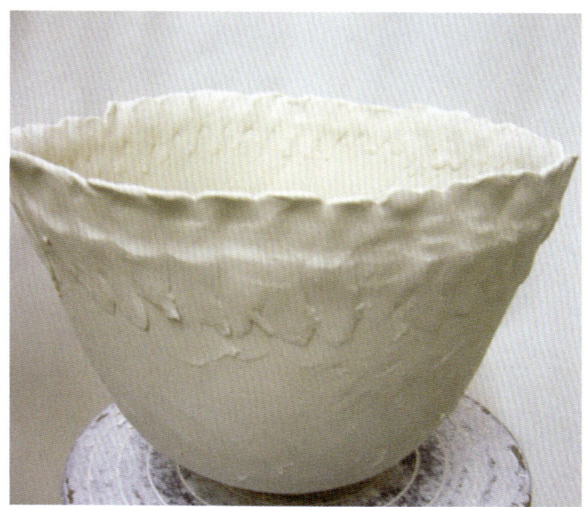

6. An integrated coil and raised rim. The wall should have an even thickness throughout.

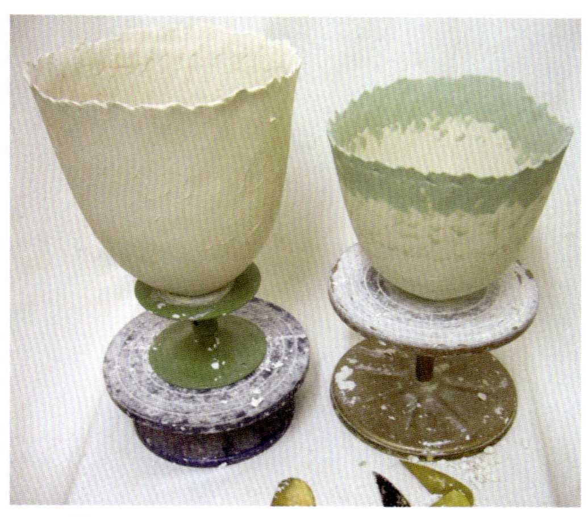

7. Building two or more pieces simultaneously, adding coils to one while the other stiffens up.

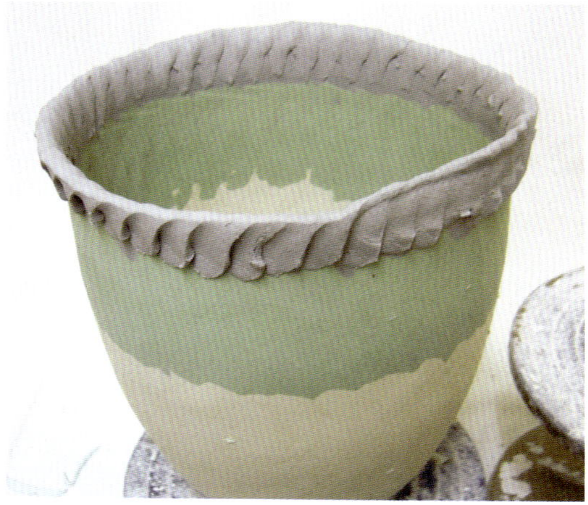

8. Add stratified layers of colored clay coils using the same technique.

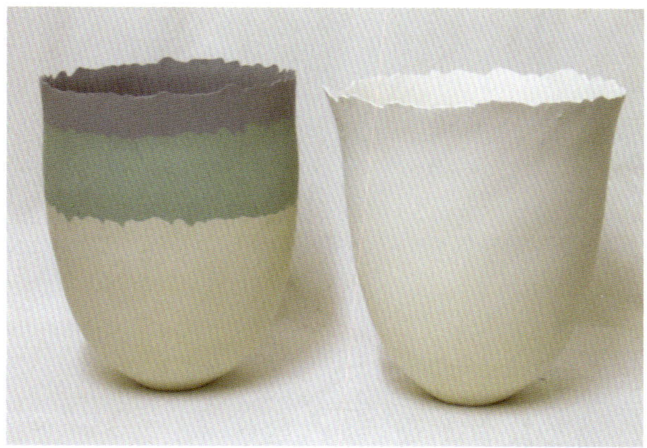

9. Blend the coils and leave an undulating rim, but smooth out any sharp edges.

smooth the rim to remove any sharp areas but leave the contour so it remains naturally undulating.

Finishing

With the building process complete, the pieces are left to completely dry. I then bisque fire the pieces to 1832°F (1000°C) in an electric kiln, after which the vessels are lightly sanded with silicon carbide sandpaper or fine sandpaper, to remove any roughness to make them ready for decorating and glazing.

1

Pinch & Coil Techniques

PINCHED TEAPOT

by Ron Korczynski

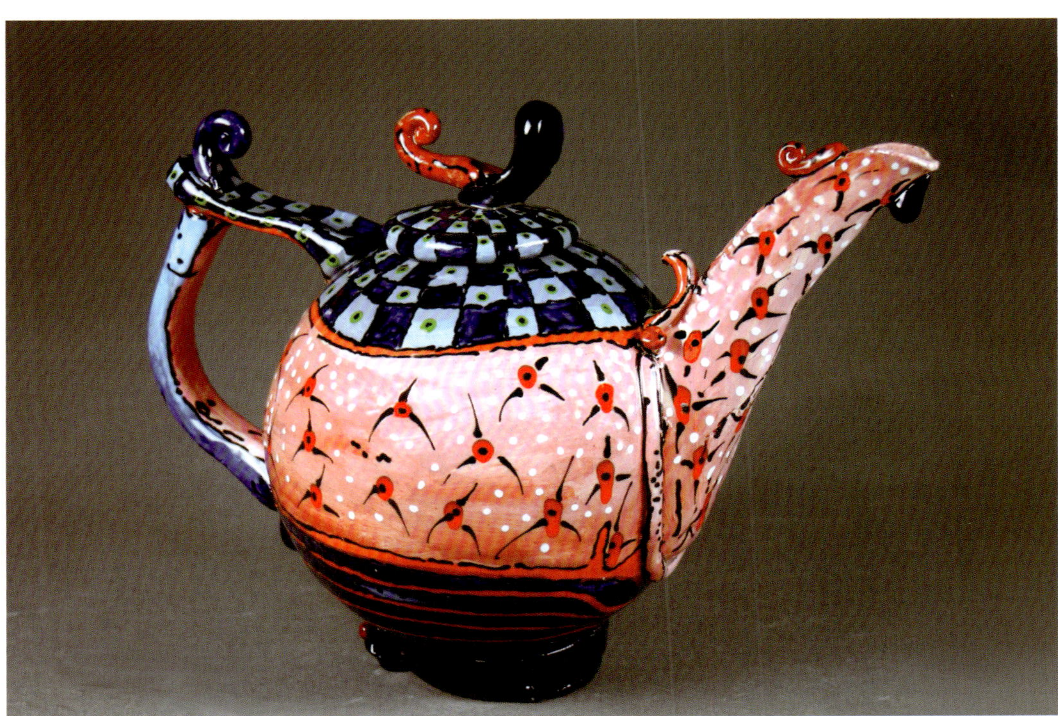

Teapots are one of the greatest challenges for any studio potter. Many elements go into their production and all the parts—the body, lid, handle and spout—need to fit together into a cohesive whole. For centuries, teapots have been produced in myriad ways and forms, and like many potters, I initially began making teapots on the wheel. But throwing and putting the parts together was a challenge for me because the forms were too mechanical so I began to experiment with handbuilding. Since I've done a lot of handbuilding using hump molds, this seemed the logical path to take. While the process here uses a spherical form, you'll soon recognize the endless possibilities with other shapes.

Getting Started

Each teapot begins with a slab draped over a plaster hump mold. I make these round plaster hump molds by taking a Styrofoam ball and cutting it in half. Styrofoam spheres are available in a variety of sizes from craft supply stores, and you'll need a 6-inch ball for a modest-sized teapot. Other forms can also work and I use the blue extruded Styrofoam board found at home centers to build up and carve molds. Once the shape is finalized, I glue it to a piece of wood or tempered hardboard that's been cut to shape (figure 1). Tip: You can finish the mold by propping it up and pouring plaster over the top. This gives you a thin, durable, absorbent layer that can be smoothed out when dry and makes a great lightweight mold.

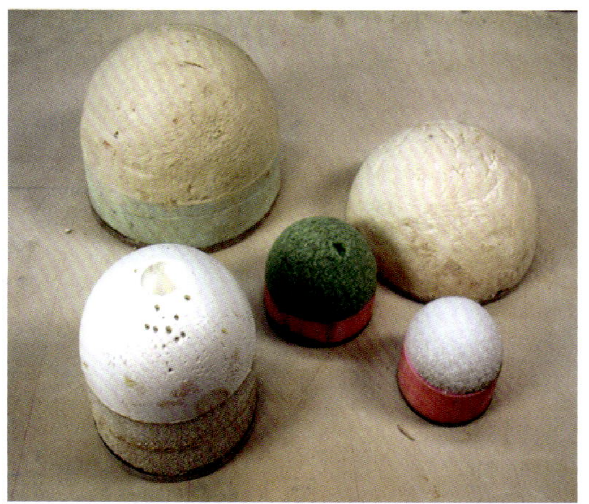
1. Make round plaster hump molds by taking a Styrofoam ball and cutting it in half.

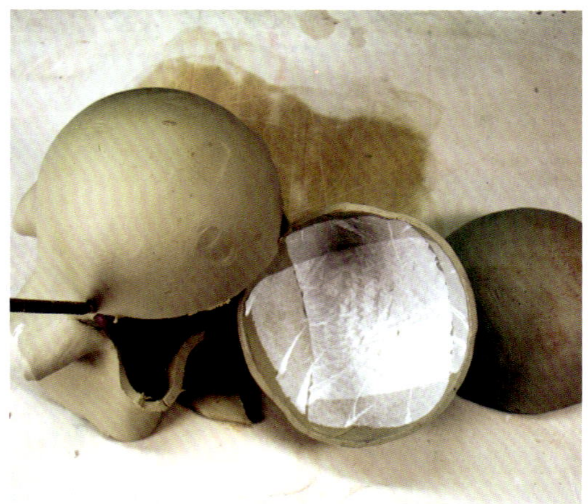
2. Apply toilet paper to the mold as a release and place a ¼-inch thick slab over it. Trim, remove and set aside.

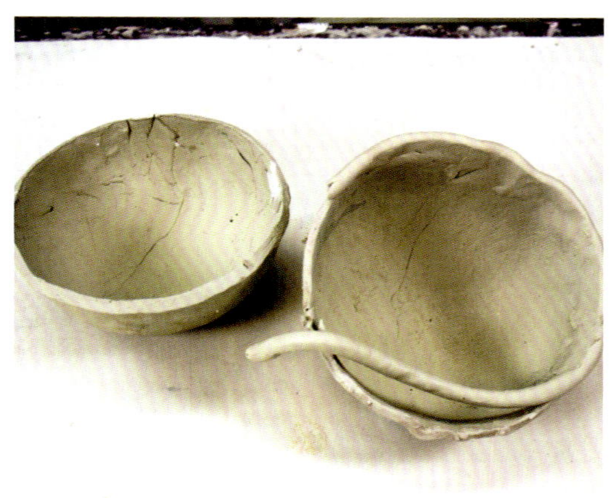
3. Make two hemispheres and allow to dry to leather-hard. Attach a coil to the edge of one hemisphere.

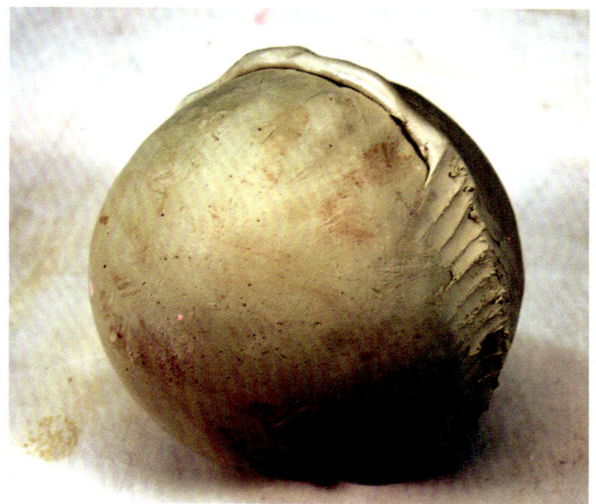
4. Attach the other hemisphere using your finger or tool to work the seam.

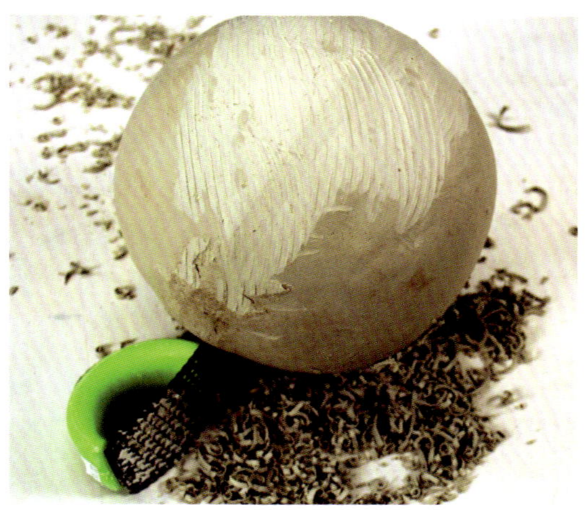
5. Use a Surform tool to refine the shape.

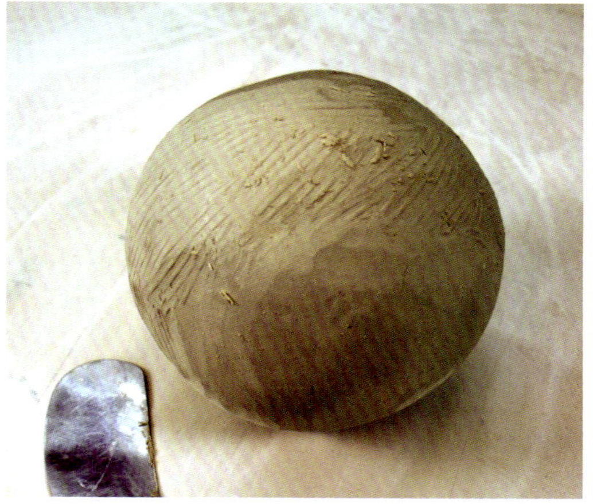
6. Use a metal rib to smooth the sphere or add different textures at this stage.

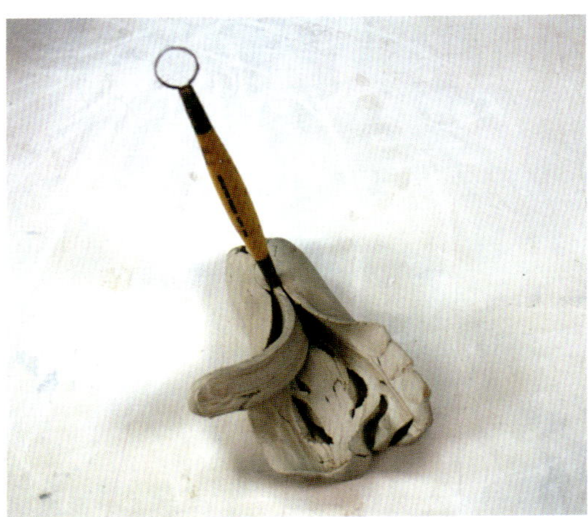

7. To create a base, use a triangular trimming tool to cut a strip from a block of clay.

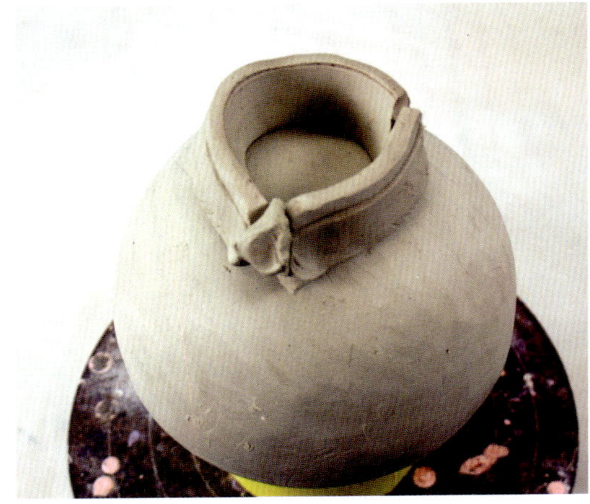

8. With the sphere resting on an empty container, attach the base and add decorative elements.

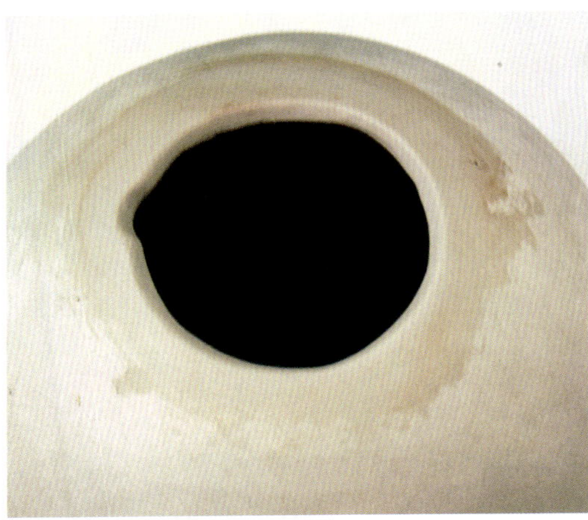

9. For the lid, cut a round opening in the top of the sphere and make a small notch in the opening.

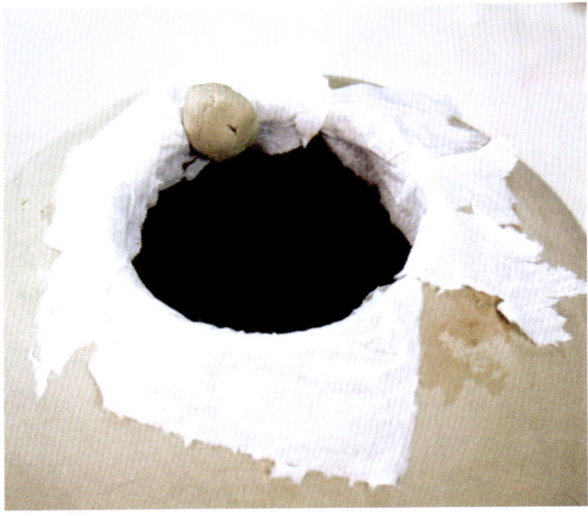

10. Place toilet paper around the edge of the opening as a separator. Place a small ball of clay in the notch.

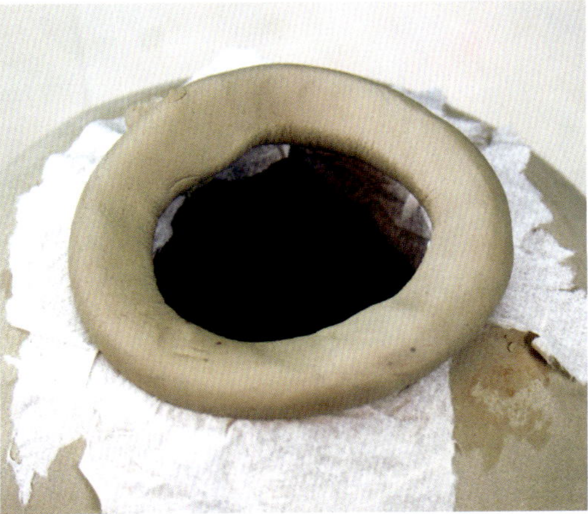

11. Add a coil of soft clay to fit into the lid opening so it slightly overlaps the opening.

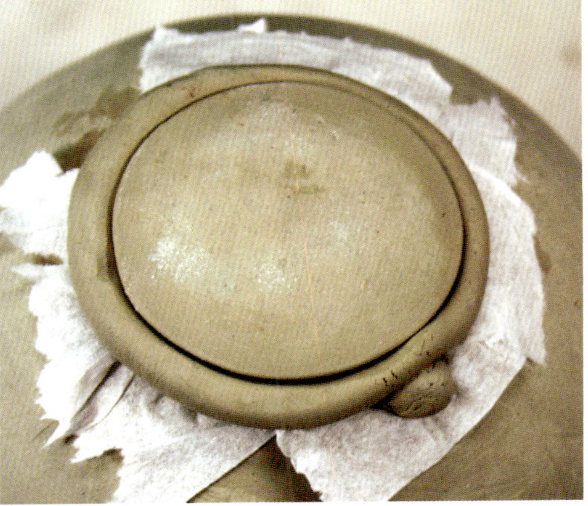

12. Take the clay piece you removed to make the opening and attach it to the coil.

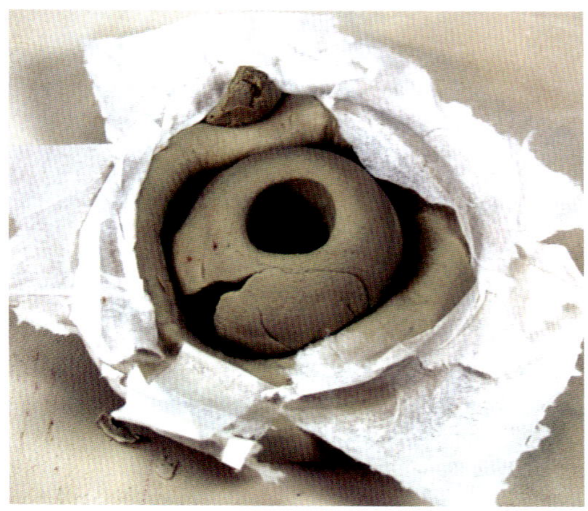

13. Flip the lid over and add a ball of clay to the underside to add weight and balance to help hold it in place.

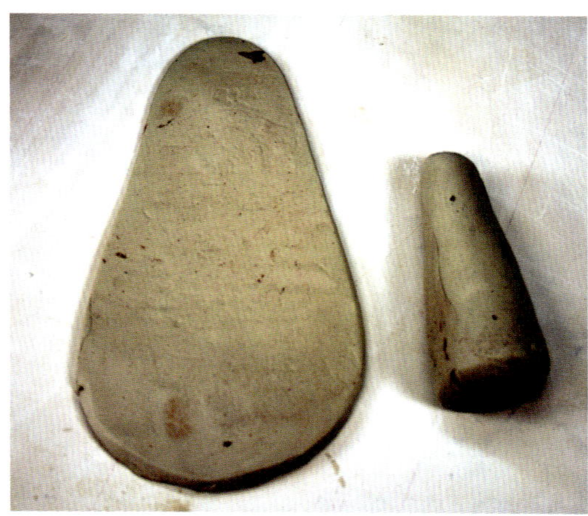

14. To form the spout, flatten a cone of clay.

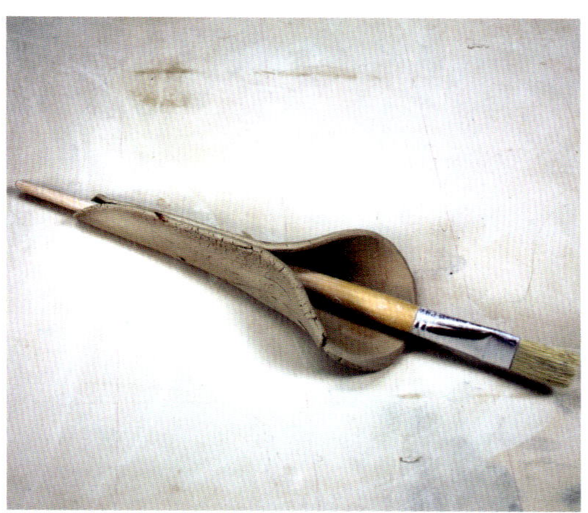

15. Form a spout around a brush handle.

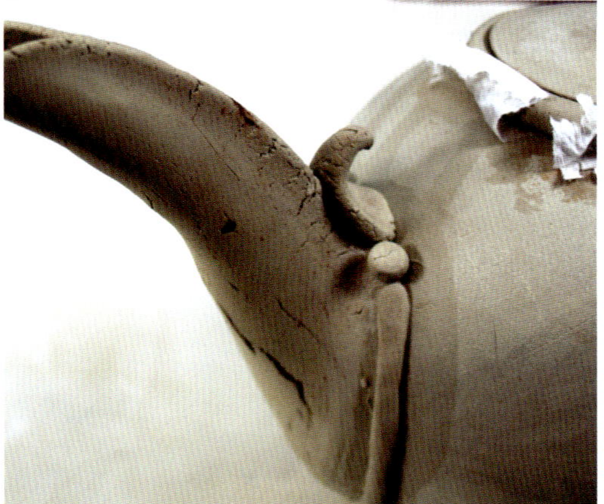

16. Trim the spout and attach it along with decorative elements to the teapot.

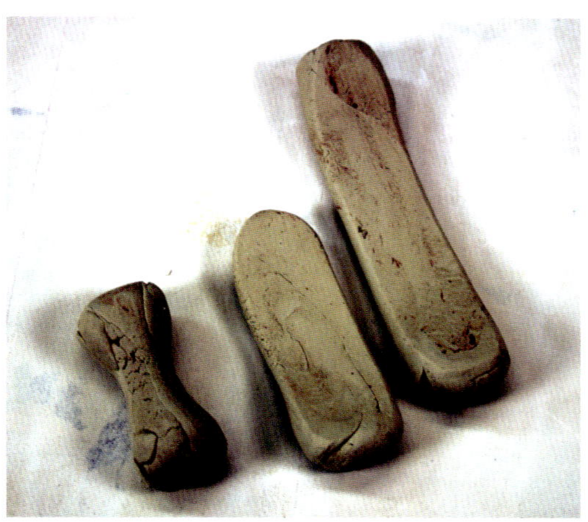

17. For the handle, make two "dog bone" shapes and flatten them, leaving some thickness at each end.

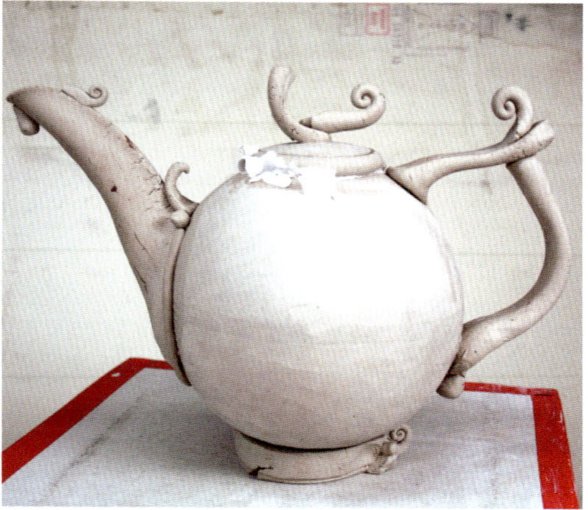

18. Assemble the handle and add a decorative element if desired. Add a handle to the lid in the same style.

FLAT COIL LARGE JARS

by Karen Terpstra

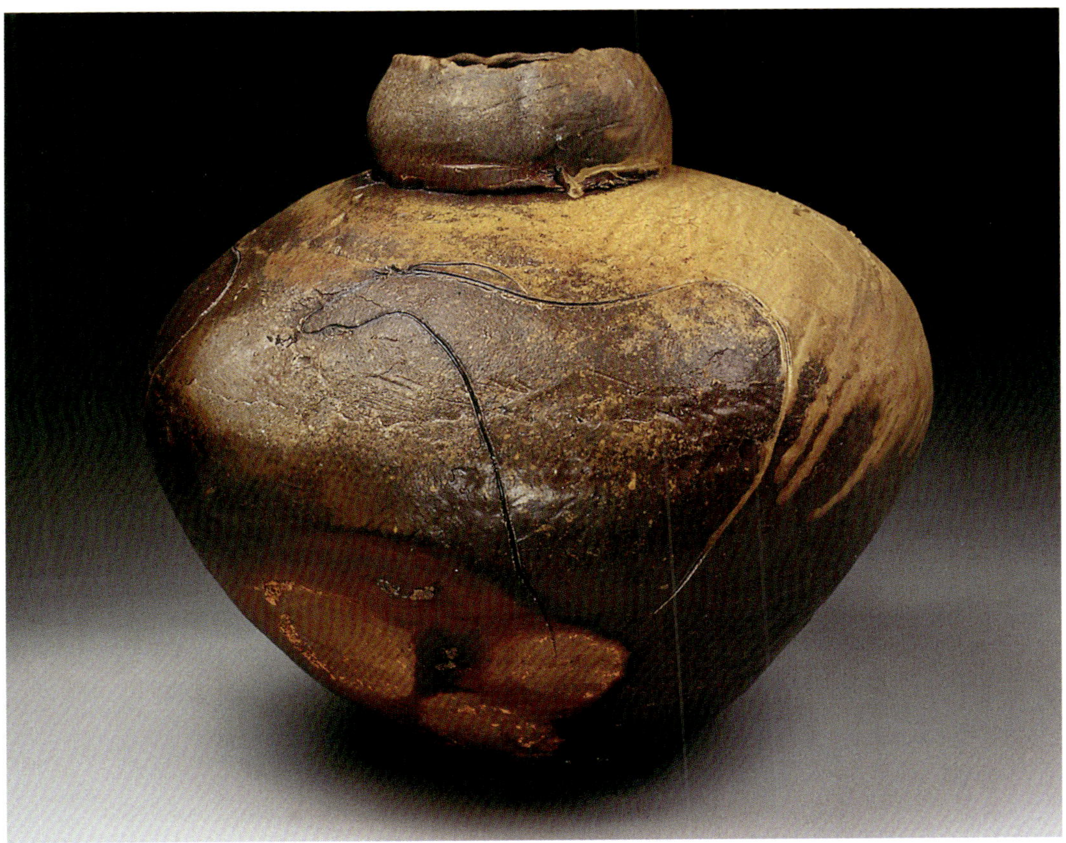

I came rather late to ceramics and my work focused on handbuilding with painterly images of the horse. As my process involved wood firing, I found the need for larger surface areas that would hold an image and be integrated with the flash and ash from the wood-fire process. Handbuilt jars that defy gravity in their form fulfill that need. Horse images with a spontaneous degree of abstraction have gradually developed from mental impressions of historical myths—others are in response to real horses I have known.

Making large jars with flat coils has been done for centuries in many parts of Asia and Southeast Asia. Master potters in Korea made thousands of flat-coiled storage jars—primarily used for kimchi, the national dish of Korea, which is comprised of pickled vegetables seasoned with garlic, red pepper and ginger. Once the basic method is learned, anyone can make large jars (or any size functional or sculptural object) with a flat coil method. I started learning with small jars and teapots, but now I make large jars that defy gravity and would normally collapse if wheel thrown. I also make many sculptural forms—horse heads, large full-body horses, torsos and columns—using this method.

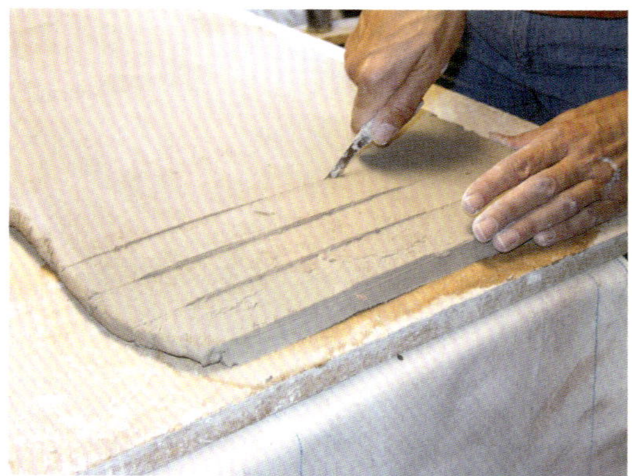

1. Cut a clay slab into flat coils about 2 inches wide for a large jar.

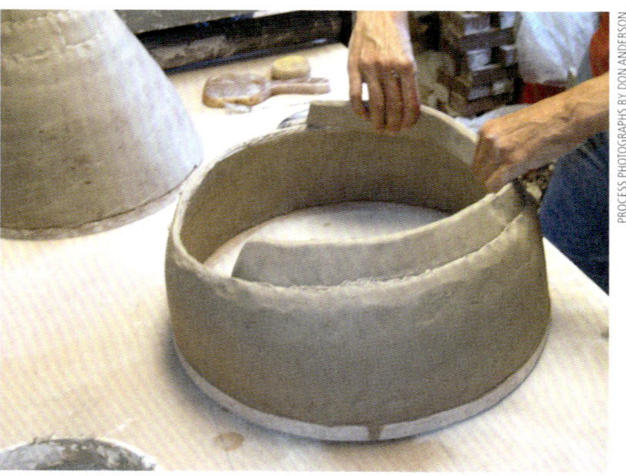

PROCESS PHOTOGRAPHS BY DON ANDERSON

2. Place the flat coil to the inside of the previous flat coil to make the diameter become smaller.

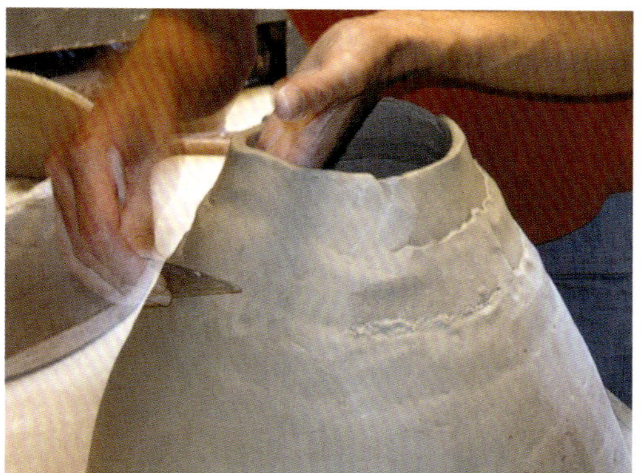

3. Smooth the seams inside and out while building.

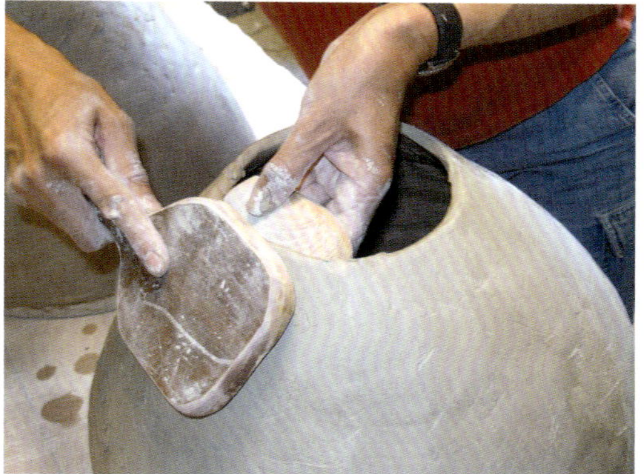

4. Use a paddle and a rounded piece of wood held on the inside of the pot.

As you can see from the photographs, one big advantage with this method is that you can change directions rather drastically by letting the flat coils become leather hard. Another advantage is the variety of sculptural forms you can make. This method also saves a lot of time by using 2-inch flat coils instead of small round coils.

It really save you time to work in a series. Build up three to six rows of coils on several ware boards at one time. By the time you're finished with the last one, the first one has set up so you can start again on that one.

Process

Roll the clay through the slab roller about $1/8$ to $1/4$ inch larger than your desired wall thickness. The walls will be thinner by the time you smooth and paddle the shape. Cut the clay into flat coils about 2 inches wide for a large jar (figure 1).

Slightly dampen the ware board or bat with a sponge for the first flat coil. Attach the flat coil firmly in place then secure another flat coil. Since you will be building the lower section of the jar upside down, place the flat coil to the inside of the previous flat coil. This makes the diameter become smaller with each row (figure 2). Also, put plastic on the inside of the jar to hold in the moisture. Smooth the seams inside and out while building (figure 3). Let the first few rows strengthen to leather hard so that they will hold the weight of additional coils. Once the lower portion is leather hard, keep it wrapped in plastic, so that it doesn't dry out as you continue to work. Once the lower portion of the jar is com-

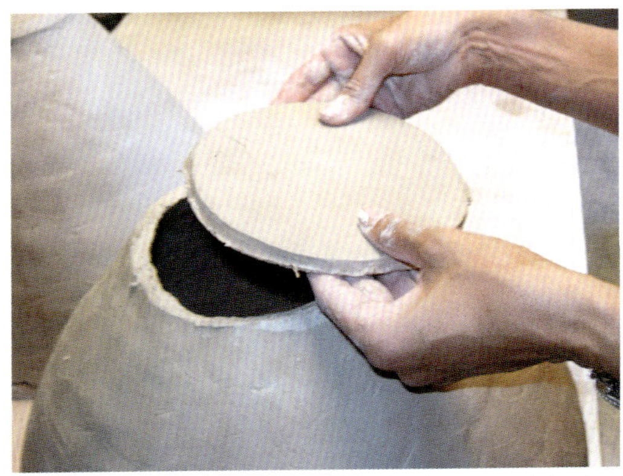

5. Cut out a circle from a slab for the bottom of the jar. Slip, score and attach the bottom.

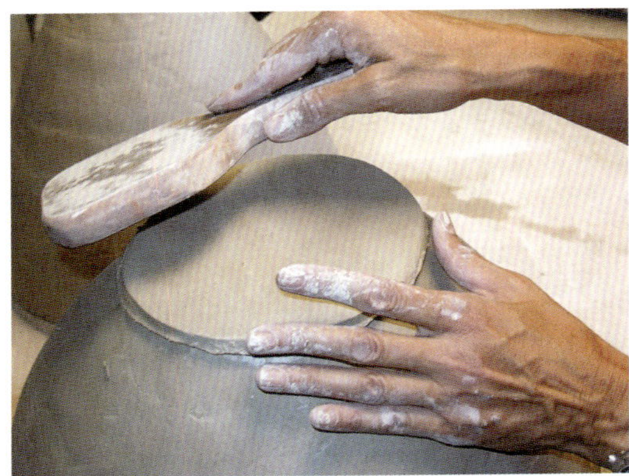

6. Paddle the circle to reinforce the seam.

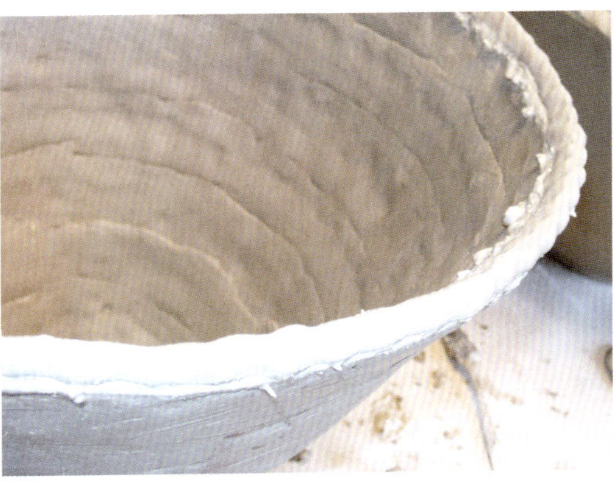

7. Add a small round coil to the edge when the form is very leather hard.

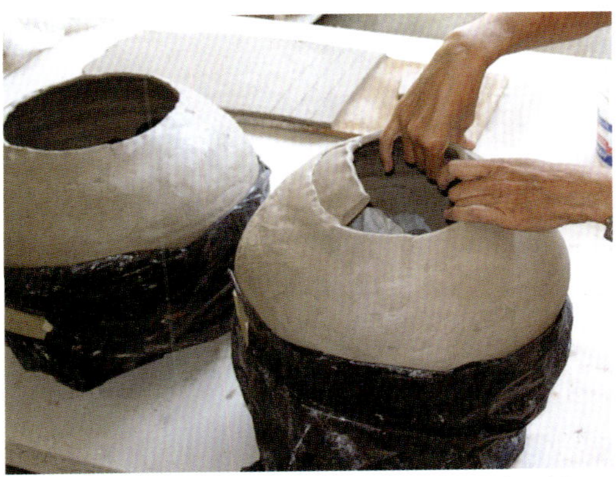

8. When the jar is right side up, you add the shoulder.

pleted and leather hard, you need to strengthen the walls. I use a paddle and a rounded piece of wood I call an "anvil," which I hold on the inside of the pot (figure 4). This technique also helps to obtain the desired shape.

Cut out a circle from a slab for the bottom of the jar. Slip, score and attach the bottom (figure 5). Paddle it to reinforce the seam (figure 6). Cover the piece and let it strengthen overnight. This also allows the moisture content to equalize.

The next morning, turn the jar over, and score and slip the edge. Since the form will be very leather hard by this time, add a small round coil to the edge (figure 7). The fresh coil provides an anchor to work off of while adding more flat coils. Now that the jar is right side up, you can add the shoulder (figure 8). Cut out a rim from a slab and attach to the top of the jar (figure 9). Sometimes I smooth the jar a bit more, or alter the rim by rotating it slowly on the wheel and using a wet sponge or rib.

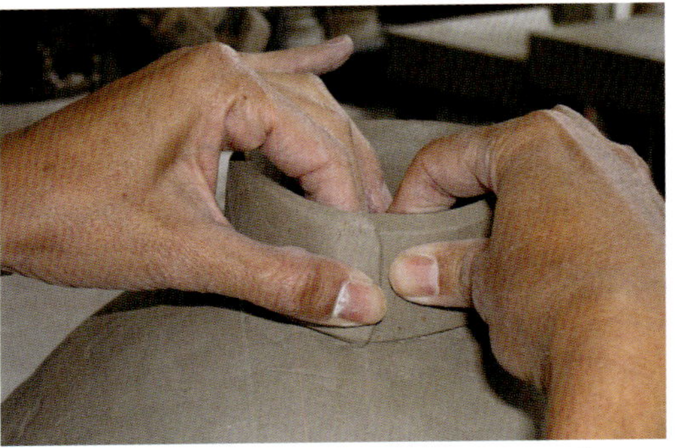

9. Smooth the jar a bit more, then cut out a rim from a slab and attach it to the top of the jar.

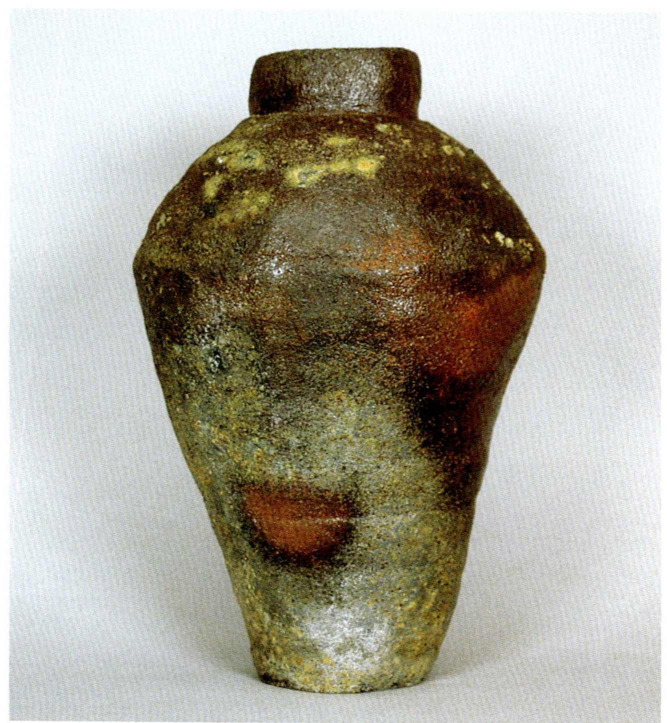

Wood-fired, handbuilt jars by Karen Terpstra. She states, "I try not to predetermine too much of the form when I start but rather let the handbuilding process determine the ultimate result. I am primarily concerned with the structure of the form, and how the shape, drawings and surface relate."

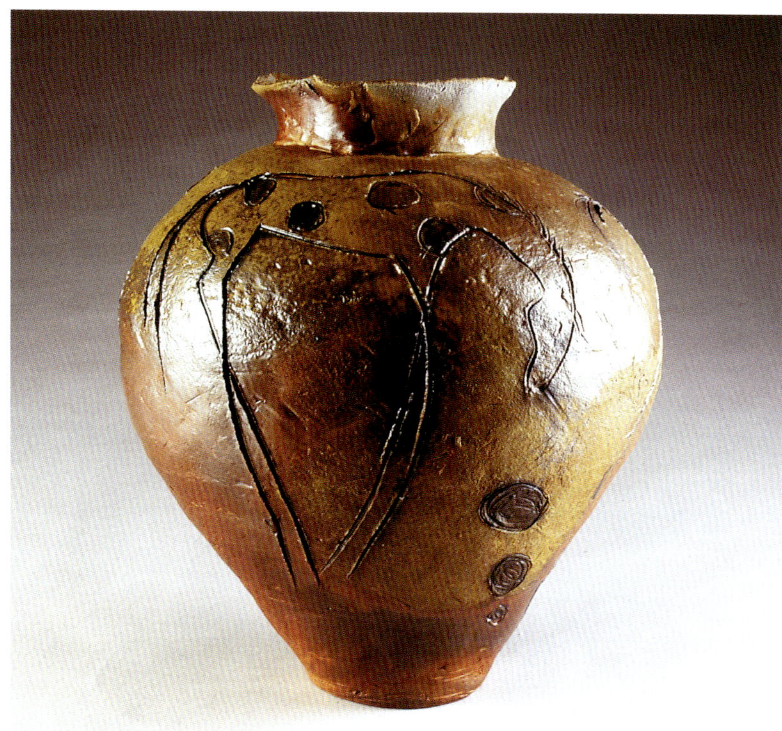

2

Plates & Platters

FOOTED SLAB PLATES

by Liz Zlot Summerfield

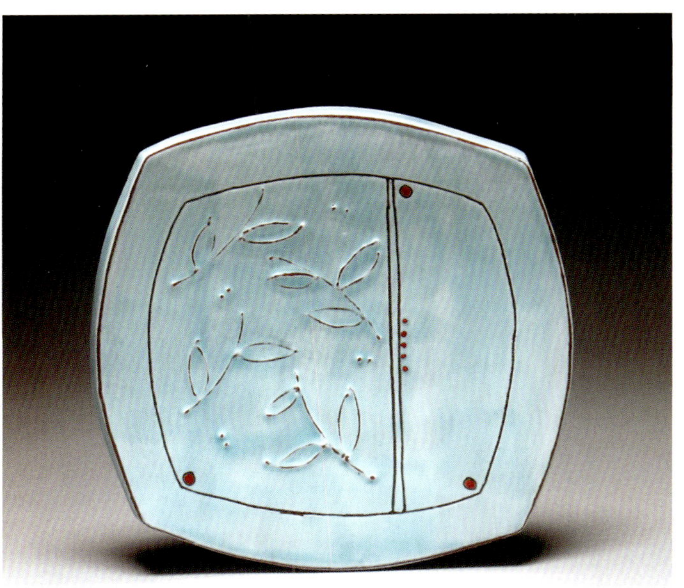

Footed plate with underglaze, slip-trailed, and sgraffito decoration.

Handbuilt slab plates are a lovely addition to any potter's repertoire. They are versatile in use, and offer an open canvas to play with a variety of surface treatments. Although they only consist of two components, a slab and a foot, they are often loaded with pesky little problems. Here's a technique that is sure to provide you with a proud product.

The Issues

The weakest link in a slab plate is the foot. It's often uneven, off center, and unconvincing. A common technique is to add a coil, place the plate on a potter's wheel and throw it onto the slab. This often leaves a bump where the coils are joined and it has a tendency to crack. The fix to these issues is to create a foot ring and apply it as one cohesive piece.

Constructing the Plate

Starting out, consider keeping the plate shape simple: try a square, circle, or rectangle. Draw and cut out the shape of your plate on paper and make two copies of this shape. Save one to cut out the plate shape, and on the other draw a foot ring—this may take some experimenting as the size of the foot ring will alter the look and stance of the plate.

Cut out the foot ring by folding the paper in half, then cutting along your drawn lines. Once the paper foot is cut out, you'll be left with a stencil to help center the foot ring on the slab (see figure 1).

Roll out a slab large enough to trace around one plate template and one foot ring template. For smaller plates, I roll to a thickness of about ⅜–½ inch. This thickness alleviates warping during the drying and firing processes. After rolling your

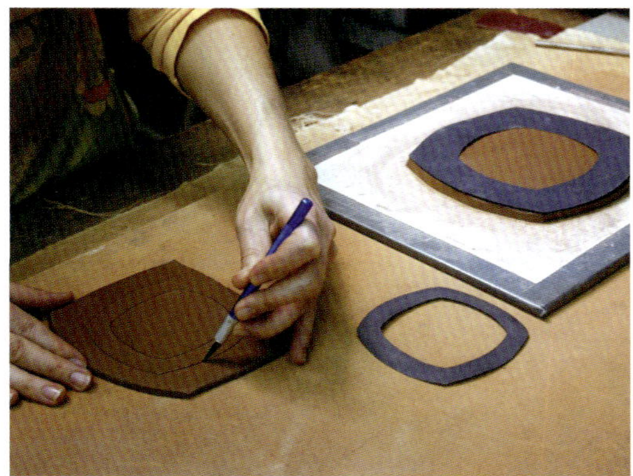
1. Create a pattern, stencil, and foot ring out of paper. Trace and cut the pattern and the stencil on a slab.

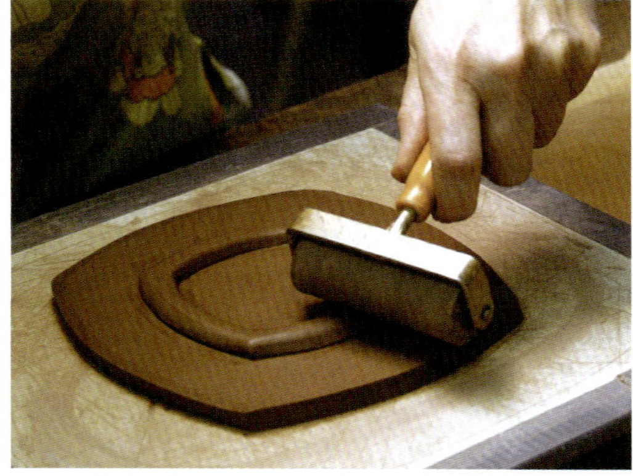
2. Attach the foot ring and refine its form to eliminate any unevenness and help connect the foot to the plate.

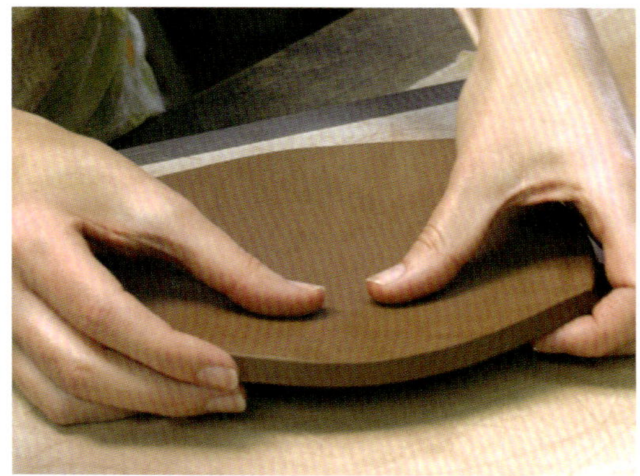
3. Gently press down in the center of the slab to shape the plate. Rotate the plate and gently lift all four sides.

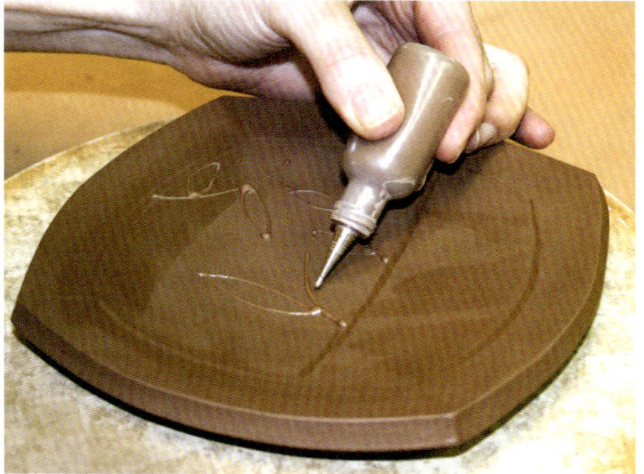
4. Use a slip from your clay body to create a raised line with a slip trailer. Allow the lines to dry.

slabs, it's important to run a rubber rib along the surface of both sides of the slab. This compresses the clay particles and removes any canvas texture from the working surface. Throughout the rest of the process, work on untextured surfaces such as drywall boards or a smooth fabric.

Trace the patterns with a needle tool before cutting them out with a knife. Hold the knife perpendicular to the slab and cut in one even motion (figure 1).

Applying the Foot

Place the stencil onto the cut out slab and trace the interior ring with your needle tool. This traced line will act as a guide as to where to place the foot ring and keep it centered (see figure 1). Since both the clay slab and foot ring are the same consistency and very wet, you only need water to attach the foot ring to the slab. Brush water onto the slab and put the foot ring in place using the traced lines for guidance. Gently apply pressure with your thumb and index finger to affix the foot ring to the slab. Refine the finished foot ring to follow your aesthetic. Avoid using any additional water as you refine it and smooth just with your fingers. A rubber-tipped tool is useful in cleaning and blending the connection between the slab and the foot ring. The final step in applying the foot ring is to use a small roller to eliminate unevenness (figure 2). Leave the plate upside down until it's ready to be flipped and formed.

Shaping the Plate

Success in handbuilding functional forms is about knowing the correct timing to touch the clay. When

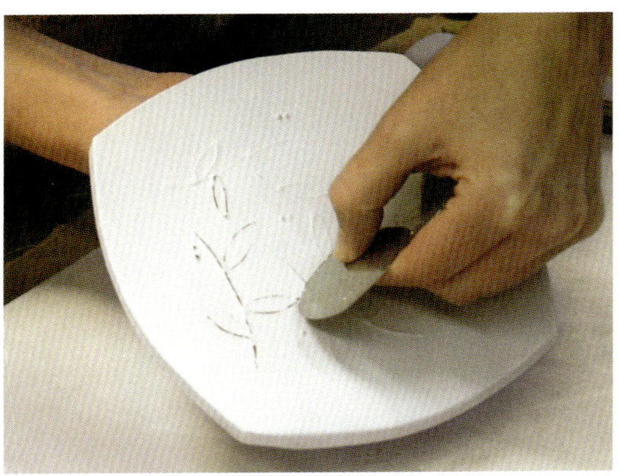

5. Apply 1–2 coats of underglaze then gently scrape underglaze off the raised slip-trailed lines to expose clay.

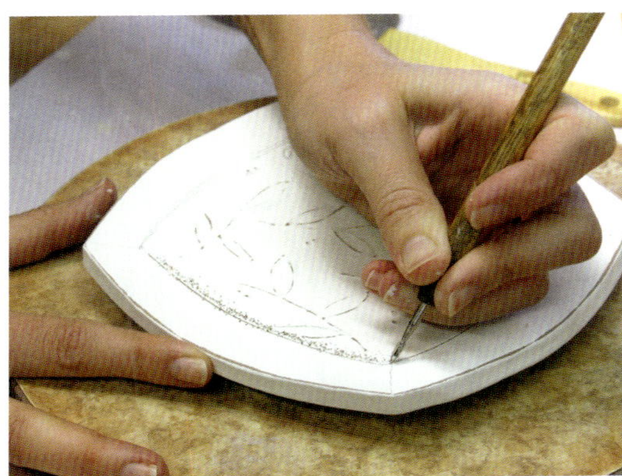

6. Carve subtractive lines using a sgraffito tool or sharp pointed tool.

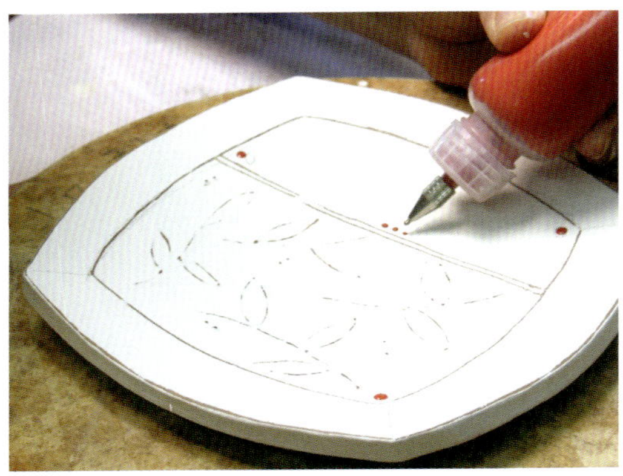

7. Add accent colors by applying underglaze using a slip trailer or brush.

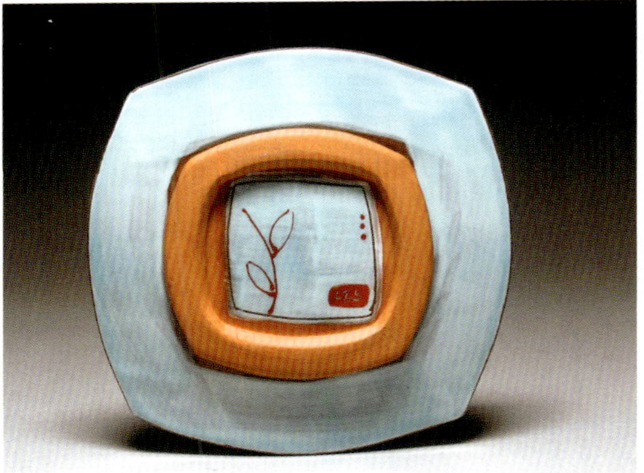

The completed plate illustrating how the foot ring becomes an essential element of the whole design.

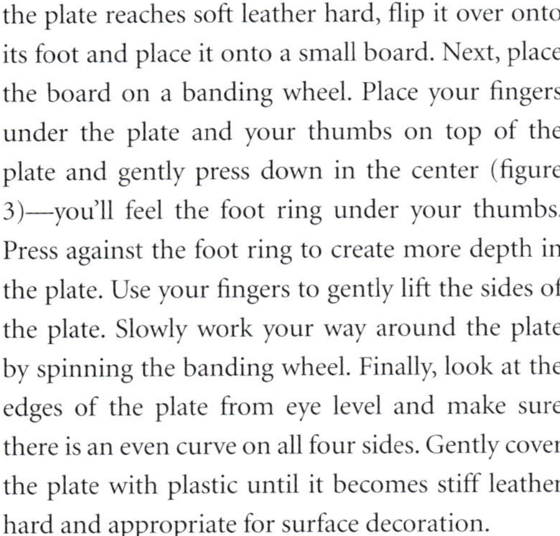

the plate reaches soft leather hard, flip it over onto its foot and place it onto a small board. Next, place the board on a banding wheel. Place your fingers under the plate and your thumbs on top of the plate and gently press down in the center (figure 3)—you'll feel the foot ring under your thumbs. Press against the foot ring to create more depth in the plate. Use your fingers to gently lift the sides of the plate. Slowly work your way around the plate by spinning the banding wheel. Finally, look at the edges of the plate from eye level and make sure there is an even curve on all four sides. Gently cover the plate with plastic until it becomes stiff leather hard and appropriate for surface decoration.

Slip-Trailing and Carving Surfaces

When the plate reaches leather hard, it's at the appropriate stage to slip trail, carve, and apply underglaze, if desired. To create a raised surface, but not a change in color, use a slip with a yogurt-like consistency for slip trail application (figure 4). Allow the lines to dry before brushing the entire plate with 1–2 coats of white underglaze. Once the underglaze is dry to the touch, take a metal rib and gently scrape it off the raised slip-trailed surface (figure 5). This exposes the red clay and accentuates the slip-trailed drawing. To contrast the raised surface, carve accent lines using a sgraffito tool (figure 6). Apply colored underglaze using a slip trailer or a brush for a small amount of accent color (figure 7). Allow the plate to slowly become bone dry under thin plastic to eliminate warping.

Once the plate is bisque fired, damp sponge to clean the surface before applying glaze. For brushing, apply 1–2 coats of glaze the consistency of skim milk with a soft moppy brush and fire.

MOLDED PLATES

by Amanda Wilton-Green

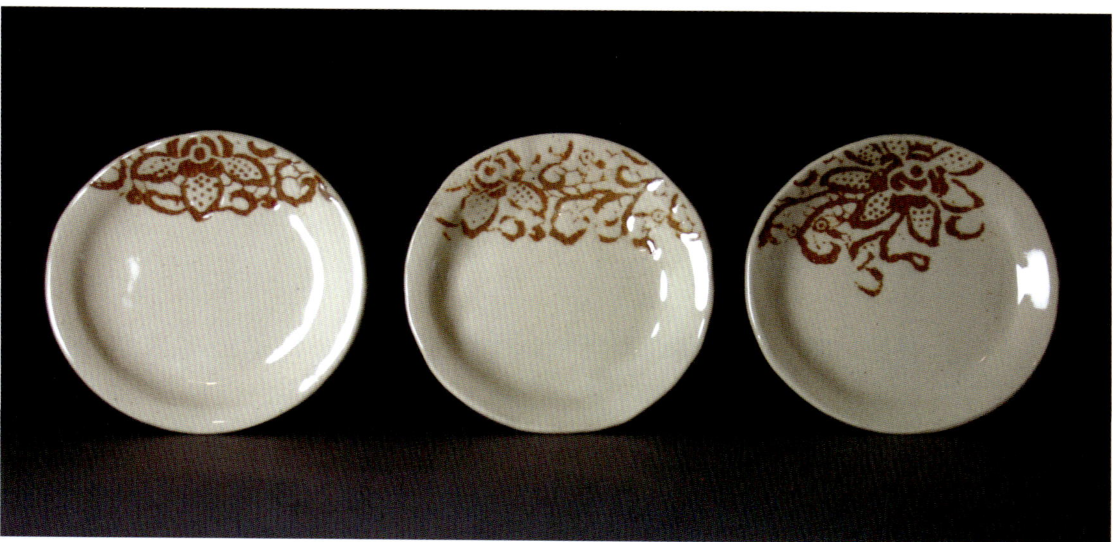

Making slab plates is a great way to develop basic slab techniques, and using Chinet® plates for forms makes this an easy project. They also make perfect surfaces for exploring decorating techniques.

Making a set of ceramic plates presents a direct and fresh slab-forming approach resulting in plates that become great canvases for surface decoration. Materials are simple, inexpensive and readily available (figure 1). After only a few hours of work, you can experience different stages of plastic clay and what the clay is capable of at each stage. You become familiar with simple slump molds and start to consider the form and function of your work. More importantly, you learn how to handle clay in a direct and intentional way.

These plates become a wonderful surface for finishing, embellishing and glazing. I have expanded this project to include experiments with paper stencils and slip decoration, but that's just the beginning. Try underglaze design work and glazing methods with this project as well. When the project is completed, you'll have a set of plates to use in you home or to give as gifts.

Process

Roll out a slab to a desired thickness of ¼ to ½ inch. When rolling out a slab, start by throwing it across the table in different directions until it is somewhere close to 3 inches thick. Roll the clay with the rolling pin, taking care not to roll over the

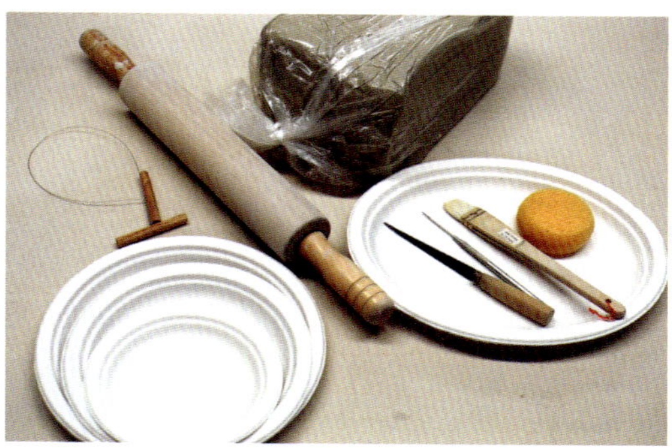

1. Tools needed include a large rolling pin, cut-off wire, sponge, 25 lbs of clay with sand or grog to reduce warping, fettling knife or needle tool, and Chinet® paper plates.

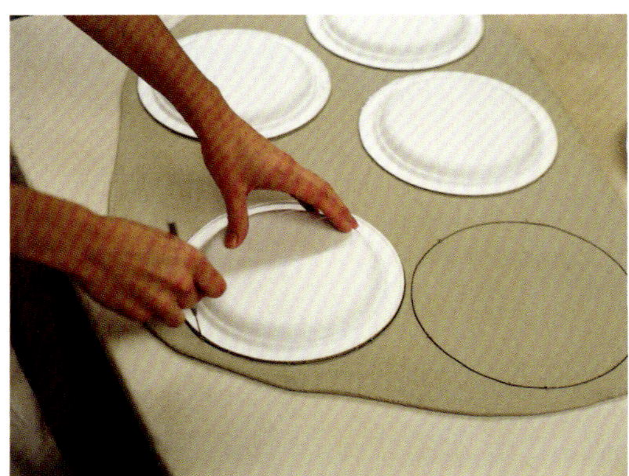

2. Using a plate as a template, cut circles in the slab.

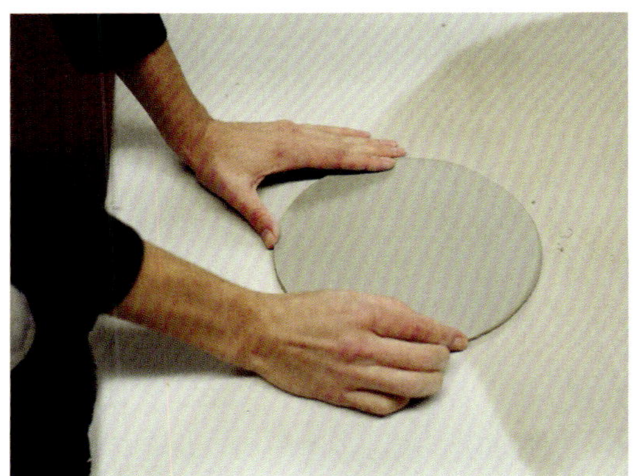

3. Remove excess clay from the rim and slide your finger across the edge.

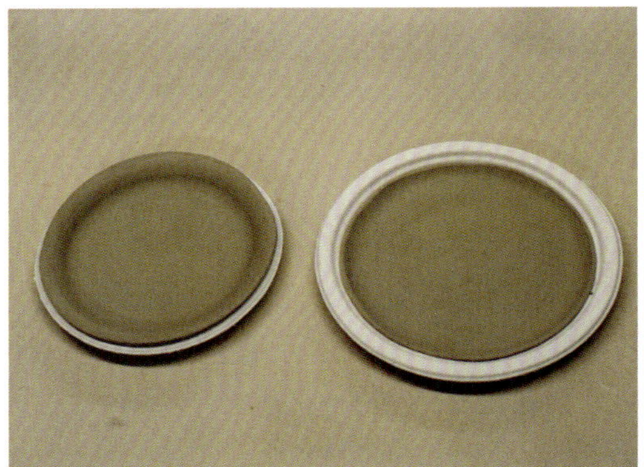

4. Flip the slab over and place it in the plate.

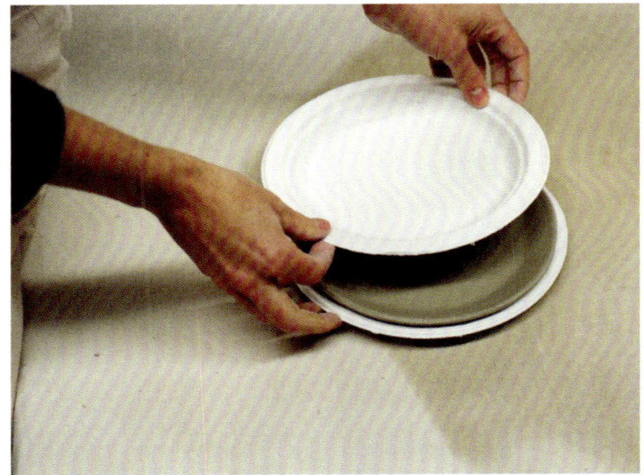

5. Press the clay with your hands or apply more even pressure by pressing with another plate.

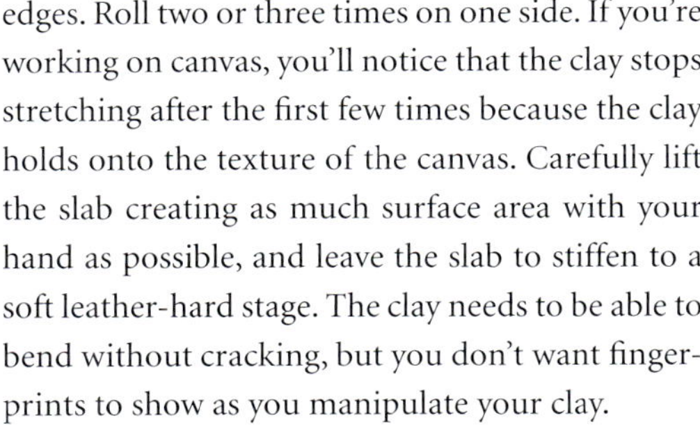

edges. Roll two or three times on one side. If you're working on canvas, you'll notice that the clay stops stretching after the first few times because the clay holds onto the texture of the canvas. Carefully lift the slab creating as much surface area with your hand as possible, and leave the slab to stiffen to a soft leather-hard stage. The clay needs to be able to bend without cracking, but you don't want fingerprints to show as you manipulate your clay.

Choose the size of your plate. Chinet® brand has dinner, salad and dessert-sized plates as well as an oval platter. Place the plate upside down to use as a template for cutting the slab (figure 2). As you cut, keep your needle tool or fettling knife perpendicular to your work surface to create a square rim.

Remove excess clay and smooth the rims. Slide your finger across the edge of the rim with firm and consistent pressure (figure 3). The sharp corner of the rim softens without flattening the edge. A damp sponge, chamois or a small piece of a produce bag also works. Stamp or sign the underside.

Flip the clay slab, smooth the top edge then place it into the paper plate, lining up the edges (figure 4). Experiment with pressing the clay into the paper plate with your hands or sandwiching your clay between two plates (figure 5). The clay will have a different character depending on your chosen method.

Allow the plates to dry to a firm leather-hard stage in the bottom paper plate. Remove the clay from the mold to check to see if the plates stack nicely and sit on a flat surface without rocking. Take a moment to look closely at the rim of each plate to do any final shaping they might need.

Plates & Platters

PLATE RING SUPPORTS

by Russell Fouts

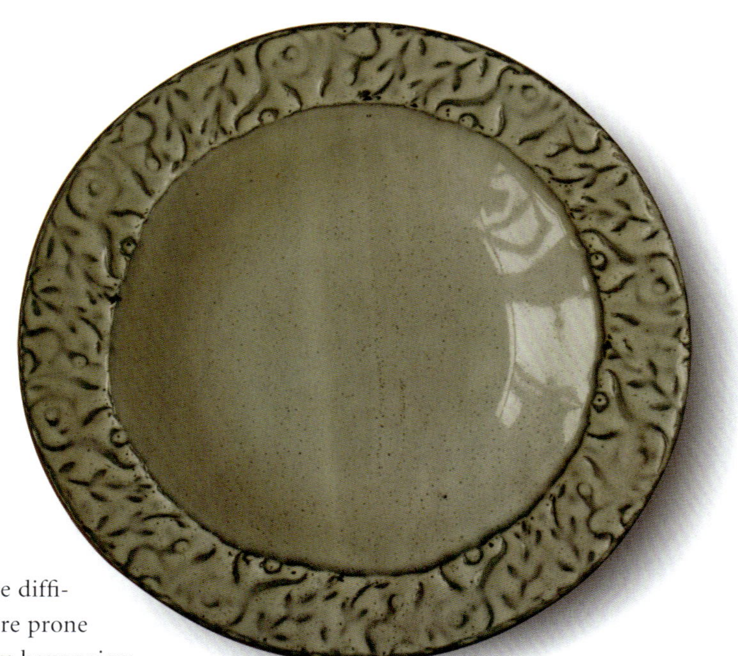

Making handbuilt plates can be difficult because low, wide forms are prone to warping. To prevent this from happening, you can make bisque-fired ring forms to support your plates while working on them. Here is a variation on a technique demonstrated by Canadian potter Walter Ostrom.

Getting Started

To make a 12-inch ring, start with about six pounds of wedged clay and roll it into a thick coil. Toss it on the table several times on each side to widen it out, then roll it back into a coil close to the diameter you want for making the initial ring (figure 1). The size of the ring you make depends on how deep you want the plate to be and how wide the rim will be. It's important to have the coil a fairly even thickness so the ring is more likely to be even when you flatten it out later.

Place the coil on a 12–inch bat and then put it on a banding wheel. The coil should overhang the edge of the bat by a few millimeters. Overlap the ends and cut diagonally through them both to remove the extra clay and provide a good surface for joining (figure 2). Slightly wet one side, rub it a bit to work up some slip, then join the two pieces together. Now, put the ring and bat on a wheel and refine the shape (figure 3).

For the next step, create a tool by wrapping a ¼ piece of brick in a chamois (figure 4). Press the brick in a regular motion going around the ring to flatten the coil down at a slight angle toward the center of the ring. Do this quickly and in three or four passes (figure 5). I like to leave the paddled texture on the surface, although it can be removed. Any texture here will end up on the underside of your plate rim. Note the angle of the surface that supports and forms the wide rim of the plate (figure 6). Following the edge of the bat, use a cheese cutter to trim off the rounded outside edge flush with the bat (figure 7).

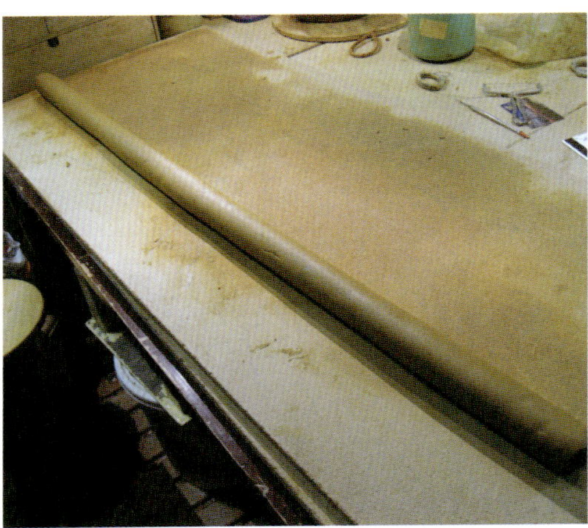

1. Roll a coil for the initial ring depending on how deep you want the plate and how wide you want the rim.

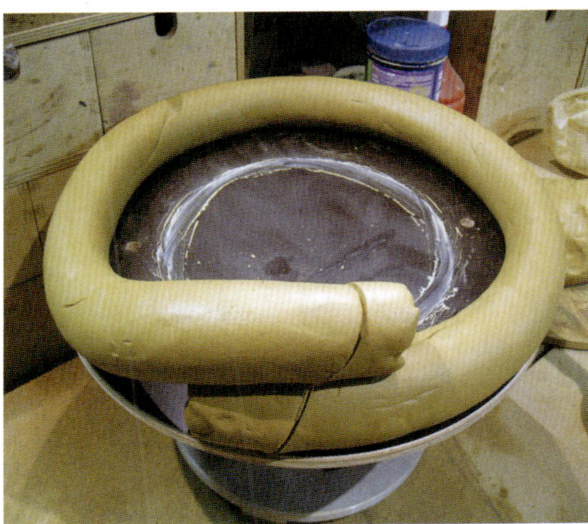

2. Overlap the two ends, cut diagonally through them both, and remove extra clay.

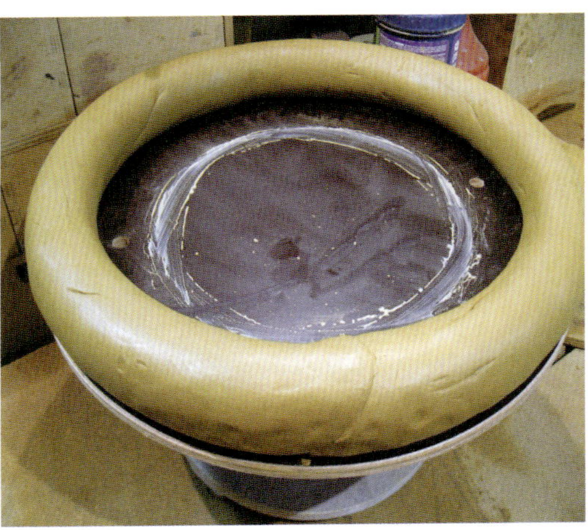

3. Slip the ends and join them, then refine the shape.

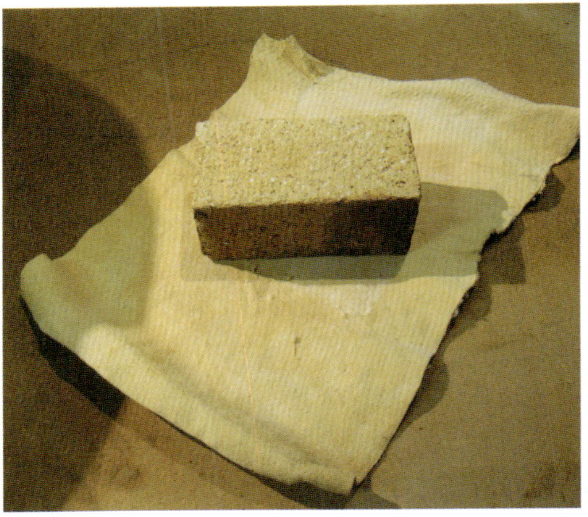

4. Create a tool by wrapping a chamois around a small chunk of brick or wood.

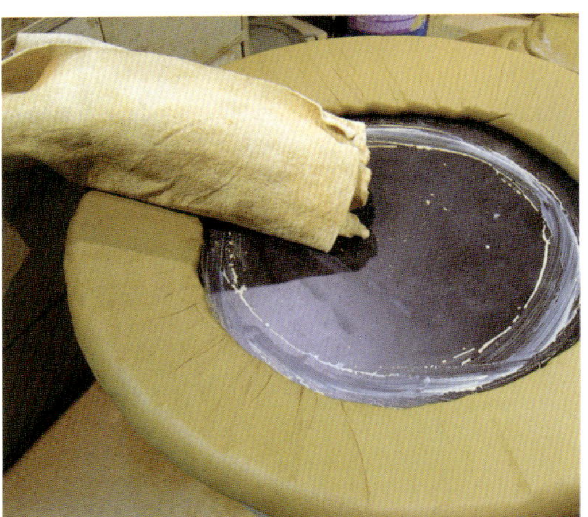

5. Beat the coil at a slight angle toward the center in a regular circular motion. Do this quickly in 3–4 passes.

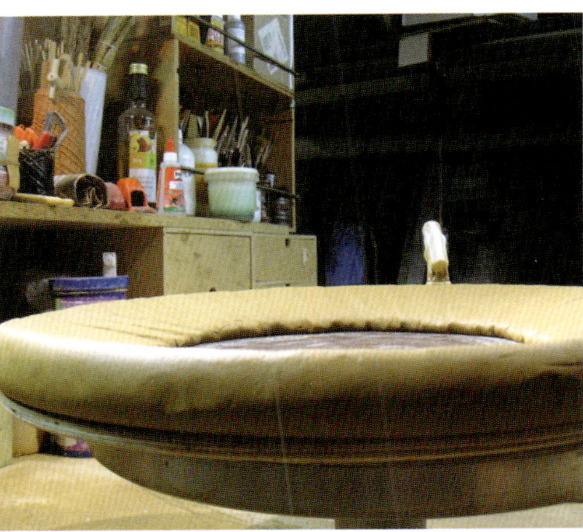

6. A view from the side showing the angle of the surface that will support and form the wide plate rim.

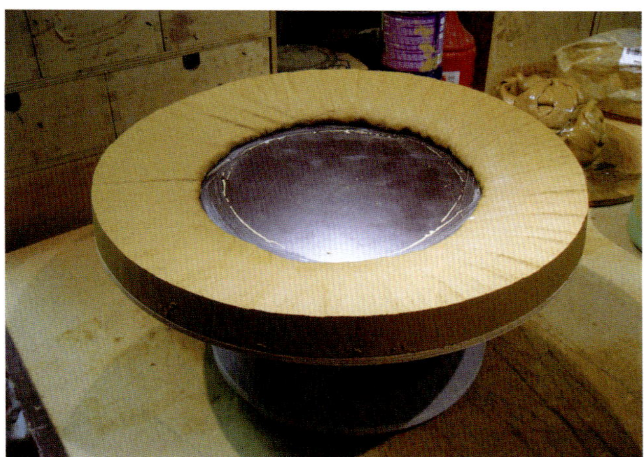

7. Use a cheese cutter or a sharp knife to trim off the rounded, outside edge flush with the bat.

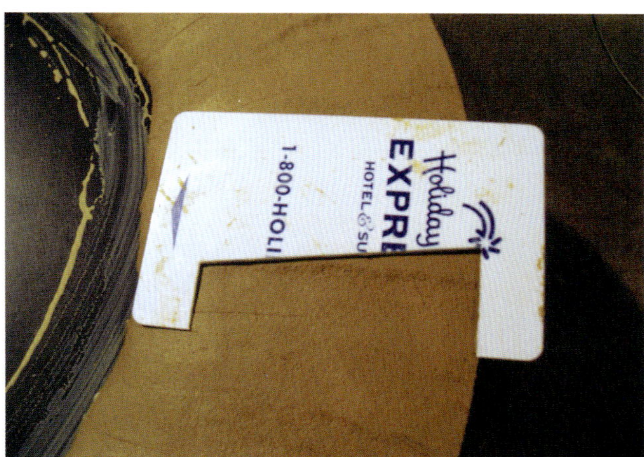

8. Cut a template shaped and angled to the size you want the plate ring to be. Use it to mark a trimming line.

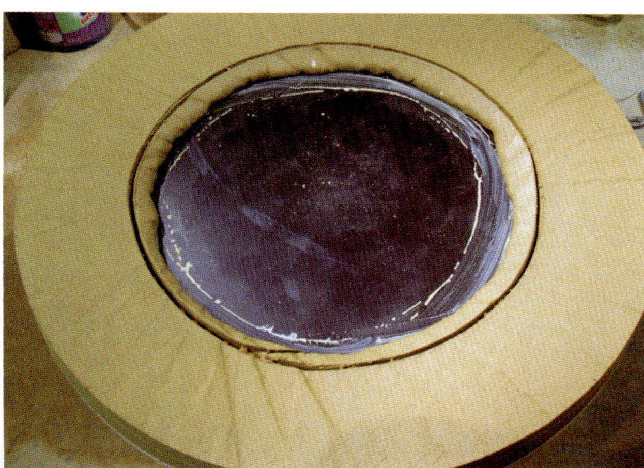

9. Cut and remove excess clay from the plate ring's interior circumference. This forms the base of the plate.

Finishing the Ring

To gauge the width of the plate ring, the angle of the horizontal rim surface, and the height, you'll need to create a profile template out of an old credit card (figure 8). The template works better and faster than calipers do. The short vertical cut is the height of the inside rim of the ring. The longer vertical cut is the height of the outside rim and the longest horizontal cut is the width that will support the wide rim of the plate.

Go around the circumference of the ring to mark a line, then go over it again with a pin tool to make the cut (figure 9). Remove the clay and the ring is essentially finished. This ring is 14 inches in diameter on the outside and 10 inches on the inside after drying and firing. This will make a deep dinner plate with a wide rim.

After the ring is leather hard, clean the edges and round them off so they are less likely to chip. Keep the outside edge as square as possible so it doesn't trap clay during drying and cause it to crack. The inside edge should be rounded to make a nice transition from the bowl of the plate to the rim. Use the template to check the angle and the height of the leather-hard ring (figure 10). I'm not worried about accuracy or repeatability here—the template is just a rough guide. The rim rises as it dries and drops again when it's fired so the rings will never be exactly the same even if they're initially made the same. My main concern is that they don't warp.

Before the plate ring dries, make an undercut around the bottom of it with a needle tool and then wire it off. Keep the plate on the bat until it's dry enough to be handled without deforming.

Test the plate ring at the leather-hard or the greenware stage by making plates on it to see if it's what you want—sometimes they may need a slight modification. Fire them flat and slowly.

Using Plate Rings

Start with a good amount of wedged clay and roll out a slab large enough to overhang the ring. One great thing about this method is that using one ring makes a deep plate but if you stack two rings, you can get a deep pasta plate (figure 11). When stacked, you can really play around with the shape of the well—straight sides, angled, curved, wide bottom narrow bottom, whatever.

When cutting a slab to use with the ring, leave the diameter a little wider so there's a slight overhang onto the plate ring. This accommodates the movement of the clay that is pressed down into the well in the ring. Put the ring on a bat on a banding wheel. The bat supports the bottom of the plate if you have to move it around during the drying. If you're worried about the bottom of the plate sticking to the bat, put a piece of newspaper between the ring and the bat. Carefully place the slab over the plate ring. Form the well of the plate by patting the center of the slab with a soft sponge or flexible rib (figure 12), being careful not to make marks. You can make the well of the plate any shape you want here; either straight or angled walls. After the well is formed, pat the rest of the slab onto the rim. Once the plate is formed on the ring, cut off the extra clay around the edge (figure 13).

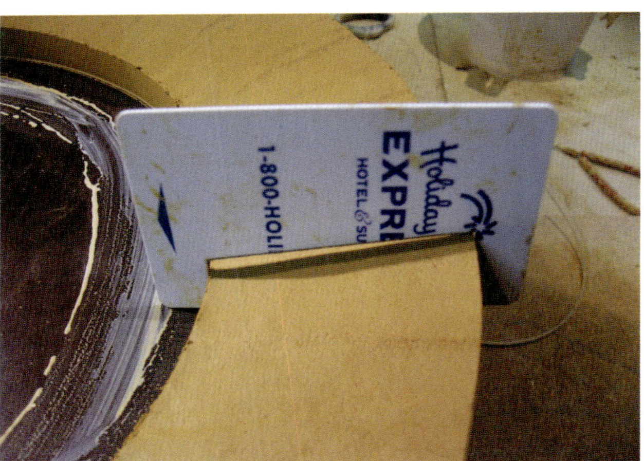

10. Use the template to check the angle and height of the ring. Smooth out the inside sharp corner.

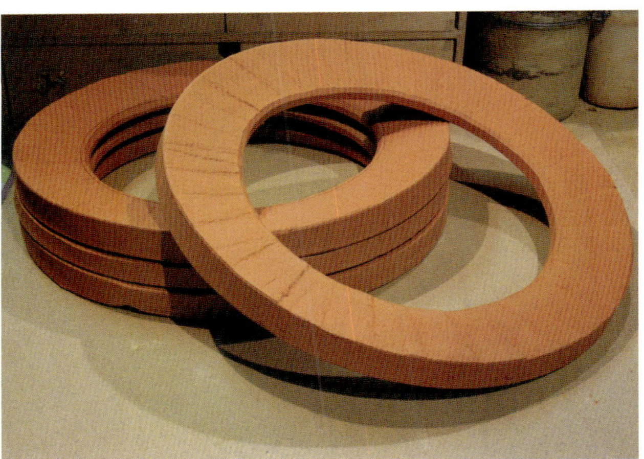

11. Wire under the ring, dry it, remove it from the bat, then bisque fire it

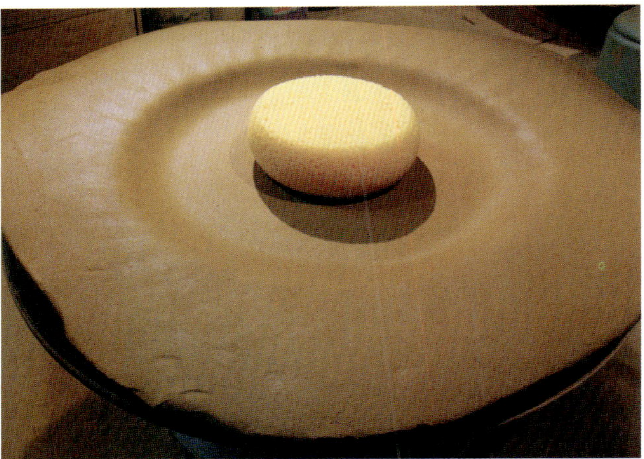

12. Put ring on a bat then on a banding wheel. Place a slab over the ring. Form the base using a soft sponge.

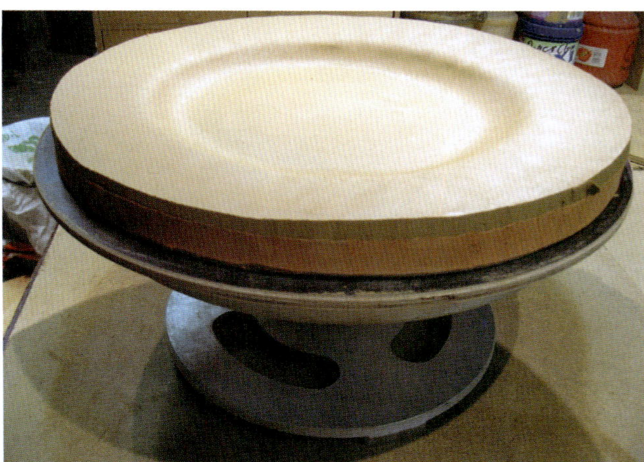

13. Cut off the extra clay around the edges using a sharp knife or a cheese cutter.

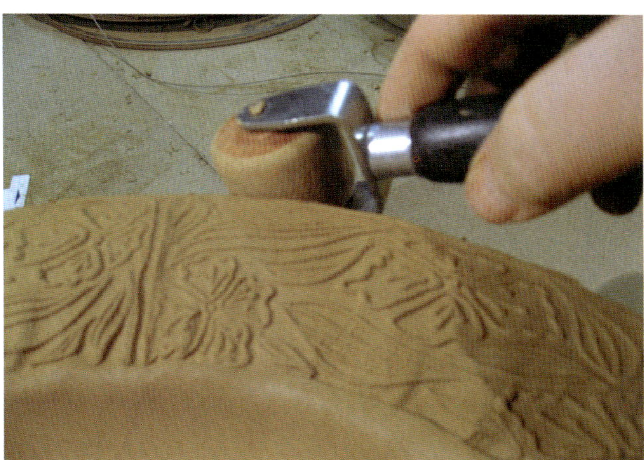

14. Add texture and create a frame by angling a roller slightly forward and very slightly inward while turning.

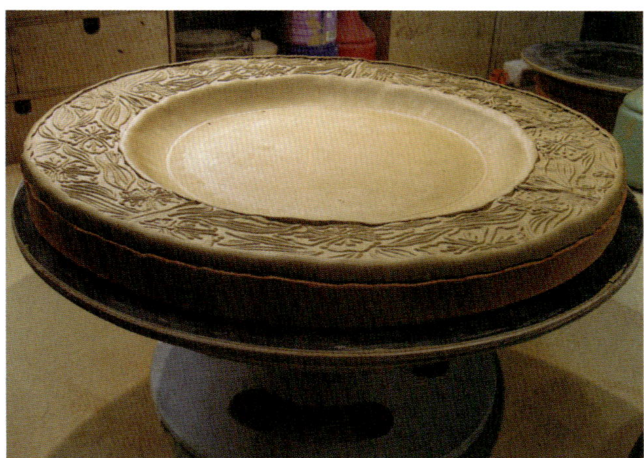

15. Pat the rolled edge down. When hard leather hard, put it face down on foam and trim. Flip it over to dry.

Creating a Textured Rim

One benefit of this method is that you can add texture to the rim with stamps, a roulette, sprigs, or whatever you want to use. I make the rims without any curves so they are flat and I can roulettes on them. You can also add texture to the slab before you put it on the plate ring, but it's easier to texture it with the added support and to maintain the detail of the texture. I've gone around the rim with the roulette, trying to keep even pressure. It's a little tricky to use a cylindrical roulette on a circular form since you have to make incremental turns as you roll it.

When you roll the roulette, the pressure causes some of the clay to squeeze out over the edge of the ring, and creates a raised edge where the rim ends and the well begins. This edge defines and frames the texture, so use a small roller to smooth it out. Angle the roller slightly forward and inward and keep it in this position while you slowly turn the banding wheel. As you turn the banding wheel, the clay is forced against the roller and, because of the angle, it rises to form a very thin lip. It only takes a few turns and not much pressure. Repeat this process on the outside edge (figure 14). Pat the rolled edge down and over so they look alike (figure 15).

When the plate is leather hard, place it face down on foam and trim the underside edge where the plate rested on the plate ring. Flip the plate back over onto a bat and put another bat on top of the finished plate to slow the drying and to keep the rim from rising too much as it dries. Leave the bat on top until the plate is dry. The bat is very light and doesn't mar the face of the plate.

Plates & Platters
ADDING VOLUME TO A RIM

by Mark Cole

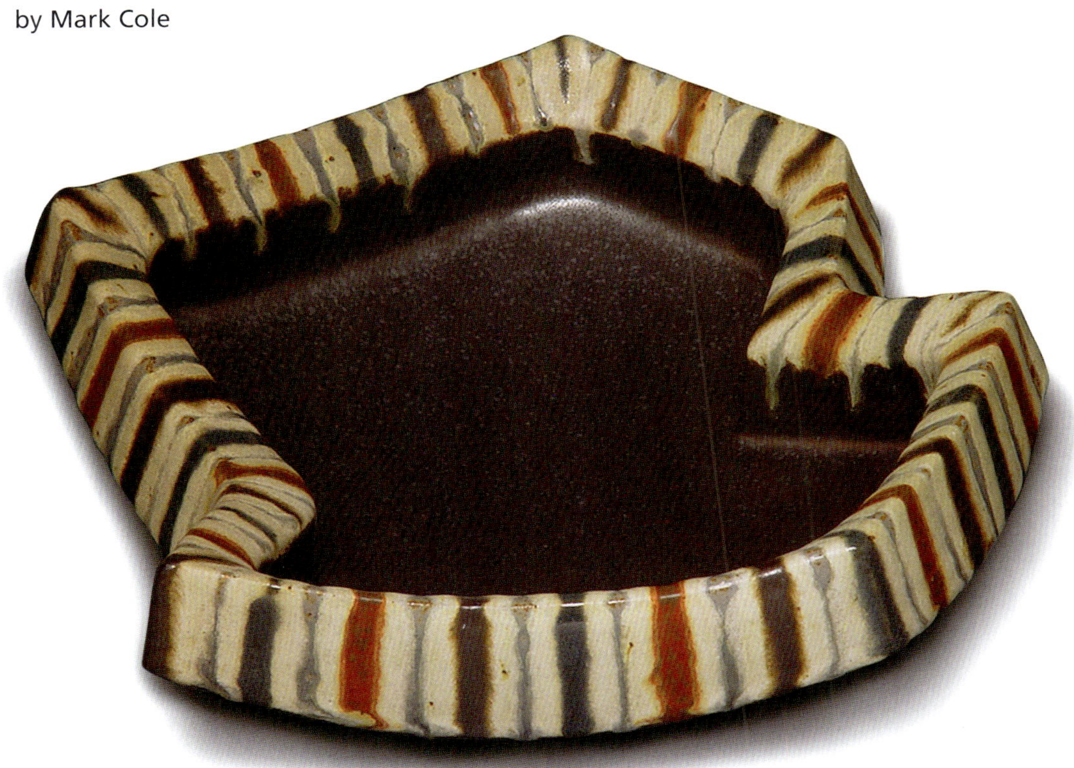

Paying attention to the visual beginning and ending at the foot and the lip of a pot is a fundamental necessity to the success of the overall form. This may include adding transitions that separate the foot from the body, leaving a little heft, and/or creating a linear element at the lip of a pot that provide a resting place for the viewer's eyes. These formal qualities help define the visual elements of a piece as well as provide a physical stability to the overall form.

Deciding the right thickness of a slab in relation to the overall size of the form can be problematic. When making smaller functional forms, the slabs can be either thick or thin, because even small hefty forms can be easily lifted. With larger functional forms, it's a different story. If a larger form is too thick, it may weigh too much for reasonable use, and if it's too thin, it may seem too fragile.

Keeping the limitations of weight (and therefore of thickness) in mind, constructing a sizeable and trustworthy functional form that incorporates distinctive visual elements can still be done in many ways. The solution I use combines slabs of uniform thickness and the constructional integrity of clay to create a visually substantial, hollow-rimmed form.

Gather Support

A slump mold provides a stable form a slab can conform to while firming up. Whether the mold is made of bisqued clay or plaster with either a flat or curved bottom, it allows a form to be safely moved

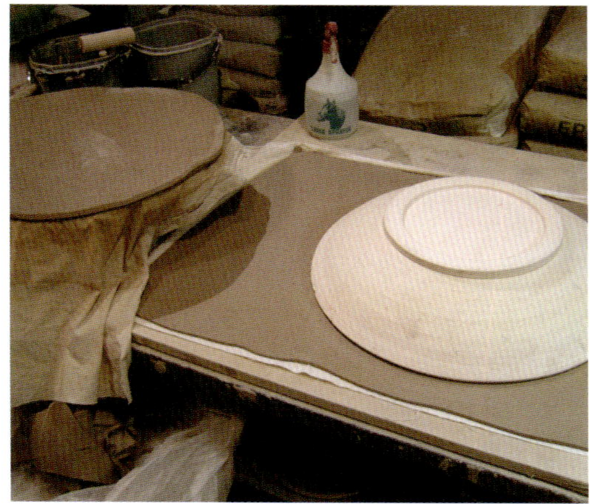

1. Tracing the diameter of my bisque slump mold onto a slab of clay.

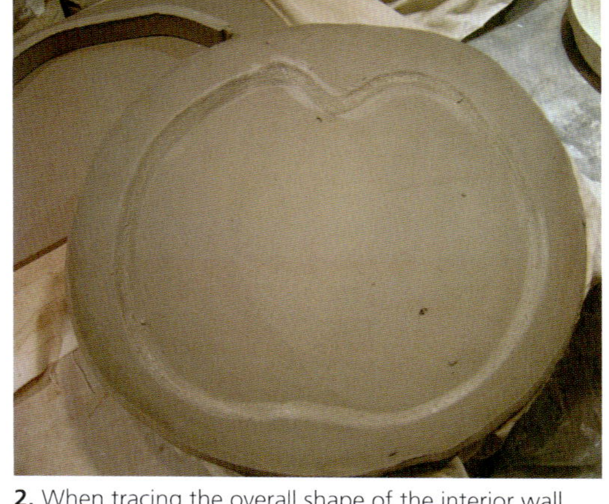

2. When tracing the overall shape of the interior wall, leave extra space for the outer wall dimension.

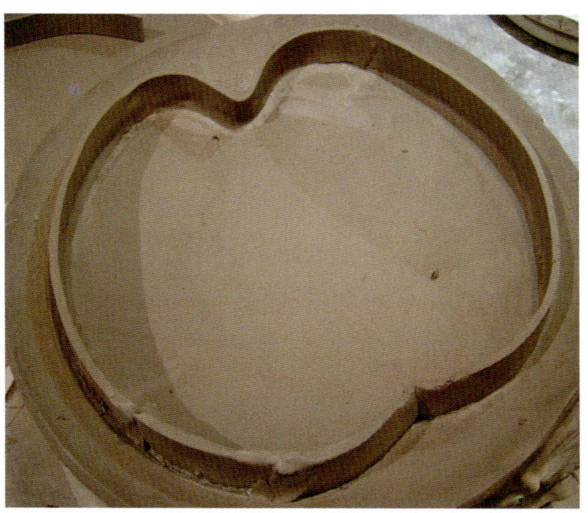

3. Attach a strip of clay for the interior wall to the bottom of the form.

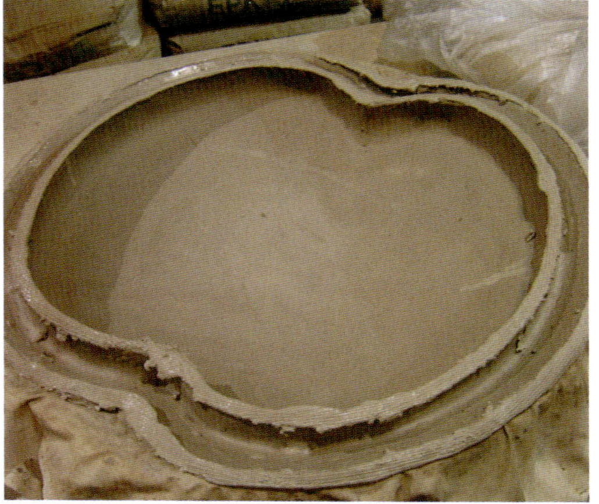

4. The scored and slipped walls are leather hard and ready for the final slab strip.

around the studio. For the forms shown here, I used a bisque slump mold made from an unaltered, wheel-thrown form (figure 1). Both bisque and plaster molds draw moisture out of a slab, so monitoring the consistency of the clay is very important.

Place a slab onto a cut section of a cotton sheet, trim the slab to size, then use the sheet as a support to lift it up and place it into the mold. The sheet remains between the clay and the mold as a separator, making it easier to remove the piece later.

Inventing the Interior Shape

At this point, the overall shape of the piece may take on innumerable characteristics. Is it curvilinear or geometric? Will the width of the hollow rim be the same throughout or will there be a wider section? Once you settle on an overall shape, draw the location of the interior wall with a scoring tool and apply slip in the scored grooves (figure 2).

Using a metal ruler as a template and a fettling knife, cut strips of clay to make up the interior wall. Being careful not to bend or fold the strips, score and slip the bottom and sides of the wall and firmly attach them to the form. Reinforce the connections with a thin coil (figure 3). Cover the form and the mold with plastic and let it sit overnight so the moisture evens out. The next day, the form and interior wall should be approaching the leather-hard stage.

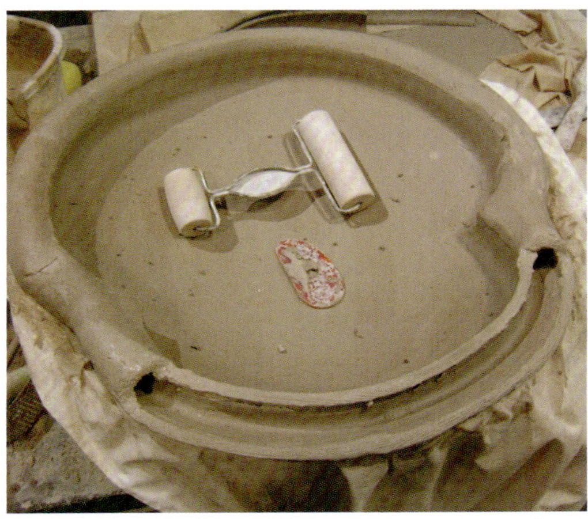

5. Place rounded strips over the two walls, then roll and rib the seams to make a firm connection.

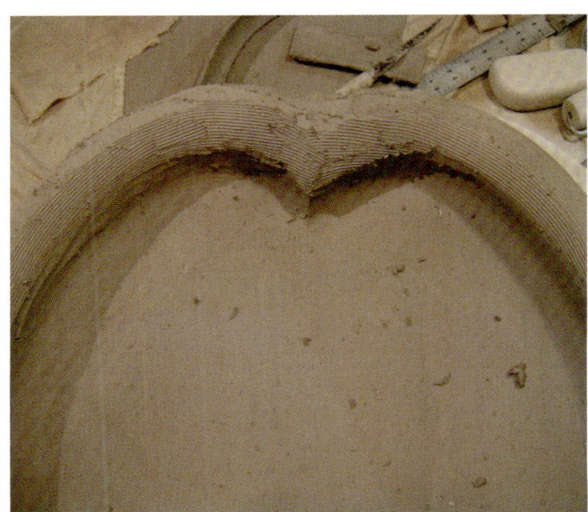

6. Once the strips are placed, score the hollow wall to move clay across the joins and even out the surface.

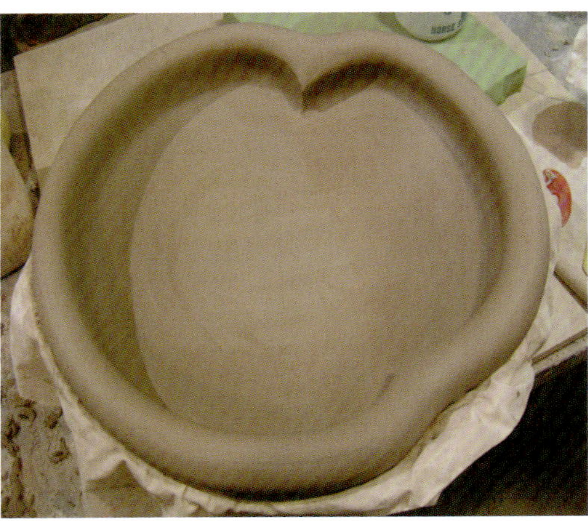

7. Using a rubber or metal rib, smooth out the rim and transitions of the hollow walled form.

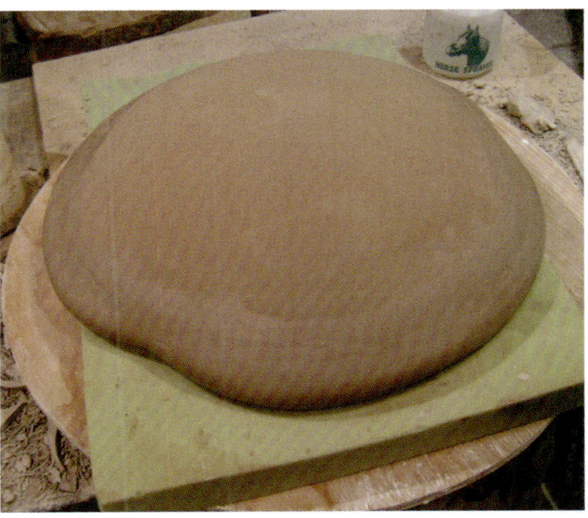

8. Flip the leather-hard form onto a foam support to finish the bottom.

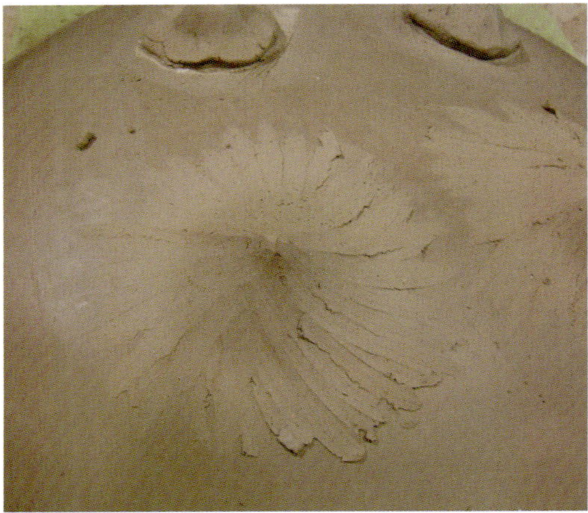

9. Add feet to the bottom of the form.

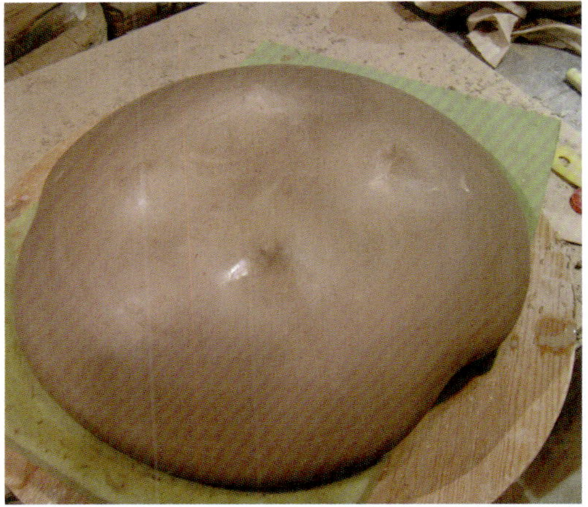

10. Use a series of ribs to smooth the feet.

Determine the location of the outer wall, draw the outline onto the form and trim away any excess clay. Then, shape the outer edge, score and slip each edge in preparation for the final slab (figure 4).

Whenever I decide on a curvilinear form, I typically also decide for the rim area to reflect this and create a rounded edge on the piece. To do this, use a large dowel and a soft rib to shape the flat slab strips around the dowel. Score and slip each side of the rounded clay strips, carefully attach them to the outer wall and then ease the strip over to the interior wall, making a firm connection. Use a pony roller and a small paddle to force these two connections together (figure 5), reinforce each connection with coils, and score the entire surface thoroughly (figure 6). Smooth the surface, first with a metal rib, then a medium hard rubber rib, and finally with a soft rubber rib, until all of the evidence of scoring has disappeared (figure 7). At this point, I cover the form and the bisque mold in plastic and let it sit a second night.

Working on the Underside

Taking the leather-hard form out of the mold and flipping it upside down onto foam, I am now ready to finish the bottom (figure 8). I first refine the texture left behind by the cotton sheet with a soft rubber rib to ensure its smoothness. Canvas leaves a very particular texture that requires more pressure to smooth out and pushing too hard during this stage can distort the form. The residual canvas texture has an unintentional effect to the glazed surface. A cotton sheet leaves a less pronounced texture that's easier to remove with a rib. After all the compression due to ribbing, you'll need to use a needle tool to poke a hole into the hollow section.

Four-footed Form

There are many different types of feet to experiment with when working with slabs. I use four understated feet made from small clay lugs that elevate the entire piece off the table, allowing me to glaze the entire form. The only unglazed part of this piece will be the four places where it sits on the kiln shelf.

Attach the clay lugs or similar feet in the location where they will best support the piece and smooth each one into the form (figure 9). Start smoothing with your finger, then with a metal rib, then with a medium hard rubber rib, then with a soft rubber rib, and lastly with a chamois cloth (figure 10). Let the piece dry slowly over the next three days.

When bisque firing these pieces, spread grog onto the shelf, and create four piles to the outside of the foot areas before placing the pieces. The grog allows the piece to shift and shrink during the firing without added stress, and the piles support the piece to prevent cracking and sagging.

Firing

I fire these forms directly on a very flat kiln shelf and let any deformation aid the overall form's ability to sit flat on a table without rocking back and forth. If a piece is not level, I simply sand down one of the feet with a palm sander until it sits properly on all fours.

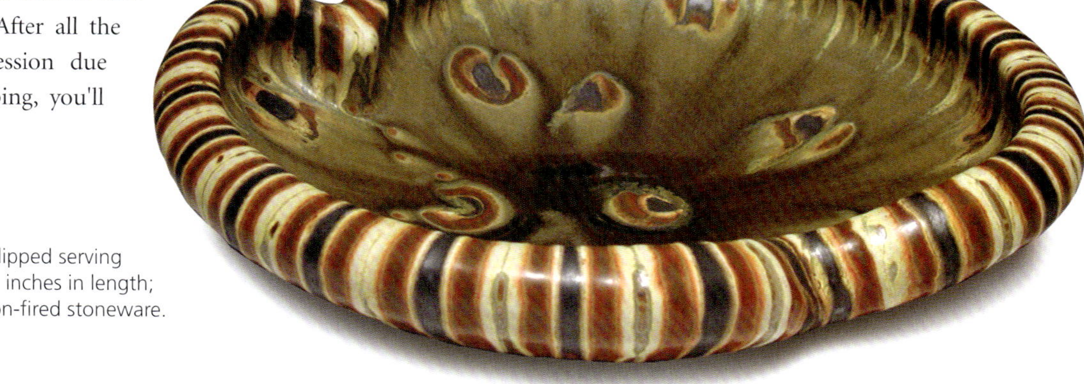

Hollow lipped serving dish; 14 inches in length; reduction-fired stoneware.

3

Slab Construction
FROM DRAWING TO CLAY

by Liz Zlot Summerfield

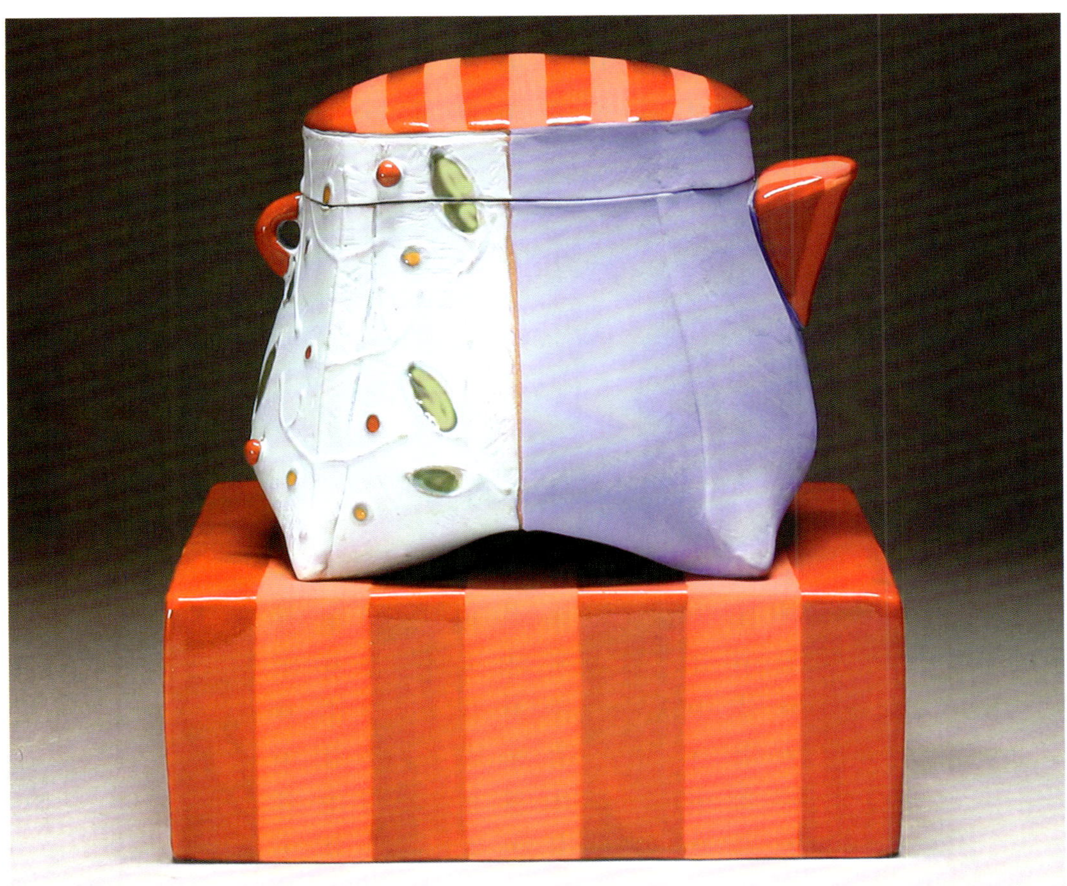

How do you journey from a drawing in your sketch book to a paper pattern? Start with a clay sketch that will become the rough draft of your pattern. Make a cylinder (either by pinching, coiling or from a slab) and attach a bottom. The cylinder should be similar in scale to the intended final piece. Draw lines on the surface of the cylinder anywhere you intend to create a seam. Cut along the lines and lay the sections out flat, creating a two-dimensional shape (figure 1). Trace the flat clay sketch onto a malleable material, such as construction paper. Cut out the paper pattern. You now have a rough draft of your pattern. To ensure proper measurements, fold the paper pattern, as you would in making a paper snowflake, and cut off any uneven edges.

To test your pattern, roll out a slab and trace the pattern. Fold the slab to create the basic form, then take note where the pattern needs adjusting. Alter the pattern and continue the back and forth between clay and paper until you are satisfied with your pattern. Trace the pattern onto a more durable

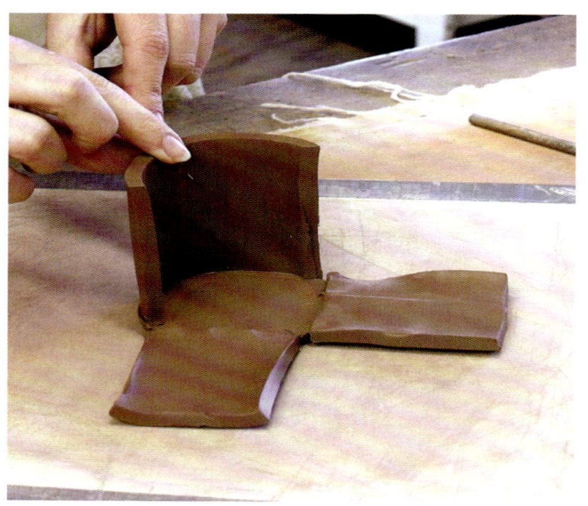
1. Make a cylinder to make a pattern. Cut it apart to give a visual from the 3-D form to the 2-D paper pattern.

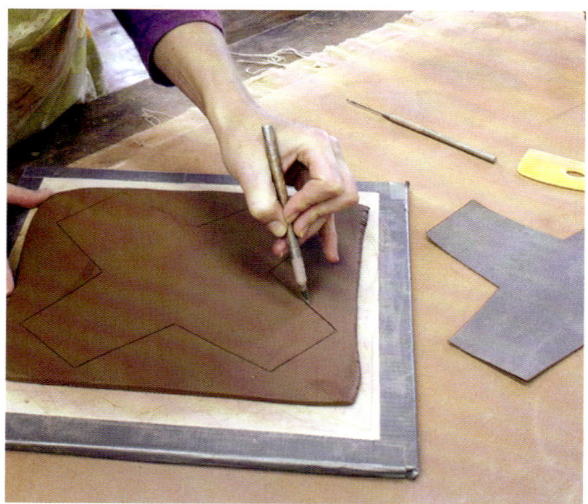
2. Trace the pattern and cut along the valley created by the needle tool with an X-Acto knife.

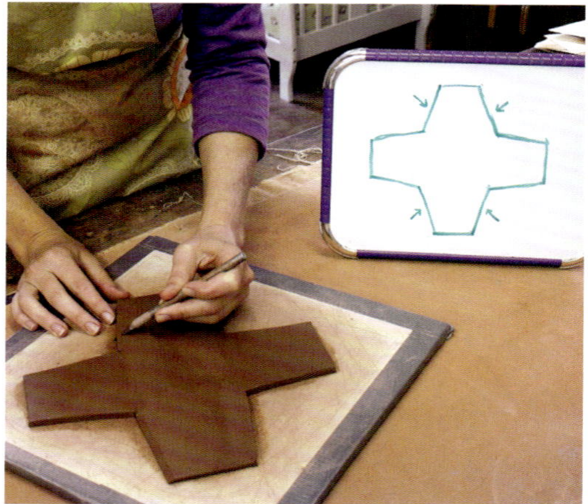
3. Bevel the edges then flip the slab over and bevel the sides adjacent to the first bevels on the backside.

material to create a master pattern. Paper patterns can easily be rescaled on a photocopier to create larger or smaller sizes of your original design.

Rolling and Tracing

Roll out a ¼-inch-thick slab large enough to fit your pattern. Run a rubber rib along the surface of both sides of the slab to compress the clay particles and remove any canvas texture. Place the pattern on the slab, and first trace it with a needle tool before cutting it out with a knife—the needle tool line creates a valley for the knife to follow. Hold the knife perpendicular to the slab and cut in one even motion (figure 2).

Beveling, Folding, and Shaping

The slab is ready to bevel and fold once it has lost its stickiness but it is still very soft to touch. To create a greater surface area for the slabs to connect, you will need to bevel the edges. Before you begin, here are a few simple hints to beveling.

Hold the knife as you would a pencil and remind yourself that your wrist should not be contorted or uncomfortable during the beveling process. If you are right handed, you will always work on the left-hand side of the piece. In order to accomplish this, you need to turn your board to orient the piece as you cut all of the bevels. One common problem with beveling is being too tentative. The knife should cut through the clay at an angle with the tip running along the surface of the board.

The following beveling instructions set the pot up in a geometric fashion; creating four equal sides. To begin, start from the top of the piece and run your knife along the edge at a 45° angle until you finish cutting one side. Repeat this step on all four sides, remembering to turn the board after each cut. Once you bevel the first half of all joins, flip the slab over and bevel the side of the seam adjacent to the first bevel. Note (with the arrows in the image) that you are always beveling on the opposite side of the slab (figure 3) to create each join.

To prepare for folding up the sides, brush the beveled edges with slip (there is no need to score due to the wetness of the slab). Lift two adjoining sides and begin to overlap the beveled edges starting from the bottom of the pot (figure 4). Gently join the slabs together, working your way around all four sides of the pot. Once the pot is standing on its own, take a rubber brayer and roll the edges together to create a firm connection. The brayer connects the seams, leaving a visible line, whereas a rib will smooth them together, eliminating the seam line. Make these decisions based on your own personal aesthetic. There is no need to add coils to the inside seams due to the wetness of the clay. You have now created your cylinder. Allow the pot to firm up to soft leather hard in order to address the bottom and add volume.

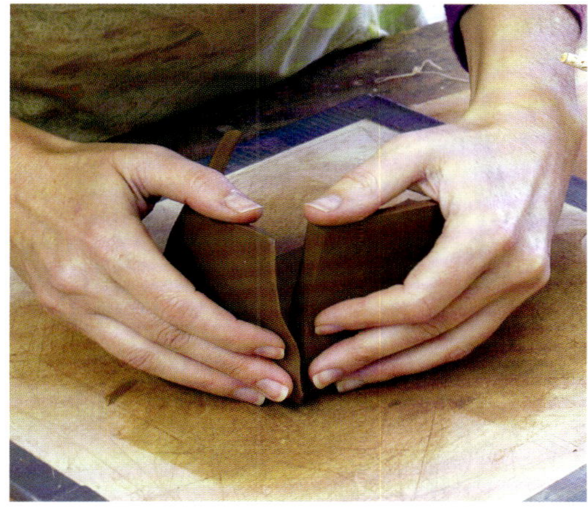

4. Gently tack the slabs together from bottom to top all around the pot. Use a rib to secure the slabs.

Adding Volume

Set the pot on a banding wheel, wet your fingers, and gently push out the inside walls. This stretches the slab and adds a curved, volumetric surface. Work around the pot until all four sides are addressed.

To form the feet, the pot must still be at the soft leather-hard stage and hold its shape. If the clay is too wet when forming the feet, the bottom will sag, and if it is too dry it will crack along the bottom. Using the fatty part of your thumb, gently tap between the seams on all four undersides of the pot (figure 5). This forces the bottom to become concave and simultaneously creates four feet for the piece to sit on. Once the feet are formed, place the pot on a level surface and bend the feet to eliminate any wobbling.

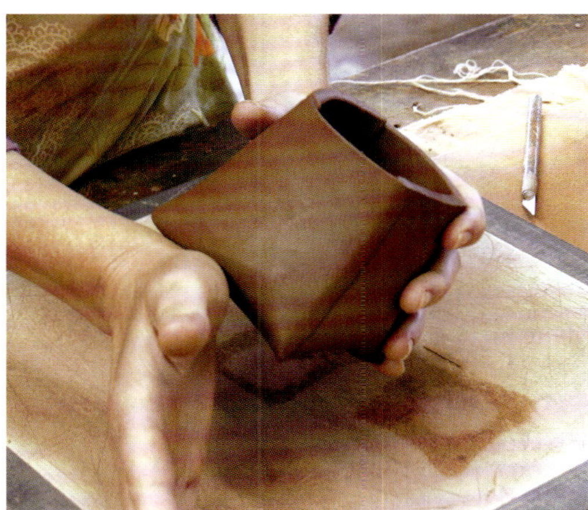

5. Tap all four edges between the side and bottom of the pot to create both feet and a concave bottom.

If you choose to stamp into the clay surface, now is the appropriate time while the clay is a soft leather hard and can accept the texture (figure 6).

Constructing the Lid, Flange, & Spout

Once the pot is a stiff leather hard, you are ready to create the lid. Prepare the pot by leveling the rim. This is easily done with a Surform tool. Roll a small ¼-inch slab about the size of the opening of the pot. Place the pot upside down on the slab and trace around the opening. Remove the pot and cut

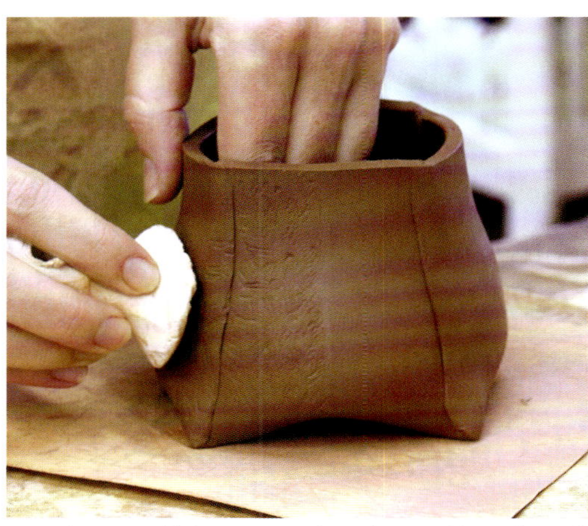

6. Push a carved bisque stamp into the outside surface of the pot while holding one hand on the inside of the pot.

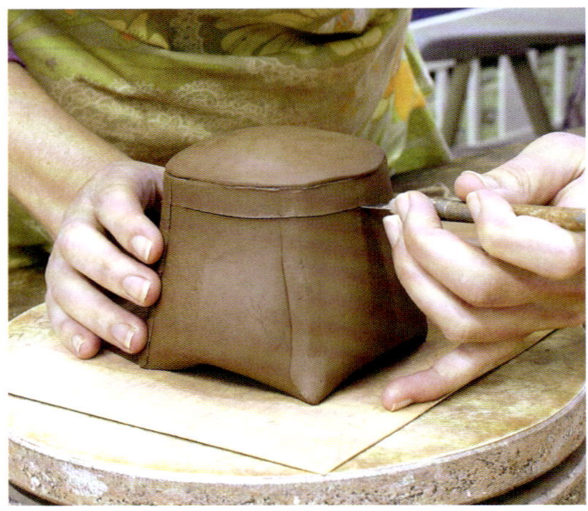

7. At the leather-hard stage, cut the lid away from the pot holding your X-Acto knife horizontal to the pot.

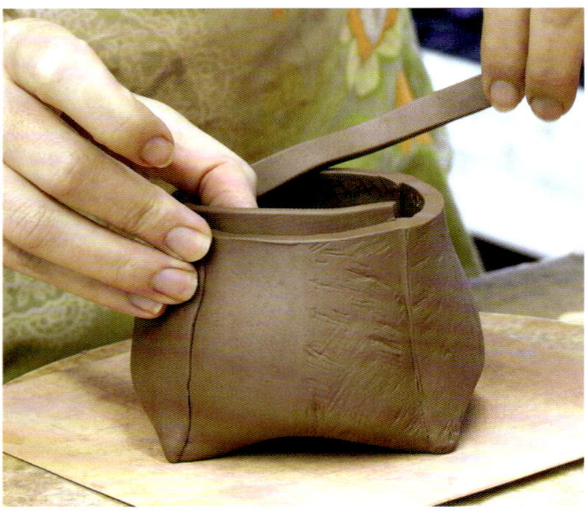

8. Finger tack a thin slab around the inside rim of the pot so its slightly higher than the top of the pot.

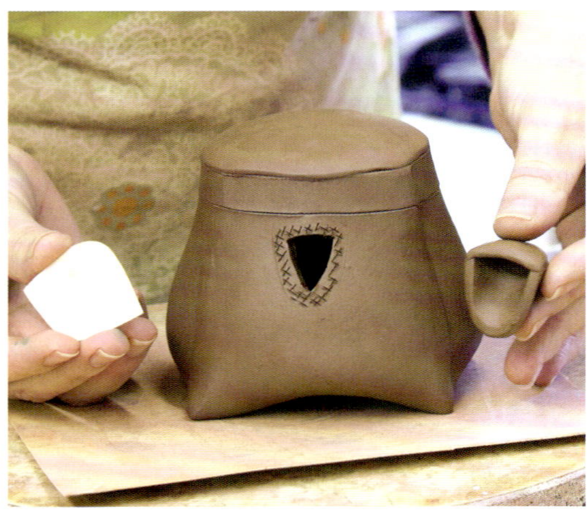

9. Cut away clay from the pot just inside the traced line of the spout,

along the traced line, then soften the cut edges, taking care not to stretch or deform the traced slab. Hold the slab in the palm of your hand and rub it with your thumb or a rib to create volume. Score and slip the pot and adhere the volumetric slab to the pot with the rubber brayer. The pot is now an enclosed, hollow form. Create a line where you intend to cut the lid away from the pot. Insert your knife perpendicular to the pot and cut an even line (do not saw back and forth) (figure 7). Slowly spin the banding wheel while you cut the lid away from the pot. Rest a finger or part of your hand against the banding wheel as you work to stabilize your hand and encourage an even cut.

It is appropriate to adhere the flange to the inside of the pot when the lid and pot are no longer in danger of being distorted from movement. Roll a thin slab (about 1/8 inch thick and 3/8 inch in height) from soft clay. Score and slip the top inside rim of the pot. Finger tack the flange to the inside of the pot leaving just a small overhang which will eventually catch the lid from sliding (figure 8). Clean up the seam between the pot and flange with a rubber-tipped tool and avoid using any water on the flange. Adjust the flange slightly inward with wet fingertips, so that the lid easily slips back into place on the pot. The lid will need to dry and fire on the pot to ensure a proper fit.

To create the spout pattern, start from a rounded triangle or ice-cream cone shape. Alter the shape of the spout by elongating or rounding the edges. Once the shape is cut from the pattern, gently squeeze the slab in half to create a trough where the liquid will flow. Add a decorative cap by attaching a small slab of clay onto the top of the spout. Mock the spout up on the pot and make sure it is centered. Once it is placed, trace the spout and cut just inside the trace line leaving enough clay for the spout to attach to the pot. Score and slip the pot and attach the spout to the pot (figure 9). Clean up the connections with a rubber-tipped tool. If you applied a decorative cap, once the piece is leather hard drill a hole through the front of the spout to allow liquid to flow.

Constructing the Pedestal Brick

The brick is a six-sided, hollow form made from leather-hard slabs. The dimensions of the brick are directly related to the pot that sits on it. This rectangular pattern consists of three total templates; two for the sides and one for the top and bottom. Roll, trace, and cut slabs as described for the pitcher form. Allow the slabs to set up until they become leather hard. Bevel all four edges of each slab but only on one side of the slab (figure 12). As you bevel, save the bevel cuttings in a plastic bag for later use. Take one slab cut to size for the side of the box and slip and score all four edges and attach it to the bottom slab. Do this for the three remaining slabs that make up the sides of the box. In lieu of rolling small coils, use the bevel cuttings to fill the spaces along the bottom and sides (figure 13). Run a rib on the outside edges to strengthen and secure the seams of the form. Allow this form to set up until the bottom is a stiff leather hard and can be flipped without sagging. Once flipped, attach the top of the brick by placing the five-sided form on the sixth leather-hard slab (figure 14). Secure and clean up the seams with a rubber rib. Poke a small hole on the bottom to allow air to escape during the drying and firing process. Place a small weighted board on top of the brick to eliminate warping while drying.

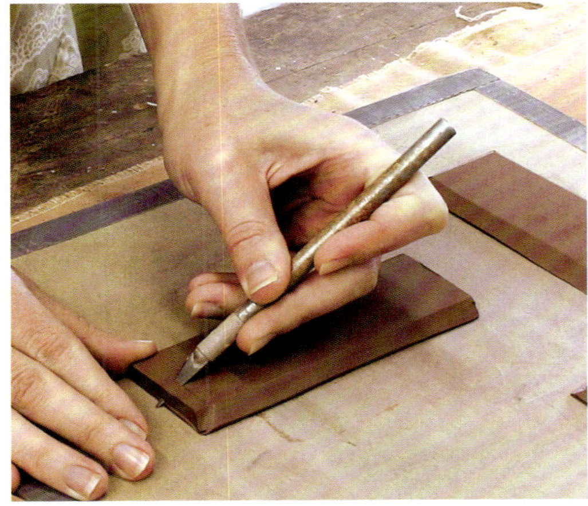

10. The slabs used for constructing the brick are stiff leather hard and beveled on all sides of the slab.

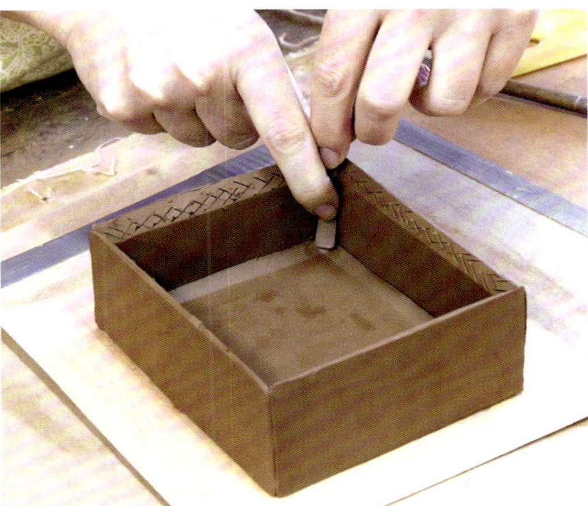

11. Attach all four sides to the bottom slab.

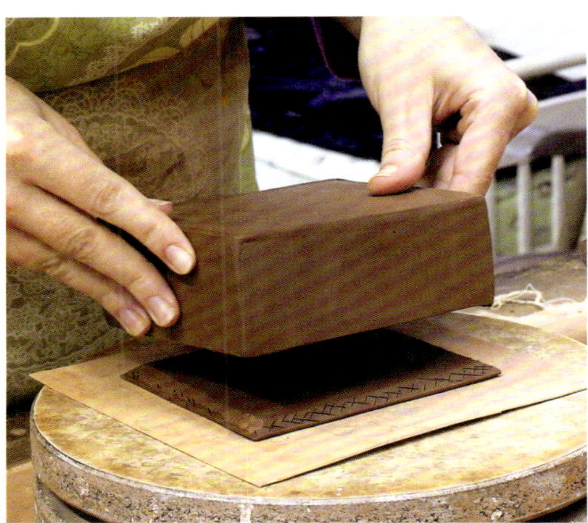

12. Once the pot sets up, flip it over and adhere it to the sixth slab. Clean and compress the seams.

Slab Construction

SOFT SLAB PITCHER

by Elizabeth Kendall

It's difficult to say which I enjoy more: the handbuilding process or the nature of the porcelain that I use. I love how porcelain behaves, how it flows and bends, and how the process allows me to explore this behavior. There is give and take between my hands and the clay, which both directs the process and contributes to the finished feel of the piece. Even making a simple pitcher allows me to express a feeling and to leave a record of my touch. I handbuild my slab forms from very soft, very thin, right out of the bag porcelain. Because the clay is so thin, I often get a little slumping during firing, which enhances the soft, relaxed look of the finished work.

Process

Every form starts with a slab, so I usually make slabs from a whole bag of clay in one session. Roll out ¼-inch-thick slabs of clay and trim to create a rectangular section (figure 1). If making several slabs, stack them with layers of plastic in between. Make sure no air is trapped between layers, and that the plastic is smooth and wrinkle free.

To produce slabs that take advantage of the bends and slumps that occur during the making and firing, use a French rolling pin and roll the slab to about ⅛-inch thick (figure 2). A French rolling pin is made from a single piece of wood, thicker in the middle and tapered toward each end. Because your hands touch the wood that's

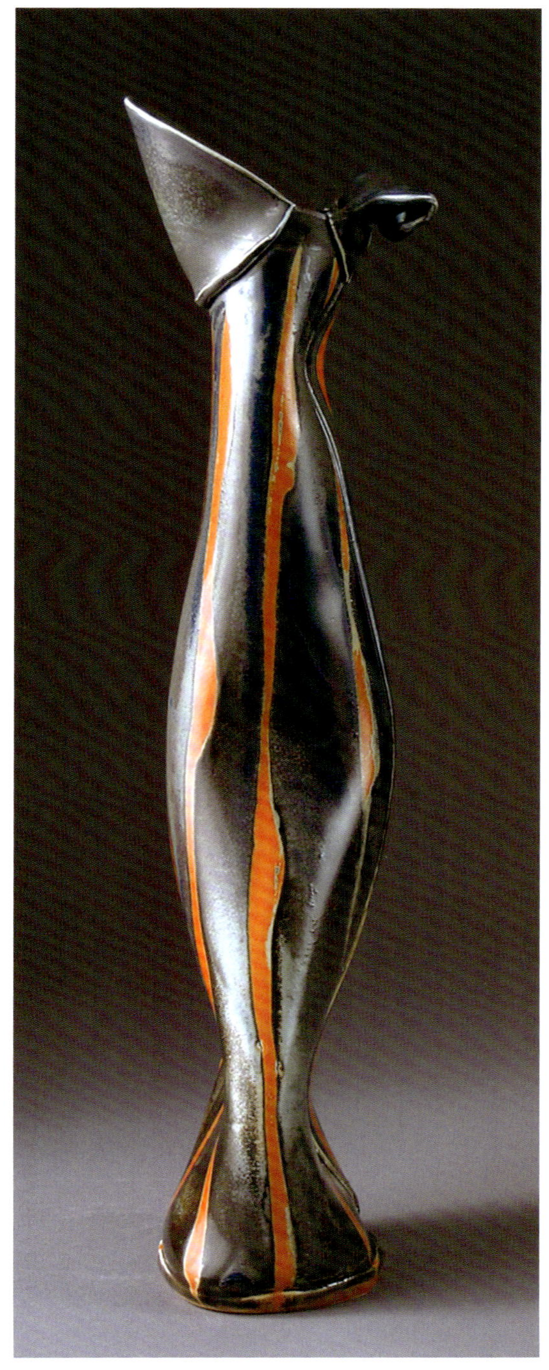

Pitcher, 14 inches in height, porcelain, soft-slab construction.

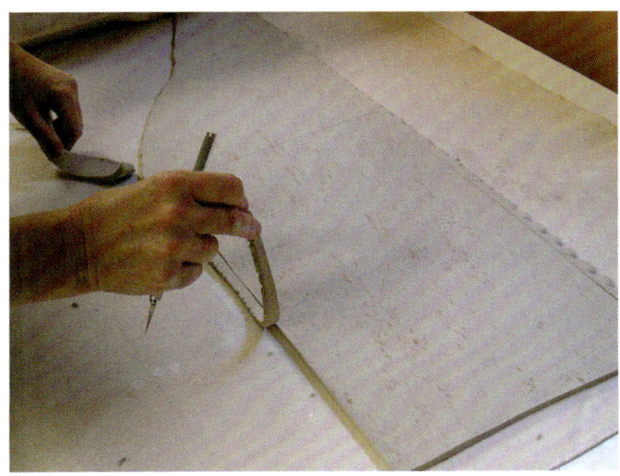

1. Roll out 1/4-inch-thick slabs of clay and trim to create a rectangular section.

2. Use a French rolling pin and roll the slab to about 1/8-inch thick.

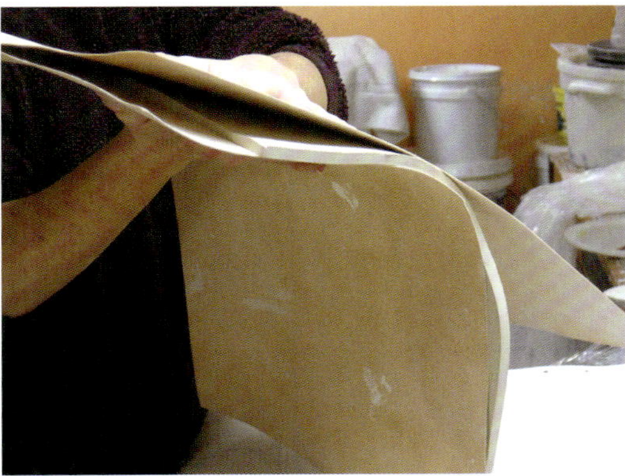

3. To prevent the slab from tearing as it gets thinner, sandwich it between two pieces of canvas or SlabMat.

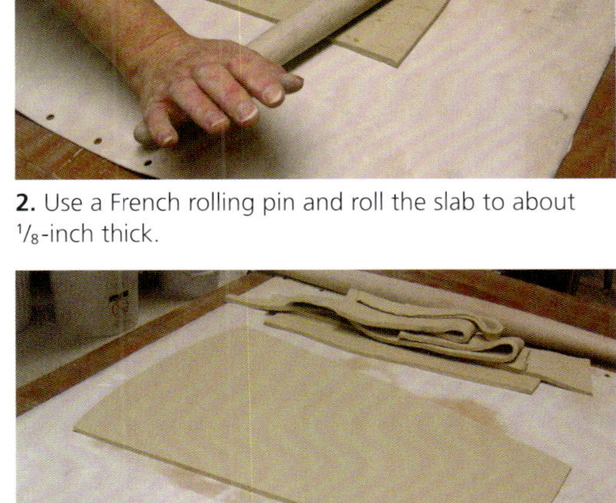

4. Cut the slab into a trapezoidal shape.

touching the clay, you'll have a better sense of how easily the clay is moving. You can also place the thicker middle of the pin directly on the part of the clay you want to thin.

After each pass, flip the slab over so it doesn't stick to the canvas, and then turn it 90° so the next pass stretches the clay in a different direction. This repeated rolling also helps to gradually get rid of excess moisture. As the slab gets thinner and flimsier, sandwich it between two pieces of canvas or SlabMat to keep it from tearing or stretching. The SlabMat is a dense paper that will not buckle when wet, and is great for flipping slabs (figure 3) and moving wet work around the studio. Switch surfaces and rolling pins as they get damp.

Cut a trapezoidal shape (figure 4), then cut a slight curve along the bottom edge. Cutting freehand guarantees distinct shapes, with something spontaneous and unexpected at the end. Before cutting, make sure the slab is not stuck to your work surface. A stuck slab will stretch and distort when you try to lift the sides.

To prevent extra thickness at the seam, use a pony roller to bevel and thin the long sides (figure 5). This gives a finished organic edge that keeps with the feeling of the piece.

Place the rolling pin on top of the slab for internal support, and slide your hand and arm under the edge of the slab without distorting or stretching the edge (figure 6). Carefully lift one length up first and onto the top of the rolling pin and then the other. Gently compress the seam with your hand and finish sealing it using a roller (figure 7). If the slab is fresh and moist, it isn't necessary to

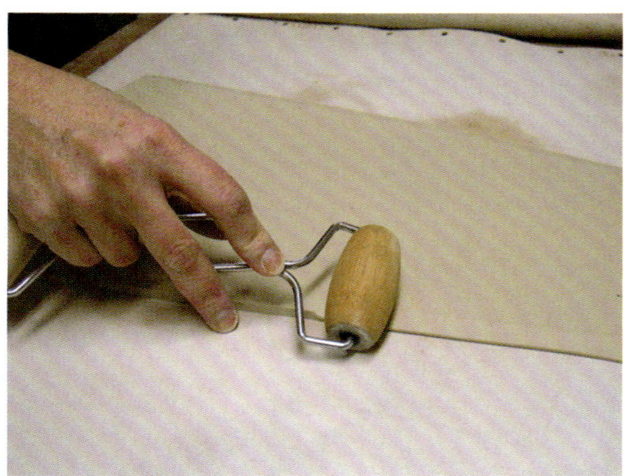

5. To prevent extra thickness at the seam, use a pony roller to bevel and thin the long sides.

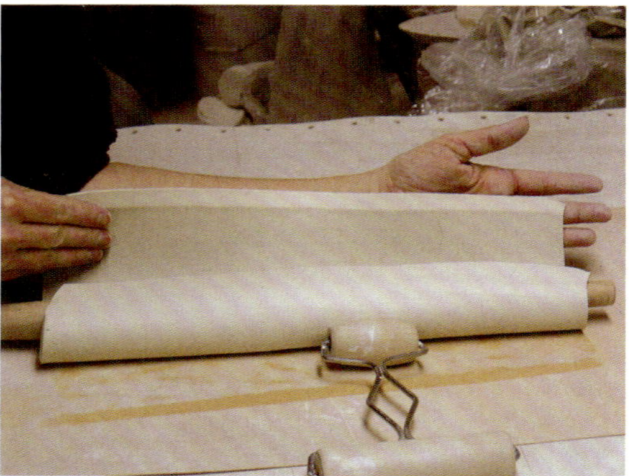

6. Slide your hand and arm under the edge of the slab without distorting or stretching the edge

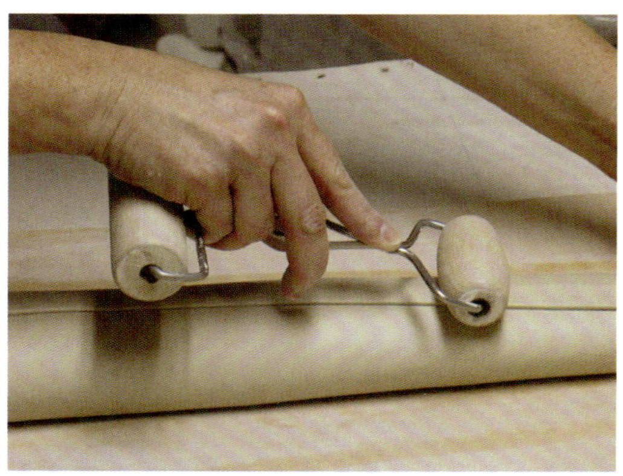

7. Gently compress the seam with your hand and finish sealing it using a roller.

score or slip the seams. In fact, it's easy to get the slab too wet. If this happens, the seam will stick or stretch.

Quickly raise the cylinder to a vertical position so it won't flatten and develop weak spots if it starts to fold. Try not to wiggle the material too much and always work with dry hands. Because the slab is so thin, you need to work fairly quickly. Place the cylinder onto a slab and cut out a piece that extends about 1/8-inch beyond the edge (figure 8). Push down gently into the base, then lift and tap the cylinder up and down to compress and attach two pieces.

While upside down, use a roller to compress the bottom onto the cylinder and to roll the edge of the base along the cylinder wall (figure 9). This provides an interesting undulating edge and ensures the strength of the union. Roll the lower corner of the newly joined base along the work surface to further compress and seal the joint and to soften the seam (figure 10). The whole profile begins to soften as it bends back and forth while rolling.

To create an undulating form with sweeping curves, gently squeeze the cylinder with the base of your hands to coax the form out of round (figure 11). Turn the form 90° and move your hand up pushing the sides in at about the point where a waist would be (figure 12). Pushing inward causes parts of the form to bulge more or less revealing a stomach and derriere. Sometimes the bulging needs to be redirected and the waist redefined (figure 13). Use a banding wheel so you can look at the work from all sides and make sure the body reference works.

Cut a small U-shape from a very thin slab for the spout (figure 14). Measure and mark the placement on the form, then bevel and thin the pouring edge with the roller. Roll along the edge of the spout that attaches to the pot. Exaggerate the flat or cut edge to echo the irregular line where the base meets the bottom wall and the exposed seam along the back. Trace the placement of the spout onto the pitcher, and cut an opening 1/8 inch on the inside edge of the tracing. Pinch the cut edge of the spout to thin and soften before attaching, and use gentle pressure to join the spout to the pitcher (figure 15).

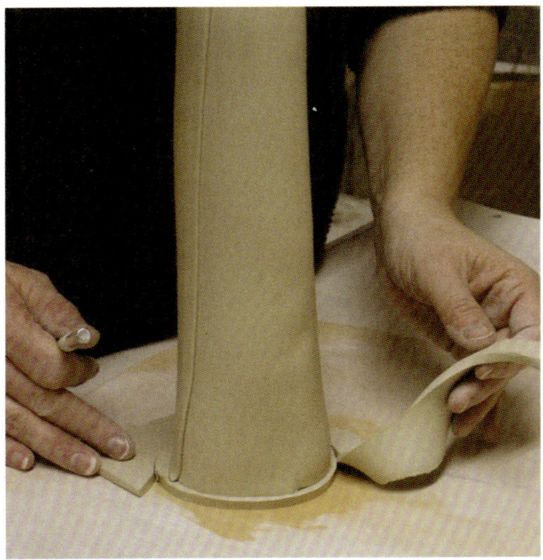

8. Quickly raise the cylinder to a vertical position so it won't flatten and develop weak spots if it starts to fold

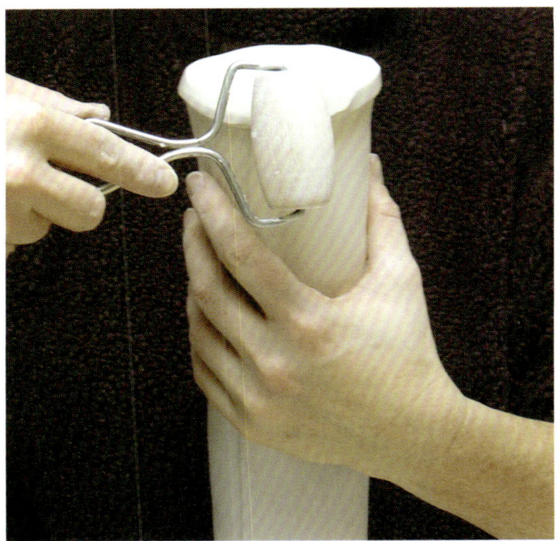

9. While upside down, use a roller to compress the bottom onto the cylinder and to roll the edge of the base.

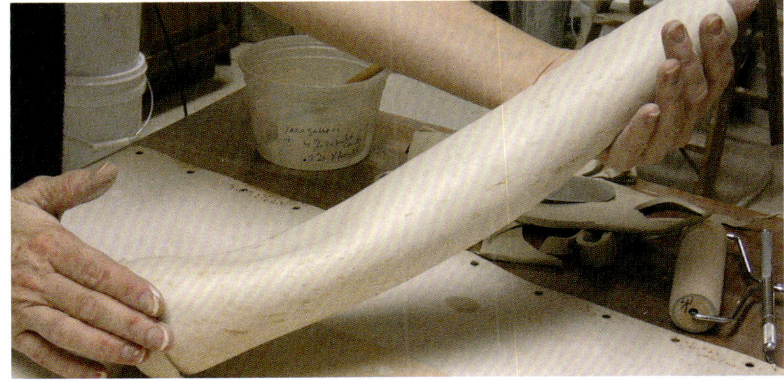

10. Roll the lower corner of the newly joined base along the work surface to further compress and seal the joint, and to soften the seam.

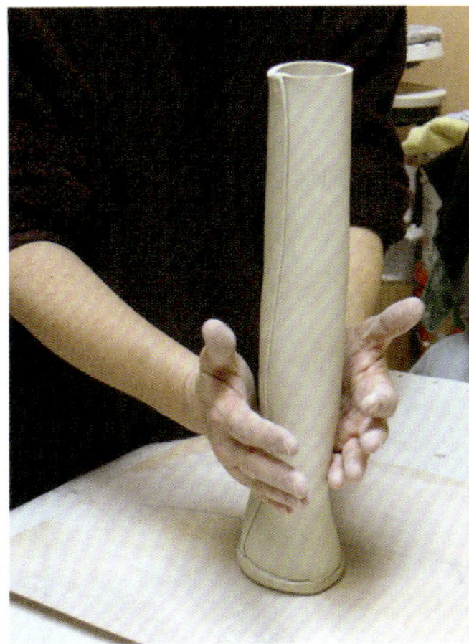

11. Gently squeeze the cylinder with the base of your hands to coax the form out of round.

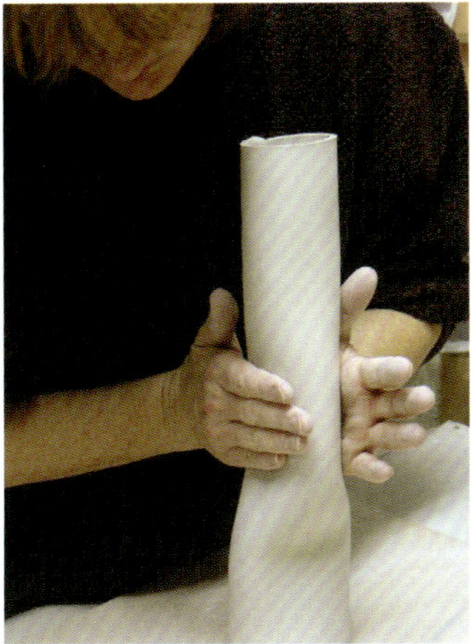

12. Turn the form 45° and move your hands up pushing the sides in where a waist would be.

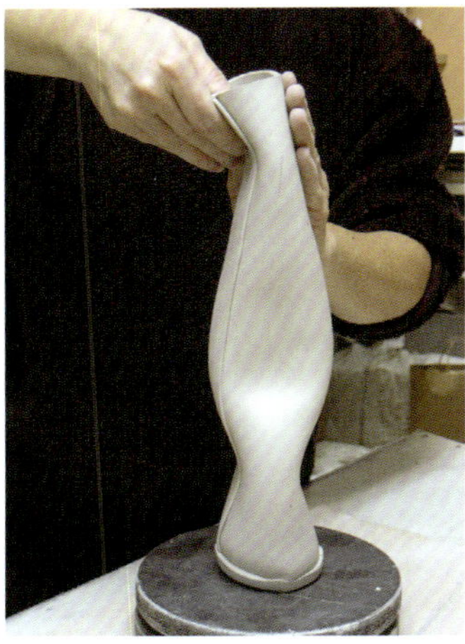

13. Sometimes the bulging needs to be redirected and the waist redefined.

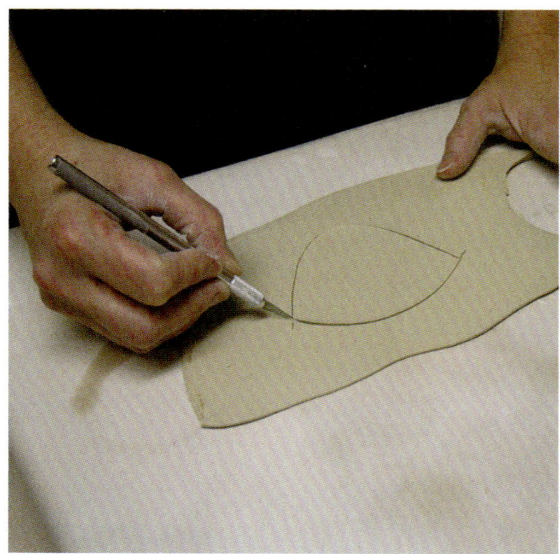

14. Cut a small U-shape from a thin slab for the spout.

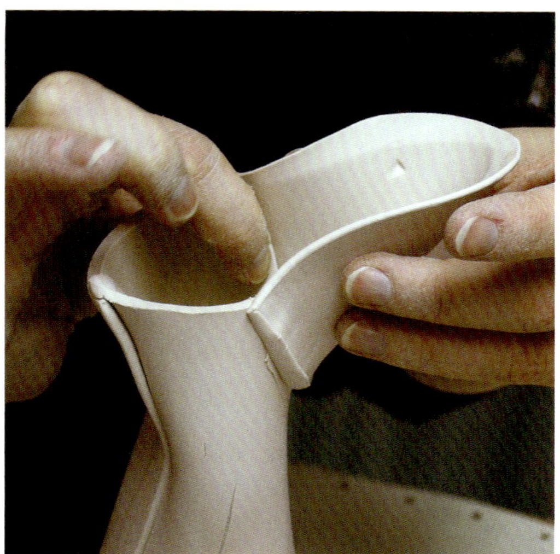

15. Thin and soften the lip before attaching, and use gentle pressure to join the spout to the pitcher

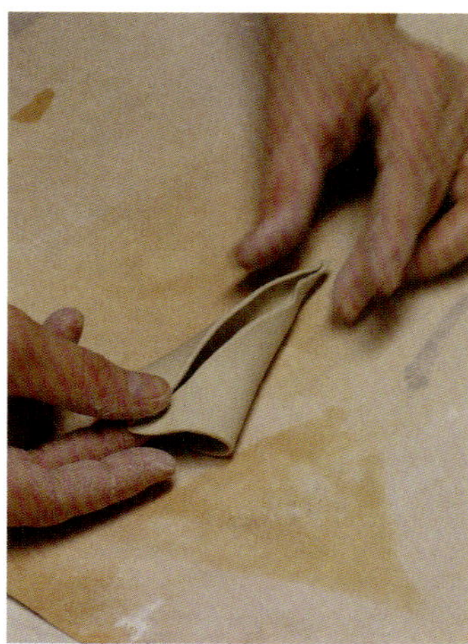

16. Cut a small triangle of very thin clay, bevel the edges, then make a cone leaving the bottom open.

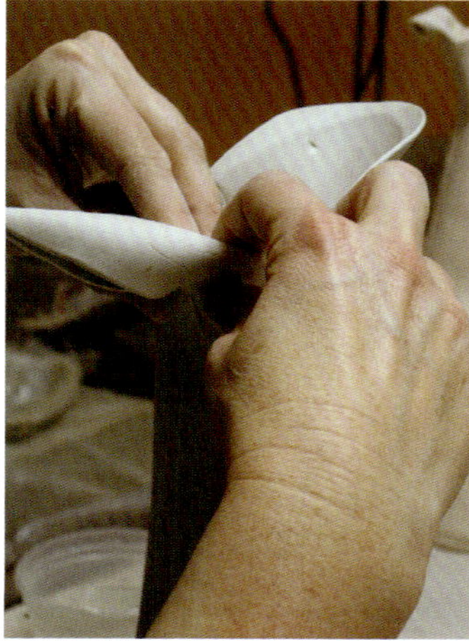

17. Sandwich the top edge of the pitcher rim inside the cone and seal with gentle pressure.

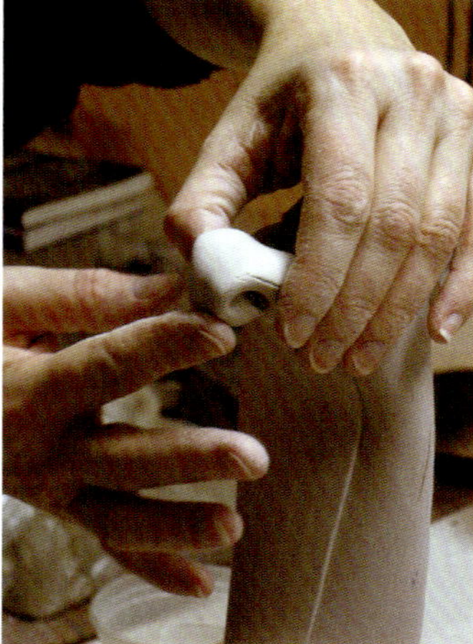

18. Roll the cone into a spiral and keep some of the air inside to capture a puffy feeling.

A small embellishment where a handle might have started can balance the forward thrust of the spout. Cut a small triangle of very thin clay and bevel the edges. Bend the two sides of the triangle into the middle making a cone leaving the bottom open (figure 16). Sandwich the top edge of the pitcher rim inside the cone and seal with gentle pressure (figure 17). Roll the cone into a spiral and keep some of the air inside to capture a puffy feeling. Support the sides of the cone with one hand while rolling the tip of the cone in and under (figure 18). The sides may open a bit and cracks may form, so watch carefully. Leave the openings and cracks if they look interesting or smooth them according to taste. Wrap the pitcher loosely with plastic to slow the drying and even out the moisture.

Slab Construction

BUILDING WITH TARPAPER

by Jonathan Kaplan

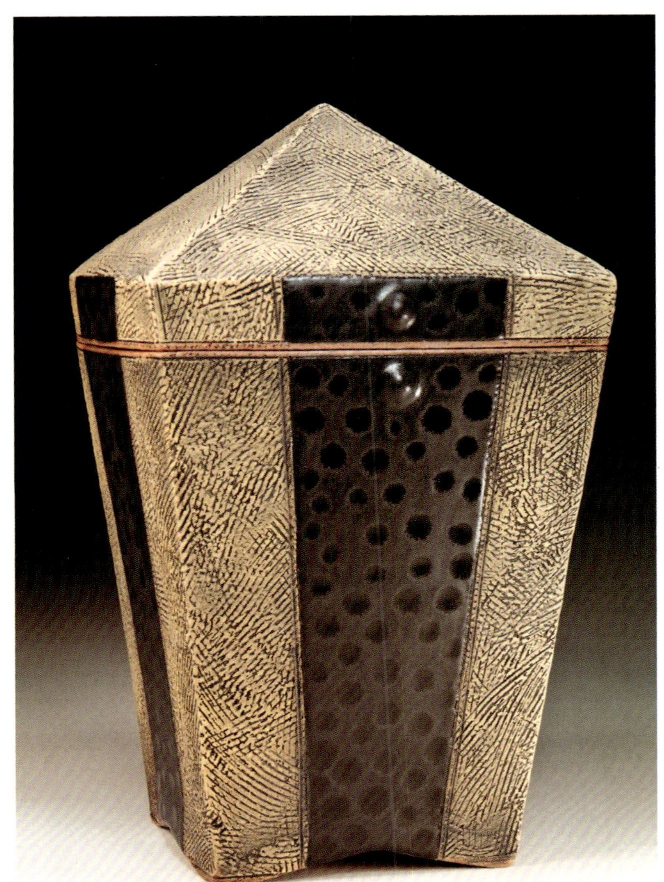

The Arrow Box, 10 inches in height, soft slab construction utilizing tarpaper templates.

Ceramic artist Lisa Pedolsky likes to think of herself as a an artist working in clay. As a designer, by the fact that her work is hollow, function becomes attached to the piece. Her work deals with the challenges of working as designed, both aesthetically and technically. Everything about her work stems from intention. For example, glazing and surface decoration are not afterthoughts; they play as important a role as the design and construction of the work. A perfectionist with attention to detail, she does not want her work to look like anyone else's. She says, "When you do what you've always done, you get what you've always gotten."

The Arrow Box Method

Lisa has developed a systematic way of making her pottery, and she likes the analogy of the sewing process where the inside of a garment is as important as the outside. Her technique follows a pattern-making process originally published in "Building a Better Box," by Anna Calluori Holcombe with Patrick Taddy in the spring 1999 issue of *Pottery Making Illustrated*.

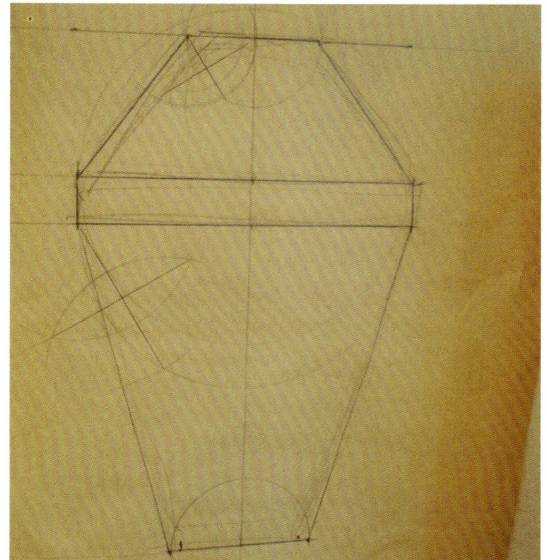

1. Start with a paper sketch and full-scale paper drawing of the design.

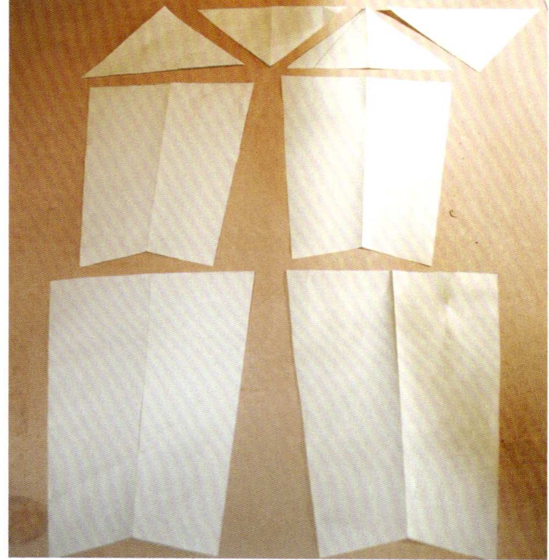

2. Create patterns for the top, sides, and bottom based on your full scale drawing.

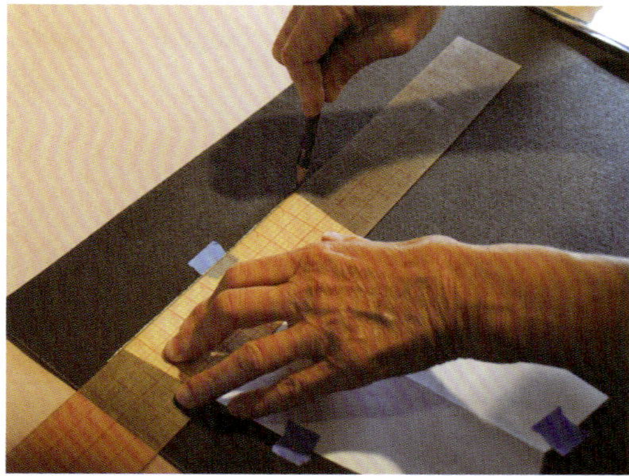

3. Affix the paper patterns to tarpaper and outline the pattern onto the tarpaper using a straight edge.

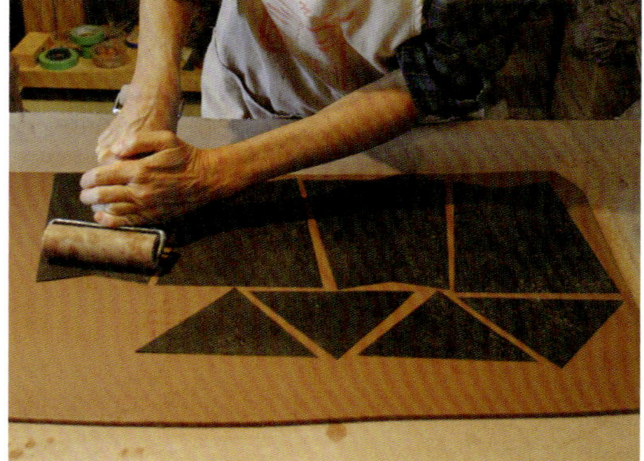

4. Use a small roller to embed the dampened tarpaper patterns making them flush with the surface.

Templates to Construction

All of Pedolsky's work begins as a sketch on paper. She sees the "potential for each piece in the drawing." Working first with sketches, she then develops a technical drawing from which the patterns are taken (figure 1). From these patterns, she designs and constructs forms that are highly structured with an architectural reference.

The initial sketch establishes a profile and a sense of scale and mass. The Arrow Box is ten inches high and six inches in the other dimensions. Using soft pencils, she refines the sketches until they make visual sense. She can spend weeks, often months refining the concept. Once the sketches are fully articulated, Pedolsky designs 2–3 pieces as a small series of works and takes 1–2 days to prepare the full-scale drawings and make the patterns. She checks everything to make sure that the proportions are correct before moving to the clay slab with tarpaper or simple paper patterns (figure 2). "The beauty of using tarpaper," says Lisa, "is that the clay can be worked at any stage, soft wet slabs or stiff leather-hard slabs."

Lisa uses a mid-weight tarpaper for most of her working patterns (figure 3). The slab can be any consistency as the tarpaper becomes the exoskel-

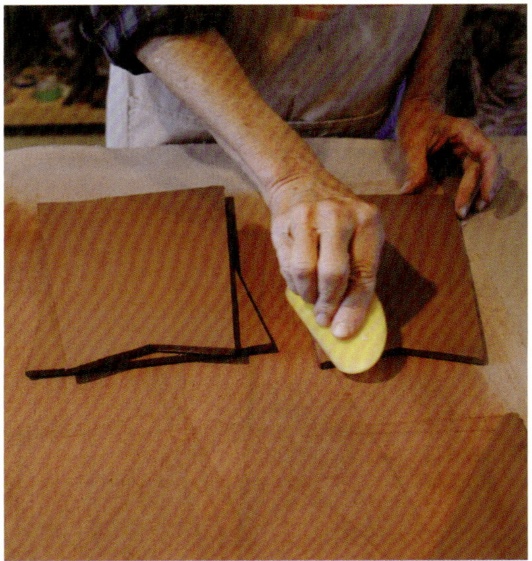

5. Leave the tarpaper attached to the cut out shapes. Compress the backs using a rubber rib.

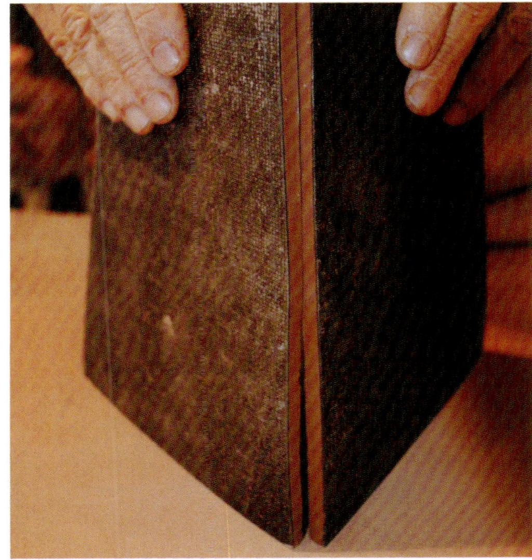

6. Assemble the sections using the tarpaper to help retain the shape of each piece as you work.

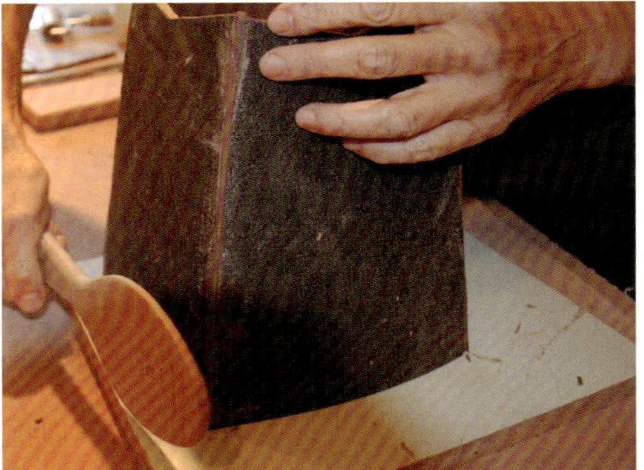

7. After joining all sections, paddle the seams to strengthen the joints.

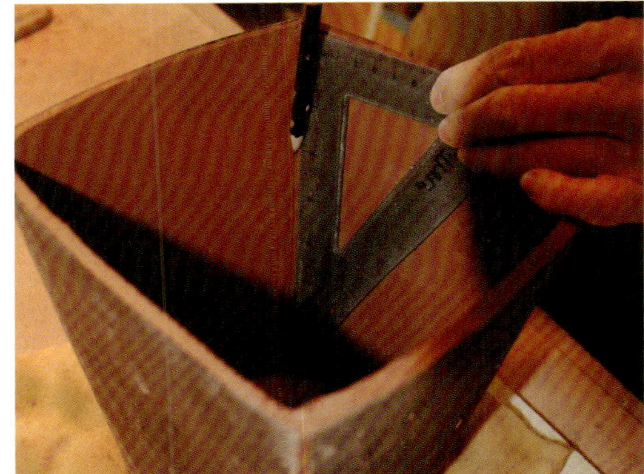

8. Using a triangle as a guide, run a dull pencil up the seam to compress and create a design detail.

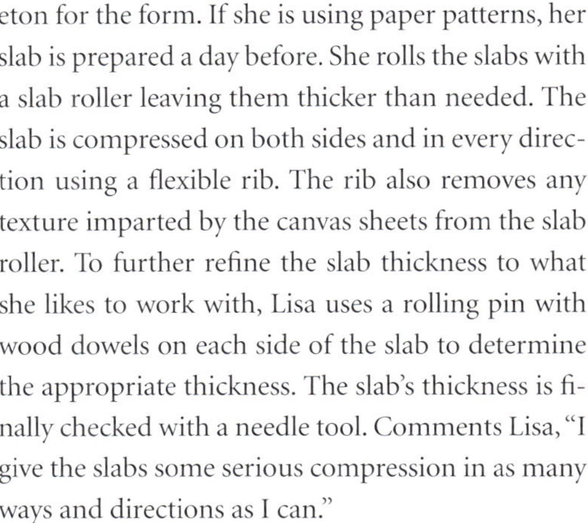

eton for the form. If she is using paper patterns, her slab is prepared a day before. She rolls the slabs with a slab roller leaving them thicker than needed. The slab is compressed on both sides and in every direction using a flexible rib. The rib also removes any texture imparted by the canvas sheets from the slab roller. To further refine the slab thickness to what she likes to work with, Lisa uses a rolling pin with wood dowels on each side of the slab to determine the appropriate thickness. The slab's thickness is finally checked with a needle tool. Comments Lisa, "I give the slabs some serious compression in as many ways and directions as I can."

Once the slab is ready, she moistens each tarpaper template. The patterns are positioned on the slab and, using a pizza roller or brayer, she pushes down to make the tarpaper flush with the surface of the slab (figure 4). Since all the components are made from the same slab, the shrinkage is uniform. Lisa then uses a dull X-Acto knife to accurately cut the clay. She also ribs the back of the cut pieces to further compress each part thoroughly (figure 5). At the same time, she cuts a long slab from the remaining slab for the lid flange and uses the balance of the slab to form the bottom of the Arrow Box. These pieces are put under plastic for later use.

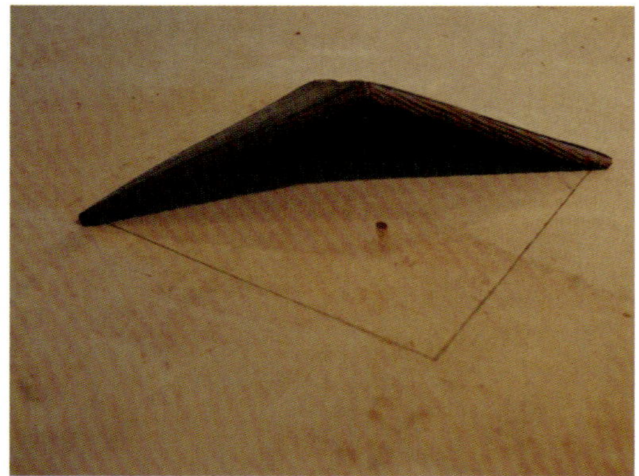

9. Assemble the triangular top sections over a drawing of the outside dimensions of the box.

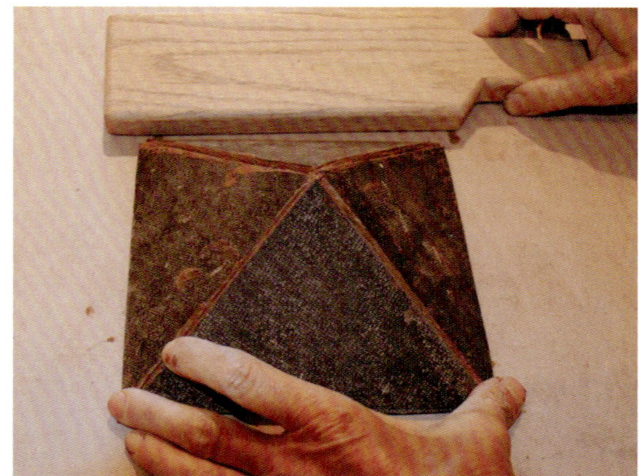

10. Once assembled, square the top over the drawing using your hands and a straight paddle.

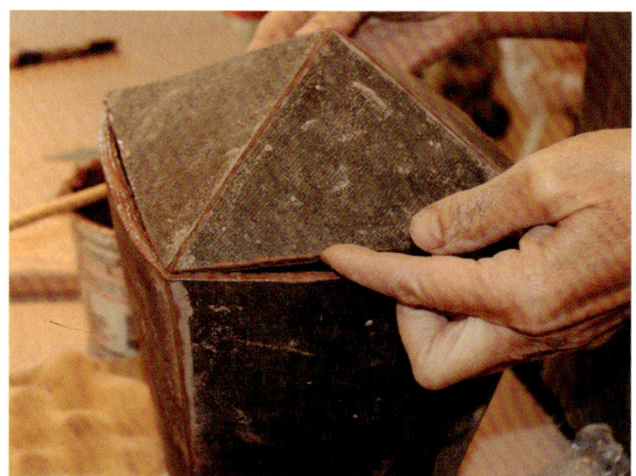

11. Score and slip the top edge of the box and the bottom edge of the pyramid shape, then join.

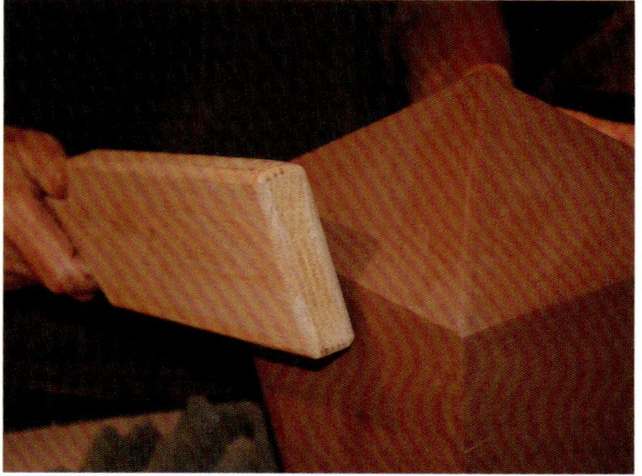

12. Remove the tarpaper and compress the seams where the body and the top meet with a paddle.

Assembling the Body

Lisa begins the assembly of the Arrow Box by cutting a shallow bevel on the long edges so that the seams can be further compressed after assembly (figure 6). After scoring the edges and applying a simple slurry of her clay body and water, she attaches all four sides of the box leaving the tarpaper in place to support the box during its construction. The assembly of all her slab components involves scoring the edges, using slip to help the joinery, ribbing the joints together, and finally paddling the seams (figure 7). The slab components become firmly wedded to each other.

After the initial assembly of the four sides, she uses a light-weight paddle on the seams. The excess clay moves into the joint as she paddles the corners. She stops when the edges of the tarpaper meet. The piece is then moved onto foam for support. Using a finger, Lisa removes any excess slip that has been forced from the seams on the inside of the box. Then using a dull, soft pencil point and a plastic drawing triangle as a guide, she creates a rounded ditch or trough and gently compresses the inside seam from top to bottom (figure 8). This small detail creates a design element that, provides a place for the glaze to pool and highlight the interior seams. Once the exterior walls are assembled and squared up, the bottom surface is sprayed with water, covered with plastic, and the piece is put aside.

Fitting the Top

With the four triangle sections cut, Lisa measures the outside dimensions of the top of the body that has just been constructed. She then draws this

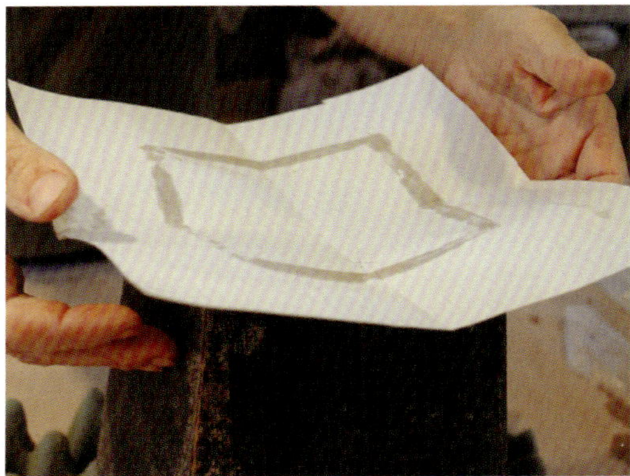

13. Wet the bottom of the box and lay a piece of paper over it to get a transferred outline of the shape.

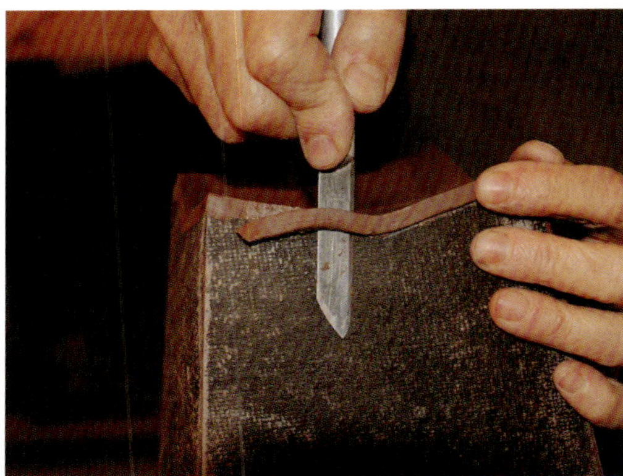

14. Attach the slab to the bottom of the box, then cut the excess clay from the using a sharp knife.

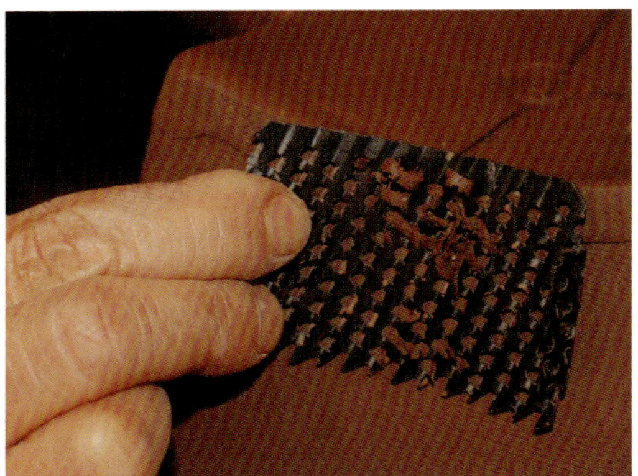

15. Remove the tarpaper patterns then smooth and refine the seam using a Surform rasp.

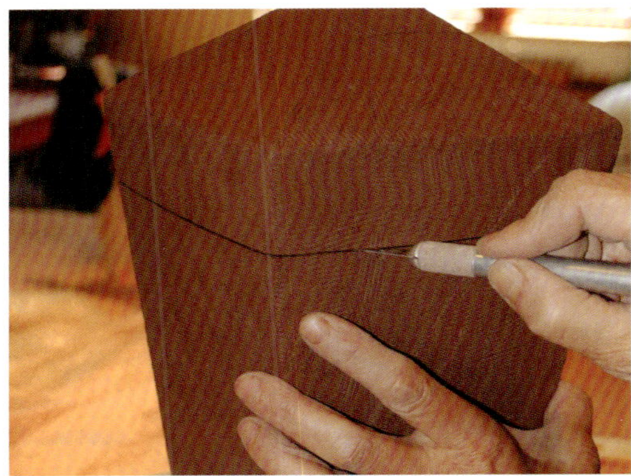

16. Measure the lid height, depending on your design and cut a straight line separating the lid and body.

square shape on her worktable and prepares to assemble each piece. After cutting a soft bevel, the edges are moistened and pressed together. The bottom edge corresponds to the square perimeter she has just drawn (figure 9) and the four top pieces go together in a logical sequence by drawing them together as pieces of a puzzle. Using a paddle with a thick edge, she squares up the top so it lines up with the drawing on the table again (figure 10). The four angled seams are paddled together, compressing and forcing the joining slip to the inside of the truncated top. Turning the piece upside down, she cleans the inside seams with her fingertip. Again, she uses a dull pencil to heal the inside seams and leave a small trough as a design element. Scoring the bottom surface of the top as well as the top surface of the body, she joins the pieces together (figure 11) and paddles them to form a secure and well-compressed joint (figure 12). After a final paddling, the assembled piece is put aside to dry slightly.

Joining the Bottom

Lisa begins working on the bottom of the body by inverting it onto a piece of foam. She takes a square piece of paper that is larger than the bottom and folds it into quarters and marks the folded lines with a pencil. After wetting the edges of the body's bottom, she centers the paper on the opening and presses down to get an imprint of the shape (figure 13). She cuts the paper to the same size as the bottom of the piece, wets both sides of the pattern so that it does not curl and places it pencil side down on a scrap slab. Using her pizza roller, Lisa rolls the paper flush with the clay surface. Remov-

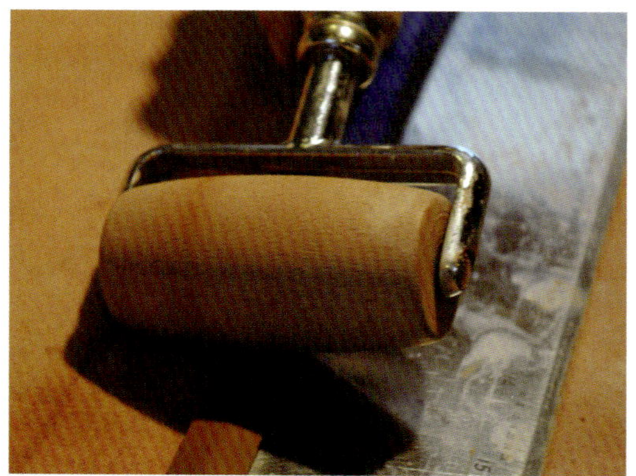

17. Cut the lid flange to the right width, then bevel the edge using a pony roller.

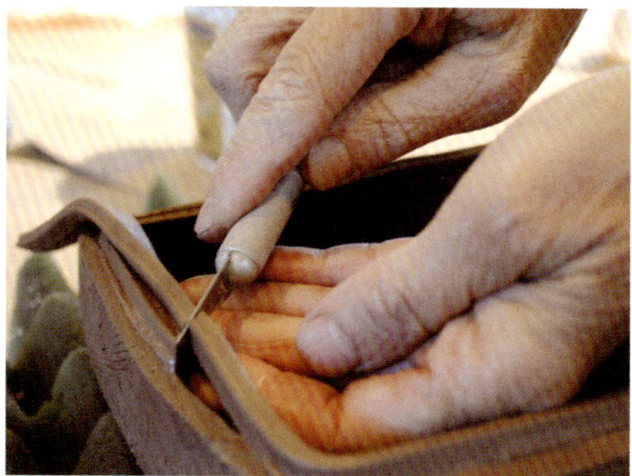

18. Attach the flange to the lid starting at the center of one side. Cut the ends at an angle and attach.

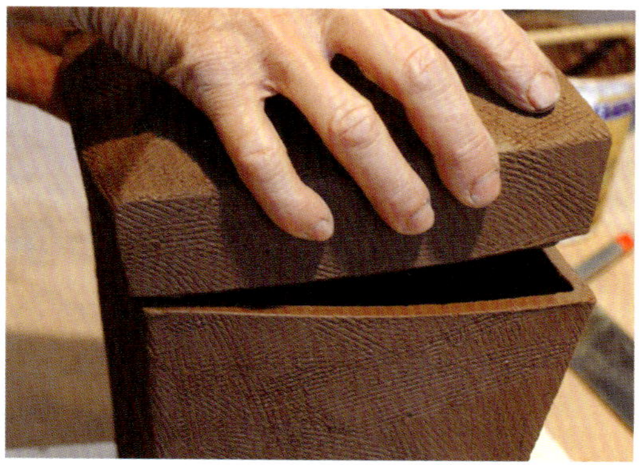

19. Place the lid onto the box to check for fit issues, and adjust the flange as necessary.

ing the paper pattern, she lightly scores the pencil lines that have transferred to the clay. The edges of the body are slipped and scored as are the inside perimeter of the bottom slab and the slab is eased onto body and pressed down to conform to the undulating shape of the base. Excess clay is trimmed with a knife (figure 14), and the tarpaper removed. The bottom edges are worked with a rib, then rolled so that some clay moves onto the sides of the body and paddled. Squaring the sides up with the paddle, any remaining high points in the area can be taken down with a Surform rasp (figure 15). She finishes the construction by using a plastic rib on the seams and then gives them a final paddle to fully compress and knit them together.

Fashioning a Lid and Flange

The piece is placed right side up on a piece of foam and all the seams are again pressed in with a rib and then paddled. To make the lid and the flange, Lisa uses a flexible ruler to measure from a flat plane up each of the four sides, marks the corners, and then connects the "dots." The lid is cut at 90° with two passes of a sharp X-Acto knife (figure 16). After removing the lid, she checks the interior seams and uses a blunt pencil to compress the clay and cleans up any excess clay scraps from the interior with a soft brush.

For the flange, she uses a long slab originally cut from the larger one at the start, and rolls it to arrive at an appropriate thickness. She then bevels one edge of the slab (figure 17) and decides on the total width of the flange, how much of it attaches to the lid, and how much projects into the body. The slab is cut to the correct width, scored and slipped around the inside perimeter of the lid and the beveled edge of the strip, and attached to the interior of the lid starting at the center. Compressing as she attaches the bevel edge, the sections are overlapped at the end and cut at an angle for a perfect match (figure 18). Using a blunt pencil, she seals the two adjoining surfaces and uses a rib and finger to carefully align the flange so its surface matches the angles of the walls of the jar (figure 19).

Slab Construction

USING BISQUE-MOLDED SLABS

by Nancy Zoller

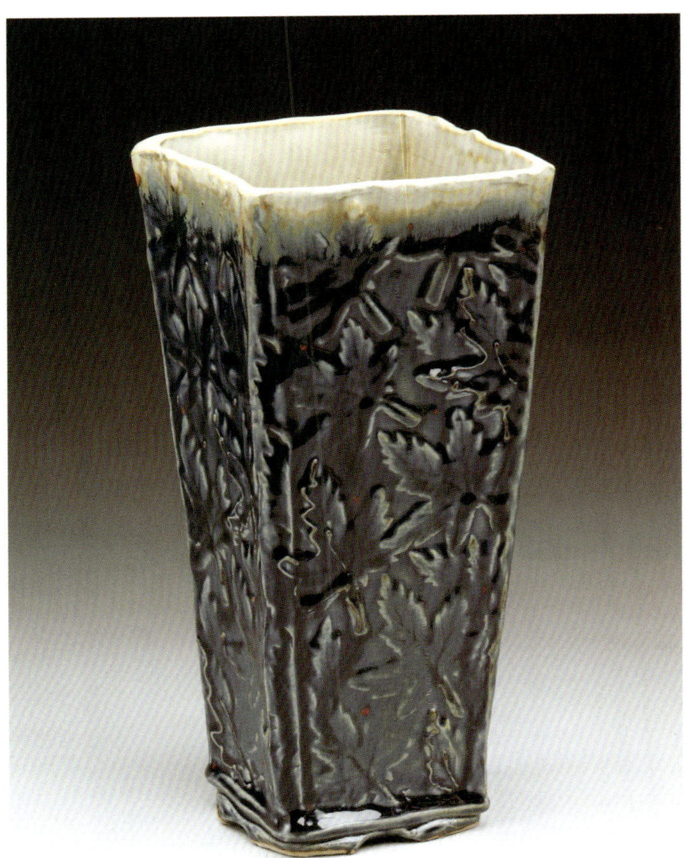

Using bisque molds both as templates and for texture allows you to easily create decorative forms

Making a vase from a bisque mold using your own designs, and adding textures and marks that speak to you personally, is a joyous adventure! Making impressions in clay never grows old for me. This technique continues to offer endless possibilities in my studio, as well as an avenue for personal discovery for my clay students. The first bisque mold served as a studio tool to make simple, utilitarian pieces such as platters, large and small dinner plates, small bowls, and the ever necessary soap dish. This line of work was designed as a signature body intended as an offering to my wholesale galleries. To keep the pieces affordable, they are not labor intensive, while still appearing visually interesting and unique.

Making the Bisque Mold

To make your initial vase bisque mold, roll out a ¼-inch thick slab of clay. Stamp your design on the surface then determine the dimensions of the finished piece. First cut this pattern out of paper then transfer it to the rolled clay. Cut or impress a pattern in the clay that is ½-inch larger than your

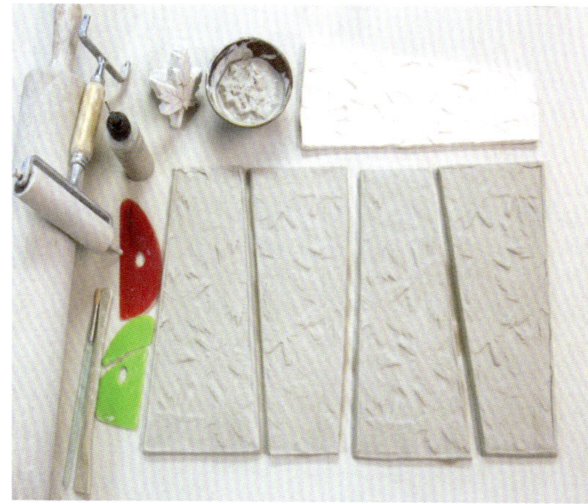

1. Cut out the four sides, then use a small roller to press the pattern from the bisque mold into each one.

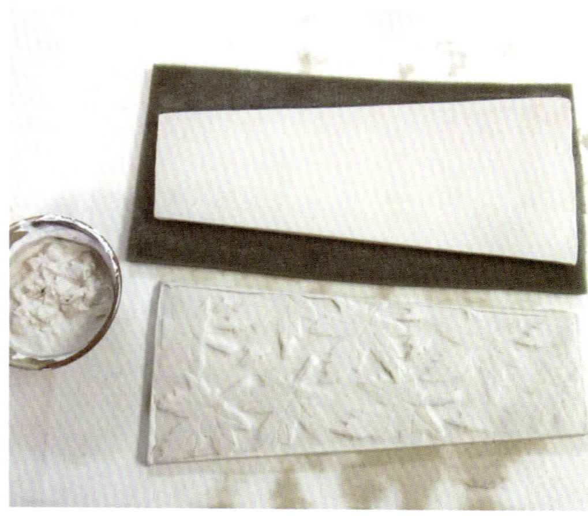

2. Place one side face down on a piece of foam to protect the pattern, then join the other sides one at a time.

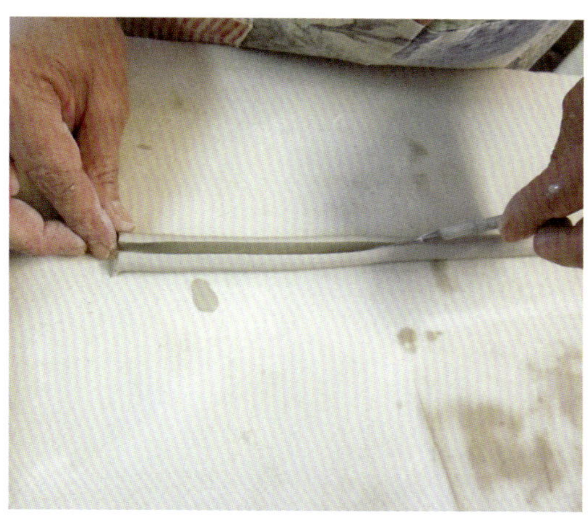

3. Cut a coil into four strips to create quarter-round beads to reinforce the inside seams.

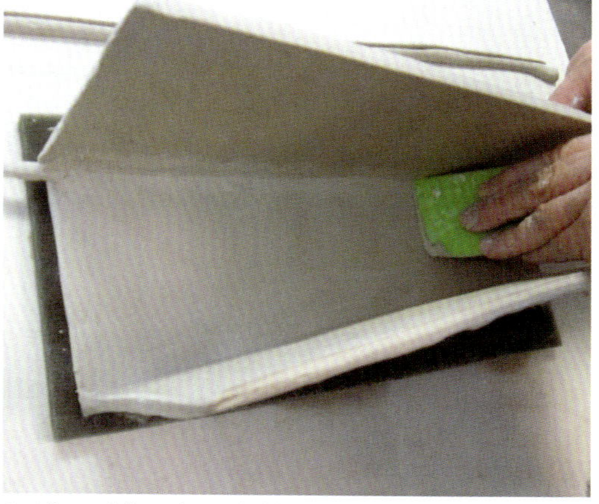

4. After adding the coil, blend it into the seam and walls using a stiff rubber rib.

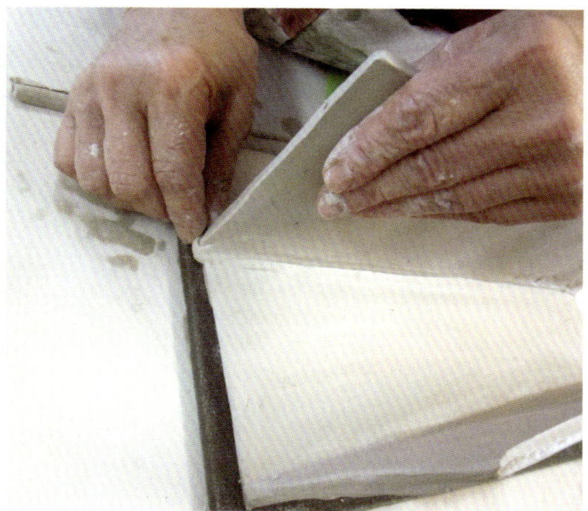

5. Extend the coil over the top corner of the two joined pieces to strengthen the corners of the top rim.

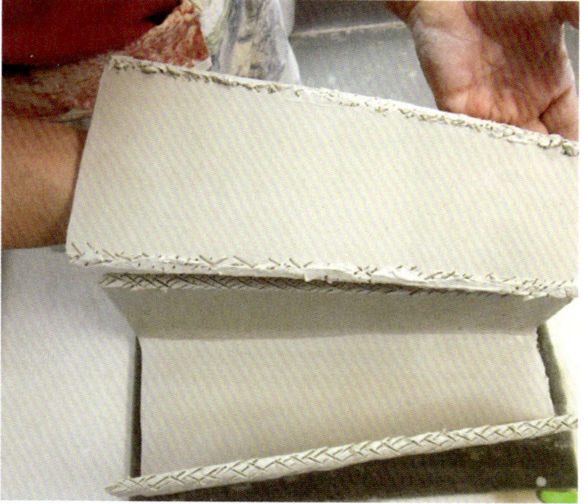

6. Score the edges, apply slip, then add the final leather-hard vase wall to the top of the two side walls.

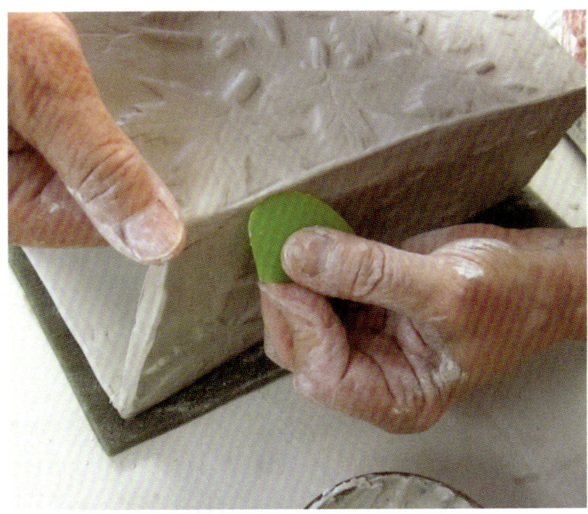

7. Reinforce and compress the outer seams using the rounded edge of a stiff rubber rib.

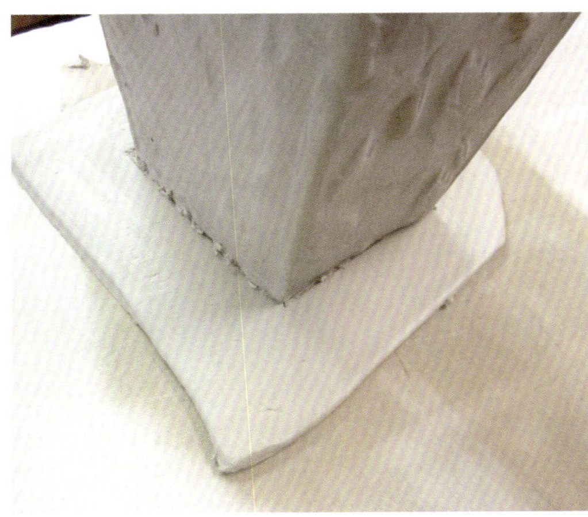

8. Place the vase right-side up on a small slab, mark the location for the bottom, then score and apply slip.

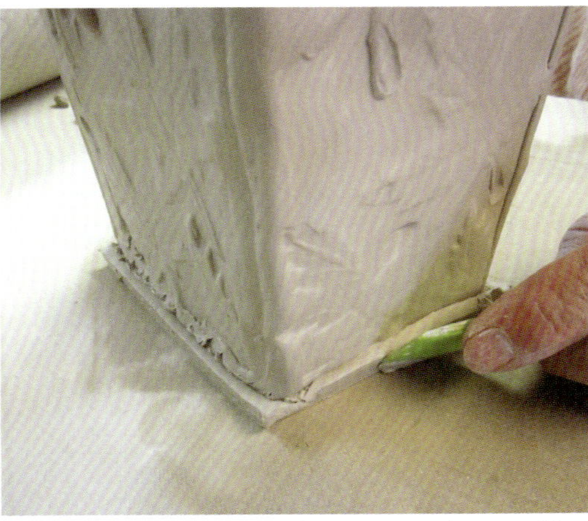

9. Cut around the outside of the vase, and use a stiff rubber rib to finish the edge.

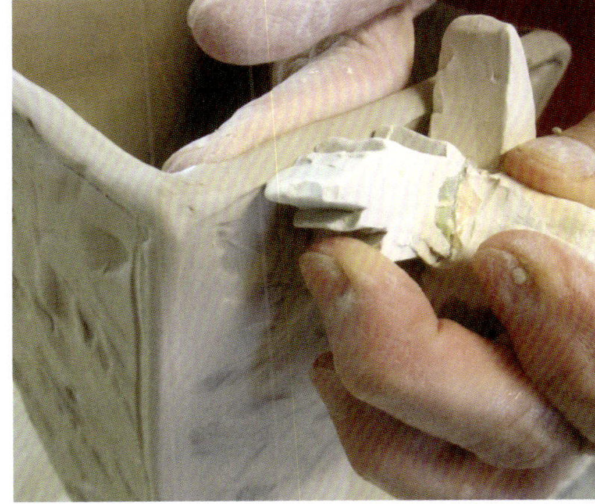

10. Press the original stamp used to make the bisque mold into the rim and over the seams if desired.

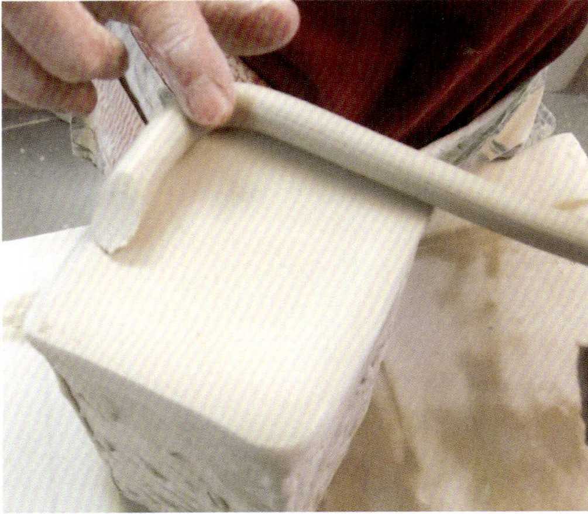

11. Add a coil to the bottom of the vase to create a foot. Angle the two ends to create a strong, even join.

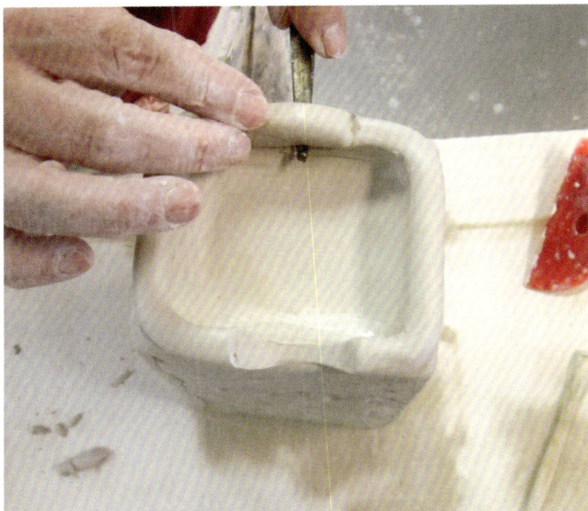

12. Carve out indentations in the foot using a fettling knife to make it visually lighter.

desired finished piece. The dimensions of my vase mold are 5 inches across the top edge, 11 inches along the sides, and 3 inches along the bottom. Allow it to dry slowly so that it does not warp, then fire the slab in your next bisque kiln.

Constructing the Vase

Roll out a large ¼-inch thick slab of clay. Smooth it with a rubber rib, making sure there are no other textures on the clay. Place the bisque mold under the smoothed slab and roll over it vigorously with a small roller. Repeat this four times (figure 1). Flip the large slab over and cut out the forms with a needle tool.

Allow the slabs to dry to leather hard so that they are firm enough to stand up straight on their own. Place the first side (pattern side) down on a piece of foam to preserve the convex leaf pattern (figure 2). Score and add slip to the edge of both pieces, then connect them. At this point, extrude a ½-inch coil of clay. With your fettling knife, cut the coil in half and then in quarters (figure 3), giving you a lovely 90°-angled, quarter-round piece to place in the inside corner of the two joined slabs.

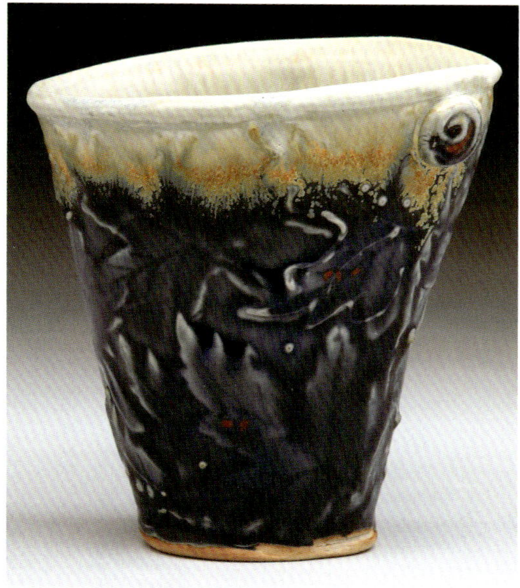

Handbuilt soft slab cup features relief decoration created using bisque mold template.

Place something behind the upright slab as you connect it to the bottom piece to provide support as you add this coil. A brick or a 4×4 piece of wood works well.

Smooth the coil evenly along the seam and blend into both slabs, reinforcing this interior connection. I like to use a flat-edge wooden tool, finishing with a firm rubber rib to finish the seam (figure 4). Repeat this on all inside edges while constructing. Extend the coil over the top corner of the two joined pieces (figure 5) to strengthen the corners of the top rim where cracking is likely to occur. Repeat this step, joining all four pieces together (figure 6).

Connect the outside edges in the same manner using a rubber rib. I use a Mudtools green rib that I cut in half, using the small round side (figure 7). This small rib fits into small spaces.

To create the bottom of the vase, roll out a small slab of clay the same thickness as the vase form and place your hollow, four-sided vessel on top (figure 8). With a needle tool, mark a square piece outlining the bottom, leaving a ⅛-inch overhang on each side. Score and slip the bottom piece as well as the vase body and attach them. Use a rib tool to move the extra clay up and over the outside of the vase bottom (figure 9).

At this point, I use my leaf stamp to enhance the top rim and portions of the side edges of the vase, adding a concave leaf design (figure 10).

Allowing the vase to firm up a bit, extrude another ½-inch coil. Add the coil to the bottom, creating a raised foot (figure 11). I like to carve the foot (figure 12) then stamp it with my original leaf stamp to give a sense of continuity, visually connecting the body of the vase and the foot. Adding a foot gives you a place to play with different designs. A foot also gives you the opportunity to glaze part of the bottom of the vase.

As a finishing touch, I like to slip trail over portions of the raised leaves adding another dimension to the clay's surface.

SOFT SLAB TEAPOT

by Margaret Bohls

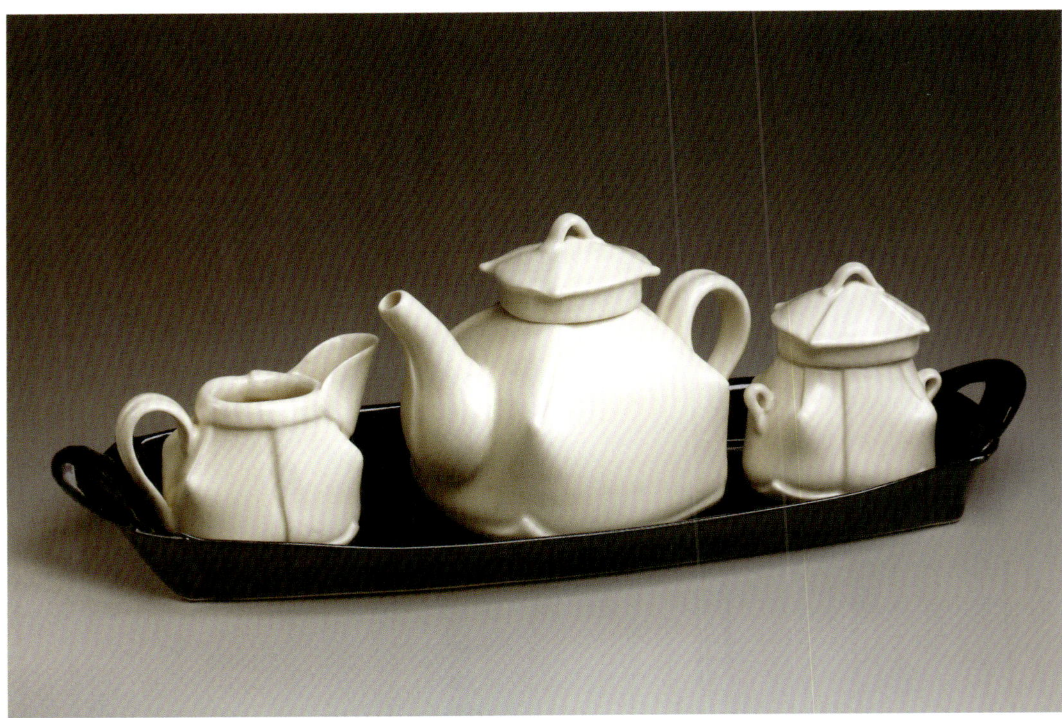

Process is a primary source of inspiration for me. A sense of inventive play while folding, cutting, and assembling clay slabs provides a stream of new information with which to work. My soft slab work is made simply and assembled relatively quickly, giving it a soft, casual simplicity. For me, each pot is like a three-dimensional gesture drawing. Each form is defined by the edges of the slabs from which it was created. These edges or lines create a drawing in space that defines each form. When making each piece, I'm conscious of the quality of each of these lines defined by its weight and direction. The form language is simple, and soft, satin and matte glazes allow one to see and feel the quiet nuances of shape and shadow.

Prepping the Slabs

I use porcelain slabs rolled out using a slab roller. Rather than canvas, I use SlabMat (www.slabmat.com), a dense smooth paper that doesn't leave a texture. I sandwich my clay between two pieces cut to fit my slab roller, one for above and one for below the clay.

After rolling the slabs and compressing them with a large plastic rib to align the clay particles, I allow most of them to stiffen slightly, flipping them occasionally, until they are about halfway between wet and leather hard. I save one wet slab for making the handle and spout. The slabs range from about 1/8–3/16 of an inch—thicker for the main volume and thinner for the spout and handle.

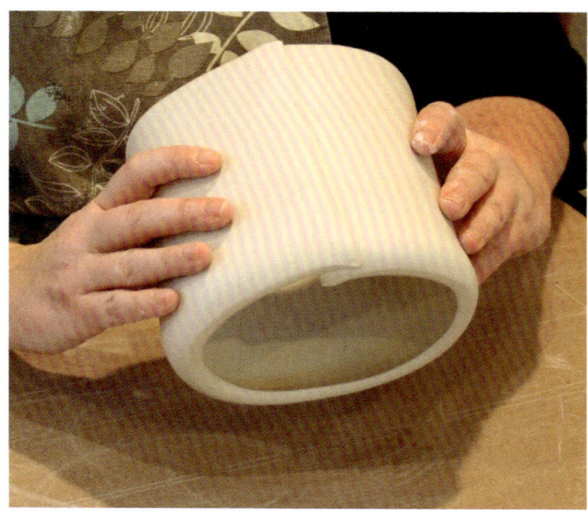

1. Roll the bottom edge of the cylinder on the table top to create volume.

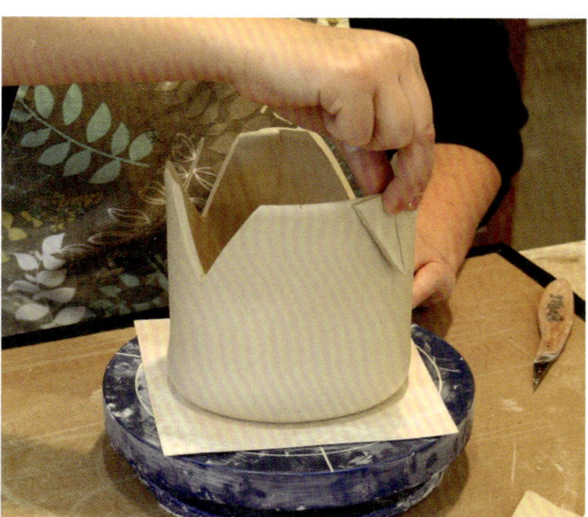

2. Cut darts out of the cylinder to close in the top.

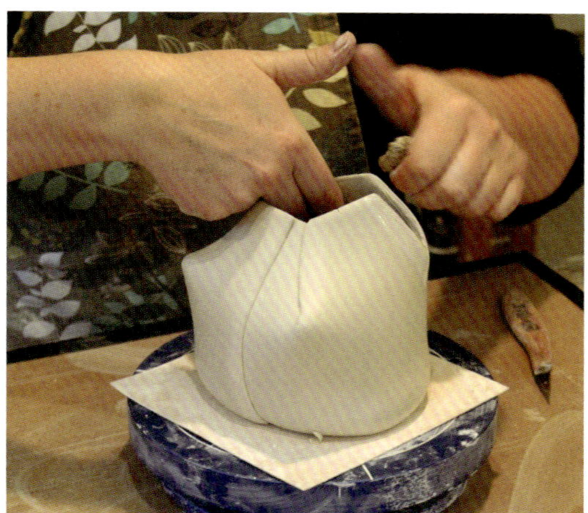

3. Join the dart seams together by slipping, scoring, and overlapping.

Building the Teapot Body

Begin by creating the main body of the pot, which consists of a darted cylinder and a bottom slab. First, cut a rectangular shape from the thicker slab. The length of the rectangle will be the circumference of the body; the width will be the height. Since the edges of the slabs are an important visual element of the finished piece, carefully smooth and compress each edge with your finger, thinning it slightly and softening it.

Rather than beveling edges, use the small end of a pony roller to further thin the edges to be joined. They will overlap so that the edge of the slab will remain visible. Score and slip the edges to be joined and assemble the cylinder, carefully pressing the edges together first with your finger from the outside, and then with a small curved rib on the inside of the seam. To create a sense of volume and to soften the silhouette of the shape, roll the bottom edge of the cylinder on the tabletop (figure 1), pushing the bottom edge in and under, and then gently drop or tap the form onto the table once or twice, making it slouch a little.

To close the top, cut four darts (figure 2). Rather than measuring, simply cut out one dart and use it as a pattern for the other three. The depth and width of the darts can vary; however, the resulting opening should be roughly the size needed for the neck of the pot. The edges of these darts are also thinned and smoothed, then scored and slipped, overlapped and pressed together (figure 3).

Cut the bottom from a slab that is just a little thicker than the slab used for the walls. Loosely trace the bottom, cutting a soft rectangular shape to wrap up over the bottom of the cylinder, softening and thinning the edges as with the first slab. Wait a bit to join these two parts.

Creating the Spout

The pattern for the spout resembles a whale tail (figure 4). This shape creates a spout that has a bulb at the bottom and a soft outward curve. The spout is cut from a fresh, soft slab, thinner than that used for the main cylinder. Once the spout is cut out, thin the narrow end of it further using a pony roller, so that the slab is thicker where it will attach to the body of the pot and thinner where the liquid will pour out.

Thin and smooth the edges, score and slip them, then gently curve the spout into a cylinder (figure 5) and tack together the larger end. Hold the spout upside down and run your thumb down the inside along the length of it. This helps to emphasize the outward curve of the finished spout.

Set the spout down on the table and gently overlap and join the edges, starting at the bottom and working your way up to the top. Use your thumb again to push out the bottom end of the spout from the inside, making it fuller and more bulbous. Using your fingers, pinch the bottom edge inward, and then gently tap the bottom of the spout on the table as you did with the main volume, making it soften and slouch slightly.

Rolling a Slab Handle

Make the handle from a rolled up slab that's then flattened on one side. Begin with a very soft slab cut into a trapezoid (figure 6). Thin and soften the edges. Be careful to rib the outer surface well to help prevent cracking. Coat the inside surface with a thin layer of slip and fold the very edge over with your fingertips making sure not to trap air, then roll it up the rest of the way using the flats of your fingers in one smooth motion. Once you have this round roll, flatten it on one side and stretch it out by slapping it on the table (figure 7), pulling it toward yourself as it comes down, in the way one would stretch a slab. Bevel the wide end and cut the handle to the appropriate length. Bend the handle into shape and set it aside (figure 8).

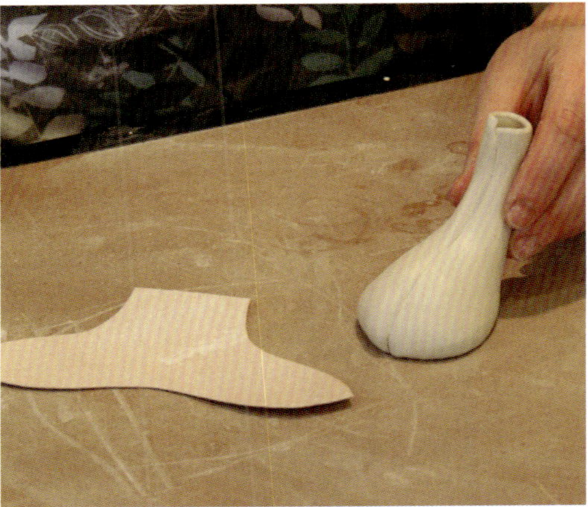

4. The template used to make the spout, shown with a finished spout.

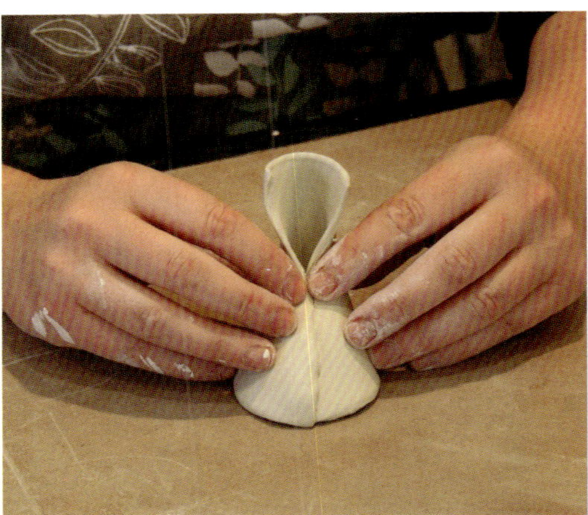

5. Cut the shape from a slab, address the edges, then join the spout's seam.

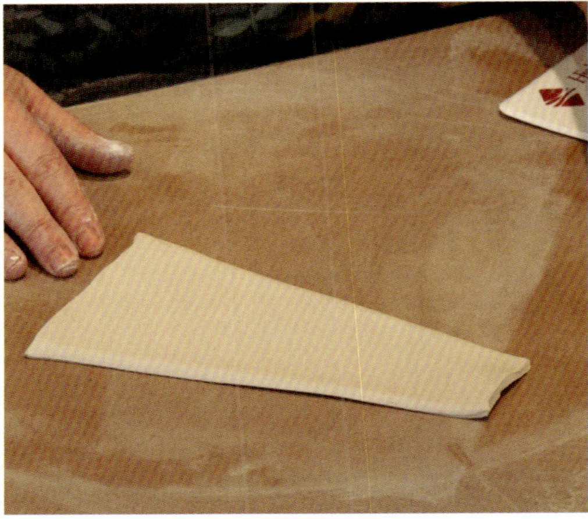

6. Cut a tapered slab for the handle and smooth the surface with a rib.

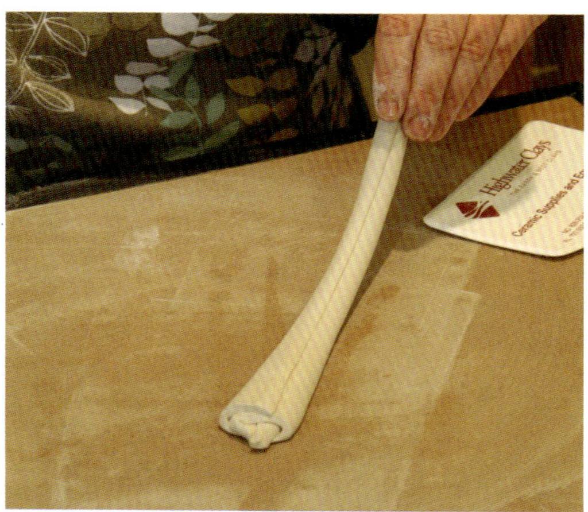

7. Flatten one side of the handle and stretch it out as you would thin a slab.

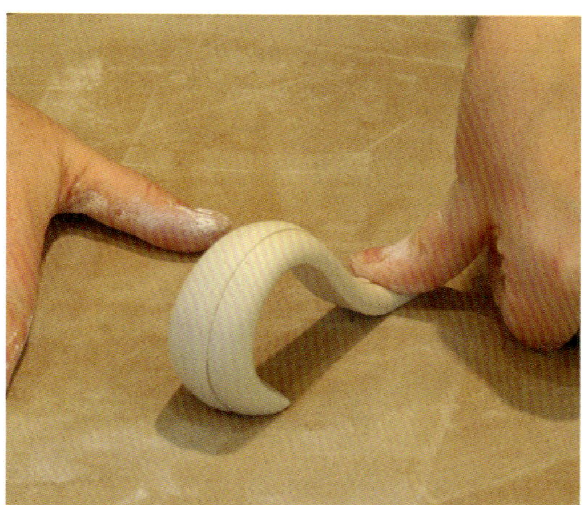

8. Bend the handle into the shape you want after beveling the wide end.

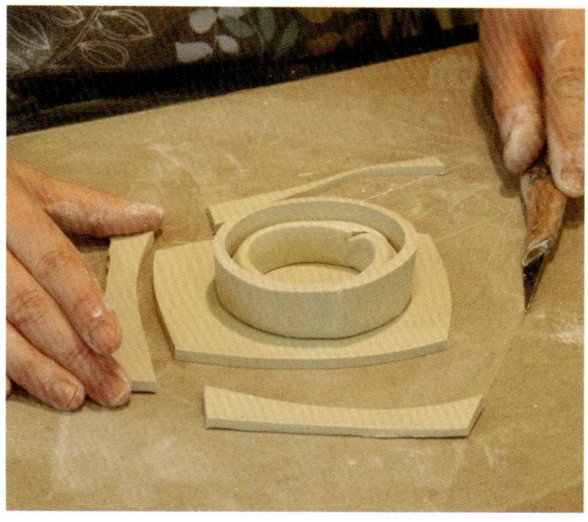

9. Cut a rounded rectangle for the lid (shown with rim and flange rings).

Making the Neck and Lid

The lid of this teapot is a cap type lid that sits down over a neck that projects up from the mouth of the teapot body. This is a very snug lid, since you can make the neck and the flange of the lid at the same time. To ensure that the lid fits well, keep the two parts together as much as possible throughout the drying and firing process.

For aesthetic reasons, the neck is made similarly to the handle. Cut a long soft rectangle of clay, soften the edges, rib the outer surface, and slip the inner surface. The strip is rolled up lengthways and flattened. This time, hold both ends of the piece while you slap it onto the table. This ensures that the piece remains consistently thick rather than becoming tapered. Curve this flattened strip into a ring that's the same size, or slightly larger than the opening at the top of the teapot body. Then bevel the ends of the strip and score and slip them together.

Cut the flange of the lid from a slightly stiffer slab. When made into a ring, the flange should be slightly taller than the neck of the pot. Smooth the bottom edge and wrap the flange strip around the neck ring. The two should fit snugly together. Note: Make the inner ring from slightly softer clay, so it shrinks a little more than the outer ring. The ends of the flange strip are thinned and softened, scored and slipped together. Make sure that the two rings still fit together.

Finally, make the top of the lid from four overlapping triangles. This creates a visual continuity between the darted shoulder of the teapot and the lid that sits on top of it. To make the four triangles, first cut a rounded rectangle of clay, slightly larger than the flange you have already made (figure 9). Cut the rectangle from corner to corner in an X, making four triangles. Then turn the rectangle slightly and cut a second X, removing the clay between each triangle (figure 10).

Smooth and thin the edges of the triangles, then score and slip them together, with each triangle slightly overlapping the one before it (figure 11).

Once those seams have been allowed to cure a little, dome the top of the lid slightly by pushing out from the inside with your fingers or a small, curved plastic rib.

Assembling

Teapot body. Now that all of the separate parts have been made, they're ready to be assembled. It's best if all of the parts are at a soft leather hard stage. Note: Especially when using porcelain, avoid joining soft clay to stiff clay.

Begin by attaching the bottom slab to the cylinder. Score and slip the bottom edge of the darted cylinder to make a print on the bottom slab (figure 12). This mark tells you where to score, and helps to avoid creating superfluous score marks.

Score the slab just on the "printed" slip ring, then apply slip. Press the darted cylinder firmly onto the slab. Lifting the piece in one hand, use the thumb of your other hand to press and smooth the edge of the slab up over the bottom edge of the cylinder. The edge of the bottom slab is stretched and thinned slightly in this process. Go over this seam with a damp sponge to ensure that it's truly joined all the way around. Use your fingers or a damp sponge to press the seam together on the inside of the pot as well.

To add the neck, first trim a small amount off the edge of the top opening and score and slip that flat edge and the bottom of the neck-ring. The two are pushed firmly together and the seam is smoothed slightly on the outside using a sponge. Join the seam more thoroughly on the inside using a round wooden tool to smooth around the inside of the joint.

For the spout and handle, first score and slip the bottom edge of the spout and press it against the pot to make a print. Cut a hole just inside the "printed" slip ring. Smooth and thin the edge of the hole, score and slip, and press the spout around the hole. Now score and slip the handle onto the other side of the pot (figure 13). To score critical areas like the handle joint, I use a scoring tool that creates deeper scoring than the serrated rib.

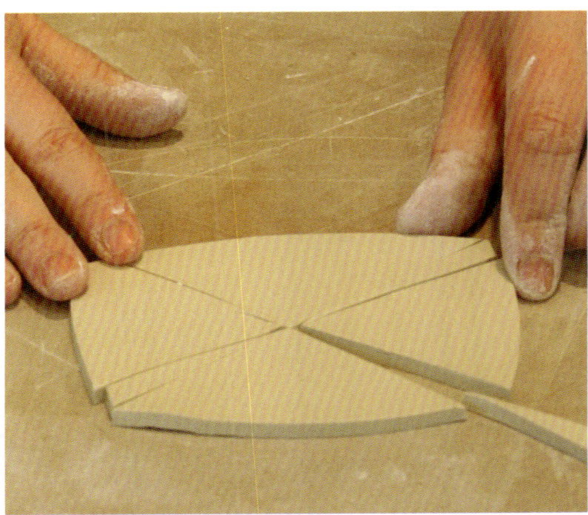

10 .Cut the rectangle diagonally into two X patterns to create even darts.

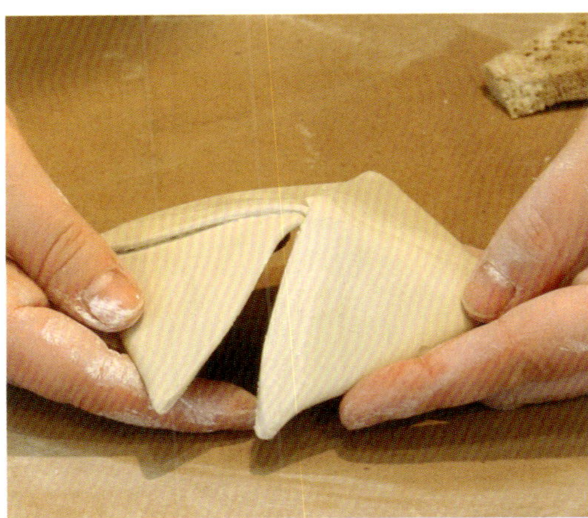

11. Assemble the top of the lid by overlapping the four triangles.

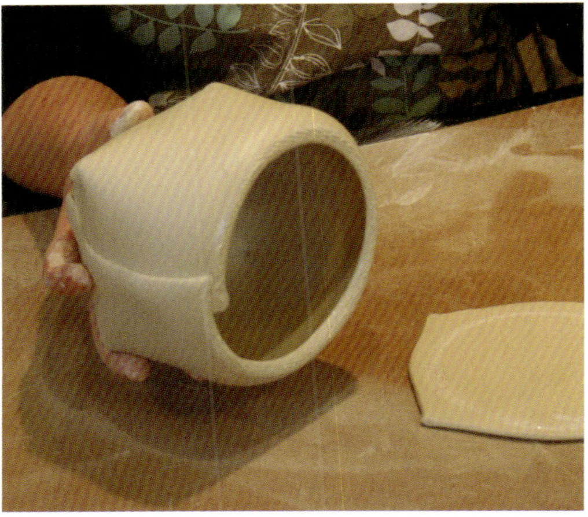

12. Make a print with slip on the slab for the bottom of the pot.

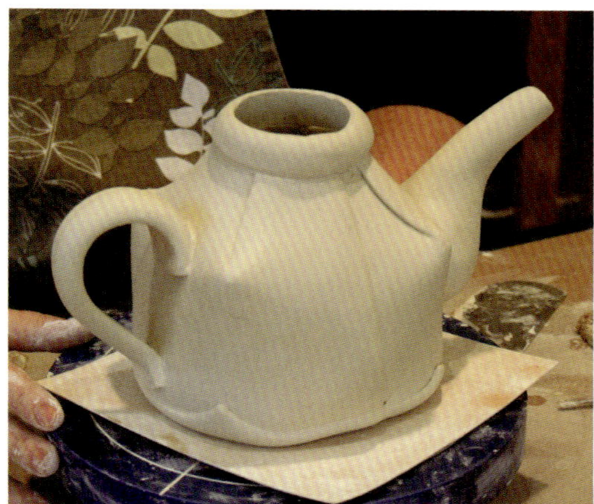

13. Attach the handle to the opposite side. Add a coil if needed.

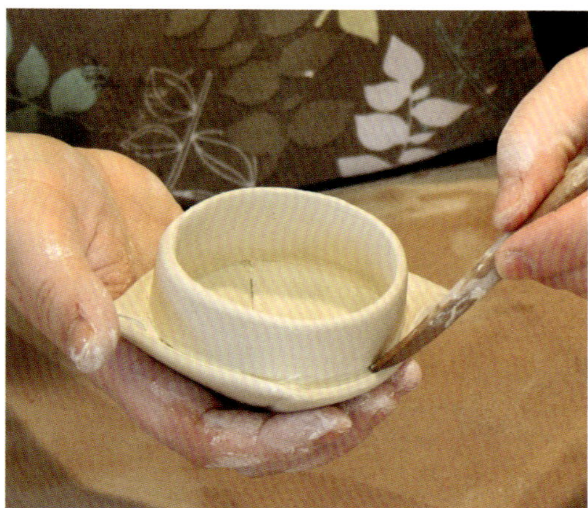

14. Compress the seam on the lid. Add a coil if necessary.

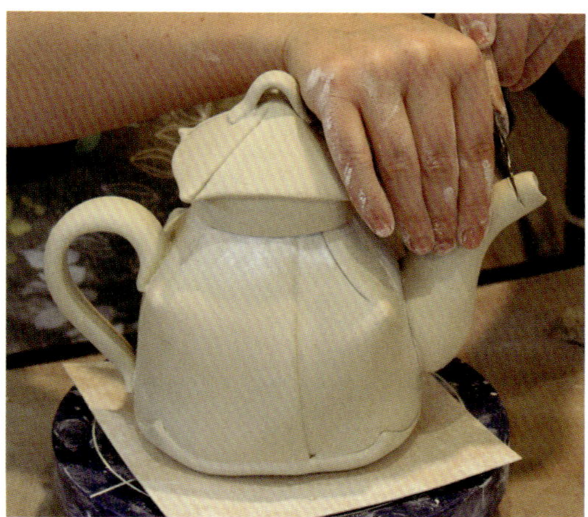

15. Trim the spout to createie a sharp edge which will prevent drips.

To join the two parts of the lid, first place the flange ring over the neck ring, already joined to the pot. Dust the surface of the neck ring with corn starch first so that the two parts do not stick together. The top edge of the flange ring should stick up higher than the neck. Slightly bevel the outer edge at the same time so that it is flush with the slanting angle of the inside of the lid. Score and slip the inside top of the lid and press it down onto the flange. Lift the entire lid off of the pot. This process helps to ensure that the flange does not warp and the lid fits snugly.

Compress the seams of the lid inside and out using a round wooden tool (figure 14), then clean them up. Thin, smooth, and shape the edges of the lid. Sometimes it's necessary to smooth a soft, thin coil into the joint between the flange and the top of the lid on the inside. After dusting both the neck of the pot and the inside of the lid with corn starch, place the lid back onto the pot and gently re-shape it to exactly fit the neck.

Finishing Touches

As a handle for the lid, make another tiny, rolled, flattened slab, then bend and attach it to the peak of the lid.

For the spout to pour well, it needs to have a sharp edge. Once the end of the spout is quite hard, but not yet bone dry, trim off the very end of the spout at an appropriate length and angle. Use a sponge to smooth and soften the outside of the spout tip, then ream out the inside of it with a very sharp knife, being sure to leave a sharp interior edge, which will help prevent drips (figure 15).

Wrap the finished pot in plastic and allow it to sit overnight before allowing it to dry completely. Lift the lid once or twice during the drying process to make certain it isn't sticking.

4

Using Templates

FORM TEMPLATES FOR ACCURACY AND STRENGTH

by Jay Jensen

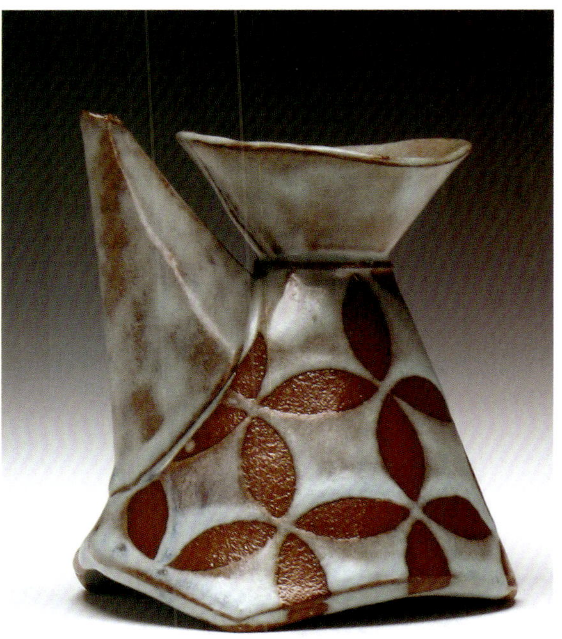

Ewer, handbuilt using computer-aided design templates. *Photo courtesy of Schaller Gallery.*

After finishing college and during a ten-year career in graphic design, I made pottery as often as possible—throwing pots and firing them in wood or soda atmospheres. It was not until eleven years later, while in graduate school, that I realized that those years of being a graphic designer could influence how I worked with clay. I started using the computer to design my pots and to create patterned surfaces. The transition to slab-constructed earthenware has been a logical direction given my experience and skills, but some of my concerns about function have been preserved from when I made wheel-thrown pots, including clay's ability to have a beautiful surface on its own. Instead of covering my work with glaze, much of the clay is left bare, similar to what I did with atmospheric firing on wheel-thrown forms.

Like many ceramic artists, I only had an electric kiln. Rather than relying on other potters to give me space in their wood or soda kilns, I decided to work with slab-built earthenware. I found that handbuilding with slabs had many possibilities. I had always struggled with the restrictions of wheel-thrown forms being round and static. Building with slabs allowed me to construct almost any functional form imaginable.

I use simple CAD (computer aided design) software to design my slab-constructed functional work. CAD is mostly used in industrial design applications and translates well to making flat pieces of material fold into three-dimensional vessels. The CAD program allows me to print out a pattern and it shows me exactly where to cut and fold to create the form. I transfer these patterns

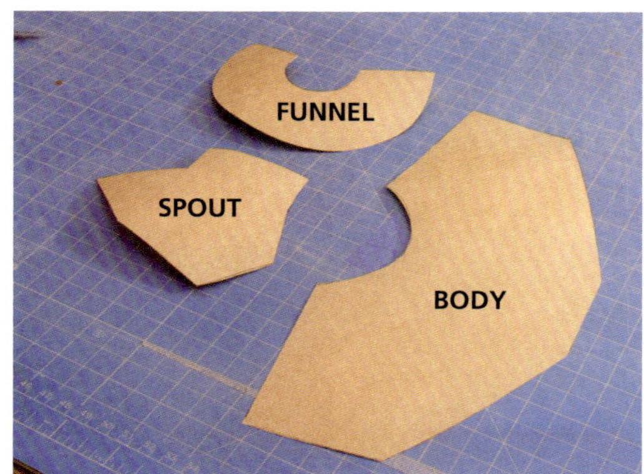

1. After making templates, cut them out in craft paper for smaller pieces or tarpaper for larger pieces.

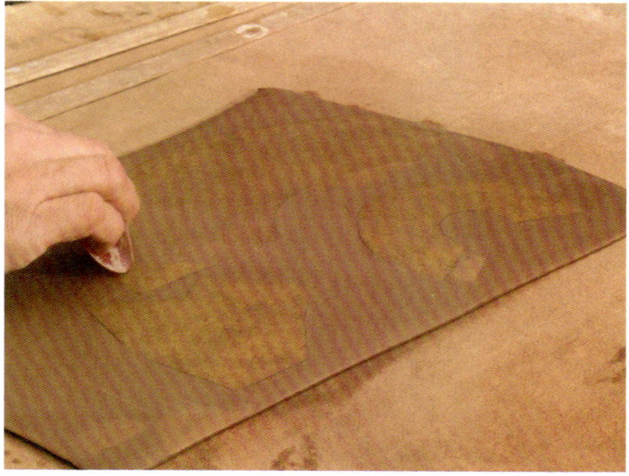

2. Smooth the paper templates onto the slabs of clay using a rib, then cut out the pieces with a sharp knife.

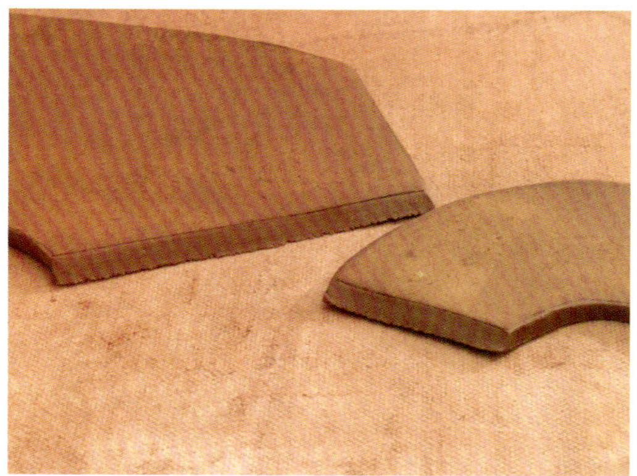

3. When cutting the pieces out, cut the joining edges at a 45° angle for a stronger attachment.

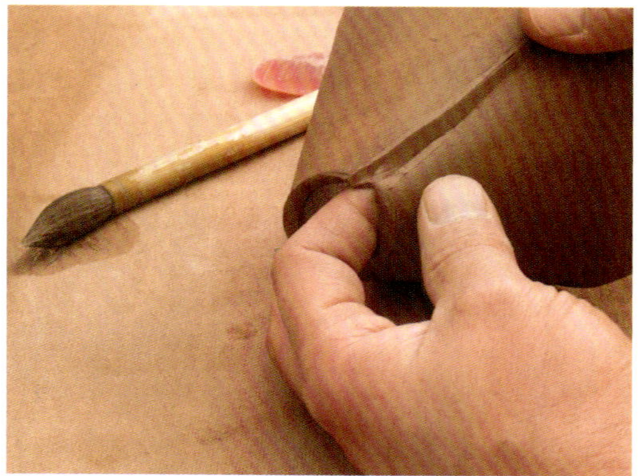

4. Score and slip all joints, curve the slabs around so the edges meet, and assemble the parts.

to paper templates that are used as guides. It's not necessary to use the computer, you can also design pots with a pencil and sheet of craft paper.

Cutting and Forming the Parts

Once you've finished the design, prepare a large slab. Most of my smaller pieces are made from ⅛-inch slabs, while the slabs for the larger pieces can be as thick as ⅜ of an inch. I use various sticks as spacers to keep my slab thickness consistent.

I transfer my CAD drawings to either tarpaper or craft paper, depending on the size of the piece. I like to use tarpaper for larger work and craft paper for smaller pieces (figure 1). For a small ewer, use paper because tarpaper fights with thin slabs as they're shaped where craft paper doesn't.

Dampen the slab and one side of the template then stick the template down firmly, ribbing the edges to stay down (figure 2). Then cut out the shapes using the patterns as a guide. Cut 45° angles into the edges where the pieces will be joined to ensure a tidy, strong seam (figure 3). It's much like woodworking, creating more surface area and a cleaner, tighter joint.

All areas to be connected are slipped and scored, then folded and joined together (figure 4). Tap the seams with a paddle to ensure a strong connection and to also reinforce the shape of each piece (figure 5). The paper acts as a membrane and gives the soft clay support while protecting the surface from fingerprints and other unwanted marks. The craft paper (tarpaper if you are using it) allows

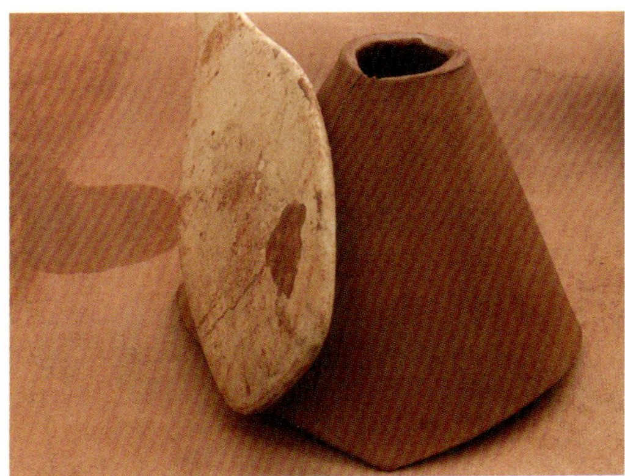

5. Lightly paddle the seams to make the joints clean and flush.

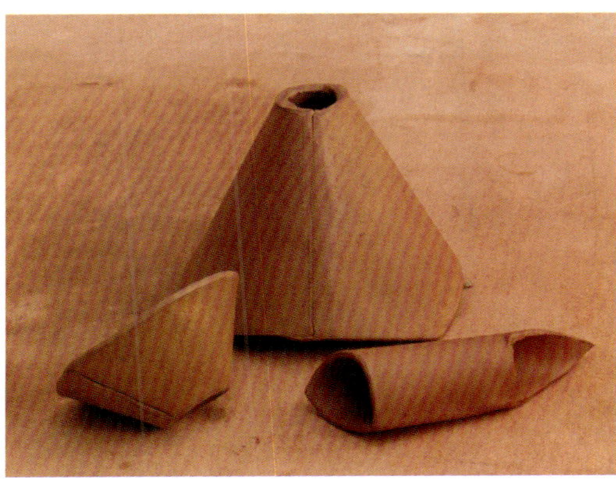

6. Finished parts ready to be assembled. Roll a slab for the bottom of the body form and attach them.

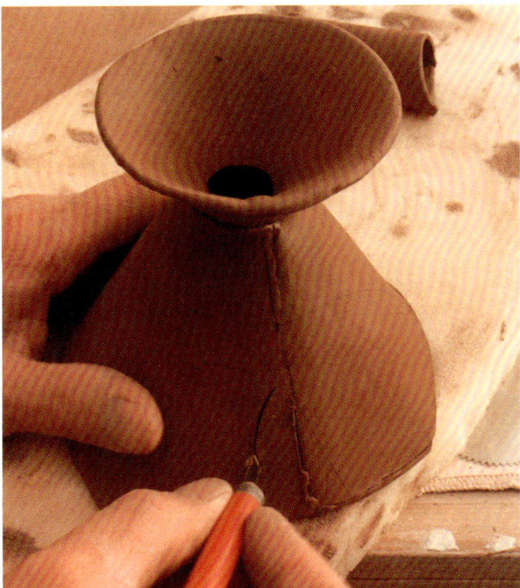

7. Attach funnel to body, then cut a hole for the spout.

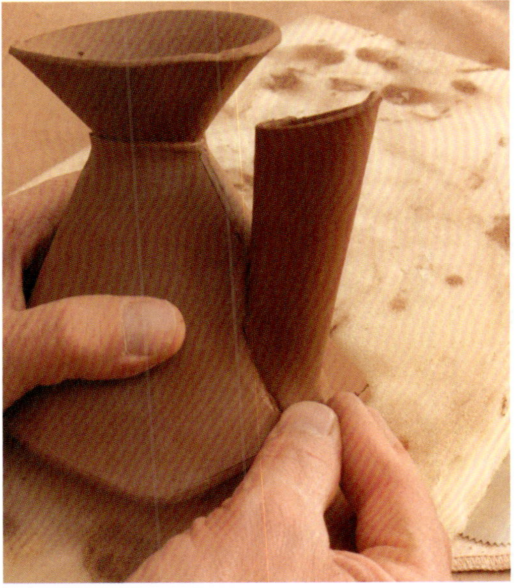

8. Attach the spout. Smooth and refine the form. Slowly dry, then bisque fire.

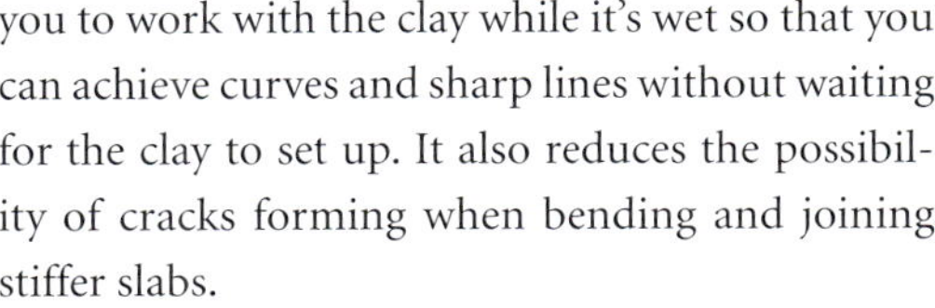

you to work with the clay while it's wet so that you can achieve curves and sharp lines without waiting for the clay to set up. It also reduces the possibility of cracks forming when bending and joining stiffer slabs.

Remove the craft paper after the parts become leather hard. Use a sponge or rubber rib to remove any unwanted texture, make certain the seams are well connected, and refine the edges of each piece. When all the individual components are completed (figure 6), it's time to assemble the finished pot.

Assembling the Ewer

Score and slip each part, then position and secure the funnel shape onto the body. Next, mark where the spout will go, cut a hole that's smaller than the mark into the lower side of the form (figure 7), score and slip its edges, then attach the spout (figure 8). Finally, clean up any excess slip and smooth out any remaining score marks or fingerprints. Let the pot dry slowly, then bisque fire it.

Using Templates

TART TIN NESTING BOWLS

by Annie Chrietzberg

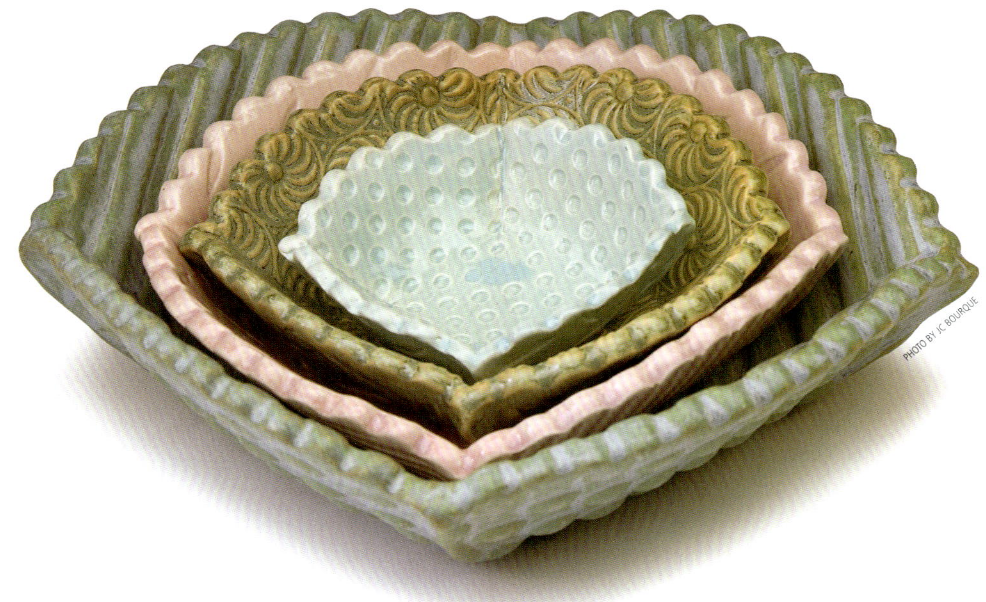
PHOTO BY JC BOURQUE

I know I'm not the only overly-involved-with-clay person out there who brings more things home from a kitchen store for the studio than for the kitchen. So, as I was browsing through a kitchen store, I came across tart tins with scalloped edges and removable bottoms (figure 1), and knew I'd found something that would be fun and easy to use. I bought four of them in graduated sizes thinking . . . nesting bowls!

To get a square-ish form from a round slab requires removing darts of clay. After experimenting with different dart ratios, I settled on somewhere between a third and a half of the radius. To make the darts template, I traced around the scallops on the cutting edge of the tart tin (figure 2). Ignoring the low points of the scallops, I cut out a circle and folded it along two perpendicular diameters, so that the folds made a perfect cross. I then found a point somewhere between a third and half way along the radius to cut the darts to. I folded the template in half and cut out a wedge, then used that wedge to cut identical darts all the way around (figure 3). Explore the possibilities of different-sized darts, different numbers of darts, and different placement of darts. As long as you keep ratios similar from one template to the next, the bowls should nest.

Clean texture tools (figure 4) before using to avoid crumbs of clay that can mar the texture, then dust clean texture tools with cornstarch so that they'll release. Smooth the slab with a soft rib. Leave an inch or so of leeway to maneuver if there are flaws in the texture (figure 5).

Place the slab onto the first texture tool, gently roll from the center towards the edge in a radial pattern, pushing down just enough to press the clay into the texture, but not so hard that you move the clay and thin the slab (figure 6).

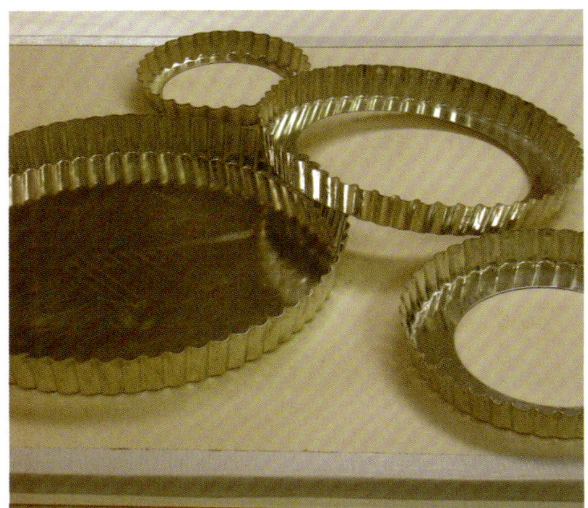
1. Tart tins with removable bottoms.

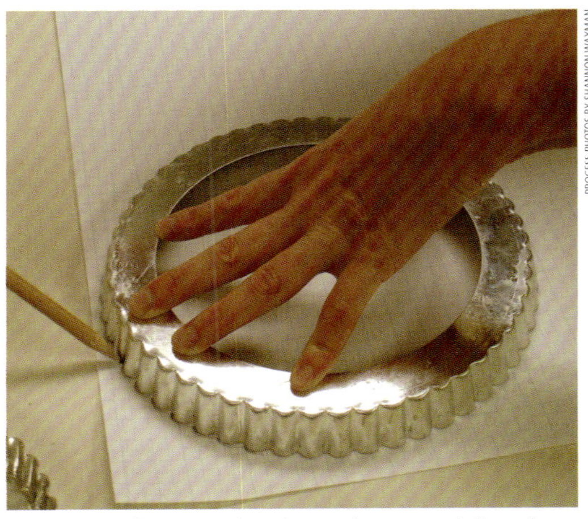
PROCESS PHOTOS BY SHANNON WAXMAN

2. Create a darts template by tracing around the edge. Ignore the scallops when cutting the circle.

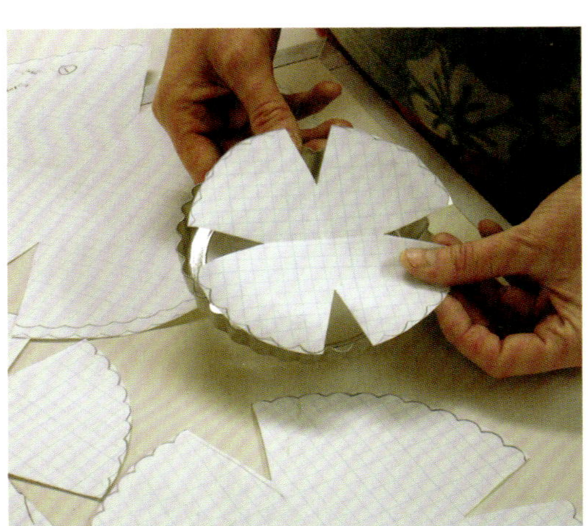
3. To make sure your bowls nest, use the same dart proportions on each template.

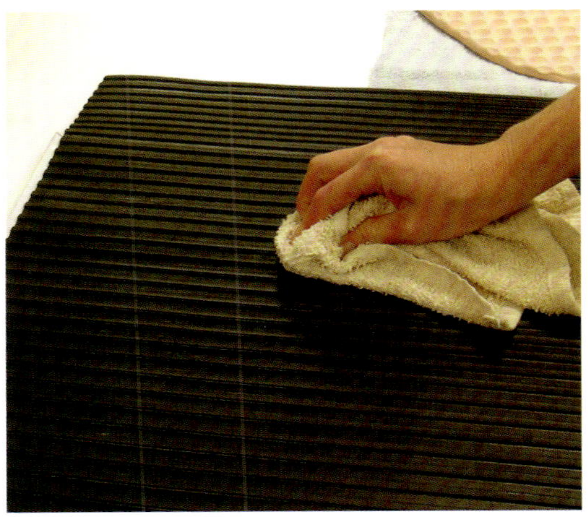
4. Clean surfaces before using to avoid crumbs of clay that can mar the texture, then dust with cornstarch.

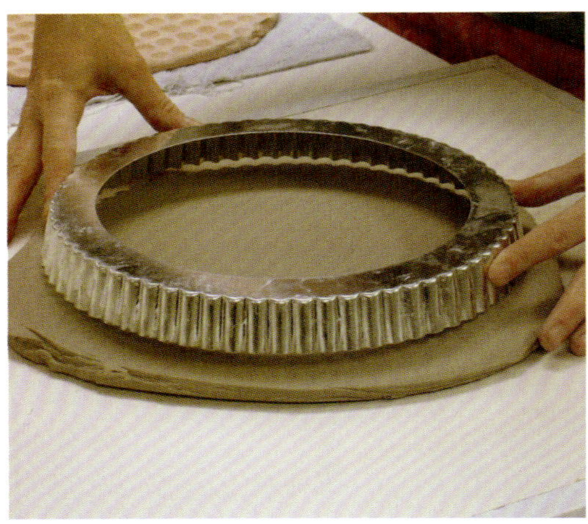
5. Smooth the slab with a soft rib. Leave an inch or so to maneuver if there are flaws in the texture.

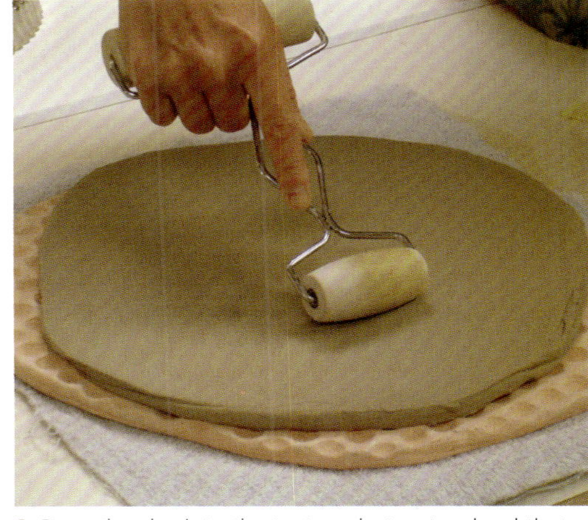
6. Press the clay into the texture, but not so hard that you move the clay and thin the slab.

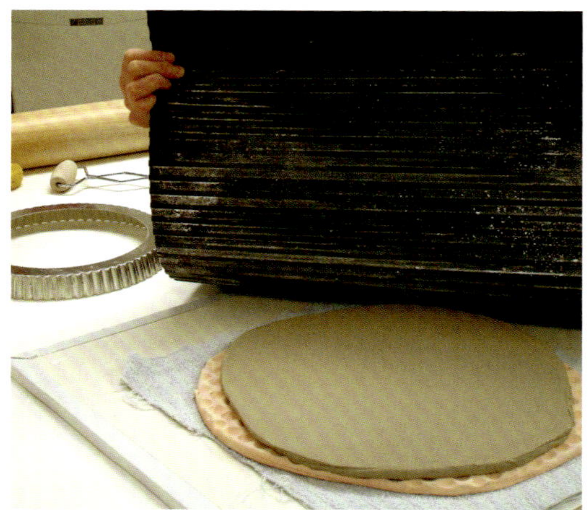

7. Place a prepared texture tool on the slab and roll using just enough pressure to transfer the texture.

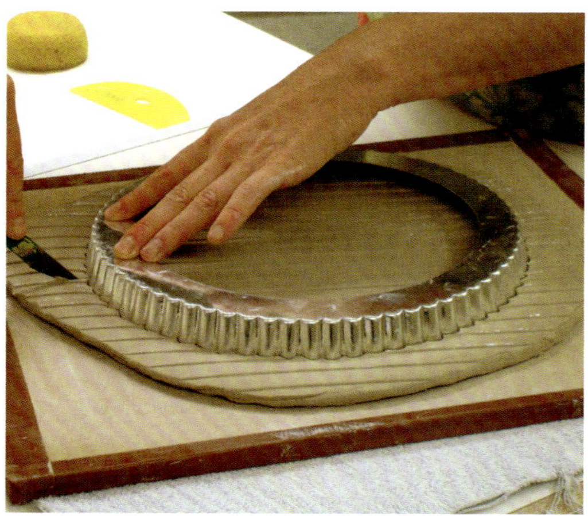

8. With the interior face of the bowl facing up, use the tart tin to cut through the slab.

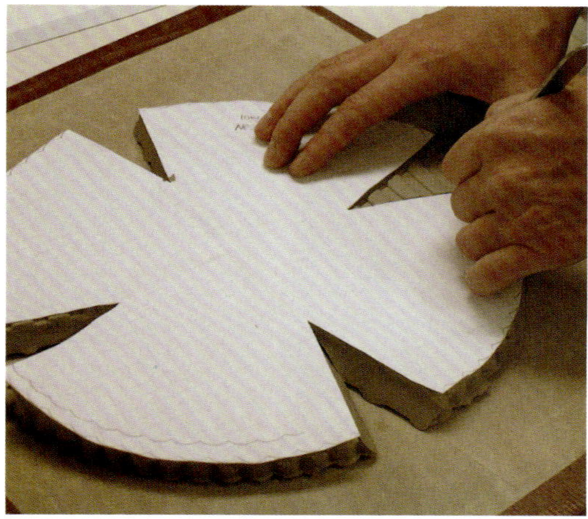

9. Cut darts with the tip of the knife angled toward the center of the dart on both sides.

Flatten the surface with a big rolling pin then carefully place a prepared texture tool on top of the slab (figure 7) and roll using just enough pressure to transfer the texture, but not so much that you thin or move the slab. Move to a wareboard and remove the texture tools, then flip the slab so the interior face of the bowl is facing up. Use the tart tin to cut through the slab (figure 8).

Slip your hand underneath the rim and place your fingertips at the edge of the slab, gently press the slab free of the cutter. Align the darts and then cut the darts with the tip of the knife angled toward the center of the dart on both sides (figure 9).

Bevel the darts by pointing the knife point towards the center on each side so you'll be switching the angle of the knife for each side of the dart. As always with slab work, score, then slip, then score again to create an interface so the seam stays together (figure 10). You may also want to add a small coil along the seams, since you're changing the orientation of the slab (figure 11). Use sponges or small pieces of foam to keep the sides of the bowl just where you want them while you work on the join.

After all four corners are well joined, turn the piece over. Anytime you need to turn a piece over, find foam if needed, and wareboards or bats, and find a way to flip the piece without touching it. Run a finger or a well-wrung-out sponge over the backside of the seam (figure 12), eliminating any sharpness and sealing it. Repeat these directions with every size tart tin and template that you have, and you will have a lovely little set of nesting bowls.

With four nesting bowls, you'll want to explore the potential using eight different textures—match textures from the top of one bowl to the bottom of the next or let the textures cycle through the set—there are so many possibilities!

The ABC's of Double-Sided Slabs

Here's how you make and use double-sided slabs, along with a few tips to help get you started. If you have two flexible texture tools, like plastic or rubber mats, pick one and lay it down, texture side up. Dust it with cornstarch (figure 14), carefully set your

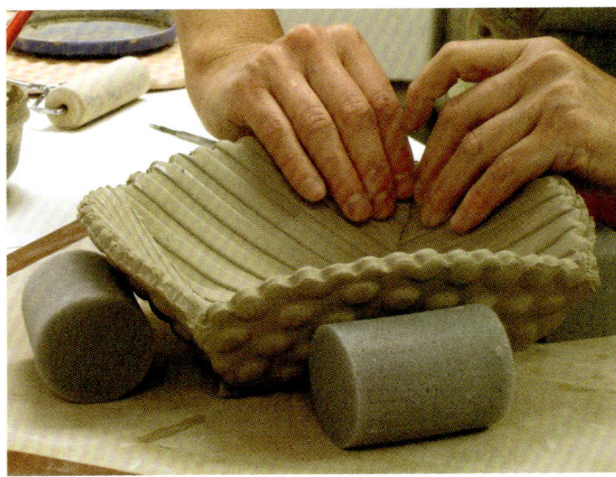

10. Score and slip the cut edges of darts. Carefully lift slab to join both sides of the dart cuts.

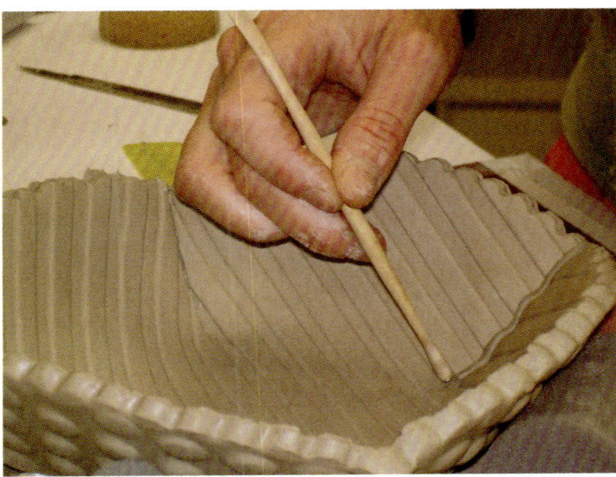

11. Remove the rough edges with a damp sponge, then lay a small coil in the corner and blend in.

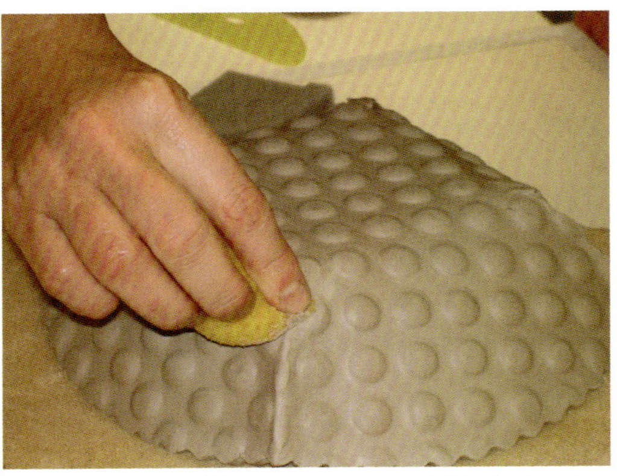

12. Place a piece of foam on the rim and flip the bowl over. Work the seams with a damp sponge

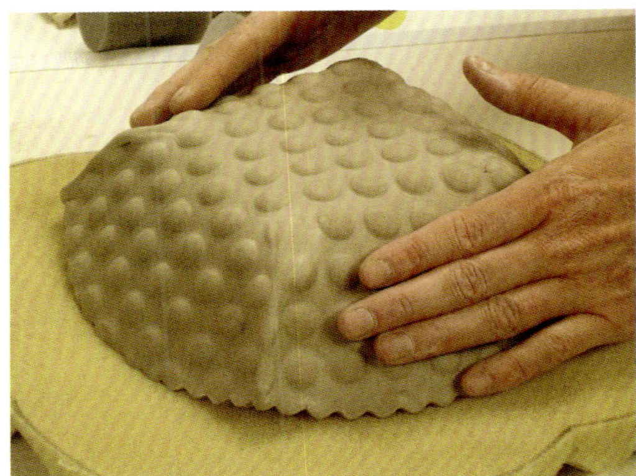

13. Adjust shape and then let dry!

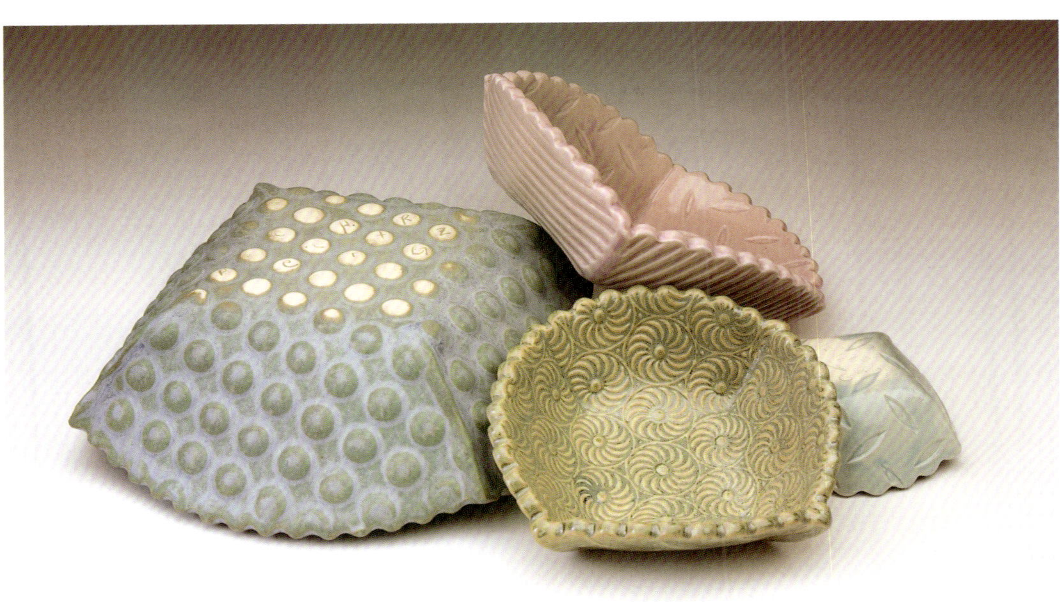

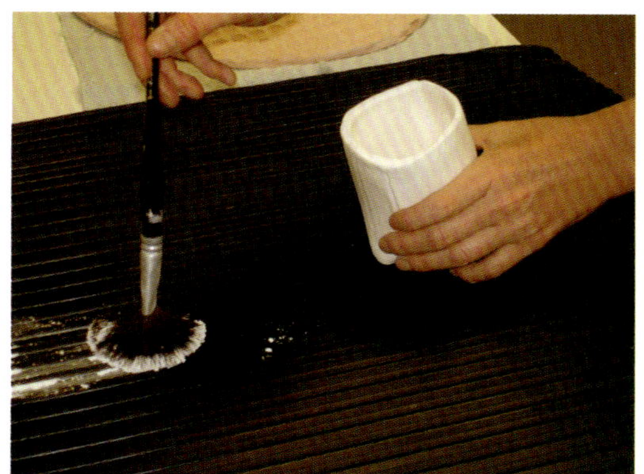
14. Dust a textured surface with cornstarch.

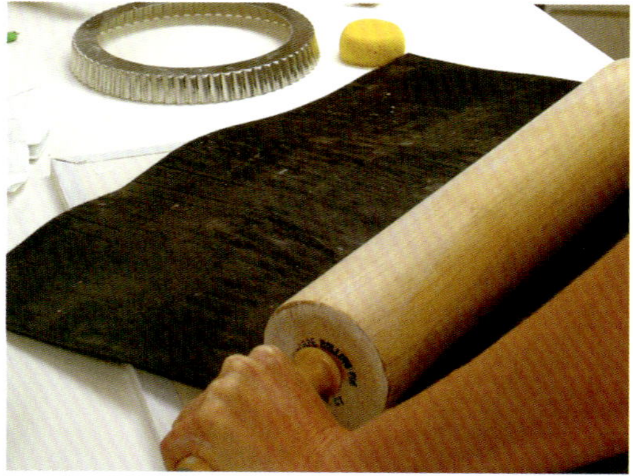
15. Dust the second texture mat, lay it on top (texture side down) and carefully roll the back of it

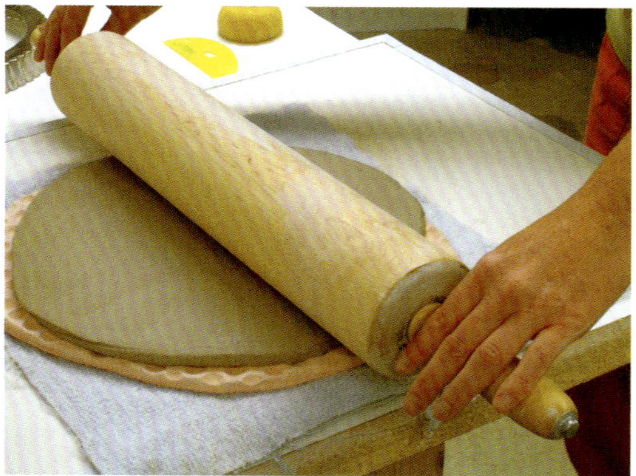
16. Use rigid textures on the bottom only, and place a towel beneath to absorb some of the pressure.

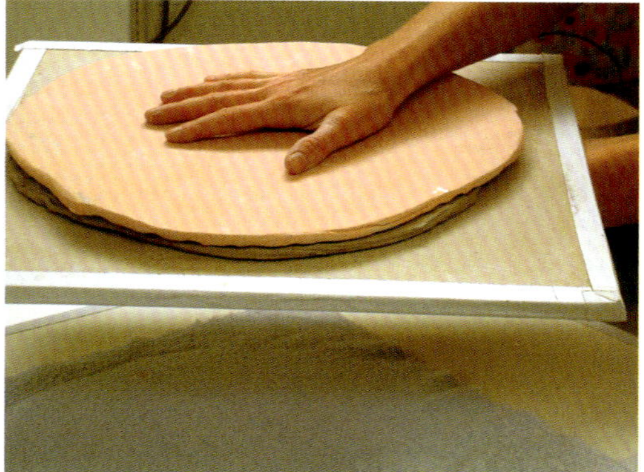
17. After peeling away the top mat, carefully set a clean wareboard on the slab and flip.

nicely rolled blank slab on top, then roll with the curved end of a pony roller, which seems to push the clay down into the texture rather than enlarging the slab. Then flatten the top with a nice big rolling pin. Dust a second texture mat with cornstarch, lay it on top (texture side down) and carefully roll the back of it (figure 15). If you're using a corduroy texture, roll with the lines, not across them. Apply just enough even pressure to get the texture to print. Rolling carelessly enlarges the slab and leaves 'tracers' of the texture as the slab moves out across it.

When using a brittle texture tool like a piece of old rusty tin, a bisque or plaster plate, or even a piece of old French patterned glass, you'll need to take more care. I only use those on the bottom, as I don't want to apply my rolling pin to the back of one, because that could mar the surface of my rolling pin or break the tool. Place a towel beneath the hard texture tool to absorb some of the pressure from rolling so as to keep it from breaking (figure 16). If you're using something nonabsorbent, like old patterned French glass, dust it with cornstarch, then lay down your prepared slab, roll, then apply your flexible mat on top of the clay, and roll again.

To remove your slab, peel away the top mat, set a clean wareboard on the slab and flip (figure 17). Remove the other texture tool. If your slab is bottom-side up, use another wareboard to flip it again.

Using Templates
CREATING HEXAGONAL FORMS

by Don Hall

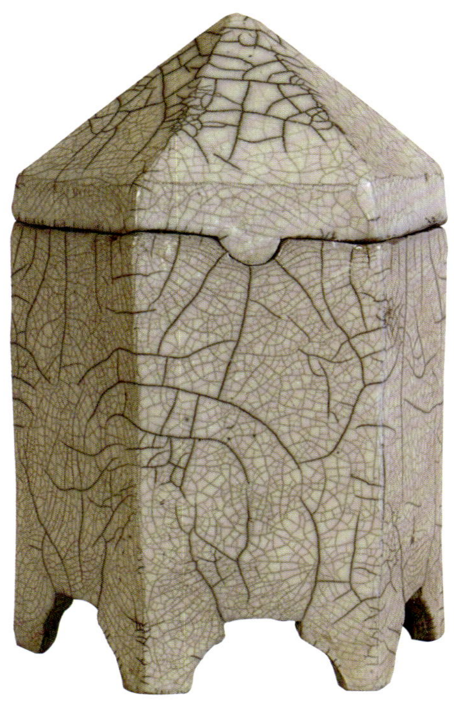

This raku box is one of many hexagonal forms you can make using a template with 60° sides and beveling seams at 30°.

Like many potters, I began learning pottery by throwing. After many years, I began handbuilding, and many contented hours followed. This project on building a six-sided box requires no throwing skills. The angles involved can be used for any six-sided form, so by adjusting the measurements, you can make a piece of any height or width.

To begin, make a template for the piece you're making. Include foot and lid pieces as needed. The box here will be 5 inches wide (figure 1). Roll out a ¼- to ⅝-inch-thick slab and allow it to dry for a bit. Make a stencil from the pattern, mark the slab and cut out. Pieces should match (figure 2).

A six-sided form needs edges trimmed at a 30° angle. You can make a wire cutter from a 2×3 inch piece of wood with a ¾×1½-inch notch (figure 3).

Dampen and score each edge. Fold up the sides and attach each one at a time to its neighbor (figure 4). The clay should be damp enough to not crack. Place coils on the inside of each seam and smooth them out (figure 5). Using a metal rib, clean up the outside of each seam (figure 6).

For the top, trim all three edges of the triangular panels to 30° (figure 7). Score and dampen the edges of each panel and assemble them (figure 8). Attach coils to the inside, smooth out then attach the lid to the base of the form (figure 9).

Now it is time to cut off the lid. Use a needle tool to score a line around the form. With a fettling knife held at an angle (upward or downward—your choice), cut off the top (figure 10). When cutting the lid, use a half circle in one side as a key so that it's easy to place the lid (figure 11). Using the 30° tool, cut the edges off the sides of each foot segment. Assemble and attach the base adding coils to the seams (figure 12).

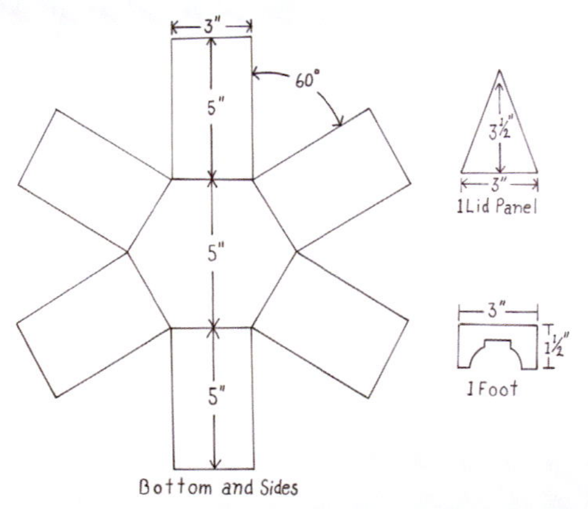

1. Make a template for the piece you're making.

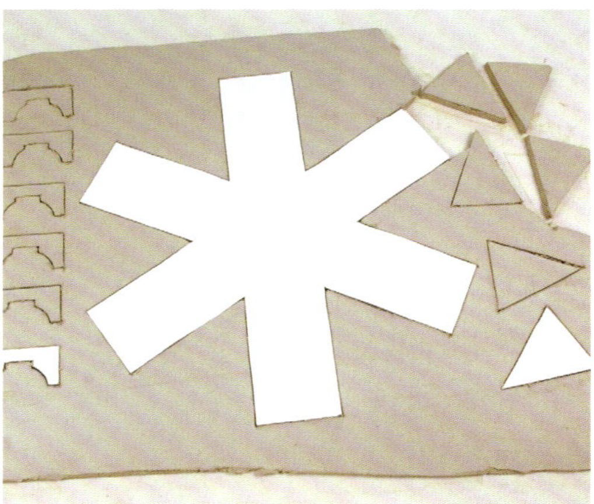

2. Roll out a slab then make a stencil from the pattern.

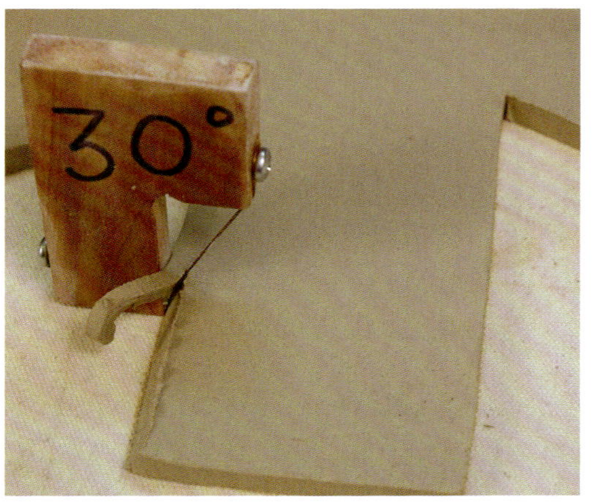

3. You can make wire cutter from a piece of wood.

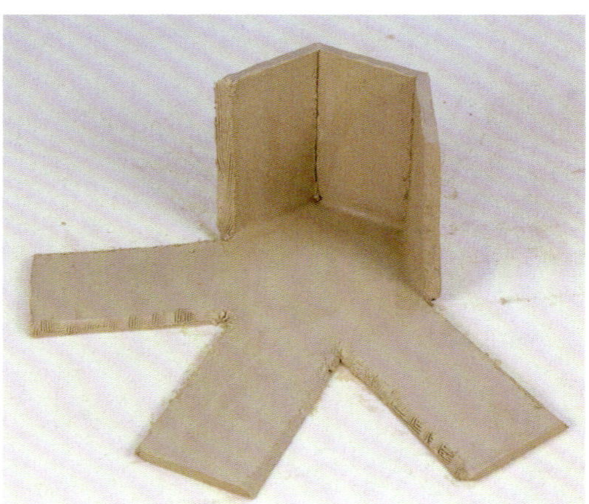

4. Fold up sides and attach each one to its neighbor.

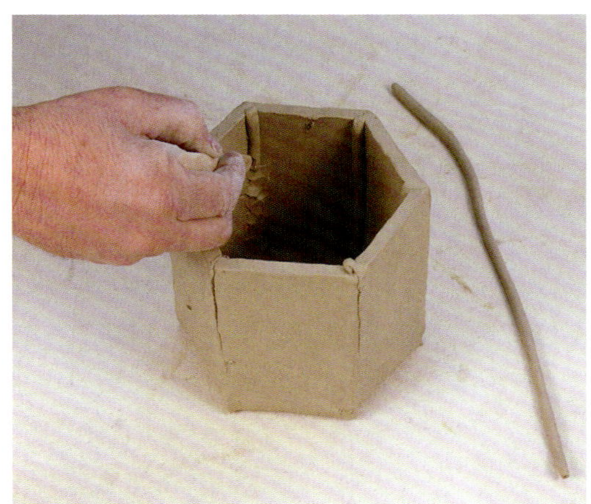

5. Attach coils to the inside of each seam.

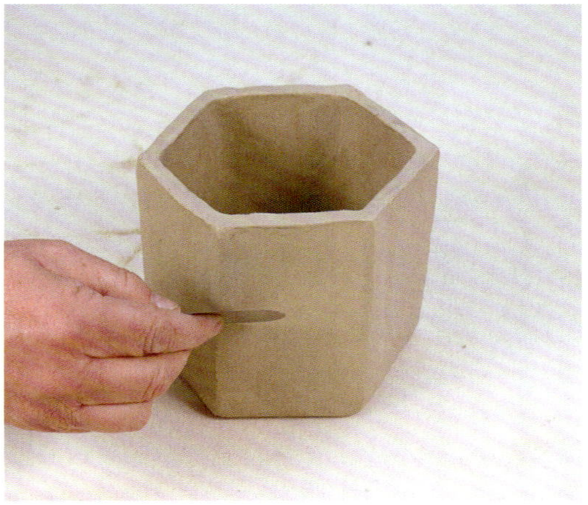

6. Clean up the outside of each seam.

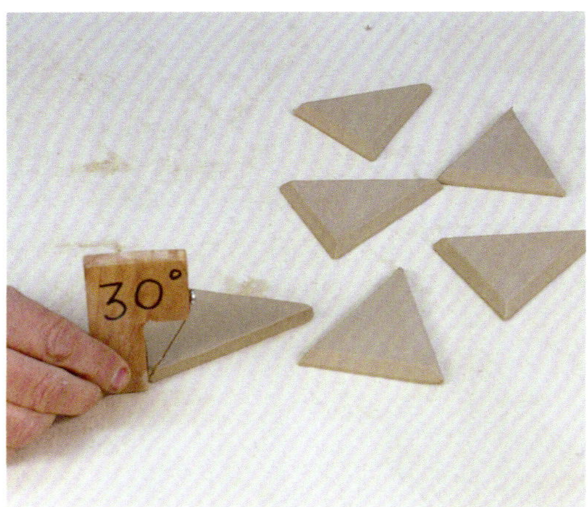

7. Trim the edges of the top panels.

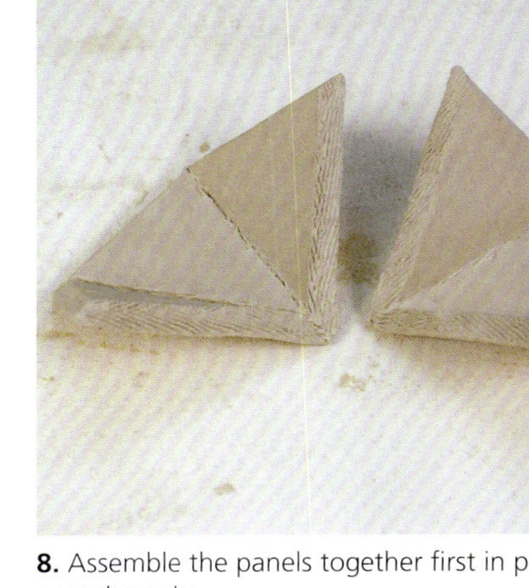

8. Assemble the panels together first in pairs then connect the pairs.

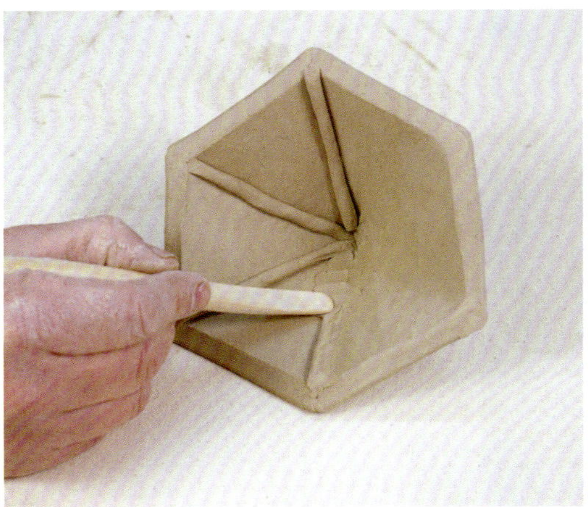

9. Attach coils to the inside seams.

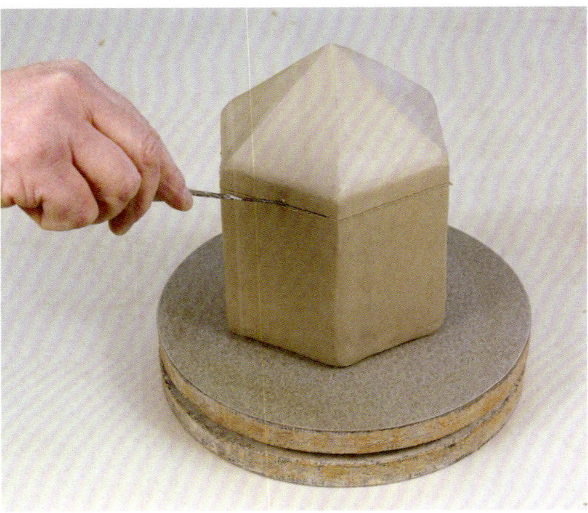

10. Cut off the lid with a knife held at a slightly downward angle (upward can work as well).

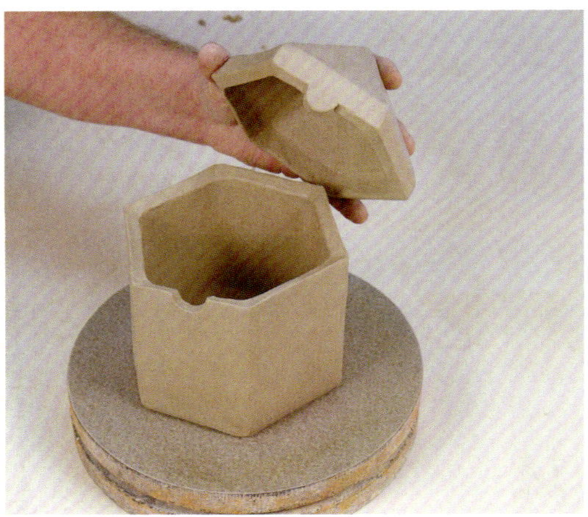

11. Use a half circle as a key.

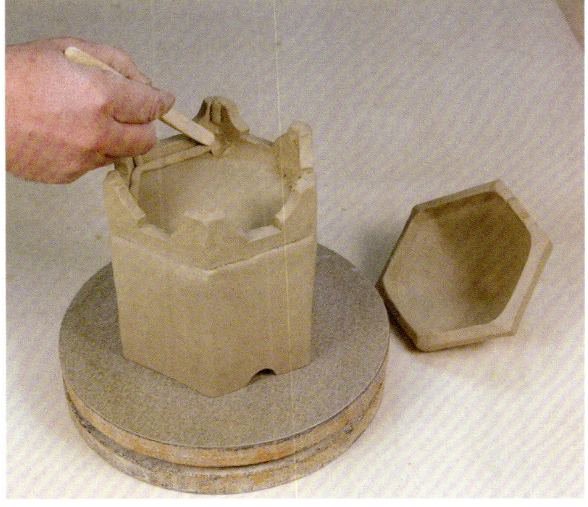

12. Attach the base and attach coils at the seams.

Using Templates
CUPS AND HANDLES

by Annie Chrietzberg

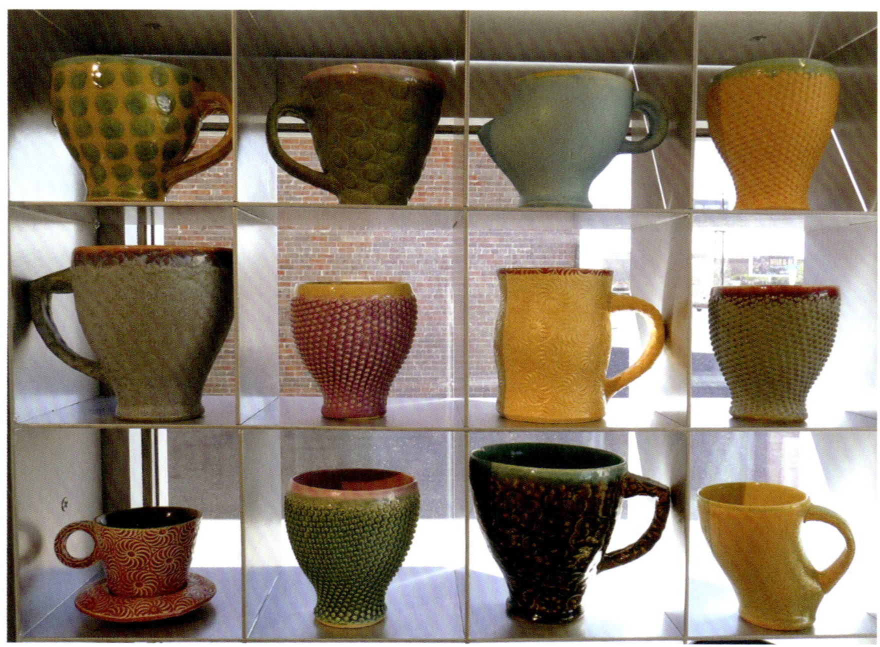

Cups are among the first pieces an aspiring potter attempts. Often they are the first part of a potter's repertoire to come into focus. Cups are a good way to get back into a making cycle after a hiatus, and a good warm up for a day of making once on a roll. Cups are the calling cards we trade with other potters, the tokens of our long days in the studio that we give to our loved ones. I attended a slide lecture given by the potter Josh Deweese and something he said stuck with me: "Cups are the potter's most successful form because they are so accessible, and therefore have the ability to truly live in people's lives on a day-to-day basis. The relationship that develops with a cup is quite intimate, and is a great way to bring art into people's lives."

Cups are taken to work, carried out into the yard, whisked off for rides in the car. Once broken, a great cup lingers in the memory as "one that got away." The really good cups migrate to the front of the cupboard, while the cups with less balance and grace end up dusty, shoved to the back corner.

Cups are small and quickly made in relation to other forms. They're great for trying new ideas and sorting through forms and textures. I choose to make each cup by hand, reinterpreting the shape of a favorite thrown form with my textured slab cups.

Cups

This technique, which I learned from attending a Sandi Pierantozzi workshop, begins by making

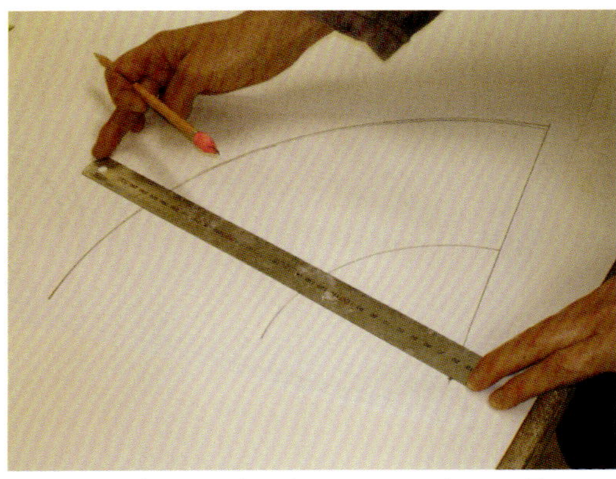

1. Begin with a template for a truncated cone. The top arc is the rim diameter and the bottom arc is the base.

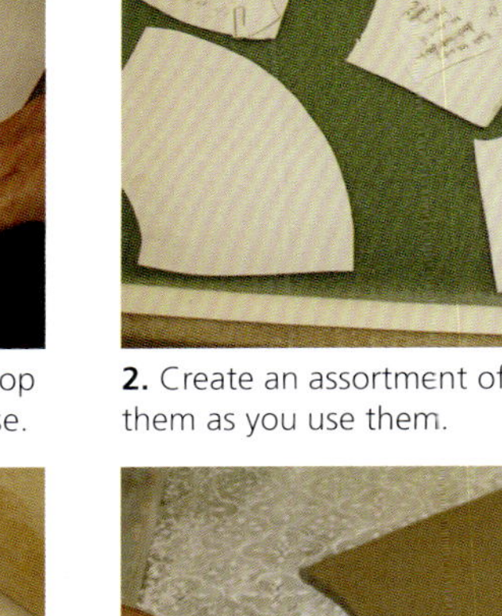

2. Create an assortment of templates. Keep notes on them as you use them.

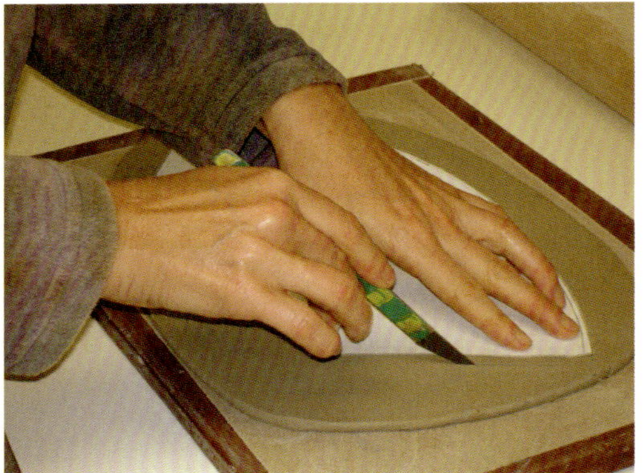

3. Roll out a slab and cut the clay leaving ¼ to ½ inch around the template.

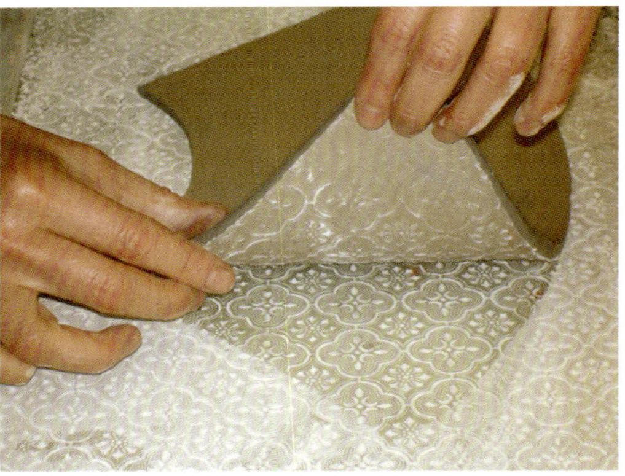

4. Place slab on a textured surface and gently roll it. Dust the texture with cornstarch so it releases.

a truncated cone template with a heavier-weight paper. Once assembled, the cone can be left with a hard line, or manipulated from the inside or outside to create or reduce the volume. If you have a particular size of cup in mind, start by approximating measurements with a measuring tape, remembering to account for the shrinkage of your clay body.

A cup pattern begins with a template for a truncated cone. The top arc is the diameter of the rim and the bottom arc is the diameter of the base. Draw a truncated cone from two arcs of concentric circles (figure 1). Use the same central point not only to draw the arcs, but also to create the sides of the template, which become the seam of the cup. Create an assortment of templates. Keep notes about what you're making on your templates, like which handle template you use with a particular cup template (figure 2). I have some templates that I use for multiple forms, and so I list the form and its related templates.

Use clay that is well-aged and plastic, but not too wet, allowing you to handle intricate texture without marring it. Roll out a slab and cut the clay leaving ¼ to ½ inch around the template (figure 3). Place the slab on a textured surface and gently roll it into the texture. Dust the texture with cornstarch for easy release (figure 4), then place the template back on the slab and cut around it angling the knife 45º on the sides (figure 5) to increase the joining surface for the seam of the cup. For these two cuts, the knife tip should point to the left. Cut the top and bottom perpendicular.

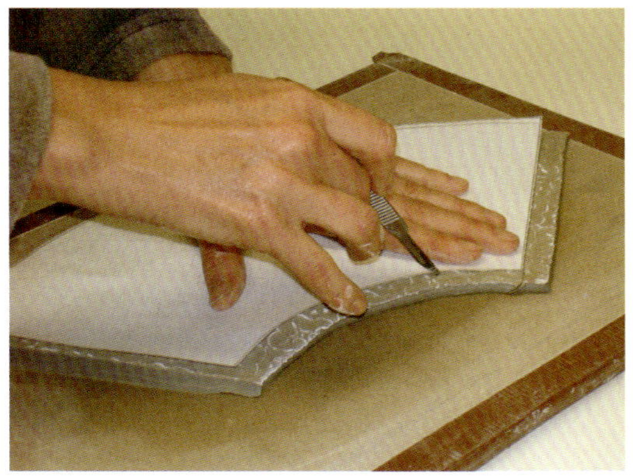

5. Replace the template and cut around it. Cut the sides at 45° angles but the top and bottom at 90°.

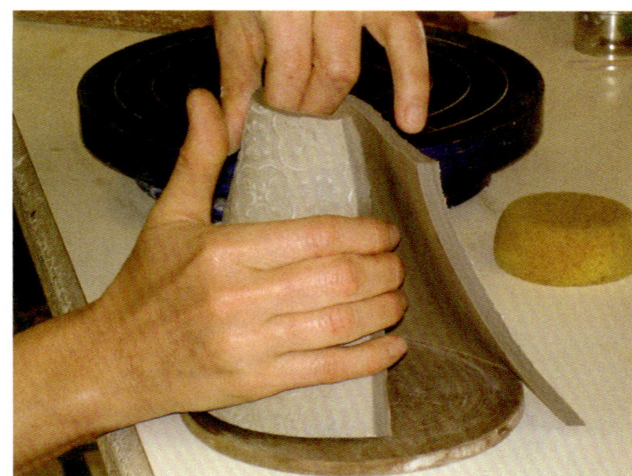

6. Set the piece on a small bat with the lip on the bottom. Use the joining edge to bend the piece around.

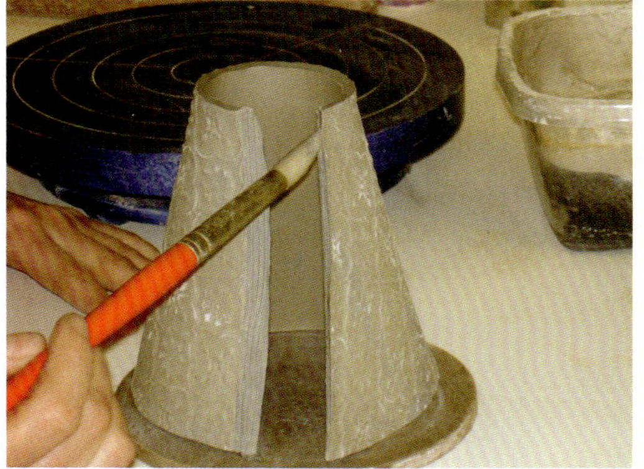

7. Score and slip both the edges and press the seam together across the beveled cut.

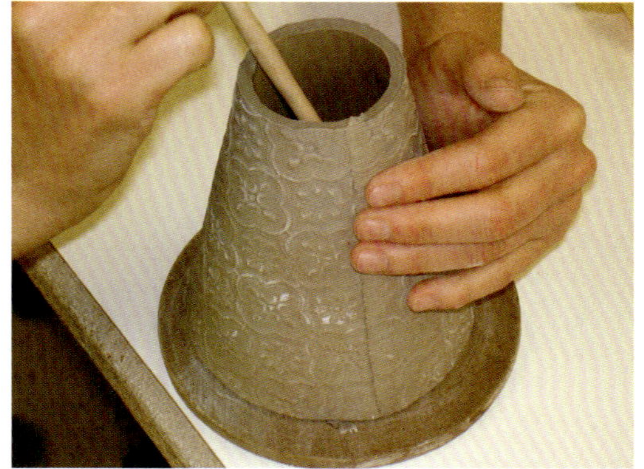

8. Use a tool on the inside applying just enough pressure that you can feel the tool moving across the inside.

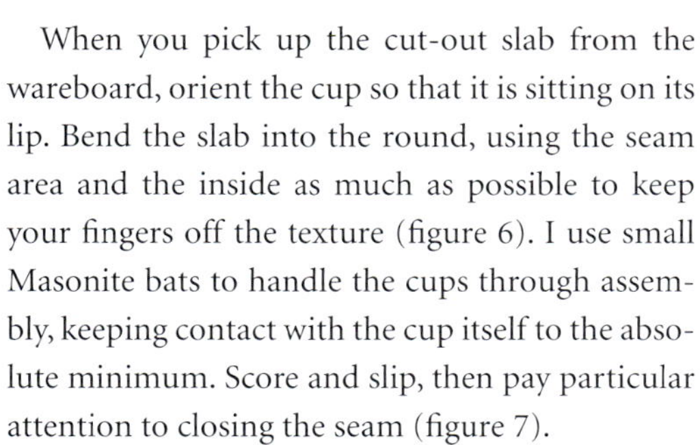

When you pick up the cut-out slab from the wareboard, orient the cup so that it is sitting on its lip. Bend the slab into the round, using the seam area and the inside as much as possible to keep your fingers off the texture (figure 6). I use small Masonite bats to handle the cups through assembly, keeping contact with the cup itself to the absolute minimum. Score and slip, then pay particular attention to closing the seam (figure 7).

When you're working the seam from the inside, run your finger or tool up, overlapping each stroke across the whole diagonal of the seam. Keep your fingers gently on the outside for support (figure 8). You should be able to just feel the tool moving on the inside of the cup. While the cup is upside down, only work the seam from the middle to the foot.

Use either a circle template or a cookie-cutter to cut a nice circle for the bottom of your cup (figure 9). For reasons of aesthetics as well as balance, I use one size larger than the bottom of the cone, and enlarge the bottom to fit. Don't pinch the bottom to enlarge. Rather, gently roll your finger over your thumb all the way around the foot a few times, until the base of the cup matches the size of the cutter (figure 10).

Prepare a small slab with your chosen texture, line up the pattern and cut your circle (figure 11). Remove the clay around the cutter, then gently press the bottom of the cup out of the cutter. Make

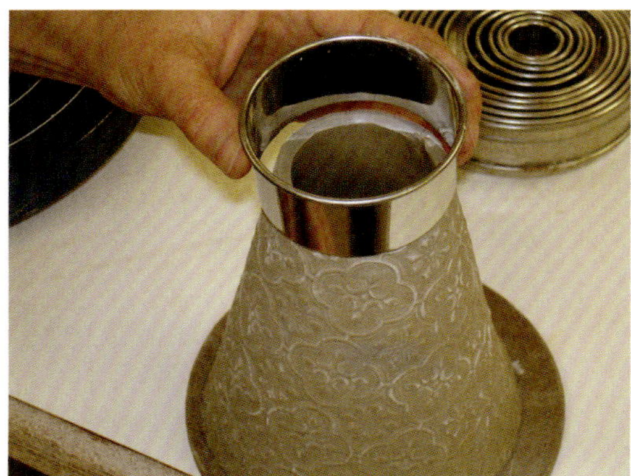

9. To make the bottom, use a cookie cutter that's just larger than the bottom diameter.

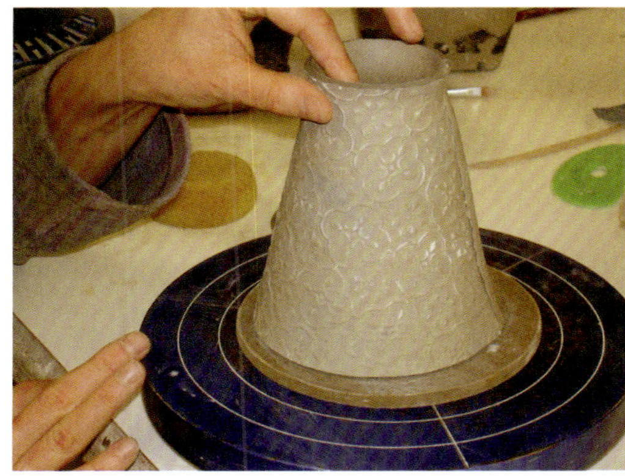

10. Enlarge the base by flaring out the edge until the bottom matches the diameter of the cutter.

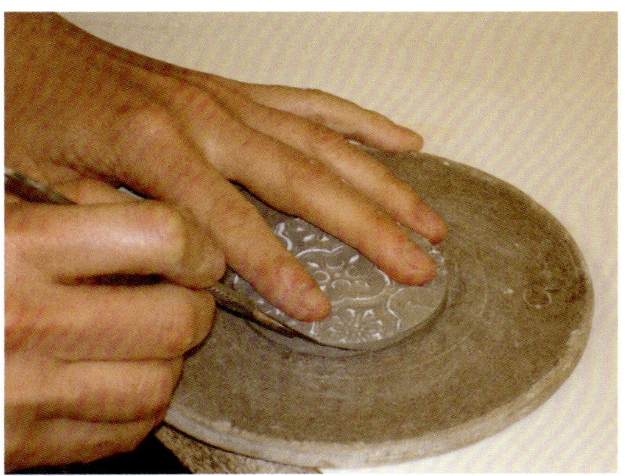

11. Texture and cut a slab with the cookie cutter. Bevel the edge at an angle to remove bulk on the seam.

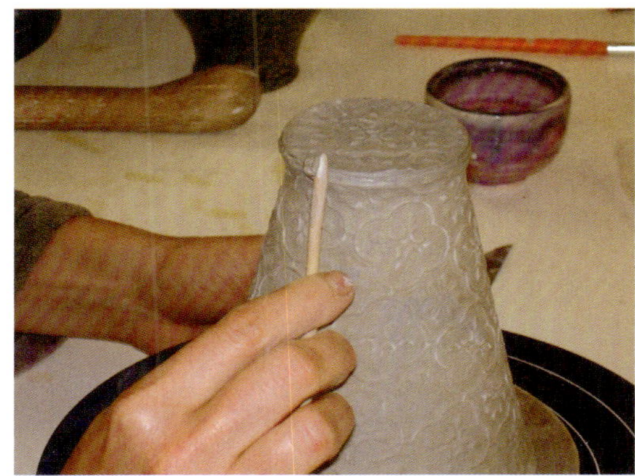

12. Attach the bottom to the flared rim. Pinch seam with clean fingers then smooth using a tool.

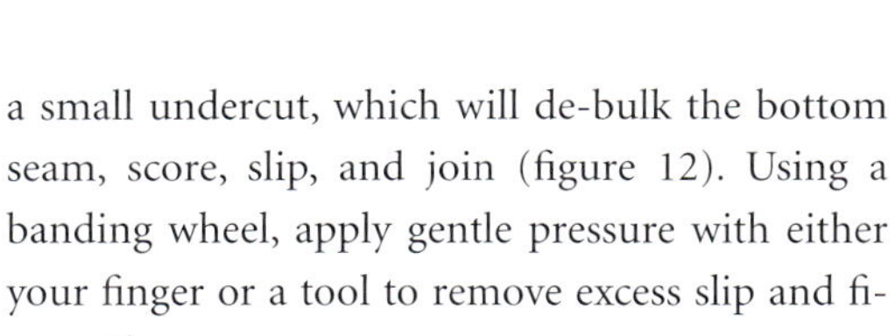

a small undercut, which will de-bulk the bottom seam, score, slip, and join (figure 12). Using a banding wheel, apply gentle pressure with either your finger or a tool to remove excess slip and finesse the seam.

Once the bottom is joined and finished from the outside, place another small bat on the bottom of the cup and flip. Now you have to finish working the seam from the middle of the cup up to the lip. If you don't work the seam properly, it will split open when you shape the cup, so don't skimp on this step!

Roll the world's smallest coil, drop it into the bottom of your cup and nudge it into place with an appropriate tool (figure 13). Press and work the coil smooth, creating a beautiful transition from the wall to the floor of your cup.

Start shaping the cup using a large throwing stick being careful to overlap each push all the way around (figure 14).

Make and apply a handle to your cup if desired and let dry. Once my cup is somewhere from the hard leather stage to bone dry, I use a piece of emery cloth lying flat on my bench to even out the rim. Then I use a sponge to dampen and a scraper to get to that nice thin lip that feels so good to drink from.

Making Handles

Slab handles are especially pleasing when impressed with a texture because they add an extra visual—as

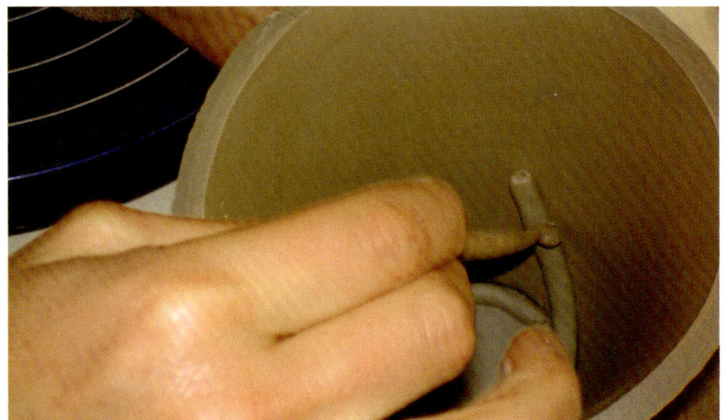

13. Nudge a coil into the bottom seam then smooth with a small brush with springy bristles.

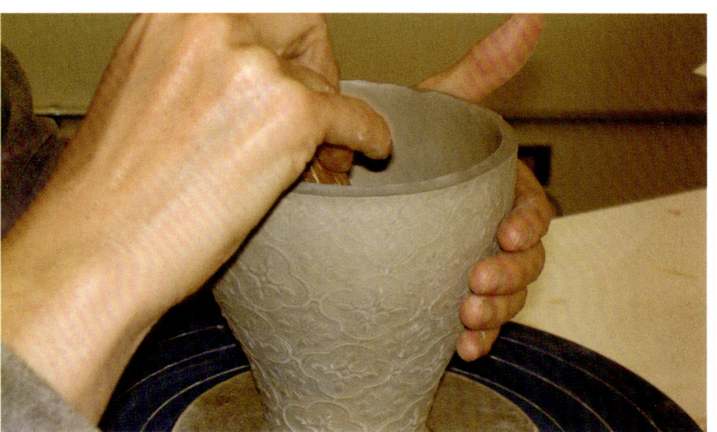

14. Start shaping the cup using a large throwing stick being careful to overlap each push all the way around the cup.

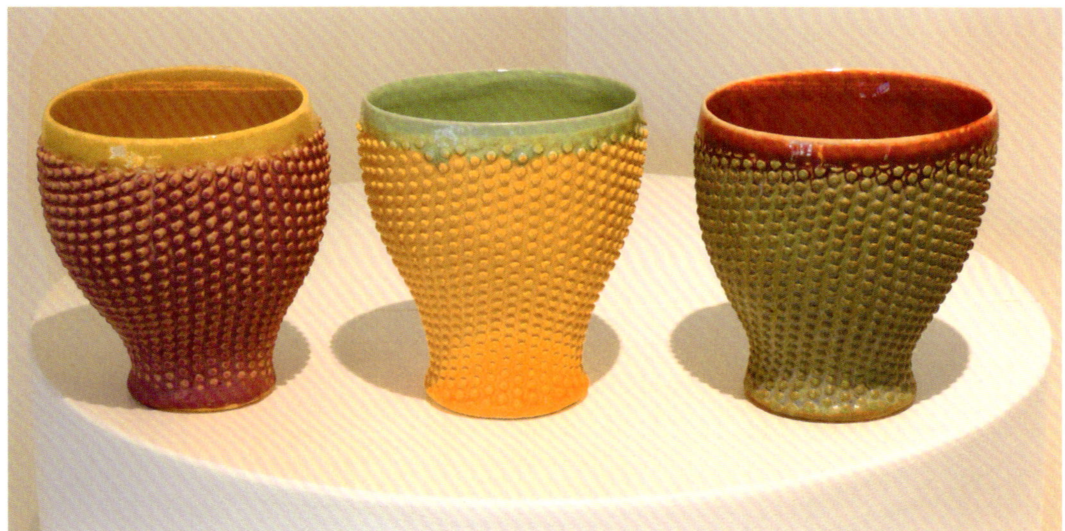

Touchy Trio. Annie prefers to make cups by hand, reinterpreting the shape of her favorite thrown forms with textured slabs, aspiring to the perfect radial symmetry of Yixing perfection.

well as tactile—zing. Furthermore, there's no waiting for slab handles to set up since they can be made and attached right after a cup is trimmed.

When I saw Lana Wilson make handles from a thin slab that she then folded over, it really looked great. The extra volume created within the slab when folded creates the perfect weight in regards to the thickness of the handle in relationship to the overall balance of the cup.

I've never had a problem with air being trapped within the handle, in part because the seam created by the fold is an informal one. There's no need to slip and score that seam, just let one side rest atop the other. The seam can be put on the inside of the handle, or used as part of the design on the outside. A vent hole can be added—just put it in an inconspicuous place—and knock off any sharpness created before firing!

I make cups in "litters" of a dozen or so. When I change the form of a cup, I'll change the shape of the handle, and also the texture. Every texture bends a different way. Just roll out a slab, then cut it into even strips, impress with different textures, and you'll see what I mean.

Start with a small piece of clay and make a thin, strong slab. Create a template that works with the

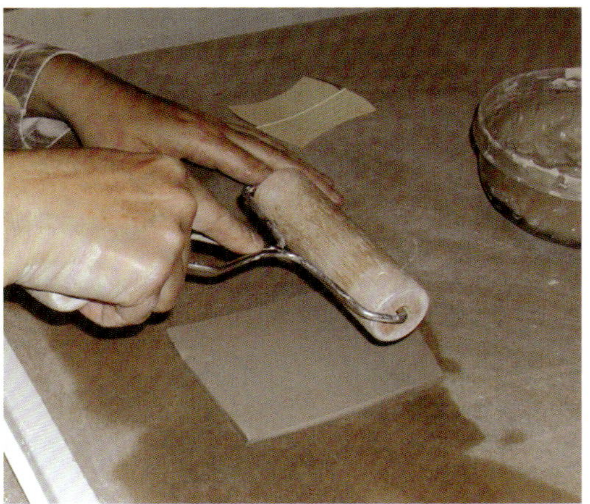

15. Use the mallet or a roller to get the slab perfectly even, then sponge off.

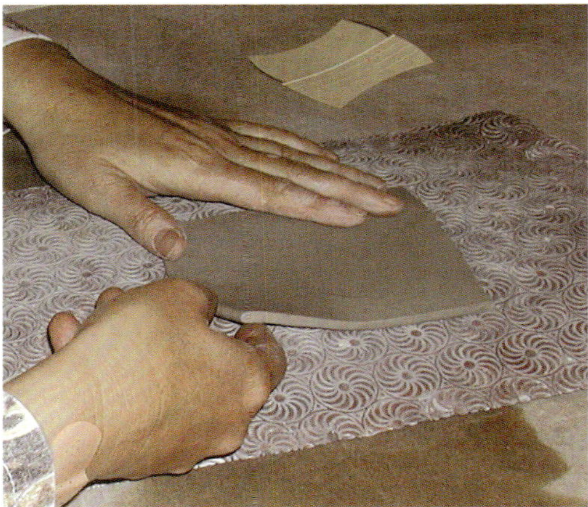

16. Align the slab with a texture. If clay sticks to your texture tool, clean off and dust lightly with corn starch.

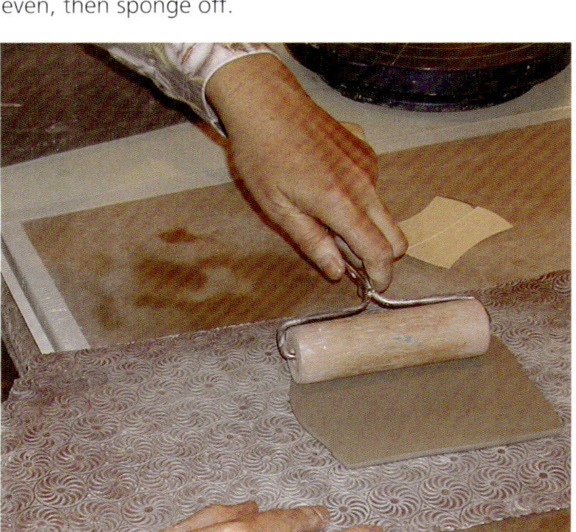

17. Roll the slab into the texture form applying even pressure like you did for the cup form.

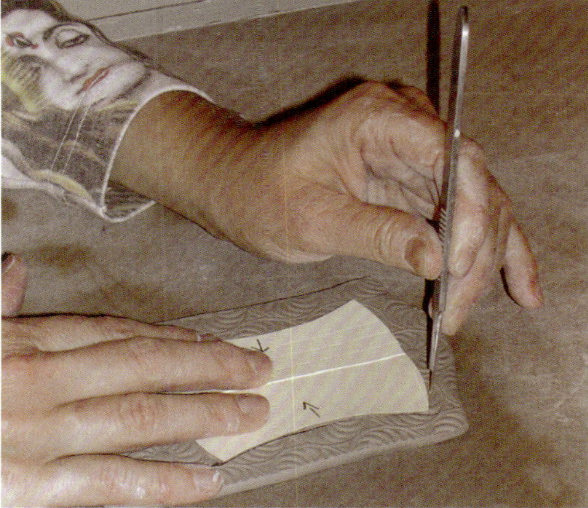

18. Cut the top and bottom perpendicular and the sides at an angle to reduce bulk at the overlap.

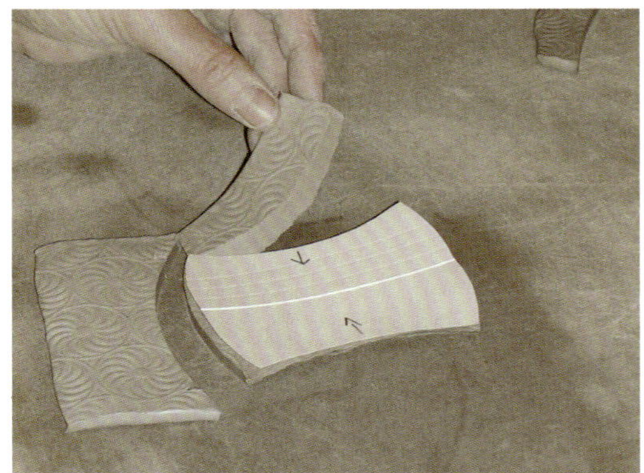

19. Carefully lift slab scraps away from handle.

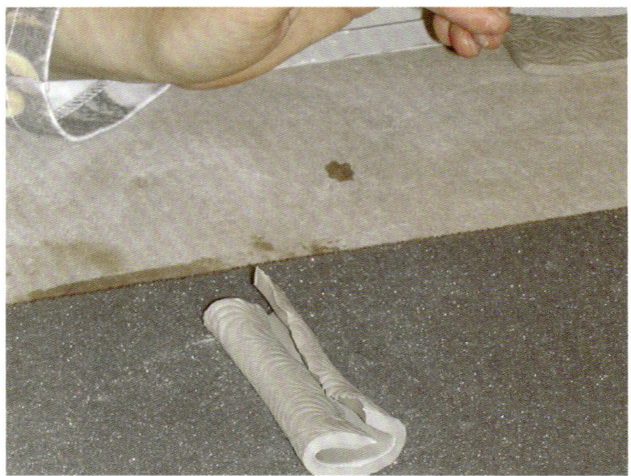

20. Fold one side into the center then roll in the second side and create an overlap—no slip is needed.

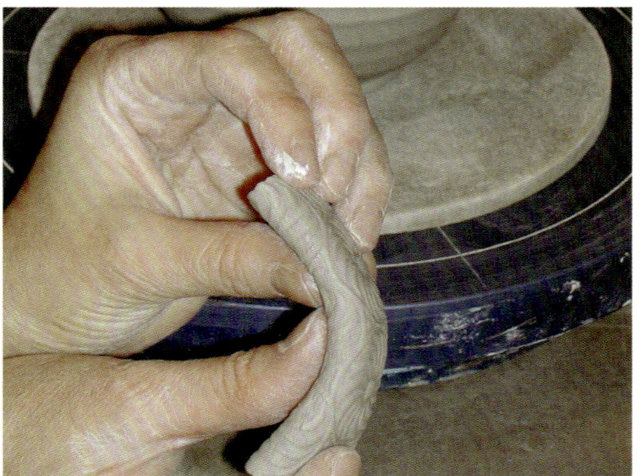

21. Shape the handle then trim to fit the form.

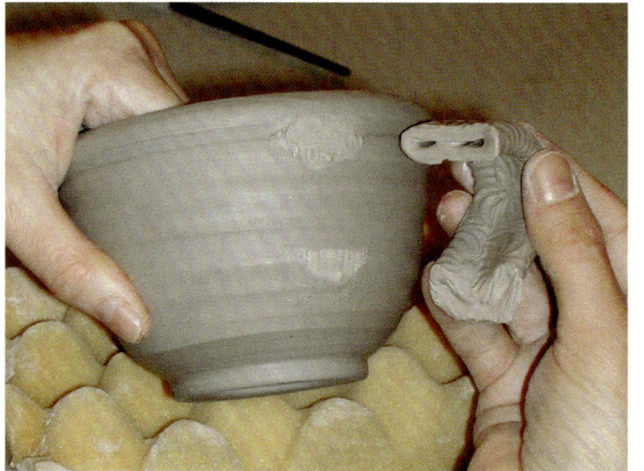

22. Score and slip the handle and the form, then apply the handle.

texture you're going to use as well as the size of the cups you've thrown. Align the template to the pattern in the texture and cut the sides with the tip of the knife pointing it in to reduce the amount of clay where it overlaps once you roll in the sides of the handle. Make sure you keep both the area you're working on and your hands free of "crumbs," otherwise they'll embed themselves in, and disrupt your texture. Crumbs tend to become even more visible when you start to shape your handle.

I slip, score, then slip, and score through the slip again, to create an interface where the handle joins the cup. Then I set the finished cup in a plastic box overnight to allow the moisture levels to even up.

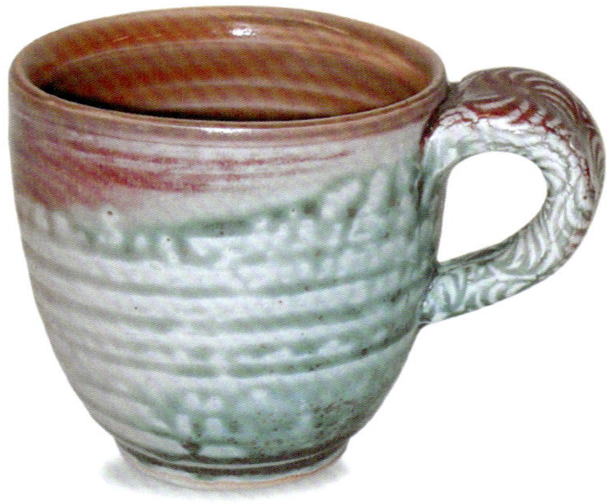

A textured handle adds interest to any handled form whether thrown or handbuilt.

5

Using Molds
KALEIDOSCOPE COVERED JARS

by Deborah Schwartzkopf

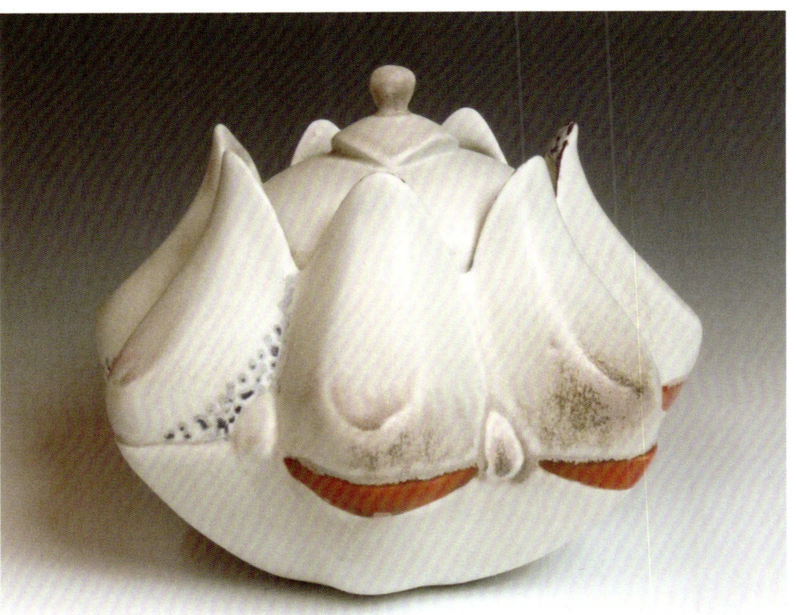

When you look into a kaleidoscope and turn it, all the colors and shapes merge, re-form, and fracture with each movement, and certain patterns come in and out of clarity. While building each of my kaleidoscope covered jars, I chase the most amazing expression of shapes, colors, and patterns possible—just as with each turn of the kaleidoscope. It's a puzzle of shapes and shadows at first, until the surface is added. Then it's all about what I want to accentuate—the seams, the bellies, the line quality, or maybe even breaking up a pattern of form with a surface pattern.

Prepping Slabs

The slabs I work with for building my covered jars are generally ⅜- to ¼-inch thick. I use a slightly thicker slab for the lower sections so they will better support the weight of added pieces.

Constructing the Base

These jars are formed by working with the slabs and a series of bisque molds. I place the mold for the bottom section on a bat before I start so it's easier to move later on. I cut out a circle from a prepared slab that will drape over the mold. To get it to fit snugly, I remove V-shaped darts of clay, beveling the edges so they overlap when put back together (figure 1).

I then gently compress the clay against the mold with a flexible rib. Since the mold is strong, it supports a lot of pressure and the clay takes on the volume and line quality of the form beneath it. Spend time making the mold, as any unevenness or dents transfer to the draped slab, especially if it's thin. Once the slab is firm enough to hold its shape, I flip the mold and slab over and then gently lift the mold up and out of the shaped slab (figure 2).

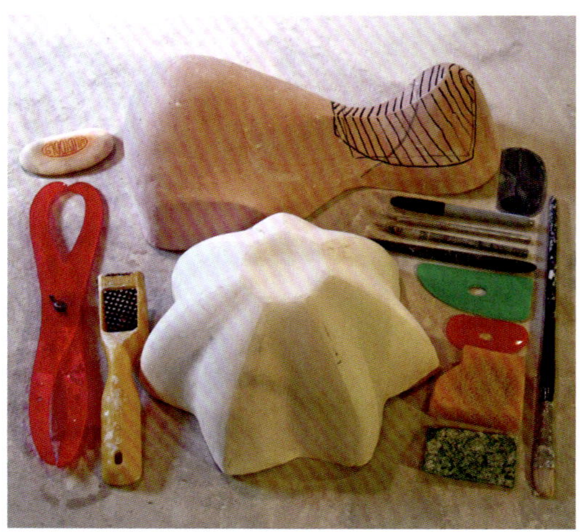

TOOLS

- *Molds*—built with clay and then bisque fired
- *X-Acto knife*—dull, this way you won't cut your hands or the canvas table covering. These work well for precision cuts, even when dulled.
- *Delicate scoring tool*—small enough to reach into small areas
- *Green Mudtools rib*—for moving clay and getting into corners to compress
- *Red Mudtools rib*—for gently pressing and smoothing surfaces
- *Metal rib*—for forming, compressing, and moving clay
- *Green kitchen scrubbing/scouring pad*—cut into small sections, good for initial smoothing and cleaning of the completed form
- *Small sponge*—use for secondary smoothing
- *Mudtools smoothing sponge*—use to get the surface flawless
- *Banding wheel*—I use a Shimpo, for the weight, smoothness of the rotation, and the height.
- *Paint brush*—long with strong bristles for smoothing small or hard-to-reach areas.
- *Surform rasp*—for evening out surfaces and defining planes
- *Calipers*—for measuring the collar, gallery, and lid diameters

Timing Is Everything

The timing of adding more sections on top of the base is crucial. If the clay is too soft, the bottom section will warp and collapse under the weight of additional top sections. If it's too firm, there will be even more cracking issues. I like to talk about the firmness of clay in terms of cheese. The bottom section should be like sharp cheddar when taken off the mold and somewhere closer to Parmesan when more sections are added. The sections forming the top should be a soft leather hard when added to the base. This is important, as these repeating sections need to hold their shape and not slump, yet remain flexible enough to work with.

To create the repeating top sections, I use a pattern that has evolved over time. I cut out seven pieces using a template, then shape each one on the same mold, one by one, letting them firm up and then removing and adding the next. I draw a line with a permanent marker around the first one, to indicate where I should lay the next six. I lay each piece on and gently flex the clay around the shape with my hands, followed with a light spray of water and then use a flexible rib to create the contours and smoothness (figure 3).

Before attaching, I trimming away unevenness with a Surform or X-Acto blade. This makes each piece very similar. I then score the bottom section's rim and the lower edge of the fluted pieces. Prescoring makes it easier to work with many pieces at once. I also add slip to all of the pieces prior to joining them so that I can hold pieces in place as I work.

Building the Fluted Top

I add one fluted top piece at a time, pressing the seams firmly together. After scoring one section, I hold the next piece in place and gauge how much to trim. I partially attach it and trim it in-place to fit the adjoining piece (figure 4). I repeat this all the way around, sizing and trimming each piece to fit. At first the pieces will not hold themselves up, but once I get three or four attached, the circle begins to support itself.

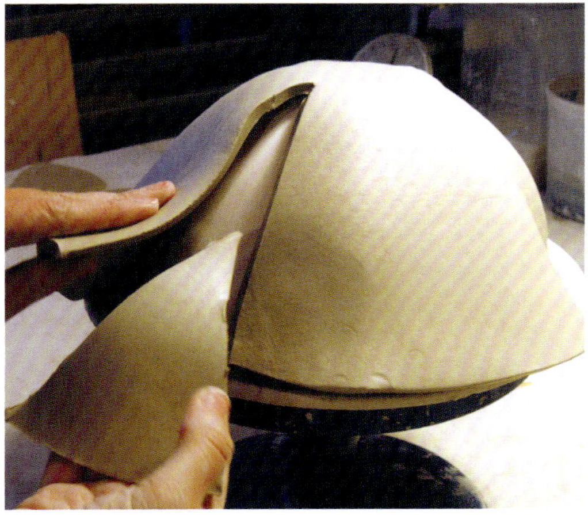

1. Draping a slab over the bisque mold and removing a dart to make the lower section of the jar.

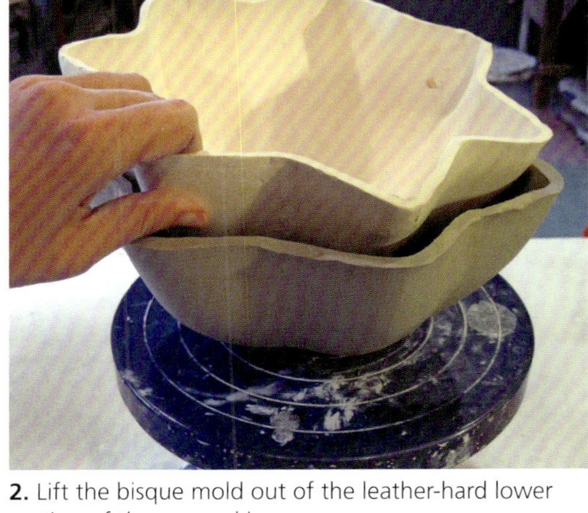

2. Lift the bisque mold out of the leather-hard lower section of the covered jar.

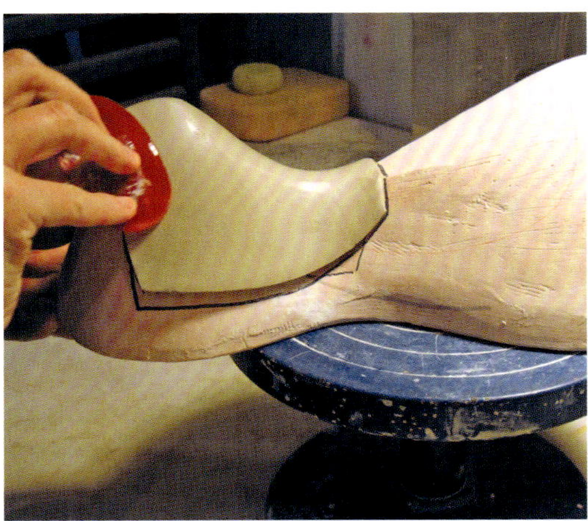

3. Create the forms for the upper part of the jar using a section of another bisque mold.

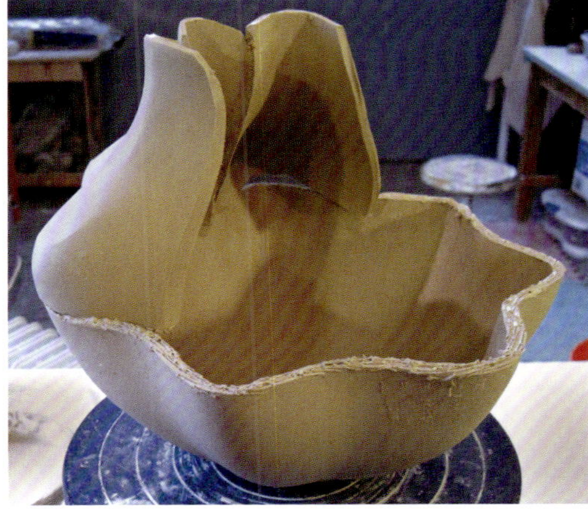

4. Add the soft-leather-hard top sections to the base one at a time, adjusting the fit as you work.

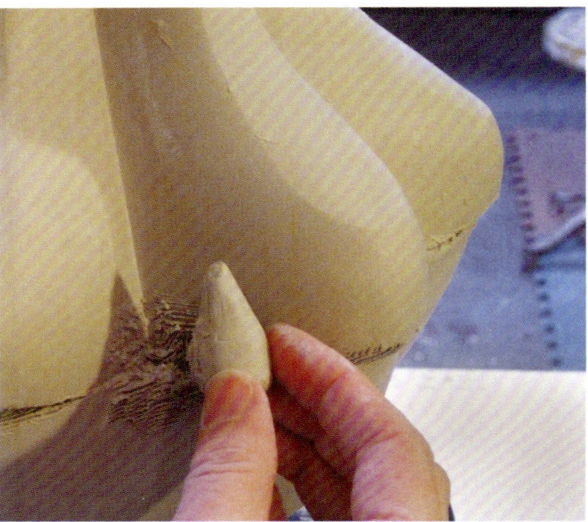

5. Add details like these tear shapes to reinforce the joints and accentuate the angular flutes.

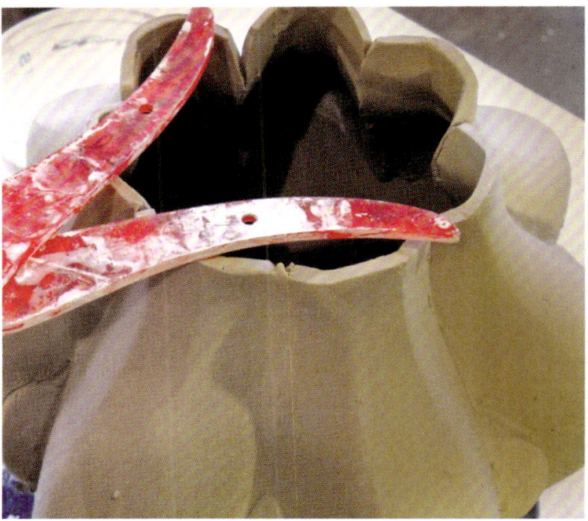

6. Using calipers, measure the rim diameter for the collar and the gallery diameter where the lid sits.

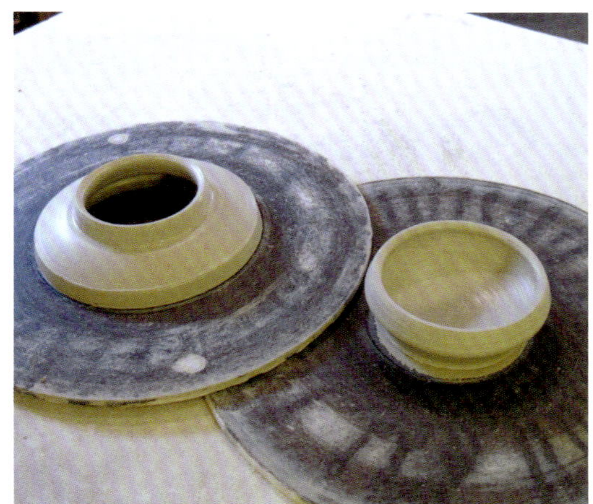

7. Throw or handbuild the collar as a bottomless cylinder and throw or handbuild the lid like a bowl.

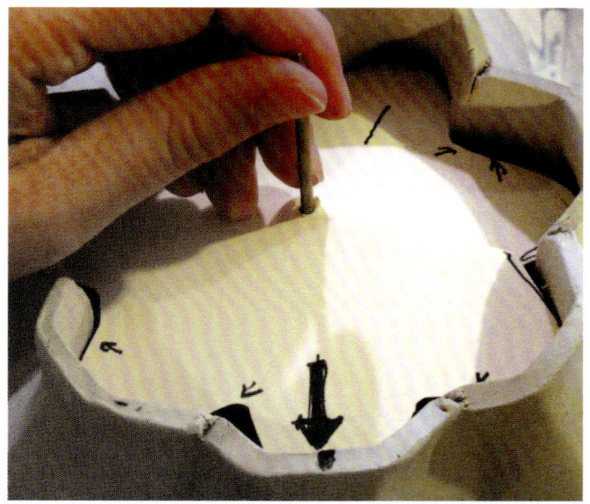

8. Insert paper into the jar, draw, then cut out the approximate shape of the edge of the collar. Refine as needed.

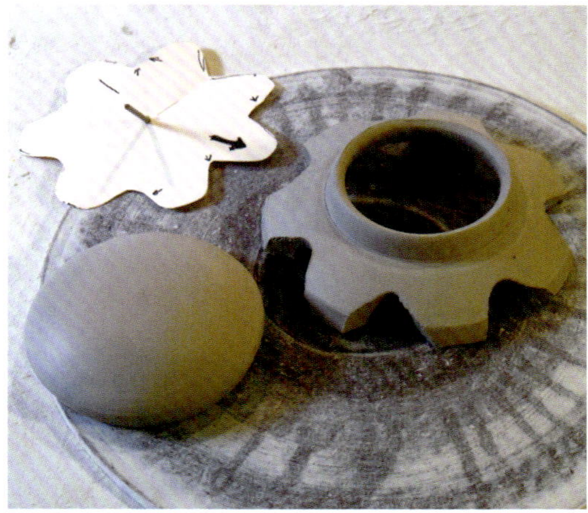

9. Trim the lid then cut the collar to fit using the paper template. Check them both for a good fit.

I spend time compressing the vertical seams between sections, adding clay where the edges don't meet well or if there's a divot or weak-looking section. All seams and gaps are strengthened and filled with soft coils of clay. I spend extra time on the inside seams at this point. It's still pretty easy to add coils and smooth before the collar is added. With the amount of time it takes to make these jars, it's worth it to take time on each seam. On this jar, I also add tear-shaped pieces of clay for an additional pattern and strength on a joint where three edges meet (figure 5). For more detailed information on the way I strengthen seams and joints, check out http://debspottery.com/Process/Process1.html.

Fitting the Lid and Collar

As soon as I have all the top sections attached and the top of the jar is complete, I use calipers to measure the widest point of the inside diameter (figure 6). I throw a collar to that same diameter so that once cut to fit, it can sit inside of the slab-built body. I throw a cap-style lid to fit over the flange on the collar (figure 7). When making the lid, I have to make sure there is enough space between the edge of the wall and the gallery for the thickness of the lid. These are left out to dry while I work on the template for the collar. Alternatively, you can handbuild a collar and lid.

To work out the final shape of the collar, I use a paper template. This saves time as I am less likely to ruin the collar if I have a guess as to how to shape it. I cut a circle out of paper, push a nail through the center to create a handle, insert it into the jar, and then trace around the inside wall of the jar onto the paper, indicating where the collar and wall will meet. I cut out this rough template and then place it into the jar again to check the fit. There are usually huge differences. I draw arrows onto the template where it should be trimmed down or added to, and draw a key arrow on it and make a corresponding mark on the rim of the pot so I can orient the template properly (figure 8). This information is transferred to a second piece of paper to create a more accurate template. It's cut out and fit into the jar.

This process of cutting and refining is repeated until the collar template fits properly.

I trim my thrown work on a foam bat, keeping the piece stable and holding it on center with my left hand. I trim the lid round and add a simple knob later on. I turn the collar upside down, place the template on it, and then trace my finger around the edge, pressing the indent of the paper onto the clay. I then trim away the clay (figure 9).

Next comes is the most challenging part of finishing the collar. It's difficult to avoid warping the curve of the collar when fitting. Transfer the arrow/mark for fitting from the template to the collar. Pre-score the inside wall of the jar where the template fits best, then score the collar. Apply slip, then insert the collar, making sure that the mark on the collar meets the mark on the jar. Draw it upward and only lightly begin to press pieces together all the way around. You will probably have to adjust it, so lightly connecting them makes any adjustments easier. After the collar is in place, reinforce the seam with a small coil, both inside and out (figure 10).

Now only the details remain. I add clay in lots of small places to sharpen lines, thicken angles, or adjust curves (figure 11). I smooth the whole surface with a scouring pad dipped in water. This works super well to take down roughness without creating dust (figure 12). I go over everything with a softer sponge to remove the marks reminiscent of cat-licked butter, and then do a final smoothing with a Mudtools super-soft smoothing sponge.

Even drying helps tremendously when it comes to preventing cracks from forming, so if you live in a dry area, give the jars more time to dry under plastic prior to uncovering them.

When designing forms like these jars, I try to imagine the progression of shapes as they rise from foot to rim, and often do this with drawing. I have, however, found this way of building particularly intuitive and difficult for me to plan on paper. Over the years of trying out different shapes, I have learned different, more direct approaches working with clay to sketch out forms that work for me.

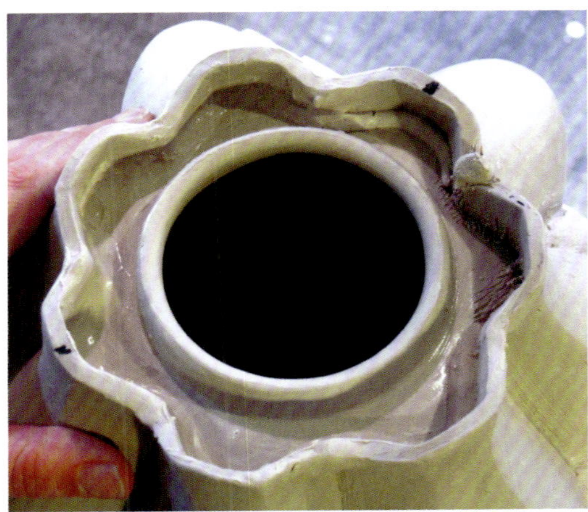

10. Lower the collar into a pre-scored jar. Press to fit, then add a coil on the top and bottom of the seam.

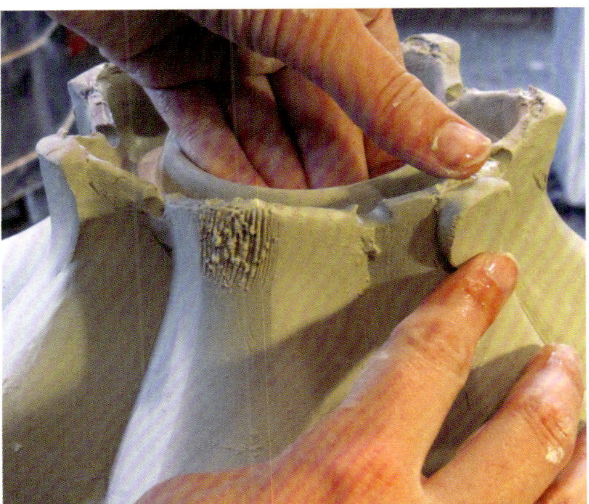

11. Add clay to create thickness on the rim and further accentuate the form's angularity.

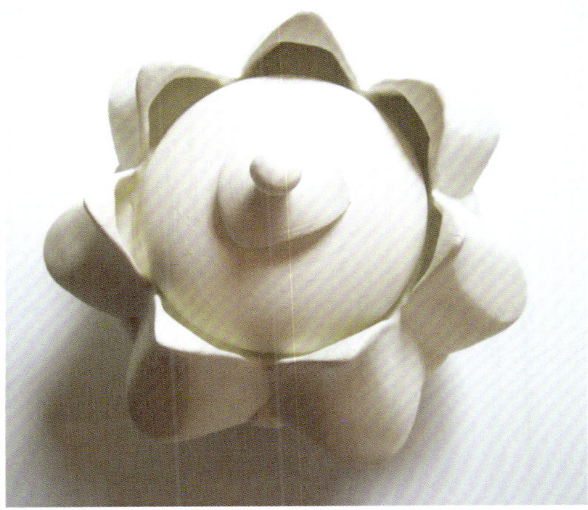

Top view of the completed kaleidoscope jar prior to glazing and firing.

VASE WITH SLUMPED SIDES

by Brenda Quinn

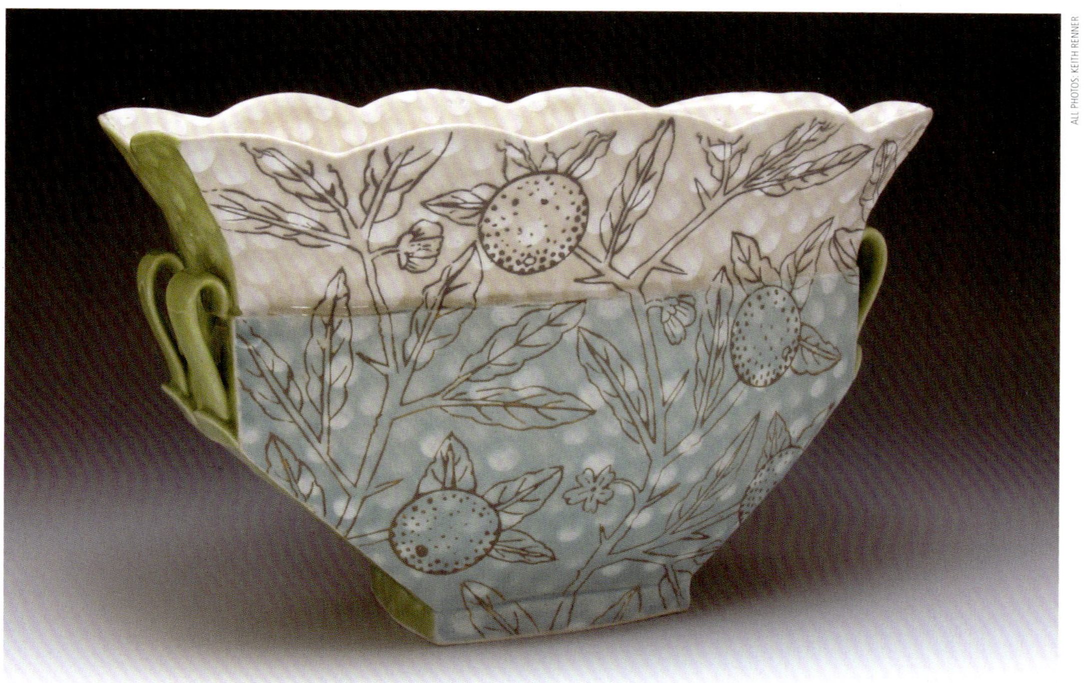

ALL PHOTOS: KEITH RENNER

Developing forms that have a utilitarian function and a dynamic design is like trying to solve an evolving equation with an elusive answer. For me, this equation becomes more complicated with the addition of an ever-expanding range of functions, techniques, and glazes to my working vocabulary. The chase for a solution is engaging; so much so that I'm often interjecting more variables into my process to keep the chase going. This is why I love learning new techniques and processes. It's like building an inventory of possibilities in my mind. I appreciate how making the same form using different techniques yields distinctly different results. The designs for my work come out of a number of practices. I begin with sketches of forms and patterns, and often pull ideas from various historical sources. My current body of work started with an assignment I had given to my students, challenging them to combine handbuilding and wheel throwing with consideration for the unique visual qualities each of those techniques carry with them. This idea evolved as I began incorporating a slumping process into my work using an octagonal mold to create a vase. The mold was originally used to make a platter. After creating the platter, it was easy to see the potential in the form to become other vessels.

Start with Slumping

To create this slab- and coil-built vase, you first need to cut an octagon out of paper to use as a slump-mold template. A variety of rigid materi-

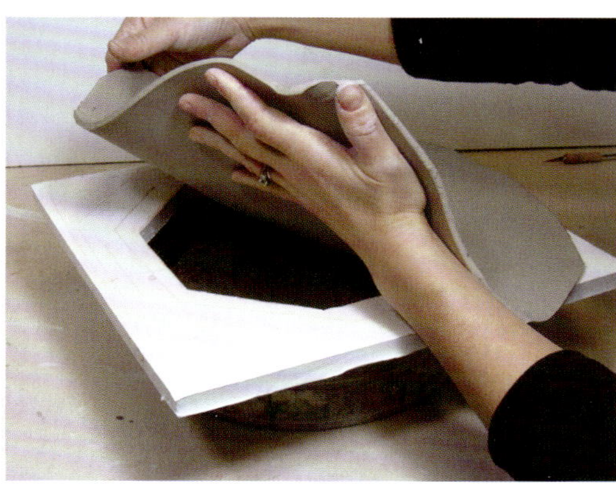

1. Cut out an octagonal template. With the template supported, drape a slab onto the mold.

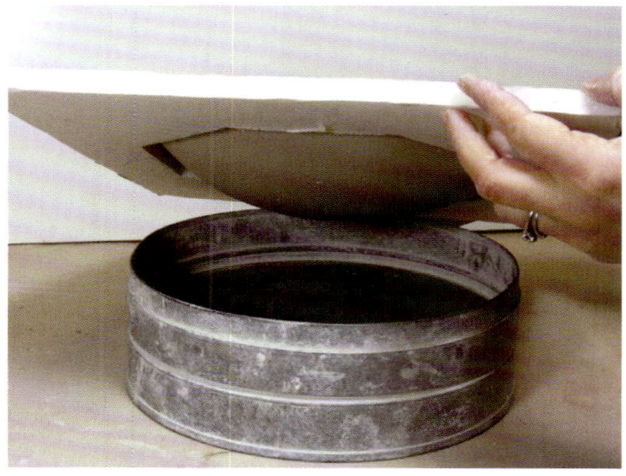

2. Remove excess clay leaving an inch overlap. Tap clay, mold, and support on the table to make the clay slump.

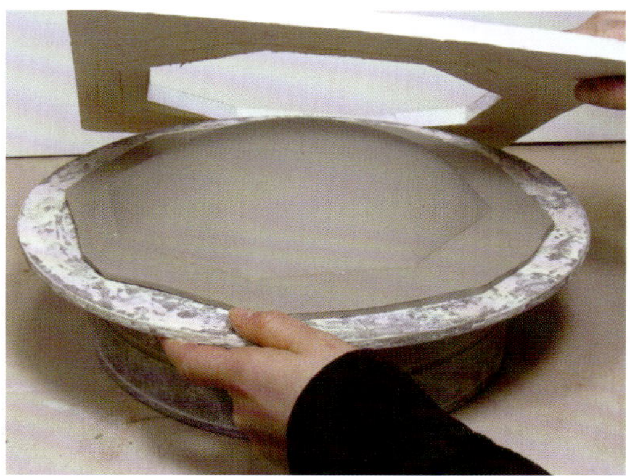

3. Using the mold board as a support, flip the leather-hard slab over and remove mold board.

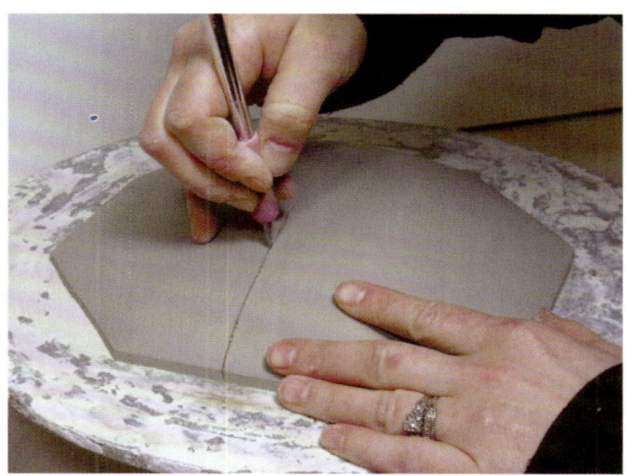

4. Trim the clay to the line left by the board. Draw and cut a line across the middle of the piece.

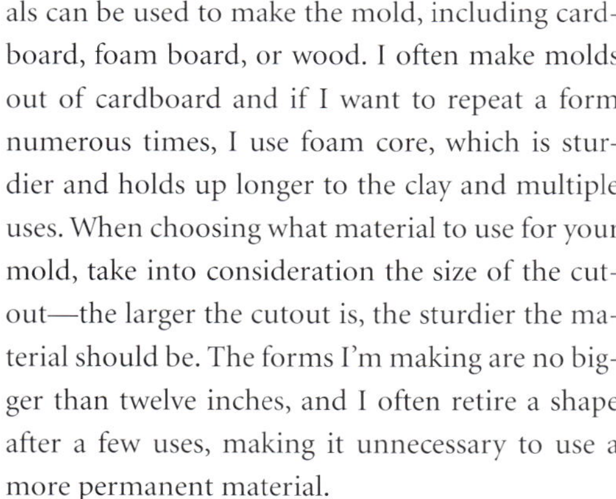

als can be used to make the mold, including cardboard, foam board, or wood. I often make molds out of cardboard and if I want to repeat a form numerous times, I use foam core, which is sturdier and holds up longer to the clay and multiple uses. When choosing what material to use for your mold, take into consideration the size of the cutout—the larger the cutout is, the sturdier the material should be. The forms I'm making are no bigger than twelve inches, and I often retire a shape after a few uses, making it unnecessary to use a more permanent material.

Next, trace the paper template onto your mold board, and allow at least an extra two inches of board around the cutout to provide support during the slumping process. Using a sharp knife, cut the shape out and mark the side of the board that you cut from—ensuring you use the side providing you with a more accurate shape. Find a bucket or box with an opening slightly larger than the size of your cutout, to support the edge of the mold as you work.

Make a slab that is at least five inches larger than the cutout. At this point you can texture your slab or to make it smooth. Carefully lift the slab and place it with the finished side facing down in the mold (figure 1). Trim away some of the excess clay, but leave an even ledge of clay about one inch wide around the edge of the cutout. This even lip helps the clay to slump evenly in the mold. If you leave too narrow a strip of clay, the clay may shift and fall into the opening during the next step.

Firmly grab the mold, slab, and support under it, lift them up, and tap it onto the table to force

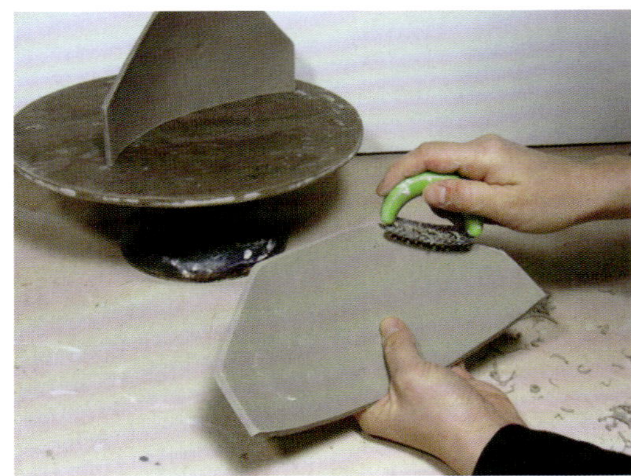

5. Use a rasp to create a 45° bevel on the edges of the two pieces. Score and slip the edges of the piece.

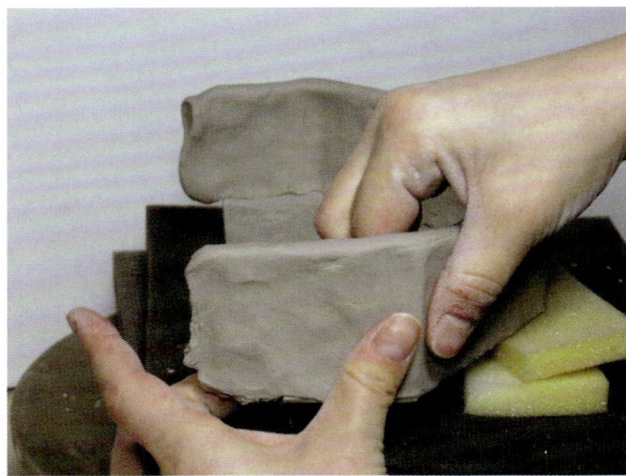

6. Attach a 2-inch-wide slab to the piece while it's supported by foam. Pinch the slab to shape and refine.

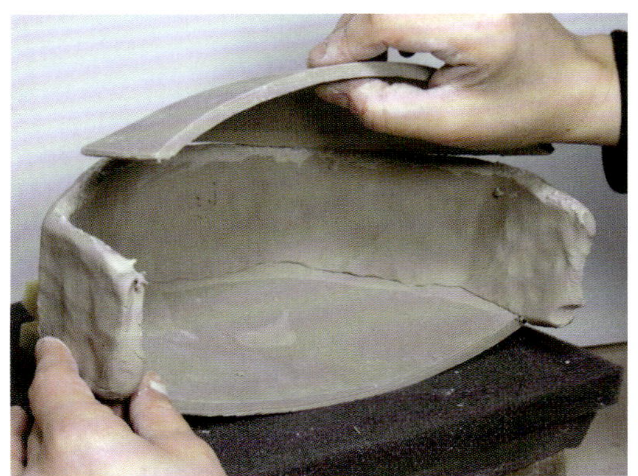

7. Score and slip the pinched slab and connect the other half of the slumped slab.

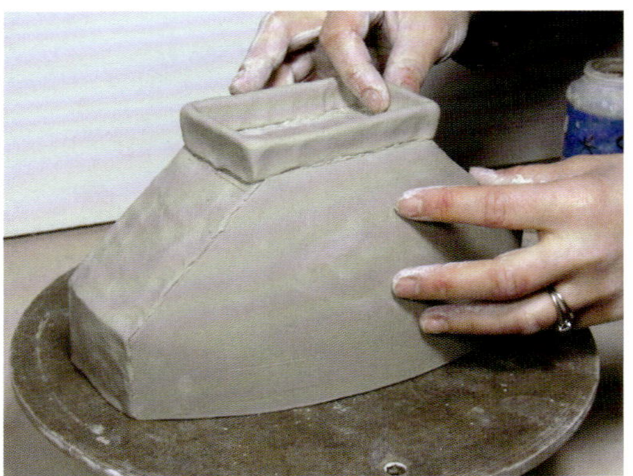

8. Flip the piece so that the opened side is facing down. Add a coil to the base to create a foot.

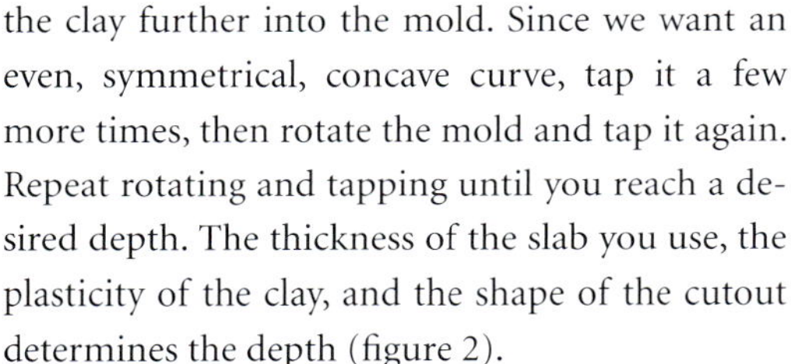

the clay further into the mold. Since we want an even, symmetrical, concave curve, tap it a few more times, then rotate the mold and tap it again. Repeat rotating and tapping until you reach a desired depth. The thickness of the slab you use, the plasticity of the clay, and the shape of the cutout determines the depth (figure 2).

Once the slumped slab reaches leather hard, put a bat on top of it and flip it over (figure 3). Cut away the extra clay and draw a line to use as a guide to cut the piece in half (figure 4).

Add Handbuilt & Pinched Elements

Use a rasp to make 45° angles on the edges of the forms (figure 5). Score and slip along the edge of the pieces, lay one of the pieces with the concave side facing up on a piece of foam to support it and add a two-inch-wide slab of clay to the entire slipped and scored edge, except the longest edge. Pinching the slab ensures a strong connection and creates texture to contrast the smooth surfaces of the slumped slab or you can make a seamless connection and a smooth surface if desired. Use your fingers to form a corner at each of the octagon's points (figure 6). Score, slip, and lay the other half of the octagon on top of the slab and repeat this same process (figure 7). Allow the entire form to stiffen under plastic. This helps to even out the moisture content and prevent the joints from cracking apart.

Next, turn the piece so it sits with the open side down. Score, slip, and add a coil to build the foot (figure 8). Make sure the foot is sturdy enough to physically and aesthetically support the weight of the piece.

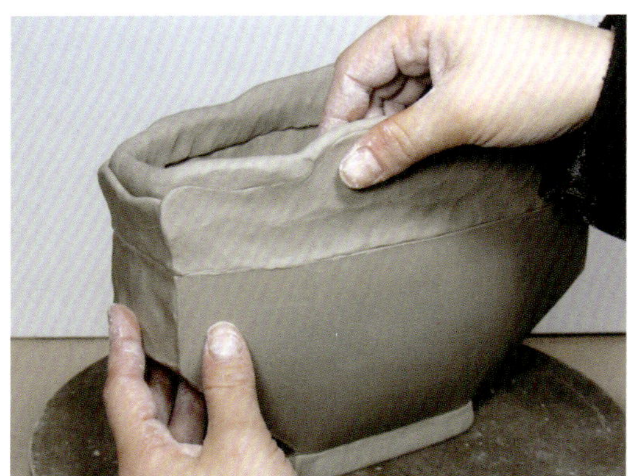

9. Turn the piece over and add coils to the rim of the opening. Pinch to combine the coils and add texture.

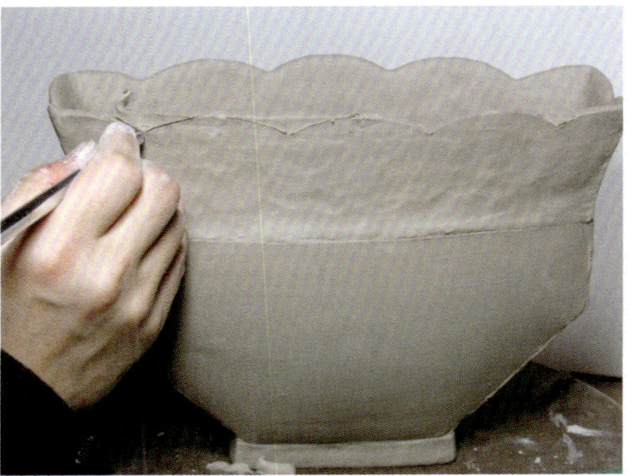

10. Cut the rim into a scalloped edge or desired pattern, and pinch the edges to refine them.

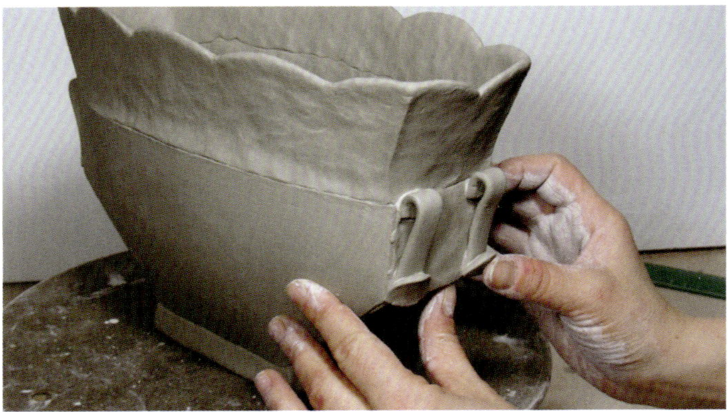

11. Create and attach four small handles and four small petal forms.

After the foot stiffens, flip the vase over. Score and slip around the rim and add a thick coil. Pinch the coil to connect it to the base and to thin it out, moving the clay up. Continue adding coils and pinching until the piece reaches the desired height (figure 9).

Consider All the Details

Using a ruler, level out the top. Finish the top edge in any number of ways, such as the scalloped edge shown here (figure 10). Consider the two-dimensional design on the surface when making choices about the three-dimensional aspects of a form. Knowing that I'll be drawing a pattern that has a leaf image with a ruffled edge led me to choose a more organic edge for the top. Looking for ways to tie three-dimensional and two-dimensional aspects of a piece together can help bring unity to a piece.

Lastly, make and attach four small handles to the sides of the piece. Using small pieces of clay, I model four petals that are attached to the bases of each handle (figure 11). I like the way these appendages add visual movement to the piece and also provide a place for an accent color when glazing. After these pieces are attached, allow the vase to dry slowly under plastic and then bisque fire it.

This technique can be used to create an endless number of forms. Make numerous slump molds of various shapes and use those parts as building blocks for new forms. By taking a slumped slab, looking at it from all angles, and thinking of cutting it into smaller pieces or adding coiled sections, you will be able to visualize how versatile these pieces can be.

Using Molds

CLOVER DISH WITH SLUMPED BOTTOM

by Joe Singewald

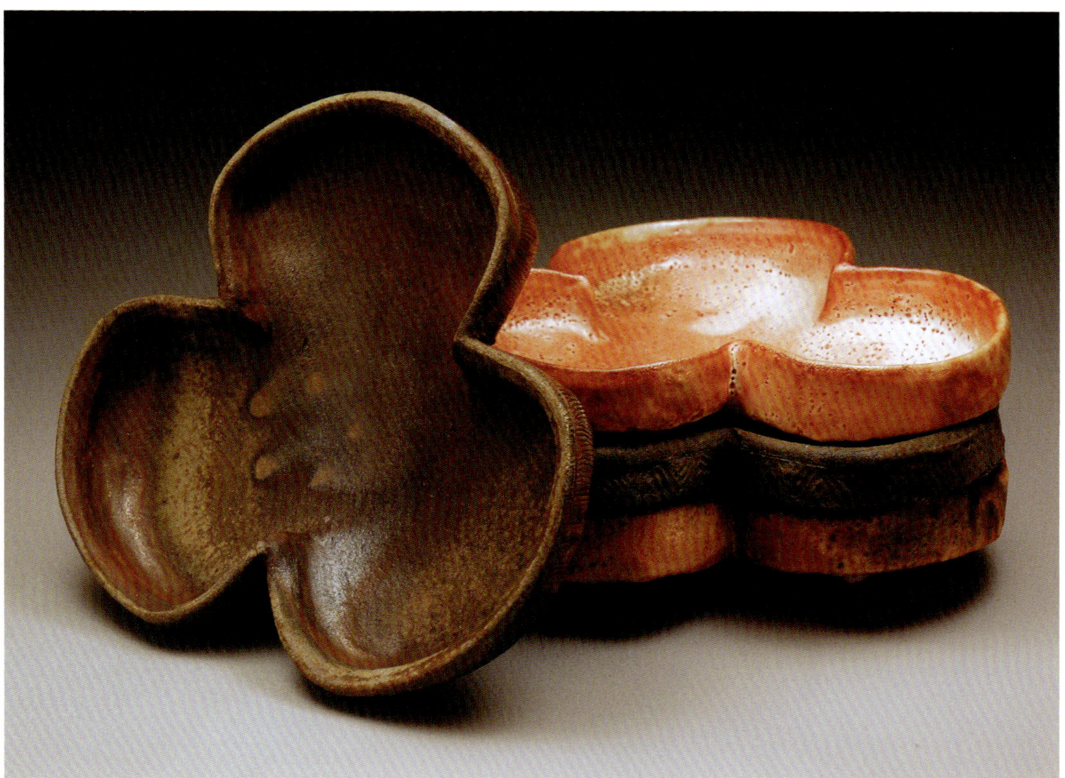

The design for the clover dish began when I decided to study ceramics with Randy Johnston at the University of Wisconsin-River Falls. Randy taught me how to handbuild with soft slabs and how the tensile strength of clay can create beautiful, gentle curves. Many twists and turns later, the first clover dish was conceived out of desperation. I was a graduate student at Utah State when asked to teach an intermediate handbuilding class. Although coil- and slab-built pottery made up a percentage of my body of work, I wasn't confident in my slab-construction forms. At the time, I asked myself, "How can I excite students about slab building if I am not thrilled with it myself?" This challenged me to develop new ideas, which resulted in the clover dish.

Making a Paper Template

My clover dishes are constructed with a slump-mold technique. Making the form requires basic woodworking tools and skills. The desired shape is first cut from a paper template to scale. It's important to know how much your clay shrinkage is so that you can compensate for it in the template. You can use any shape, symmetrical or asymmetrical, large as a serving platter or as small as a soap dish.

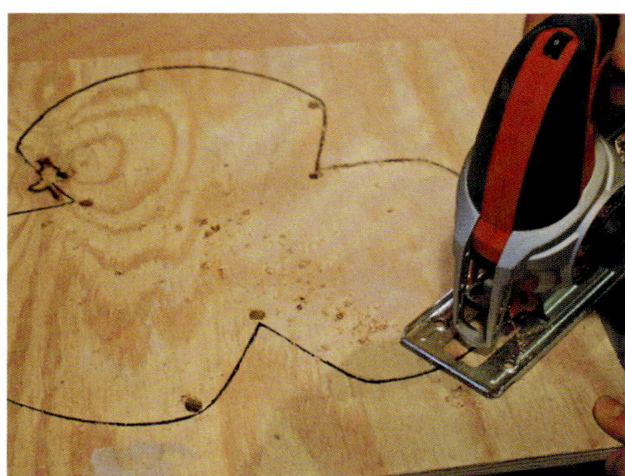

1. Drill holes just inside the traced form, then use the jigsaw to cut a precise slump mold.

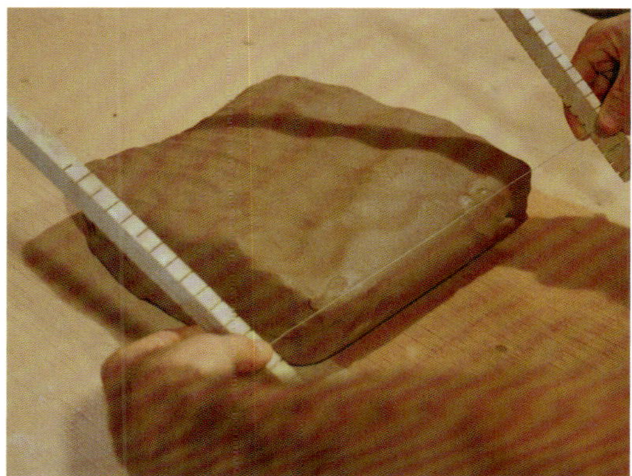

2. To make a slab, stretch a wire between two notched sticks.

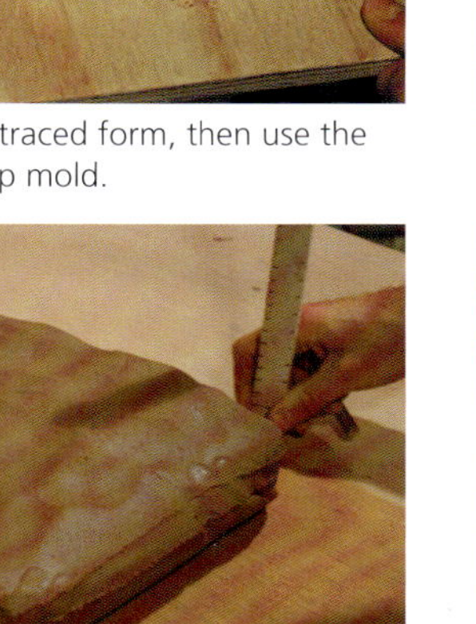

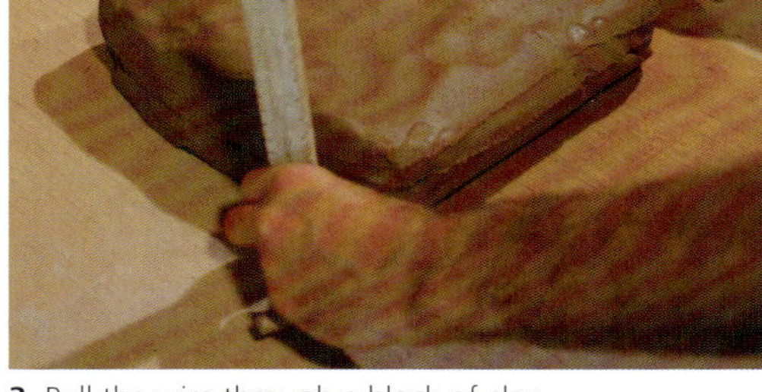

3. Pull the wire through a block of clay

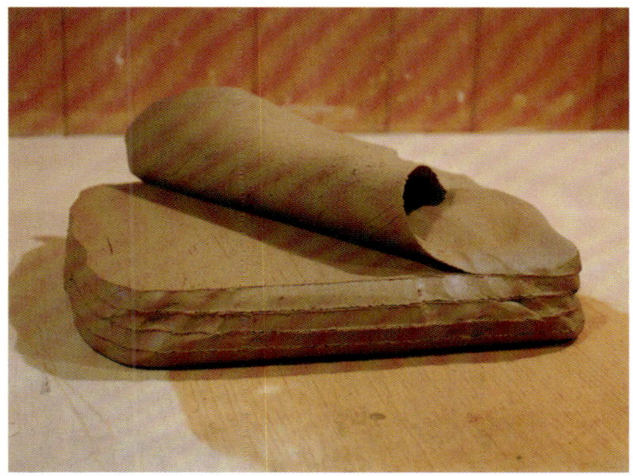

4. Each slab thickness is determined by the space between the end of the stick and the notches.

Cutting a Wood Slump Mold

With a marker, transfer the paper pattern onto a piece of ¾-inch thick plywood that is at least one inch larger than the paper pattern in all dimensions. Use a drill and jigsaw to cut out the pattern (figure 1). Start by drilling a hole just inside the traced form with a drill bit that is wider than the a jigsaw blade. Sometimes several holes make cutting complex forms easier. In this case, I cut three holes at each of the inner clover points. Next, slide the saw blade inside a drilled hole and slowly begin cutting along the pattern. Once the form has been cut and removed, hand sand the inside edge. Softening and slightly rounding this edge helps prevent unwanted shearing of the clay. Now your slump form is ready to use.

Preparing a Slab

Roll a slab out to at least 1½ inches larger than the cut hole in all directions. The clay will stretch and thin as it slumps into the form so make the slab ½ inch thick. To reach the desired thickness, either use a rolling pin and wooden thickness guides or cut the slab using a "pocket slab roller" (figures 2 through 4), a handy tool I made after seeing Randy Johnston's. To make a pocket slab roller, tape two scrap pieces of wood together, measure and mark them, then cut notches at regular intervals with a band saw. My sticks have different spacing on opposite sides, allowing different slab thicknesses depending on the project.

Next, compress each side of the slab with a firm rib and then texture one side. I make bisque clay

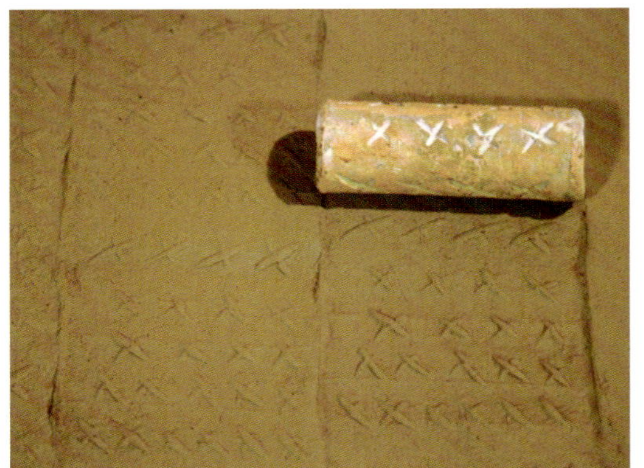
5. Compress each side of the slab with a firm rib and then texture one side.

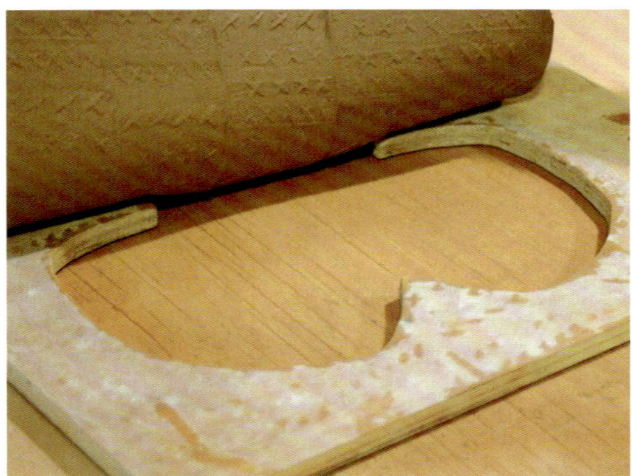
6. Carefully drape the slab, texture side down, over the plywood slump mold.

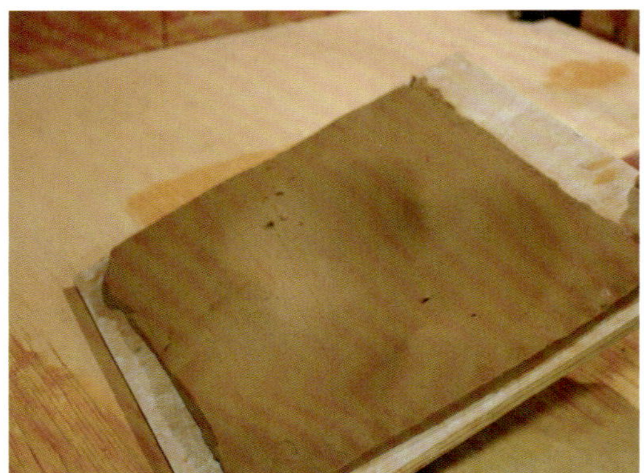
7. Tap all four of the edges of the mold against the tabletop to slump the clay.

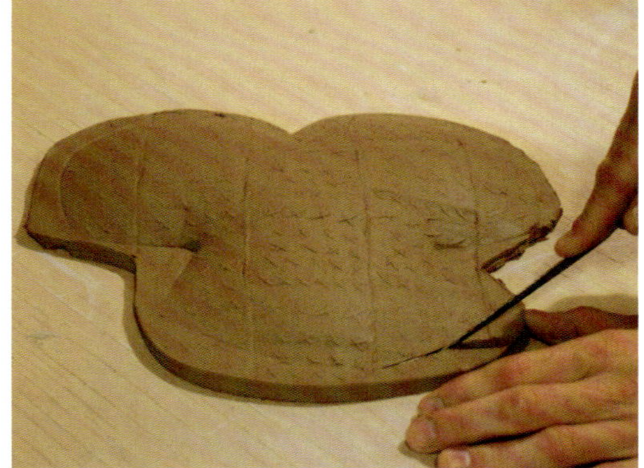
8. Cut a beveled edge, angled inward, ⅛ inch from the outside edge along the line made by the mold edge.

rolling stamps, or cords for texture (figure 5). The great thing about handbuilding with soft clay is how easy it is to impress while flat.

Slumping a Slab

Once textured, the clay is ready to be put in place. Drape the slab, texture side down, over the slump mold (figure 6). Lifting the clay-covered form from the tabletop immediately allows the clay to take shape. Tilting the form and tapping all four of the edges on a tabletop promotes further slumping (figure 7).

Now set the board and slab on wooden blocks or kiln posts that are tall enough so the draped clay doesn't touch the table surface and allow the clay to become leather hard. I typically cover the slab with plastic and return the following day. The wooden form will absorb some of the clay's moisture overnight. Once leather hard, remove the slumped slab from the mold and gently flip it onto a table. Next, bevel the edge ⅛ inch from the outside edge. You will see a distinct line created from the wooden form (figure 8). After placing foam on the mold (I re-use cone pack foam) return the clay to the form (figure 9). The foam prevents the clay from falling through after being cut.

Adding Walls

To add the walls, start by flattening coils of clay and cut them into equal widths. An extruder works great if you have access to one. I make extruder dies from Masonite by cutting the wall cross section with a jigsaw in the same manner the clover mold was made. A string can be used to determine

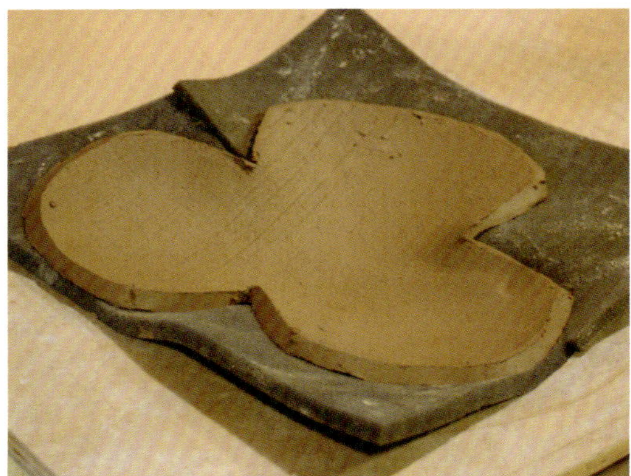

9. Return the cut-out slab to a foam-lined slump form. The foam prevents the slab from slipping through.

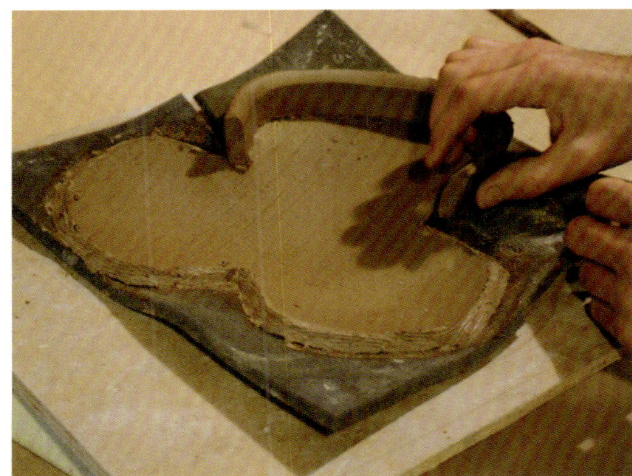

10. Flatten clay coils and cut them in equal widths, then attach after slipping and scoring both parts.

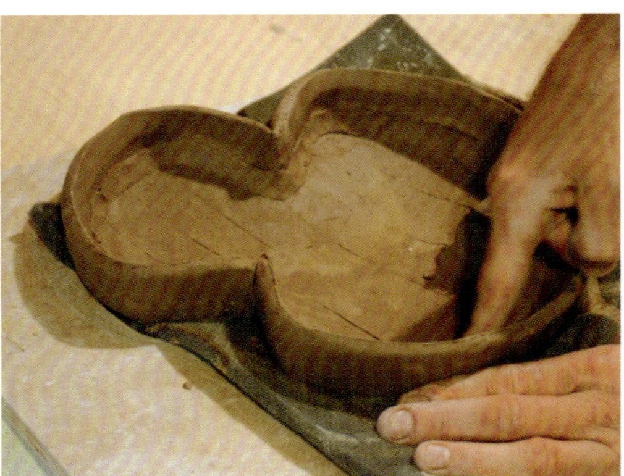

11. Add a coil to fill in the inner seam where the walls connect to the base and to each other.

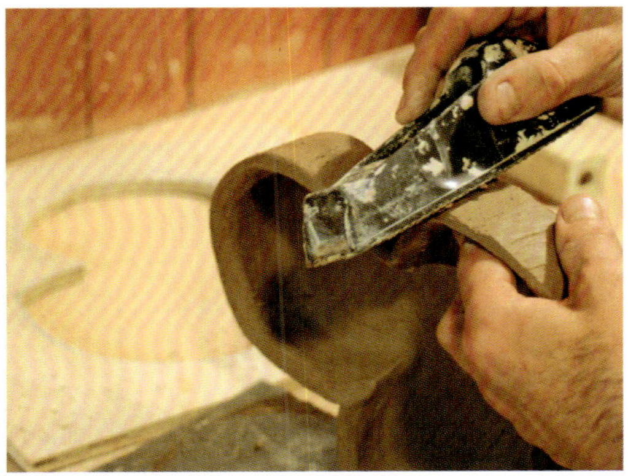

12. Use a Surform to true up the sides and to create texture. Then pinch and refine the lip.

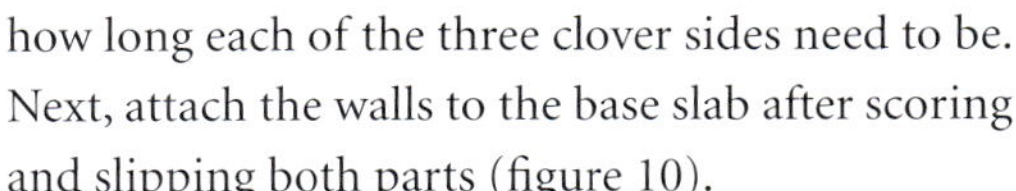

how long each of the three clover sides need to be. Next, attach the walls to the base slab after scoring and slipping both parts (figure 10).

Cover the dish overnight, allowing the walls to become leather hard. Once this has occurred, add a worm-sized soft coil to fill in the inner seam where the walls connect to the base and where they connect to each other (figure 11). I often texture the exterior walls with a paddle or rolling stamp. In this case, I used a Surform to true up the sides and create texture (figure 12). At the same time, I pinch and refine the lip.

Adding Feet

The final step is adding three feet. Flipping the dish over onto foam protects the lip while feet are added. Roll out three angled coils, score one end of each, then score three spots on the bottom of the dish. Apply slip, then attach the coils. Be careful not to attach the feet too close to the center, as the form will become unstable and could tip during use. While the feet are still soft, flip the dish over and set it on a banding wheel. Turning the wheel, make sure the dish's lip is level and adjust as needed. Return the clover dish upside down to the foam and wait for the feet to become leather hard (again, I cover the piece and return the following day.) Once the feet are leather hard, cut and define their shape (figures 13).

Making these forms requires several days and patience. It takes time for parts to become leather hard and it's best not to rush. I work on them in a series of three, making slight alterations to vary each one from the other.

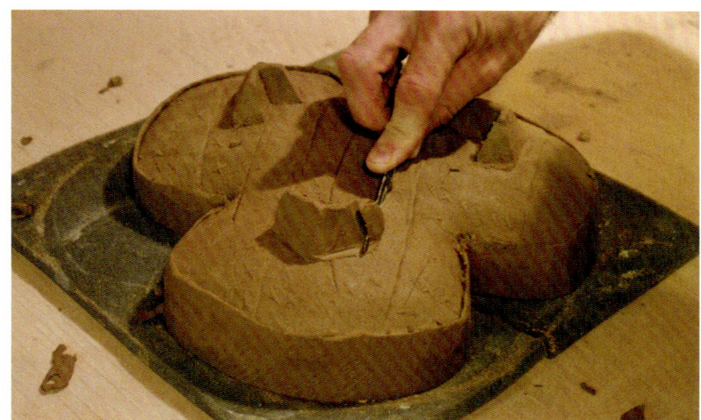

13. Score, apply slip, and attach three angled coils for feet. Once they're leather hard, cut and define their shape.

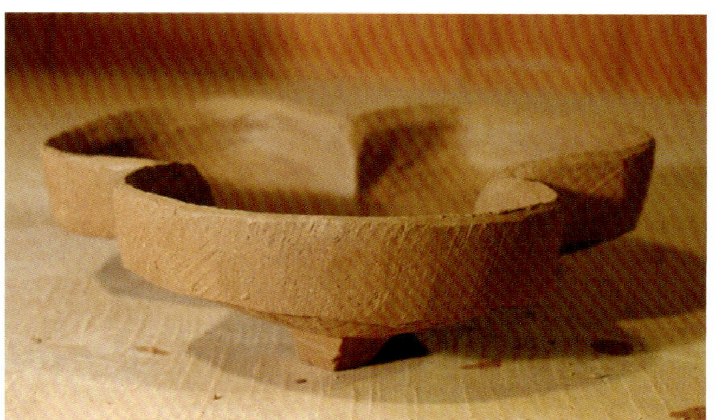

The finished form showing the side profile view and a detail of the surface texture and shape of the feet.

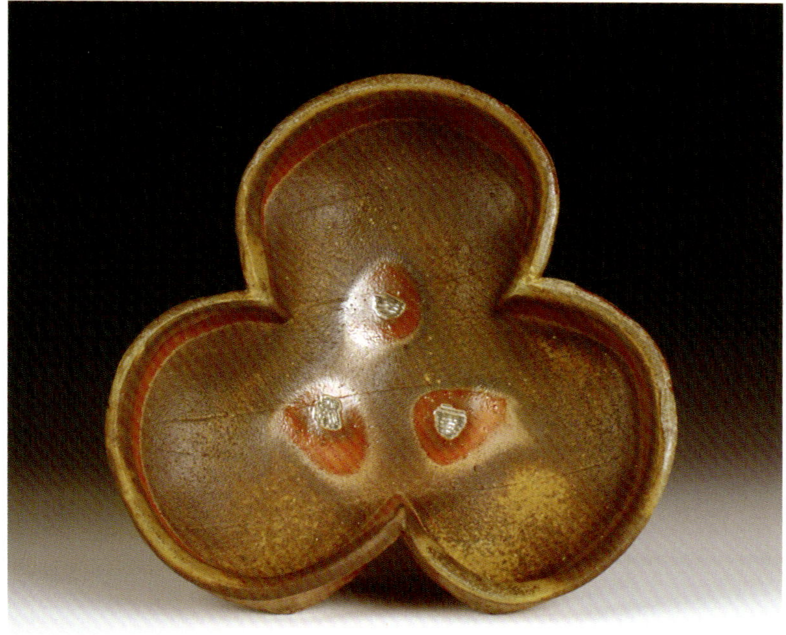

The finished wood-fired clover dish showing the top profile.

Using Molds
ADDING VOLUME TO A FORM

by Ben Carter

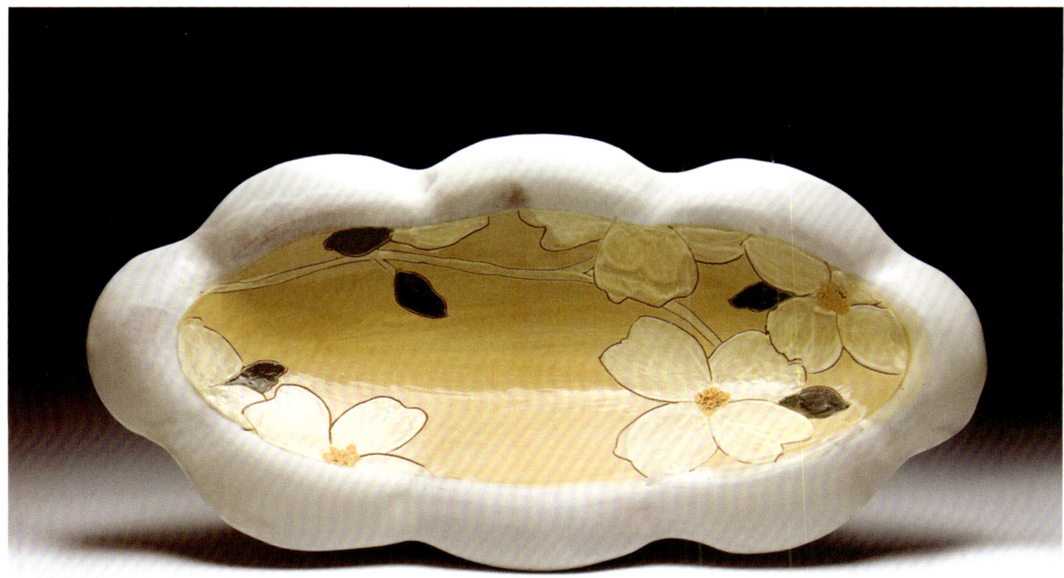

Dogwood Oval Platter, 20½ inches in length, created using templates and a slump mold technique, earthenware, painted slips, sgraffito, and glaze, fired to cone 3.

I begin a large platter by making a template in the shape and pattern of the rim of the platter, creating the template using tarpaper. Tarpaper can be used repeatedly because it's impervious to water. Cut the interior section of the template at both ends for easy registration on the form (figure 1).

Next, create a slump mold from stacked layers of closed-cell foam (the kind used for home insulation). The thickness of the mold depends on the depth of the recessed area required in the finished piece. I'd suggest making the mold at least 3 inches thick for strength. Mark the outline of the template on the top of the stack. Individual sheets can be secured together using double sided tape. To create the recess in the slump mold, measure 1½ inches in toward the center from the two long ends and the two middle lobes of the outline and make a mark at each spot. Draw an oval connecting the dots, then use a serrated knife to cut out the shape.

Use the tarpaper template to aid in creating small cloth forms that sit on the rim of the foam mold. The cloth forms are comprised of eight semi-circular sections that form a wavy rim for the platter. Make each cloth form using two pieces of canvas sewn together and filled with heavy grog. Pin the thinnest edge or point of the cloth form to the foam using T-pins (figure 2).

Making a Platter

Cut a $\frac{3}{16}$-inch thick slab using the tarpaper template. Bevel or soften the edges of the slab and use a soft rubber rib to compress each side of the slab in both directions. Place the slab onto the stacked

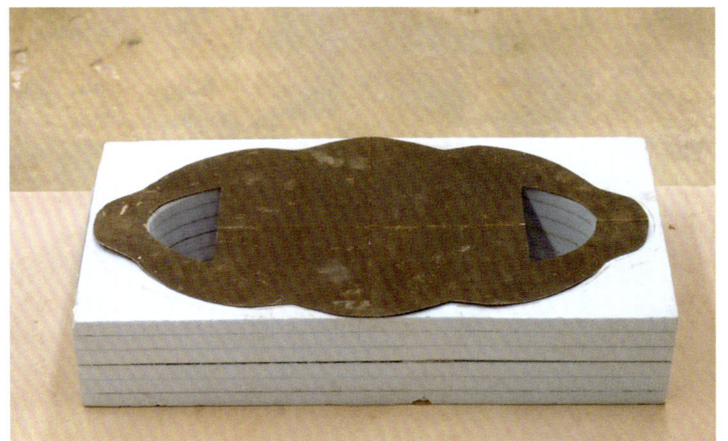

1. Create a tarpaper template of the platter. Make a stacked foam slump mold. Cut an opening in the foam 1½ inches in from the template's edge.

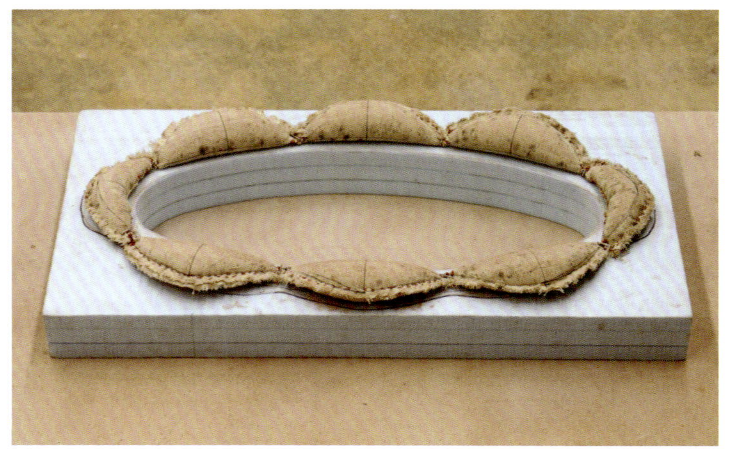

2. Use the tarpaper template to create a cloth mold that sits on the rim of the foam mold. Pin the cloth mold to the foam stack using T-pins.

cloth and foam forms so that the slab edge lines up with the outside edges of the cloth form. Work the slab into the form using a soft rib and working both from end to end and side to side (figure 3). The advantage of this form is the ability to bend the slab on more than one axis, so take time to work the clay down into the curves.

Let the slab firm up to a leather-hard. Place a bundle of soft padding and the section of blue foam that was removed earlier into the platter's interior. Flip the whole stack over (figure 4). Make sure the rim rests parallel to your work surface and is elevated a few inches above it.

Make a ring to form the foot. Curve the wall of the foot into a slight "C" shape with the curve flaring away from the center of the piece. Try to match the volume of the foot to the volume of the rim. Allow the foot to set up to the same leather-hard consistency as the piece before attaching it by slipping and scoring (figure 5). After the foot has set up and can hold up the rest of the platter without slumping, flip it over and remove the padding and foam. Smooth out any marks made by the foam.

Allow the piece to dry slowly under a loosely wrapped layer of thin plastic. Dry larger pieces, like platters, for about a week before bisque firing. Since pieces longer than twelve inches in any direction have a greater chance of cracking during the bisque fire, lightly sprinkle the kiln shelf with fine sand and place the piece on top of the sand.

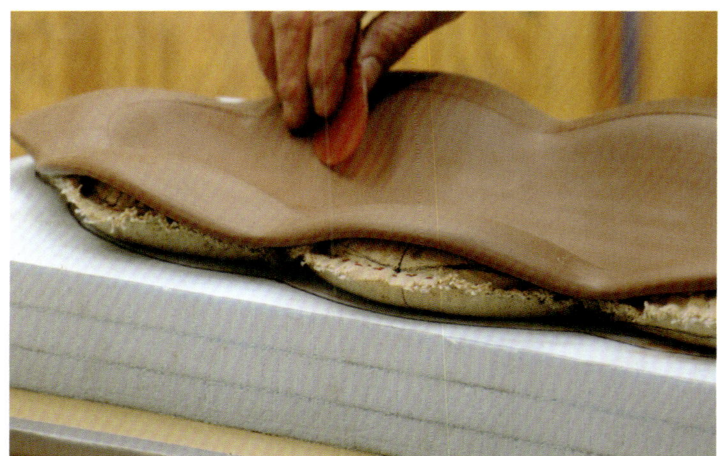

3. Roll out a slab and trim it to the size of the tarpaper template. Place it so that the clay edge lines up with the edges of the cloth. Rib the slab into the mold.

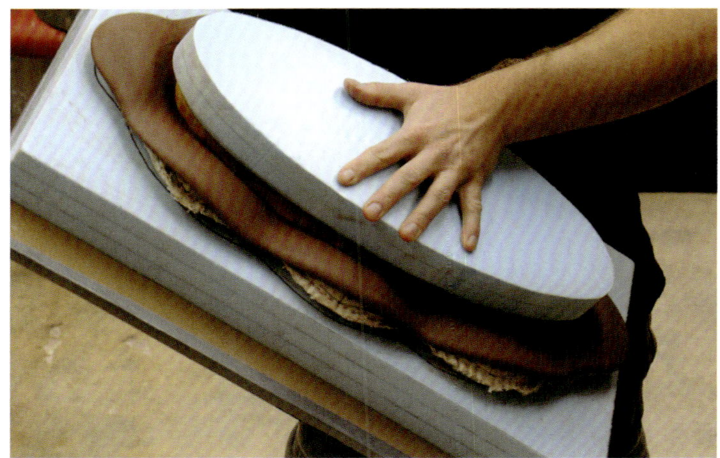

4. Sandwich the removed oval section of blue foam, the cloth, and the platter (still in the slump mold) between your hands, then flip the piece.

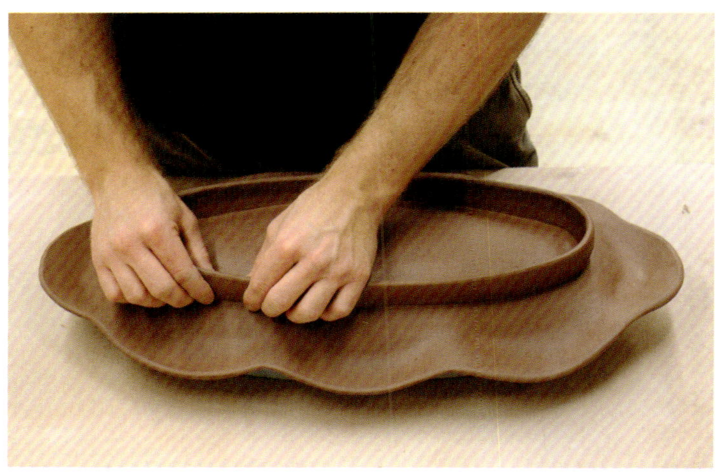

5. Be sure the rim sits parallel to and several inches above the table. Add a foot to the bottom of the piece and allow it to firm up.

Using Molds

RECYCLED PLASTIC MOLDS

by WangLing Chou

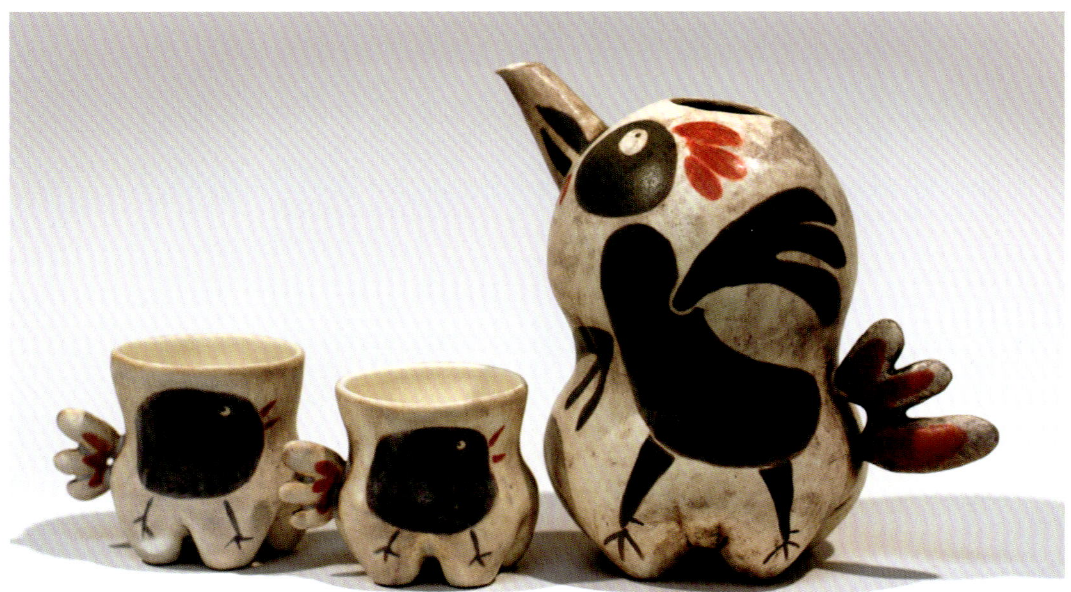

The inspiration for a series of teapots comes from wanting to reuse and recycle materials, a practice rooted in my experiences as an international student. During that time, I traveled light, carrying all my possessions in just two suitcases. These circumstances forced me to get extraordinary use out of limited materials. I would use objects multiple times and in some instances, find new uses for a particular object.

Now, my past manifests itself as I take used plastic bottles and give them a new life, saving them from the landfill. The commercial design of the bottles serves as a mold to provide the basic form of each piece, to which I add my own creative touch. Ultimately, I seek to highlight the original industrial design by retaining its form, yet through my human touch, give each work its own unique character.

Preparing the Plastic Mold

Collect any interesting forms of plastic to be used for potential molds such as soda bottles and food containers. Clean and rinse the plastic with soapy water. Next, use a utility knife or saw to cut out the portion you want to use for the mold.

Coat the inside of the plastic mold with a very thin layer of WD-40 and spread it evenly then wipe out the form with a chamois. Avoid using excess WD-40, as it will make the surface of the mold overly slippery and will penetrate the slab.

Drill a small hole in the bottom of the plastic bottle to allow air to escape when the slab is pressed inside the mold. Roll out a slab of clay and cut it into shapes to cover the inside of the mold (figure 1). Several sections of slabs will need to be connected together when pressing the inside of a

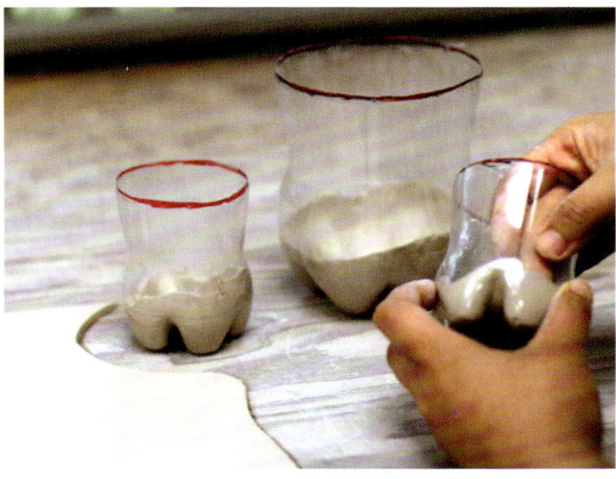
1. Cut plastic bottles, apply a mold resist, then fill the inside of the mold with slabs.

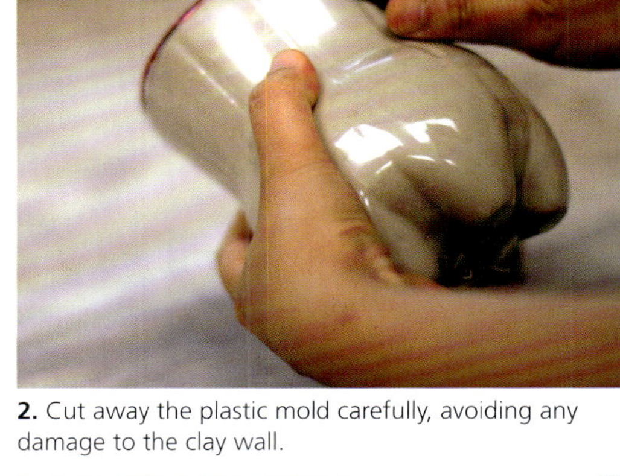
2. Cut away the plastic mold carefully, avoiding any damage to the clay wall.

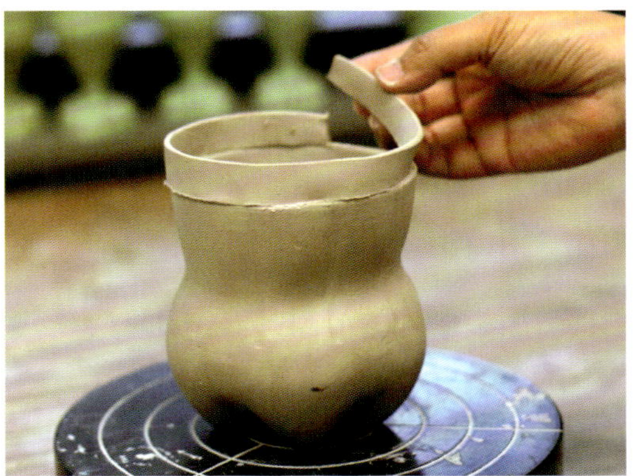
3. Use coils or slabs to add height. Score both parts then blend the seams.

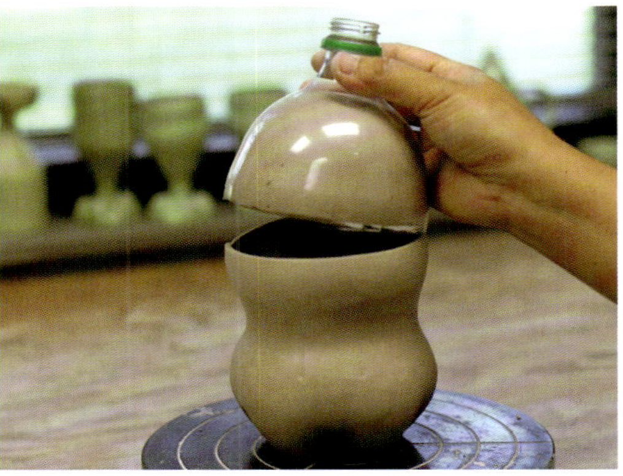
4. Use the top portion of the plastic bottle as a mold for the top of the vessel. Connect the two halves.

curved plastic bottle and the number of sections will vary according to the size and shape of the form. Press the slab against the mold evenly and then smooth the inside as much as possible before removing it from the mold.

Forming a Zoomorphic Teapot

Wait until the pressed clay is stiff enough to hold its shape, then use a utility knife to carefully cut the soft part of the plastic bottle allowing the form to release from the mold (figure 2).

Smooth out the seams and remove any unwanted texture. During the leather-hard stage, you may model the form further by pushing out the curves, squeezing the excess clay, or cutting and reconnecting some sections to alter or even exaggerate the profile. You can use coils or thin slabs to extend the vessel or alter the proportional balance and overall form for the teapot to a desired shape (figure 3).

Use the top portion of another plastic bottle as a mold for the top of the teapot (figure 4). This gives the form a more gradual rounded top as opposed to an abrupt flat one. Make the press mold for the top just as you did for the bottom.

Before adjusting and refining the size of the top hole, clean the interior while there's still a big enough hole to access the inside of the teapot. This ensures the joined pieces are well attached and the seam is smoothed.

Making the Spout and Handle

To create the basic spout form, use a tapered dowel, either short or long depending on the size spout you need. Roll a clay slab around the dowel and

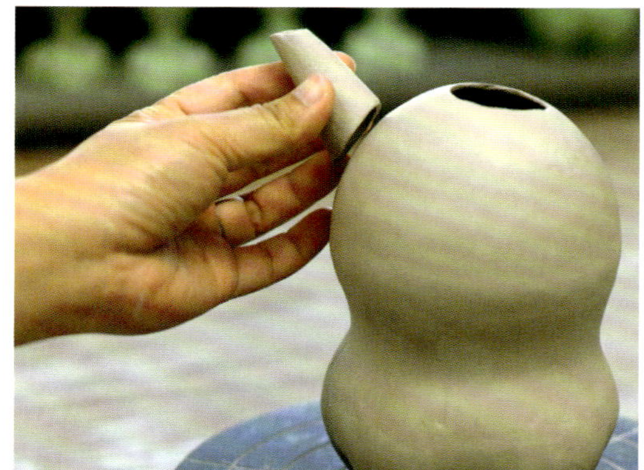

5. Adjust the size of the hole at the top of the pot and make a spout. Shape it to fit the form, then attach.

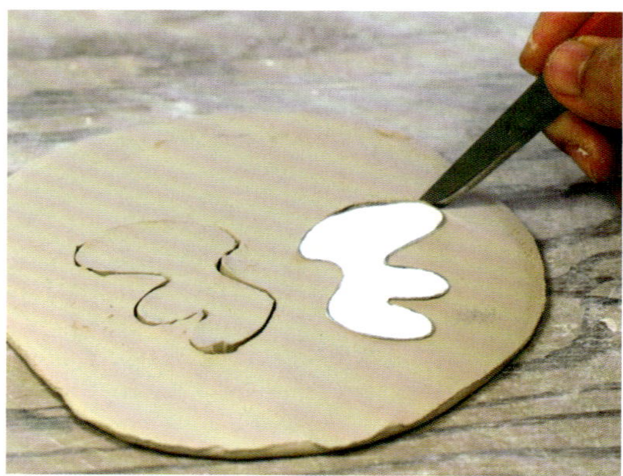

6. Draw a pattern for the tail on paper and cut it out. Use the pattern to cut out both sides of the tail.

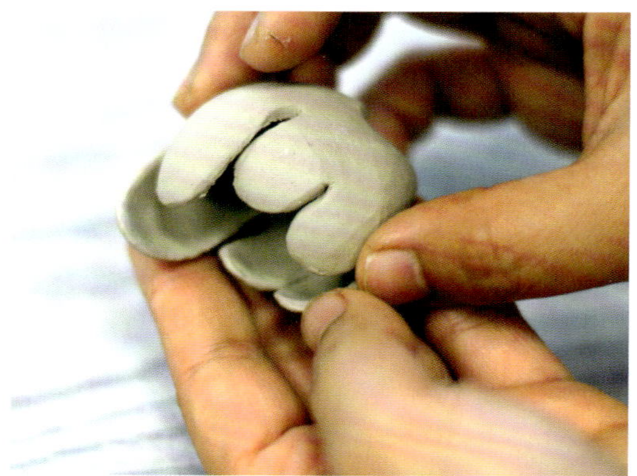

7. Curl the two sides inward and connect them to create an inflated appearance.

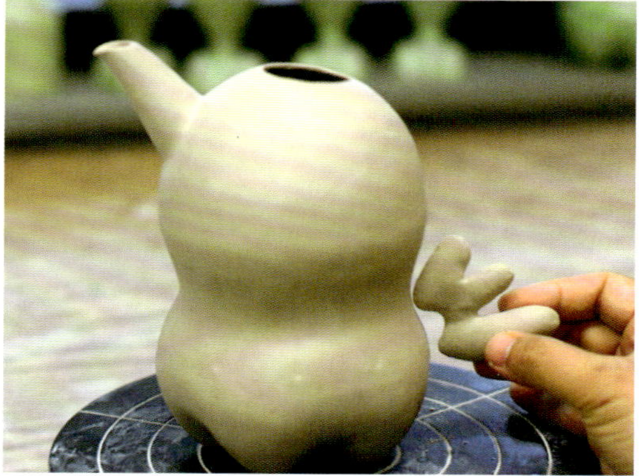

8. Attach the handle in a position where it will resemble tail feathers. Score and slip both parts and attach.

use it to shape the spout. To give the spout more of an organic feeling of an actual chicken beak, try to pull it into a slight curve, then cut the spout to size and attach it to the teapot (figure 5).

The construction of the tail, or handle, involves two mirrored parts formed together to give the impression of an inflated balloon. Cut out the two abstract forms similar to a chicken tail using a pattern to ensure the proportions of each side are the same (figure 6). Next, curl the edges inward in order to achieve the puffy appearance, then connect them, making sure to leave a hole for the air to escape (figure 7).

Finally, attach the tail in an appropriate place that gives the impression of tail feathers (figure 8). This tail not only serves as part of the chicken but also suggests a teapot's handle.

Decoration and Glaze

To decorate this vessel's surface, I started by staining the form with a thin layer of Amaco Velvet Jet Black Underglaze, then used a damp sponge to remove the underglaze from the highest spots. I then sketched the basic outline of a chicken drawing over the stained base glaze. The design of the figure should flow well with the shape of the vessel. In order to achieve this, distort some of the proportions and exaggerate the gesture of the chicken in order to create a composition that complements that shape. Use black underglaze for the chicken and Amaco Velvet Bright Red Underglaze for the tail and comb. Finally, I glazed the interior with a food-safe opaque white glaze, allowed it to dry then sprayed the exterior with the same opaque glaze.

Using Molds

WOOD BLOCK MOLDED DISH

by Tom Quest

I use wood forms and wood stamps to create my pottery designs. This dish uses an old wood moth stamp I made years ago for part of the surface design, and a wooden drape mold for the depth and shaping.

Tools to Make

After sketching a new idea, I work through test pieces of clay with a stamp before making templates, additional stamps, and a drape mold. For templates, I use plastic sheets used for quilt layouts found at fabric stores. I prefer this to tarpaper because I can see through it for registration. For this design, I created two templates—one for the outside shape and a second one for the pattern that creates a border and defines the interior areas (figure 1).

While you can use many types of materials for drape molds, I normally choose wood. For this project I created a mold by cutting a 2×6 board to the shape I wanted then rounded the edges with a router (a Surform tool works well also). In designing a mold, be sure to consider the size of the object you want to make in order to determine the best size of your slab-to-form ratio for supporting the rim.

The type and age of clay is also important. I use a smooth, plastic clay body, which tears less when you stretch it over a form. New clay, which is generally less plastic, tears more than aged clay when stretched; older clay tends to be more plastic and forgiving. I do not use clay with grog because the impressions don't show up as nicely, and dragging grog across a surface can ruin the surface decoration.

Creating a Textured Slab Bowl

Roll out a ¼–5⁄16-inch-thick slab of clay. Smooth both sides with a soft rib to remove any canvas marks or surface flaws. When lifting and turning the slab, be careful to fully support it so you don't create a "bad memory" that causes it to warp in the firing. Lay the larger template on the slab and cut out the shape (figure 2). Next, lay the second template with the cut-out hexagon on the slab and use a wood tool to push the plastic evenly into the clay around the perimeter (figure

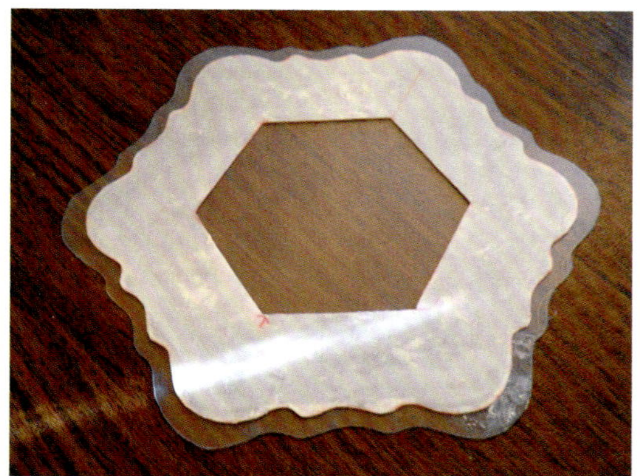

1. This project uses two templates—one for the form and one for defining sections for surface decorations.

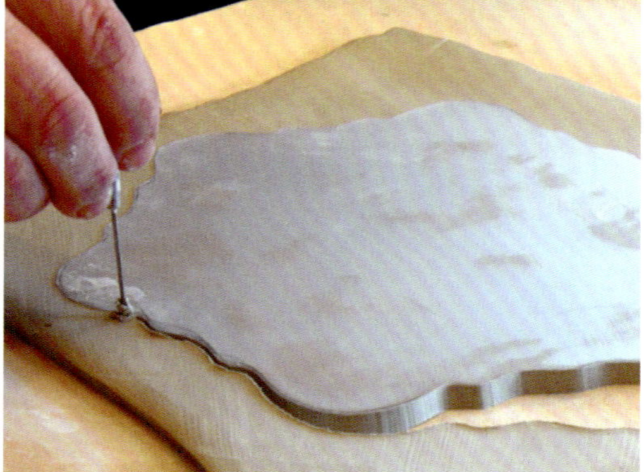

2. Roll out a 1/4–5/16-inch-thick slab of clay, and cut out the form using the large template as a guide.

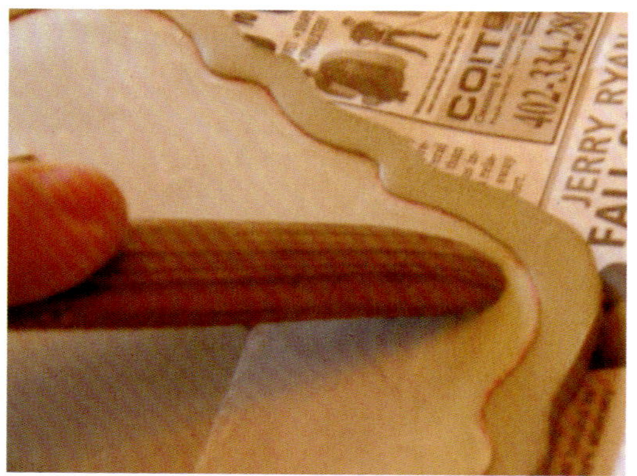

3. Place the smaller template on the slab and use a tool to press the edge of the template into the clay.

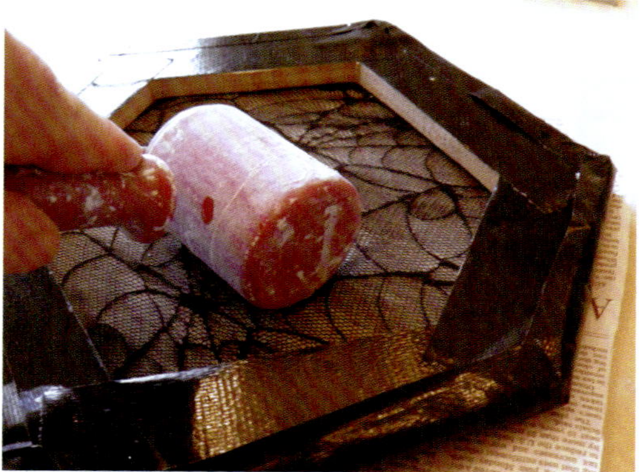

4. The small template also serves as a mask when adding background texture to the center of the slab.

3). This defines the border and leaves a nice glaze transition line in the clay. Leave the template on the clay for the next step.

As part of my design I wanted a visual "gathering point" for the moths in the center of the bowl. While shopping in a costume shop, I found a nylon stocking with a spiderweb design. I stretched the stocking material over a wooden frame (figure 4) then used a small roller to transfer the design. The template acts as a resist and only allows the impression in the hexagonal center (figure 5). Round over the edges with a damp sponge, then carefully remove the template.

I created the moth stamp with a scroll saw and added details with a woodburning tool. The advantage of using wood stamps is that you can cut, carve, drill, sand, file, and wood burn what you need for your design while the clay is still wet. Spraying wood stamps with cooking oil or dusting them with cornstarch keeps them from sticking to the clay (figure 6).

Firmly press the stamp into the clay, repeating the pattern all around the form (figure 7). Note how the "unstamped" portion of the clay between the moth and the spider web creates an interesting design with contrasting positive and negative space. Add additional details to complete the texturing.

Center the mold on the textured slab (figure 8). For larger pieces, spray the mold with cooking spray or even lay a piece of newspaper cut to the same size as the mold to serve as a separator.

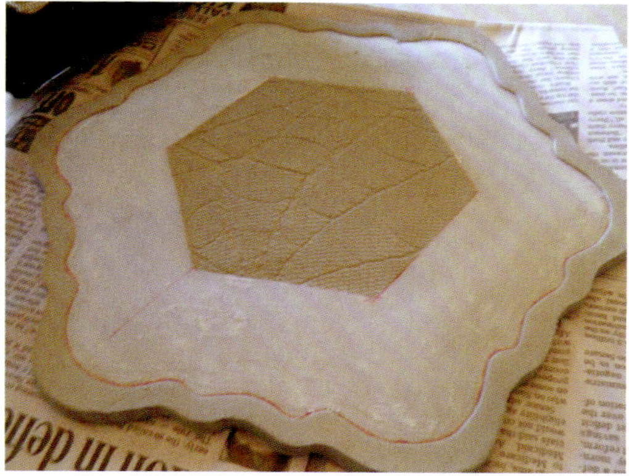

5. With border and central areas defined, and background texture in place, gently remove smaller template.

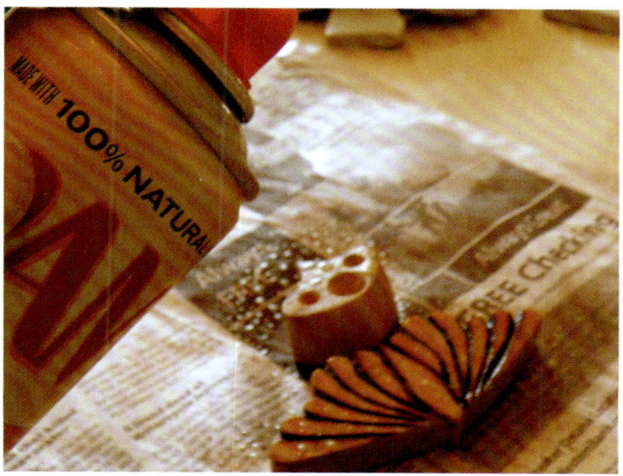

6. Lightly spray wooden stamps with cooking spray so they won't stick to the clay.

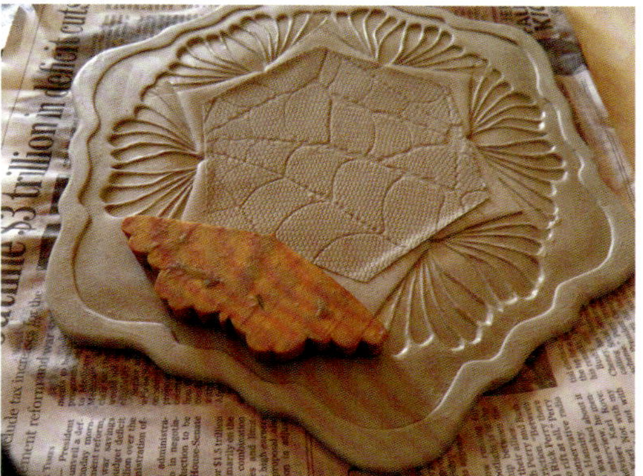

7. By planning ahead and creating accurate templates, the stamped pattern fits the overall design.

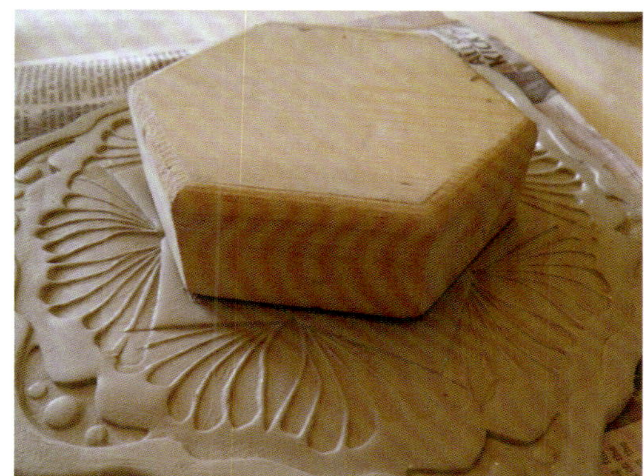

8. Carefully place a drape mold in the center of the slab. Place a board or bat on top and flip the slab over.

Carefully lay a second work board on top of the hexagonal block and lift the work up using the original large working board under the slab. Quickly flip the sandwiched block and slab over without altering the registration between the clay and the wood. Carefully remove the original board (which is now on top) and the newspaper. The newspaper sticks to the clay so peel it back slowly so the registration of the hexagon block and the clay won't shift. At this point the clay begins to slump over the mold.

When you look carefully at the clay you'll notice how the stamped image has translated through the clay and is now visible on the bottom, in some designs this is helpful as to the location of pressure you use when forming. You'll also notice some wrinkles made by the newspaper, but these will be worked out later.

At this point it's very important not to rush! Moisten your fingers, then slowly apply gentle pressure on each corner of the piece (figure 9). Use a banding wheel and rotate the piece to evenly apply a small amount of pressure to each corner. Move in very small, even steps otherwise the piece will warp when fired. Notice the position of the thumbs in relation to the outside shape and the hexagonal mold, which is clearly visible even though it is under the clay. Move your thumbs evenly up and down at each corner and continue to dip them in water to reduce drag. It's important to know when to stop; you want a slope to the sides of the bowl but don't overwork the clay

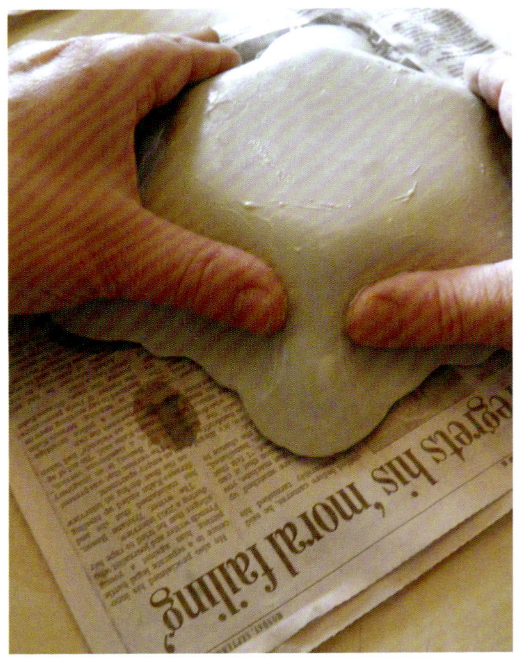

9. With moistened hands, slowly work the slab over the form as you rotate the piece on a banding wheel.

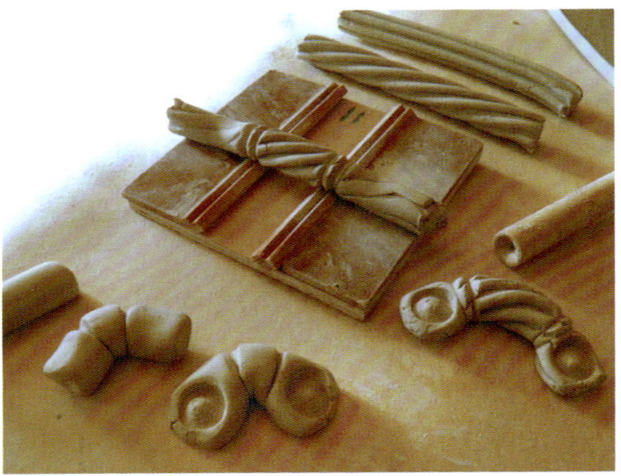

10. Feet can be formed using different strap handle techniques. The possibilities are endless.

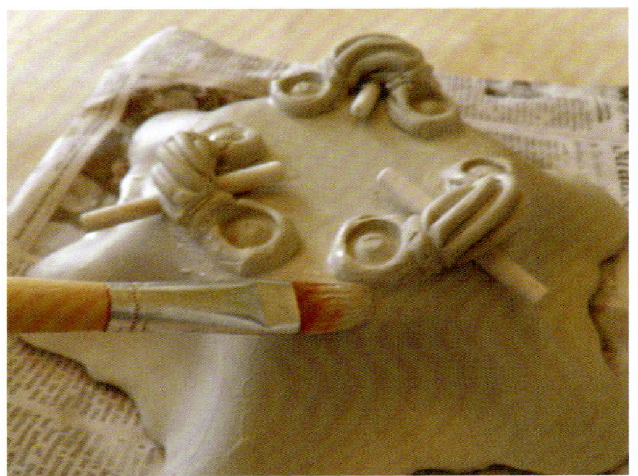

11. Strap feet serve a dual role in they can be used as lugs for picture hanging wire.

until it cracks. As you do more projects with this technique, you'll discover how much you can feel through the clay where the impressions have been made.

Finishing Touches

To create the feet, there are many methods you can use. You can make a decorative coil foot by starting with a coil then rolling over it with a square stick at two opposing angles to segment it, then flatten the ends and press with a stamp (figure 10).

I've created a collection of dowels with drilled countersinks in the ends. These are perfect tools for creating decorative touches as well as securely fastening feet or handles to your work. Another type of foot begins with an extruded ribbed coil. When twisted, it has a "barber pole" pattern. When you take this coil and roll it on a raised board that has parallel ridges as shown, it forms a decent end ring to visually finish the foot. Attach the decorative coiled feet to the bottom of the form using dowels to maintain an opening (figure 11). Strap feet allow a user to display a form as a decorative hanging object. Lay a small light board on top to flatten the bottom surface that will contact the table then remove the dowels. Cover the piece to allow the moisture to even out.

Most of the trimming on the rim is done at the leather-hard stage to give it a nice rounded edge, and the entire surface is checked for cleanup. I usually allow the piece to dry for 10 to 14 days before bisque firing.

Using Molds
HANDBUILDING WITH SPRIGS

by Kate Maury

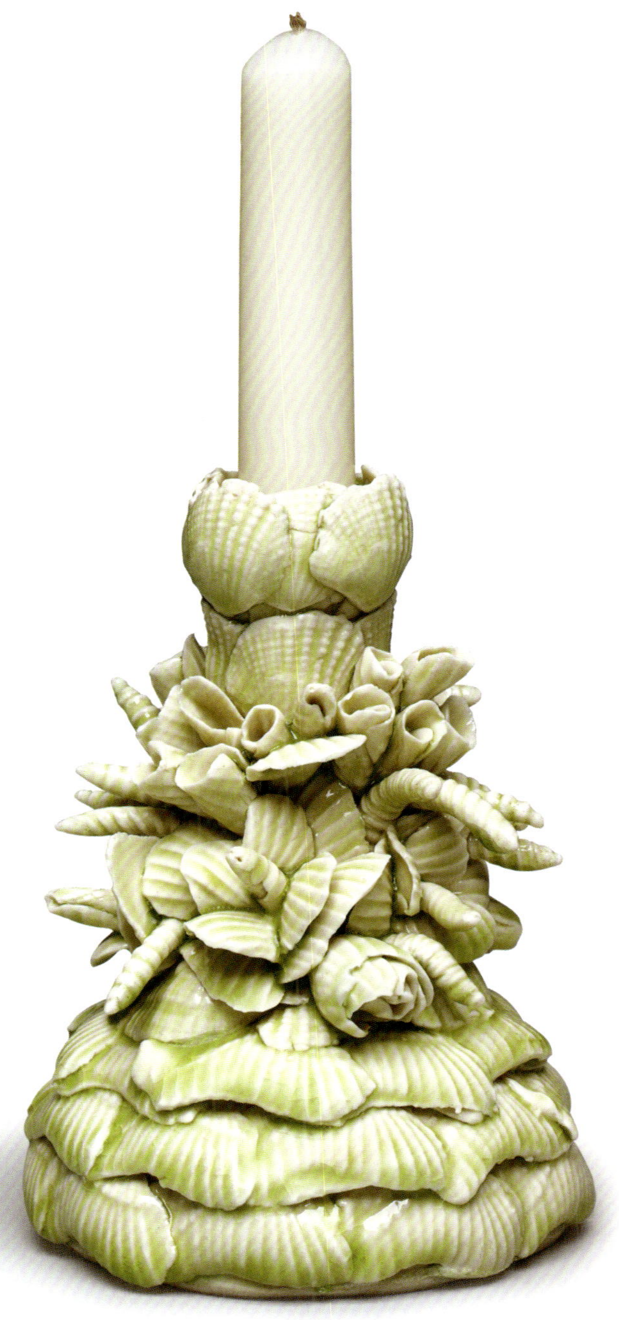

Candle holder, 7 in. (18 cm) in height, porcelain, handbuilt with sprigged components. *Photo by Peter Lee.*

Commercial molds can easily be overlooked when making your personal artwork. Repurposing the elements offered within these molds, and the variety of options they provide, can be used to improve the surface of your form.

Various textures and elements of these molds can be pressed into small pieces of clay and applied as sprigs. The sprigs quickly create low- or high-relief embellishments and add a new visual dimension. Sprigs rapidly establish rhythm, patterns, and dynamic details on a form that can be further amplified by a fluid transparent glaze.

Repurposed commercial molds, or even quickly made clay molds, can produce sprigs that can easily establish high-relief surfaces, highly textured elements, or detailed work in a minimum amount of time.

Making Sprigs

I use cone 6 Super White pre-mixed clay from Continental Clay Company, but just about any clay can be used for this process. Clay sprigs can be pressed and cleaned ahead of time and stored in plastic containers with plaster in the bottom (figure 1). Detailed forms can be quickly finished with sprigs when you have damp boxes stocked with a variety of these textured shapes. Such damp storage can keep

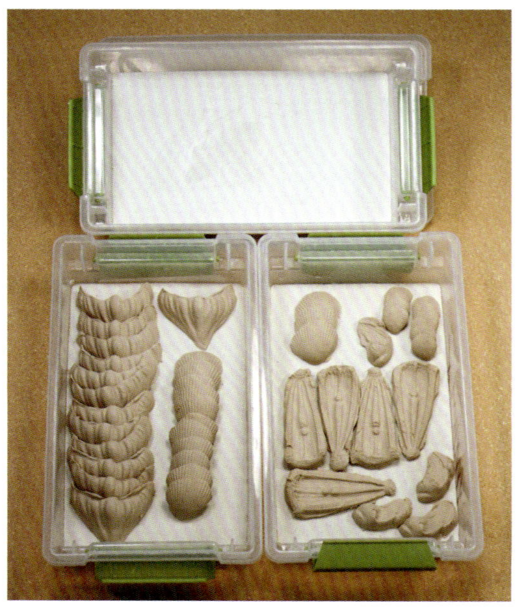

1. Make sprigs ahead of time and store in a damp box made from a plastic container with a plaster bottom.

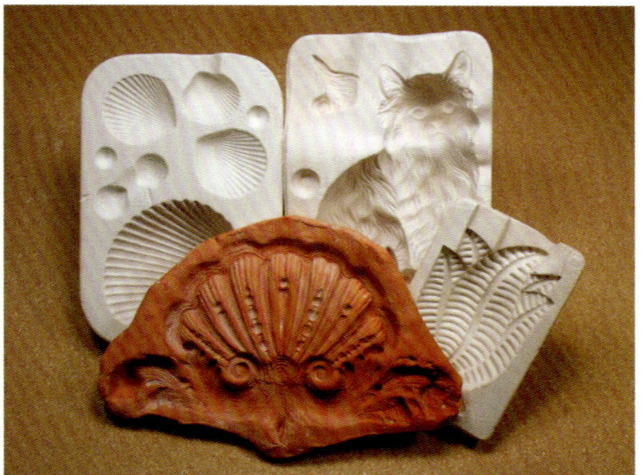

2. Look for sprig molds that have texture, movement, and volumetric shapes.

the sprigs moist enough to work with for weeks at a time. These damp boxes are simple to make. Fill the bottom of plastic snap-lid containers (the type of resealable containers work best for damp storage) with at least 1 inch of plaster. Allow the plaster to cure with the lid off. Dampen the plaster as needed to keep your sprigs ready for use.

When making sprigs from commercial molds I look for molds that have texture, movement, and volumetric shapes (figure 2). Some sprigs can repeatedly overlap vertically, horizontally or diagonally to give the appearance of dynamic movement. Other sprigs can be used to build separate forms to be applied as floral embellishments.

Building a Form to Embellish

One of the forms that I make and then embellish with sprigs is a candlestick holder. Start by making the base. Place a slab of clay in a slump mold and cut away the excess clay from the edges. If you don't have a small slump mold, a small thrown bowl or even a pinch pot will work. Allow the bowl to stiffen up enough to be handled. Roll a ¼-inch slab for the hollow base, cutting a shape ¼ inch wider than the slump mold's diameter. Score and slip the outer edge of the base slab.

Roll a ¼-inch-thick coil. Attach the coil ½ inch in from the edge of the base slab. After letting the slump-molded clay and base slab stiffen to leather hard, place the slump-molded form on top of the base and press them together toward the inner coil (figure 3). Seal the join by scoring and slipping a coil over the seam (figure 4). Trapped air helps stabilize the sealed form while attaching the decorative sprigs onto the base. Wait until the entire form is built before poking an air hole into the form.

Applying the Sprigs

Begin to apply the sprigs around the base. Make sure to score and slip both parts before attaching them together. When choosing sprigs, consider their shapes and textures while working from the bottom to the top of the form or clockwise versus counterclockwise. Overlapping sprigs can also change the visual effect (figure 5). Consider your options and try different approaches; this helps you see different outcomes with each attempt. Leave the top bare for the candlestick pillar.

Forming a Candlestick Pillar

Insert a dowel lengthwise into a tapered 4- to 5-inch coil. The widest end should be about 1

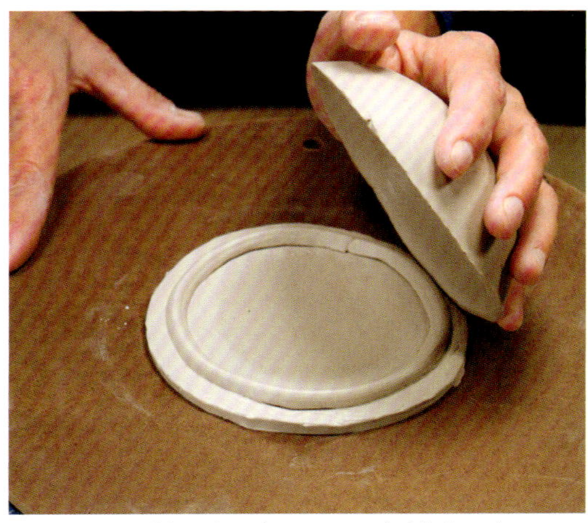

3. Form a small bowl and cut a round slab for a base, attach a coil ½ inch from the edge, then attach the bowl.

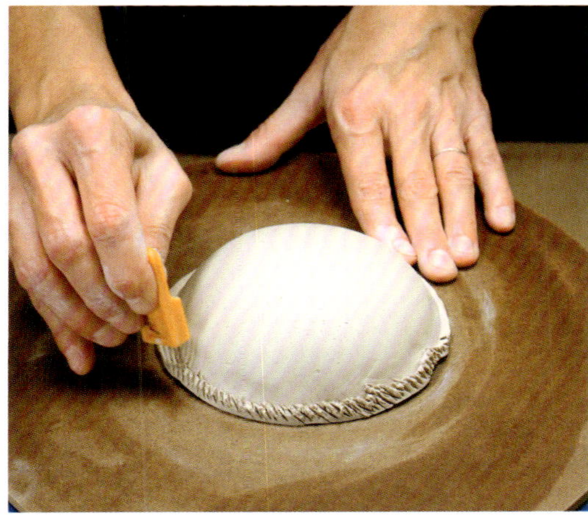

4. Press the bowl form toward the inner coil and seal the two parts together well.

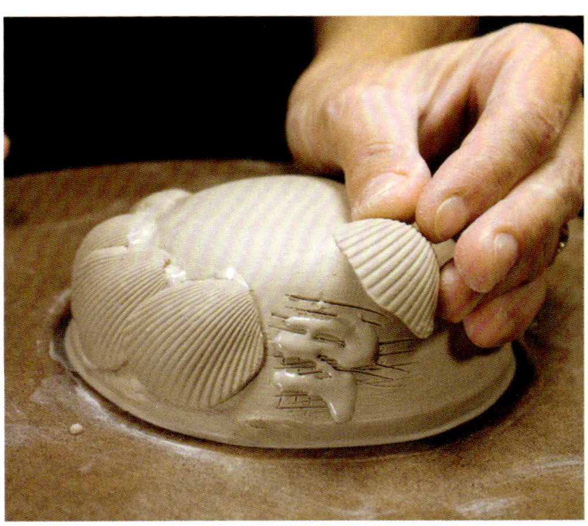

5. Apply sprigs from bottom to top. Leave the top of the form bare for placement of the pillar.

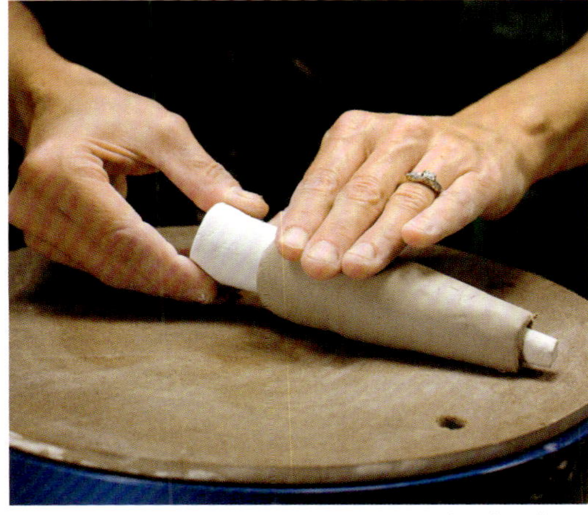

6. Insert a dowel lengthwise into a tapered coil. Roll to open interior of tapered coil then trim ends.

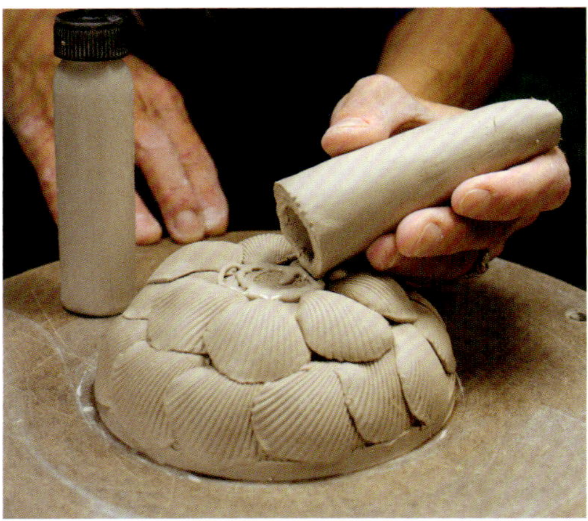

7. Score both ends and attach to domed base. Press firmly so the pillar is secure and standing vertically.

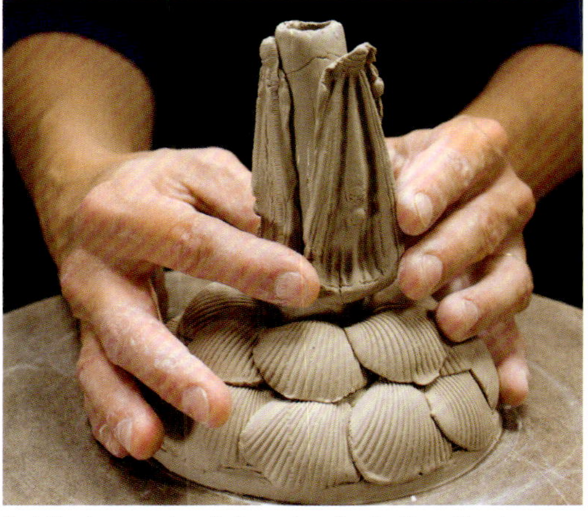

8. Attach scored and slipped sprigs to the pillar to decorate and complete the stem of the candlestick.

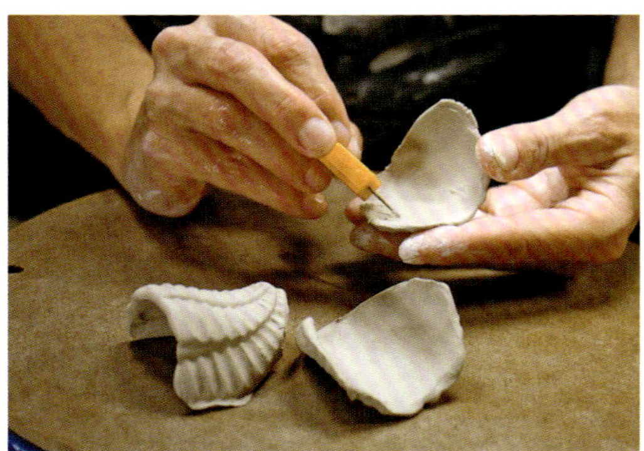

9. To make the candle holder cup, configure sprigs in a clockwise fashion.

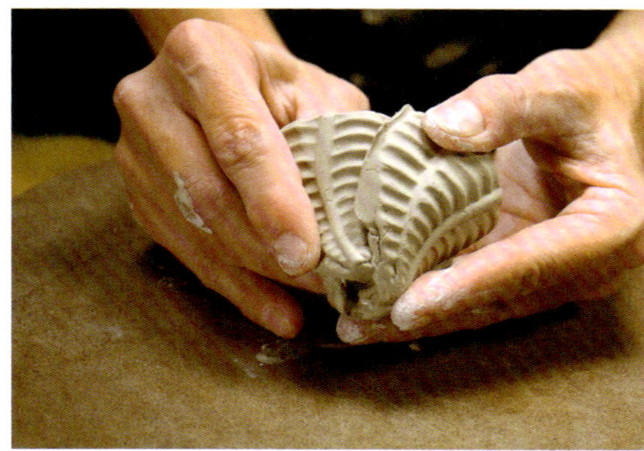

10. Press overlapped edges firmly together.

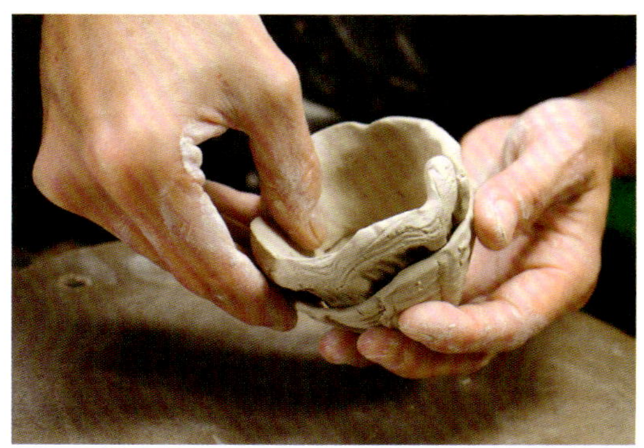

11. Layer sprigs into a cup shape then insert a ¼-inch tapered, textured coil vertically to secure candles.

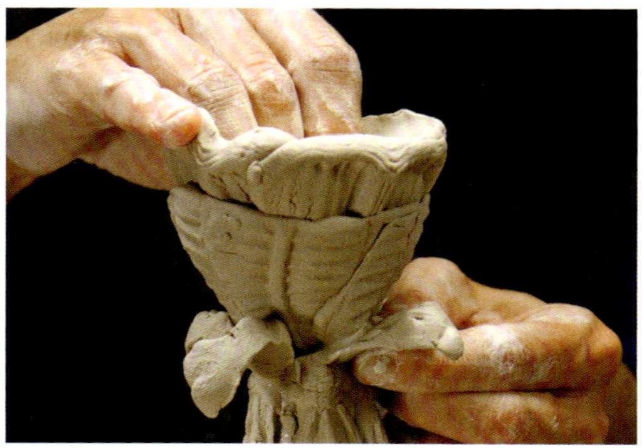

12. Add sprigs to cover the seam between the cup and the pillar. Poke holes in any pockets of air.

inch. Roll the dowel to open up the interior of the tapered coil (figure 6). Stand the conical form on end and let it stiffen to leather hard. After scoring both parts, attach the widest end of the pillar to the domed base (figure 7). Once the attachment has had a chance to firm up, add sprigs to the pillar by again scoring and slipping both parts (figure 8).

Constructing a Candle Cup

Candlestick holders can be made in various ways, with elaborate, wide bases, or with heavy tops that balance out similar-shaped bases. This one has a cup shape at the top to hold the candle and its melted wax.

Configure sprigs together in a clockwise fashion to form a cup-like shape (figure 9). Press the overlapping edges firmly and smooth the seams. For a layered look and proportional solutions, sprigs can be placed as layers within the cup shapes to add height (figure 10–11). Place the finished cup on soft foam until it's leather hard.

Place a ¼-inch, tapered, textured coil vertically inside the cup to secure candles after its fired. Score and slip the top of the pillar and press the cup firmly into place but be careful not to push too hard and dent the base. Add sprigs to cover the seams and embellish where necessary for visual effect (figure 12).

Dry the entire piece slowly to reduce cracking. Remember to poke a hole in any area where pockets of air have been trapped. I bisque fire the candlestick to cone 04, then I dip or spray a high-gloss, cone 6, transparent glaze and fire to temperature. I generally place work on ¼-inch-thick slabs made from kiln wadding for easy release if my glaze runs during the firing.

Using Molds
SHAPING AND SHAVING

by Shoko Teruyama

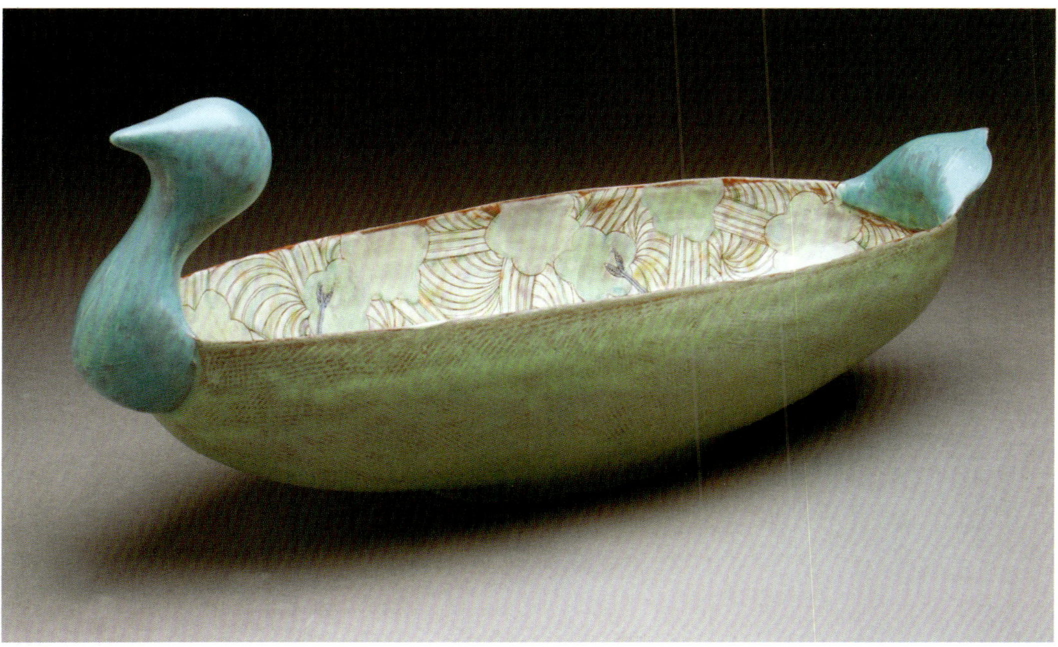

I create handbuilt forms using bisque molds. The premise of using bisque molds is not to quickly produce a lot of work, but quite the opposite. It's about slowing down the process, examining the form, and touching everywhere to create well thought out pots. I like my work to have a thicker wall on the bottom and taper to a thinner rim on top. I touch the entire form to make sure there's a smooth and consistent transition from thick to thin. In addition to the changes in wall thickness, I work with contrasts in surfaces. The textured area on the outside is a place for your eye to rest and contrasts with the highly decorated surface that will be on the inside.

My bird boat form was developed in response to a historical wooden boat that had a bird figurehead on the bow. At the time, I was using bird imagery in my surface decoration and wanted to incorporate the imagery into the actual form. I am interested in how the three-dimensional bird head points in a given direction, and how the head and tail combined elongate the boat, and activate the form.

Getting Started

I use a variety of bisque molds as a starting point. They are made by mounding stoneware into a desired shape, carving them out, and bisque firing them. It's important to use a porous clay body and only fire it to bisque temperatures so it will absorb moisture from slabs wrapped around the mold.

It is very important to begin with an even, well compressed, and thick slab. Make your slabs ½-inch thick by pounding a ball of clay with a wooden mallet or paddle (figure 1). The repeti-

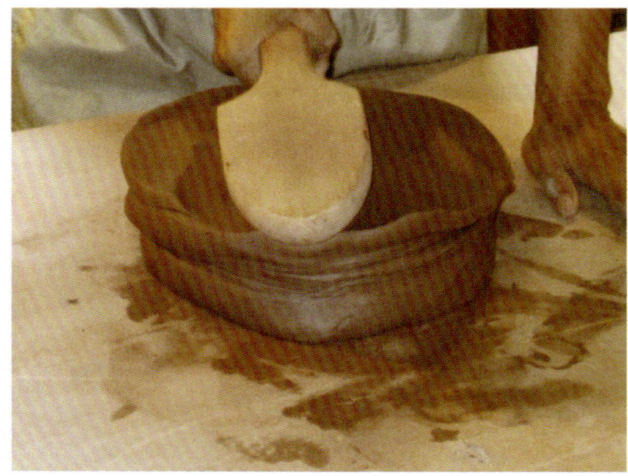

1. Pound out even, compressed slabs from a block of clay using a wooden paddle.

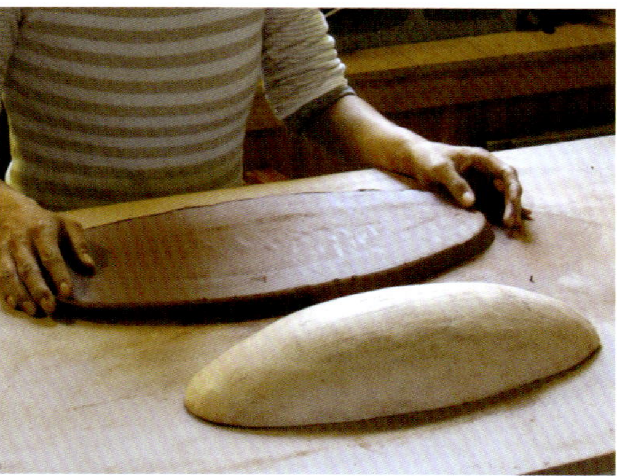

2. Make the slab 1/2-inch thick and 2 inches wider than the bisque mold.

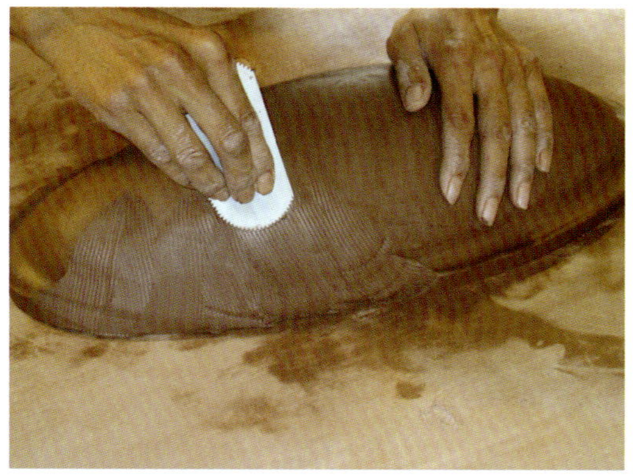

3. Smooth excess clay from around the indented area at the bottom of the mold into the form.

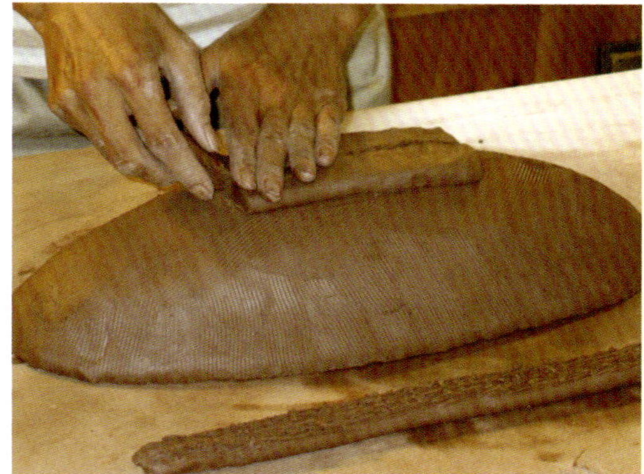

4. Attach two flattened coils to the bottom of the boat and level the foot.

tion of pounding and flipping compresses the clay particles and creates a strong slab that will not crack. For larger slabs, pound two or three balls of clay together. Make your slab two inches wider than needed to cover the bisque mold (figure 2). Use a rolling pin when you are done pounding to smooth the slab out.

Making the Form

Place the slab over the mold. Use both hands to press the slab against the mold, removing all trapped air. Use your finger to compress around the edge of the mold and make a slight indent. Cut outside the finger mark and remove the excess. To strengthen the edge of the slab, first merge the clay flange in toward the mold and then up into the slab using a serrated rib (figure 3).

The finished piece has a foot that elevates the form, so score and slip a row of coils on top of the dome (figure 4). Use a wooden disk to smash the coils down evenly and level to create a flat base. Use a serrated rib to merge the base into the slab, making a smooth transition into the body (figure 5). Using coils to build the solid foot works much better than using a slab because the coils do not trap pockets of air when they are attached. Working the serrated rib in a crosshatch pattern erases the clay's memory of being coils and no cracks appear during drying or firing.

Leave the form and the mold together until the form is a soft leather hard, or firm enough to hold its shape. Remove the boat from the mold and cover it with plastic overnight to even out the moisture.

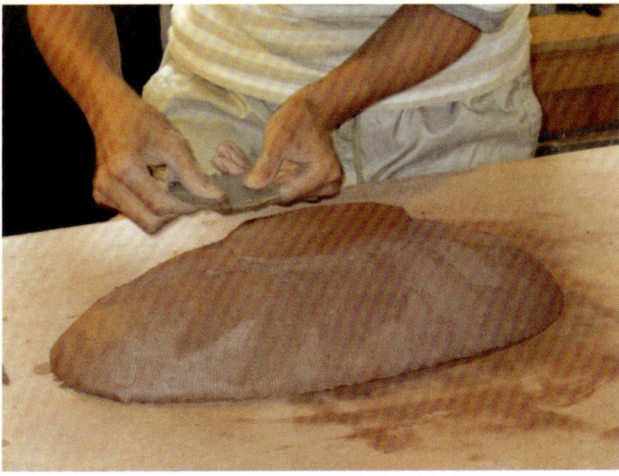

5. Smooth the foot onto the form with a serrated rib. Work from the foot towards the rim.

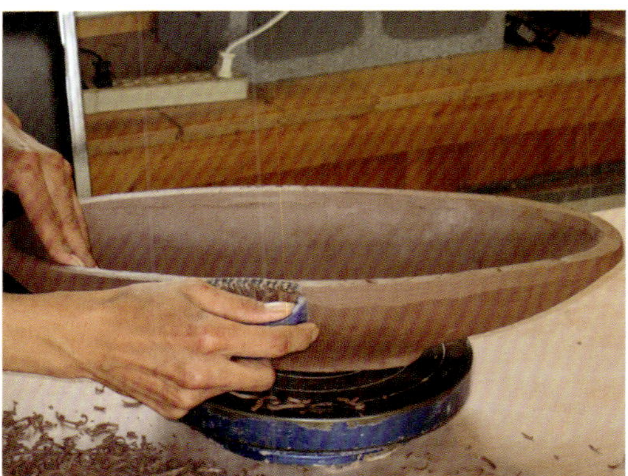

6. Flip the boat form over, trim and shape the form, and taper the rim using a Surform.

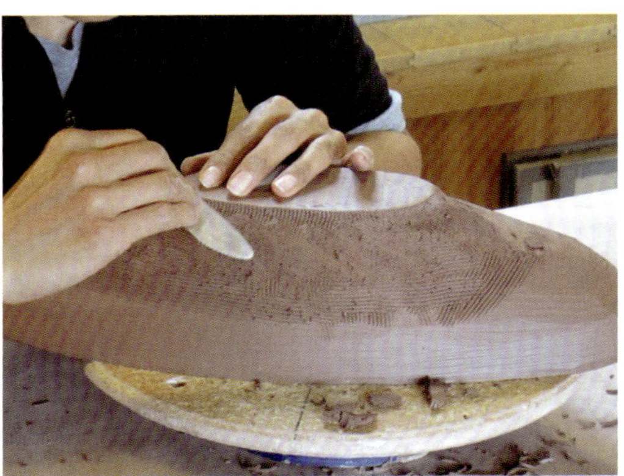
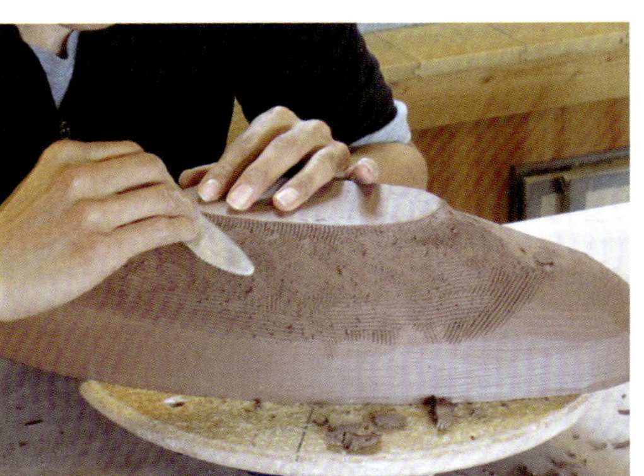

7. Smooth the transition between the foot and the form using a serrated metal rib.

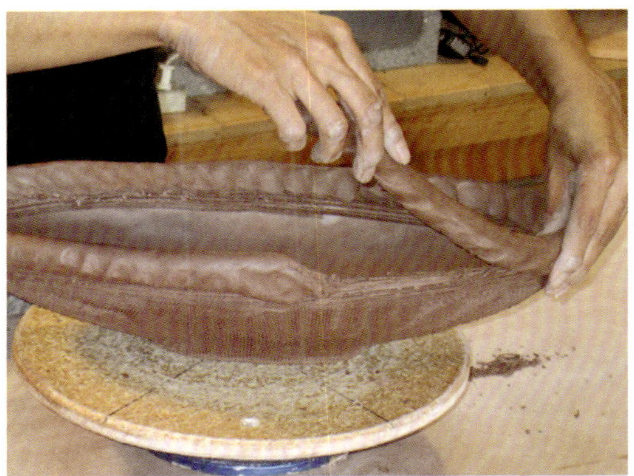

8. Add coils to the rim to increase the volume. Score the edges and securely attach the first coil to the slab.

Refining the Form

When the boat is soft leather hard, use a Surform to shave away excess clay, remove bumps, and create a strong curve (figure 6). Define the foot by trimming it with a stiff serrated rib. Continue to use the rib in a crosshatch pattern to refine the form and create a texture on the surface (figure 7).

When the form is turned right side up, attach two coils to the rim to add extra volume (figure 8). Curve the coils in slightly to add height and enclose the volume. Use a Surform and serrated rib to refine the inside of the form once it has become leather hard.

Making the Bird

Using a ¼-inch-thick slab, cut out the shape of a bird head and tail using a tracing paper stencil. Cut out two of each shape. Both halves of the tail and bird head need to be mirror images (figure 9). Bevel the edges at a 45° angle. Push out the middle of each piece to give them volume, score the edges and attach the two halves together (figure 10). One edge on each piece is left open. Use a small coil to reinforce the inside of the joint. Push a little more from the inside to give a puffed feeling. I use a wooden spatula to tap the bird head gently and make it more three-dimensional. Leave both parts uncovered until they reach a soft leather hard.

The head and tail are dry fitted (without scoring and slipping) to the body by cupping the opening around the rim (figure 11). Once the head, body, and tail are lined up, trace around the joints. Score within the traced line, apply slip and reat-

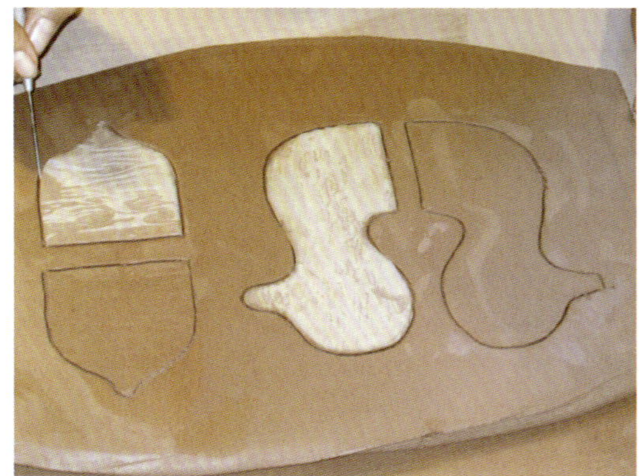
9. Cut two bird head and tail shapes from a slab. The head shapes should mirror one another.

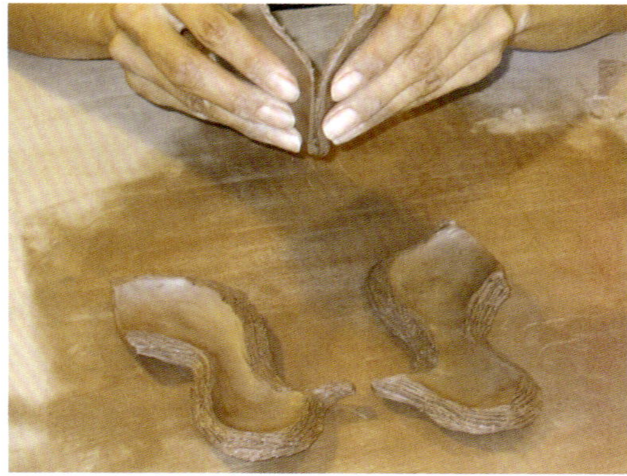
10. Puff out the shapes, score and slip them together leaving one side open.

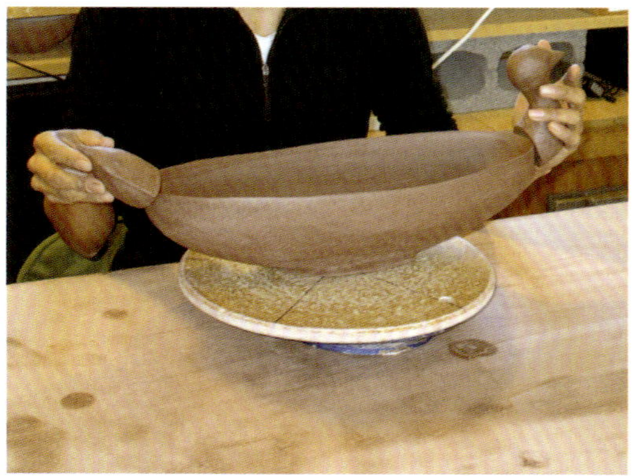
11. Determine the placement of the shapes and mark a line around each onto the boat for attachment.

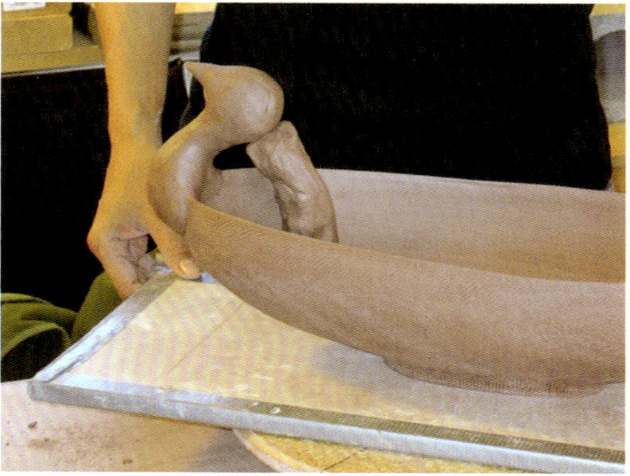
12. Attach the head and the tail. Support the head with clay while it dries.

tach. I leave the attachment edges exposed instead of working them in to keep the definition of each part visible. The head is supported until it becomes leather hard (figure 12). Poke a hole into both the head and the tail to allow air to escape during drying and firing.

Designing the Surface

As soon as the piece reaches leather hard, I apply green slip over the bird head and tail and brush white slip onto the interior surface with a fluid motion. This creates depth in the slip that is revealed after the glaze firing. Allow the piece to dry slowly and completely.

At the bone dry stage, sketch out a decoration onto the white slip with a pencil. I often use flying birds in the decoration as focal points to lead the viewer's eye around the form. Between the birds are different patterns of motion that allude to wind or water. The two motifs create rhythm and activate the interior space.

Use an X-Acto knife to scratch through the slip revealing the red clay. The process creates a lot of fine dust and it is important to not blow the dust away and into the air where it can be inhaled.

I use translucent colored glazes over the sgraffito decoration so the marks stay visible and thicker opaque glazes over the textured areas for contrast.

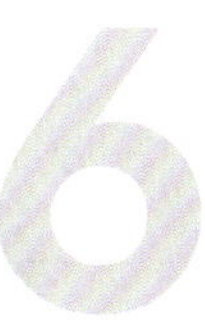

Advanced Techniques

BELLY-BOTTOMED DISHES

by Birdie Boone

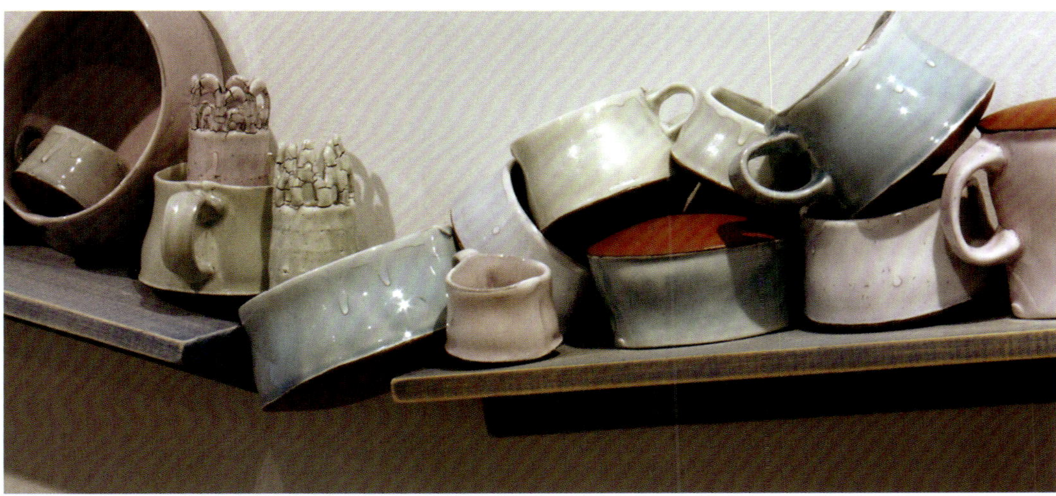

I once read that certain monks had an eating habit that restricted the amount of a meal to what would fit into the volume created when both hands were cupped together. I looked down at my own cupped-together hands to see just how much food I could eat were I a monk, and I realized that hands were the original vessels used for consuming sustenance, and that the next best thing would be dishes that fit just so into that curve formed by two hands cupped together. Since then, "belly-bottomed" dishes have become a significant part of my work.

I use a mid-range red clay body from New Mexico Clay called Sandia Red and fire it to cone 5–6 in an electric kiln. The clay contains a lot of fine sand so it's easy to handbuild with.

I prefer to use a darker clay body because it allows me to create a greater depth of surface with the layered slips and glazes. The slip and glaze naturally break (separate) over edges and other high points, revealing the darker clay beneath. In addition, the crackle slip cracks along seam joins, calling attention to each step that took place in the making process. These three elements work very well together to emphasize the subtleties in my work in a way that a light-bodied clay simply can't. I like to think of red clay as humble, as opposed to porcelain, which has tremendous historic ties to social division and wealth. For me, the humbleness of the red clay fits well with the idea of a simple meal cupped in the vessel that my hands form.

Gathering up the Pieces

My basic construction methods are slab building and coil pinching. I like to work on blueboard, (a type of drywall), because its smooth surface is denser than regular drywall and the paper covering is more durable.

When making a cup with a handle, I join two slabs together to form the walls of the pot, add the bellied bottom and a handle. To make a piece like this, begin by rolling out a few slabs. Try to work with slabs that are ⅛- to ¼-inch thick (thicker for plates or larger forms). If you don't have access to a slab roller, use a rolling pin to refine a thrown/stretched slab.

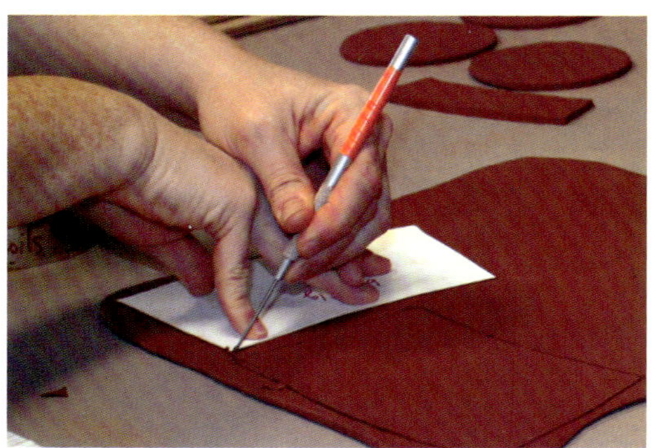

1. Use paper templates and cookie cutters to cut out shapes from fresh clay slabs.

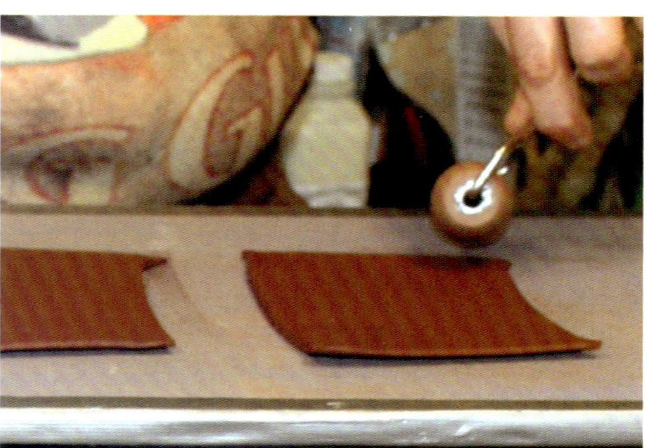

2. Bevel the seam edges and thin out the lip edges with a pony roller.

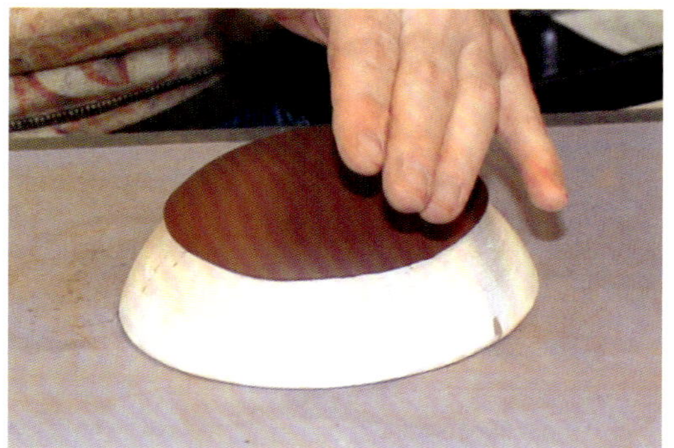

3. Pat the belly bottom pieces into curved forms over a plaster or bisque hump mold.

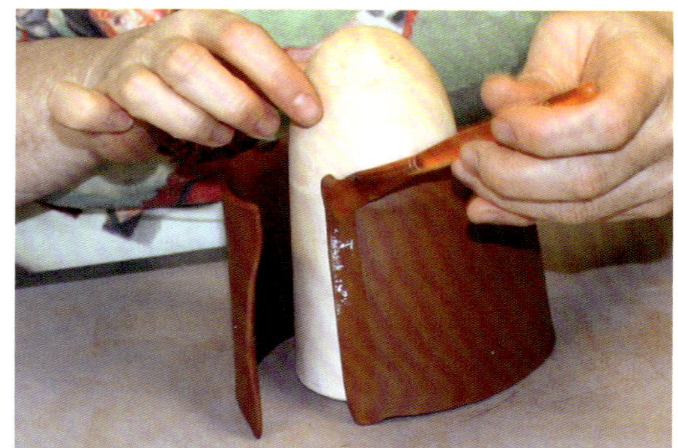

4. Curve the walls of the cup to form a cylinder, apply magic water, and join the seams.

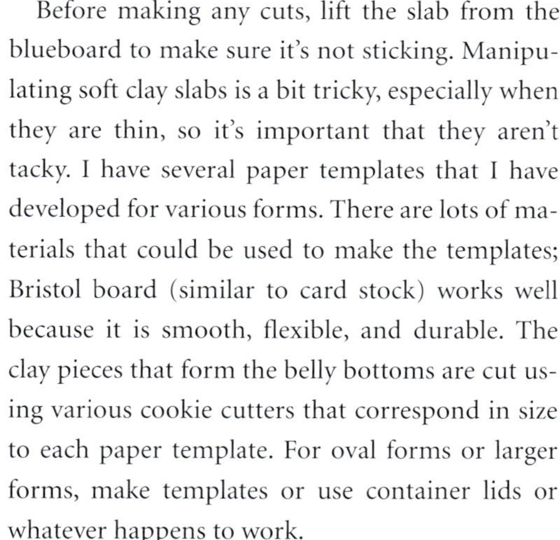

Before making any cuts, lift the slab from the blueboard to make sure it's not sticking. Manipulating soft clay slabs is a bit tricky, especially when they are thin, so it's important that they aren't tacky. I have several paper templates that I have developed for various forms. There are lots of materials that could be used to make the templates; Bristol board (similar to card stock) works well because it is smooth, flexible, and durable. The clay pieces that form the belly bottoms are cut using various cookie cutters that correspond in size to each paper template. For oval forms or larger forms, make templates or use container lids or whatever happens to work.

Lay the templates down on the slab and carefully cut around them with a needle tool while gently holding down the edges of the template (figure 1). Once the cuts are made, remove the excess scraps and allow the pieces to firm up just a bit. Carefully move each piece to a smaller section of blueboard that sits on a banding wheel. Using a pony roller, bevel the seam edges and thin the lip edges (figure 2). For me, it's important to have a quality banding wheel (one that turns effortlessly) so that the manipulation of clay is fluent as you use the pony roller. If you do this successfully, there is no need to clean up/soften edges once the pot is finished.

Try to work in a series, making several of a given form at a time. By the time you have finished a step with the last one of the series, the first one is ready for the next step and you can proceed without having to wait for the clay to firm up or the need to re-wet. The quantity to work with depends on the complexity of the form.

Next, place a convex plaster or bisque hump mold on the banding wheel and form each belly-

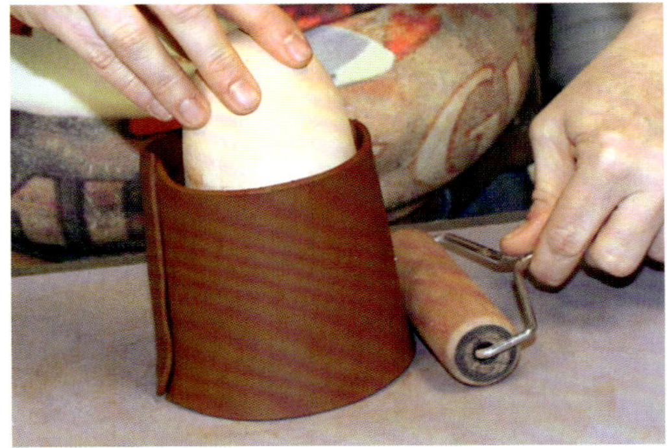

5. Compress the seam with the pony roller. Use a form or a curved paddle to support the seam's back side.

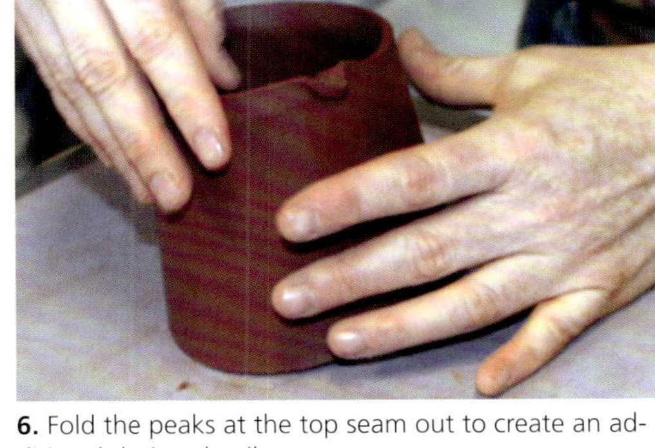

6. Fold the peaks at the top seam out to create an additional design detail.

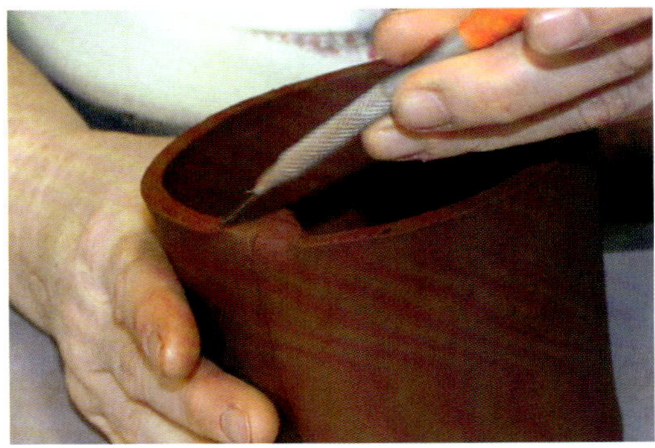

7. Flip the cylinder over and fold the rolled seam edges in. Score cylinder and belly bottom seam edges.

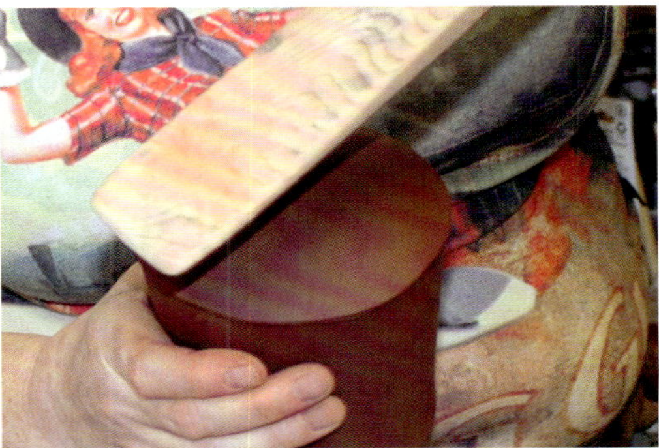

8. Use a wooden paddle to compress the seam. Since the bottom is dryer than the walls, seal the attachment.

bottom piece over it by patting gently with your hands as the banding wheel turns in response to this action (figure 3). Smaller pieces can be removed fairly easily and quickly from the mold without distorting the curve; bottoms for larger forms require more time on the mold or a quick blast with a hair dryer to firm up enough to be moved without distortion. If the hump mold starts to get sticky with absorbed water, dust it with a little cornstarch or take a break and allow it to dry out. Lay each bellied pot bottom directly on the blue board to continue firming up. They need to be at least medium leather hard to hold their form during the assembly process.

Fitting the Pieces

Once all the pieces are cut out and the edges thinned, you can begin to assemble them into a form. To do this, gently bend each piece into a cylinder that will stand up. Use a little Magic Water as a joining medium—it works like a charm and isn't messy. (Make Magic Water by adding 3 tablespoons liquid sodium silicate and 1½ teaspoons soda ash to 1 gallon of water. Dissolve the soda ash in 1 cup [reserved from the 1 gallon] of boiling water before adding to mixture.) Because this is wet clay and you're applying plenty of pressure to ensure sound seams, you don't need to score (unless you're joining two pieces of unequal dryness). Using a paintbrush, apply the Magic Water to one side of each joint (figure 4) then position something firm (try using a plaster mold) behind the joint, and use the palm of your hand or a pony roller to compress the seam from the outside (figure 5). Apply enough pressure to make sure the clay particles are mingling nicely, but not so much that the visual line you've created is marred.

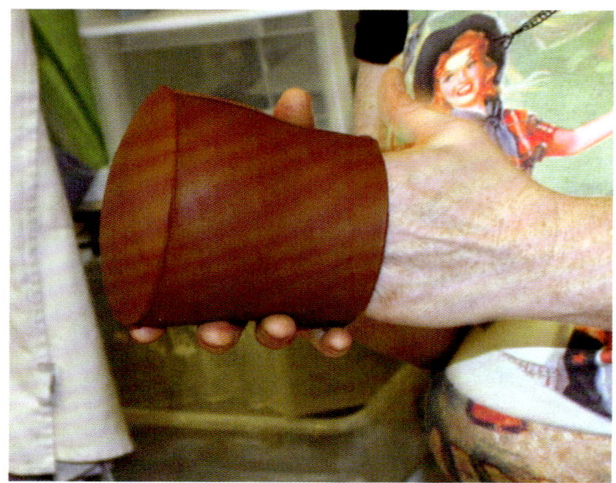

9. Use your fingers to stretch the wall from the inside to add volume and further define the form.

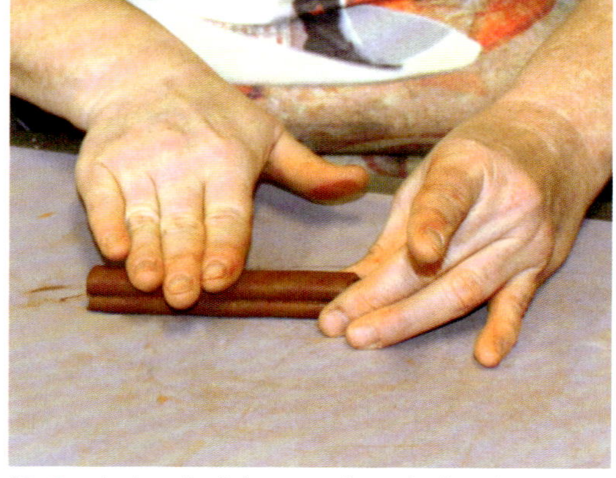

10. For the handle, join two coils and roll each side with a pony roller to the desired thickness.

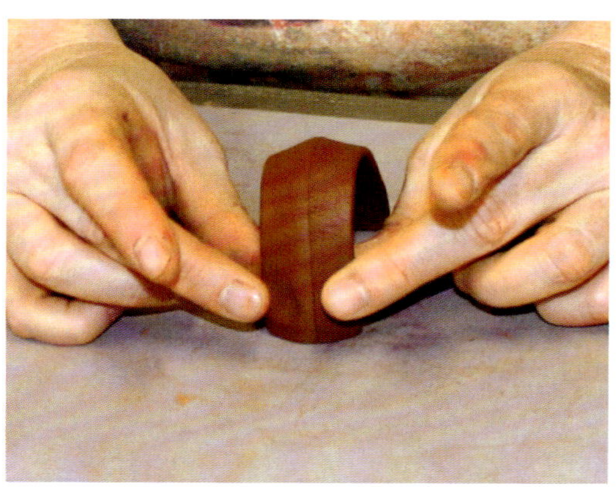

11. Reinforce the faux seam with your fingers. Plump the ends between your fingers and the table.

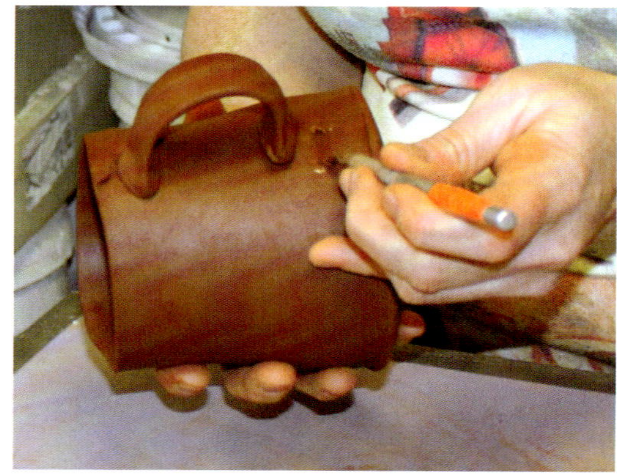

12. Hold handle up to the cup to determine if size is right, adjust if necessary, then attach.

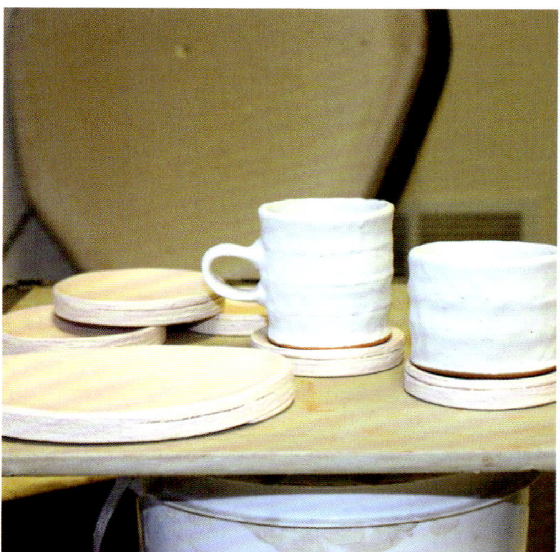

13. Glazed pots sitting in 'slump crutches', ready to be loaded into kiln for glaze firing.

The following steps create subtle, but important parts of what makes these pot forms special. One of the effects of rolling the seam edges to miter them is that some of the clay moves, forming little peaks at the ends. When joining your two pieces together to form the wall of the cup, try to preserve these bits of clay and then fold them down to the outside of the pot's wall (figure 6) once the two pieces are joined. Next, flip the cylinder upside down taking care not to squish the rim. Instead of folding these bits down as you did the ones on the rim, you will fold them in toward the center of what will be the interior of the cup (figure 7) so that they are on the same plane as the bottom of the cylinder wall. Once the cup is completely assembled, they will be visible in the bottom interior of the cup. These can now be considered part of the bottom edge, which you will vigorously score along with the bottom piece. Gently set the belly bottom down over the cylinder and work your way around the seam to make sure it's aligned before applying pressure. Holding the form, use a paddle to compress the seam well to prevent cracking during the drying process (figure 8). Next, shape the wall into a curve.

For smaller forms like cups and small bowls, hold the form in one hand and use your other hand to stretch the wall from the inside, turning it as you work (figure 9). For a larger pot, set it upright on a piece of foam on the banding wheel and use a soft red Mudtools rib to stretch the wall from the inside while supporting the wall from the outside with your other hand. Once you're satisfied with the shape, check the rim and re-shape it if any distortion has occurred.

Holding On

To make a handle, start with a coil or two of soft clay. For this handle, two coils are joined with a little Magic Water. Place one coil on top of the other, press them together (figure 10) and then begin to stretch them back out by rolling with the large end of the pony roller. Once you have the width you want (it should still be thicker than the end product), roll each side with the small end of the pony roller until its edges are about the same thickness as the rim of the cup. Form a fake seam-line down the middle of the handle that creates a visual repetition of the wall's seam. I tend to wing it when it comes to handle length; cut a length that looks close, then plump the ends for a solid attachment (figure 11). Once you decide where to place the handle, score both cup and handle and join them. Apply pressure to the joints firmly but gently to make sure the attachments are sound (figure 12).

A handle adds a little extra weight and, since the bottom is not flat, the cup will tend to list in the direction of the handle. To correct this, re-balance the cup by slightly shifting where the curve of the cup's bottom meets the surface of the table, opposite from the handle.

Functional Supports

A strong and durable pot is fully vitrified and to become so, it needs to be fired to maturity. When the clay particles are starting to melt together, this can cause physical shifting in an unstable form. If the body of the pot has too much weight for the belly bottom to bear, gravity will attempt to flatten it. To keep the bottom bellied, it needs support. To support curved forms, I use a *puki*, a bowl-like form used by Native Americans to support a rounded base while coil building (figure 13). These support forms are made with a cone 10 stoneware (I glaze fire to cone 6) so they don't vitrify right away. I use the same cookie cutters and oval templates as I use for making my pots when I form these. I make them over the same plaster hump molds so they have the same or similar curves, but they don't shrink as much, so the pots sit well in them for several firings.

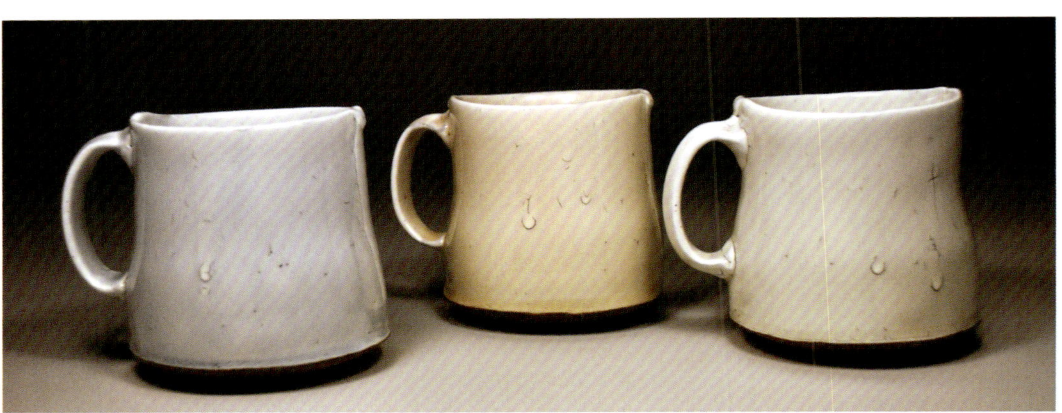

Advanced Techniques

SCALLOPED FLOWER VASE

by Allison McGowan Hermans

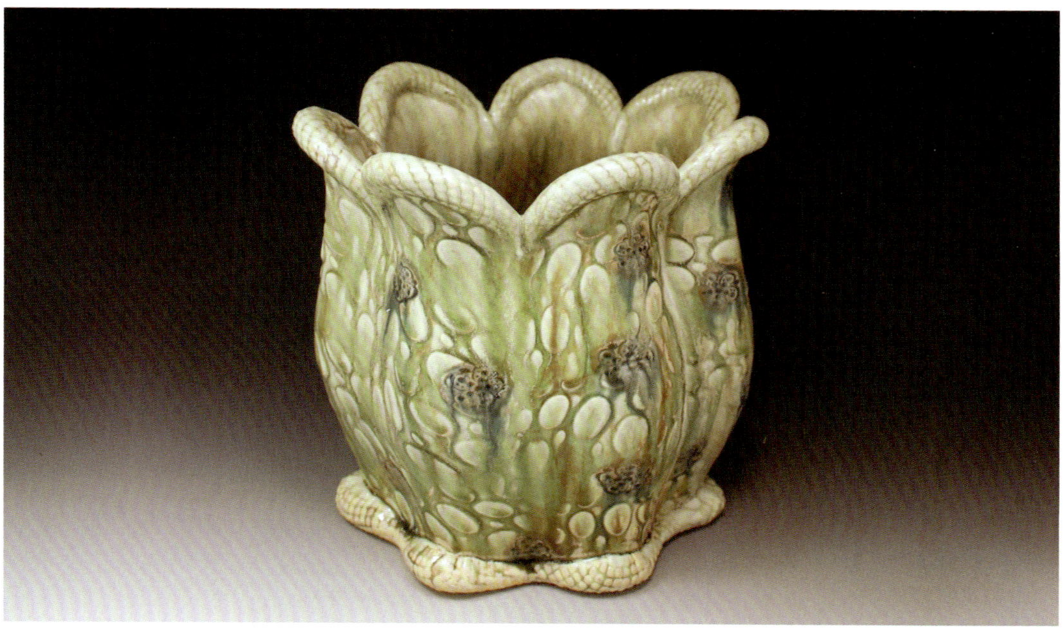

Making handbuilt porcelain vases comes naturally to me as a ceramic artist, lover of nature, and avid gardener. I love the minute formal challenges these porcelain vases bring within the parameters of function. My inspiration comes from sewing, nature, the basic structure or architecture of plants, Art Nouveau architecture, traditions in ceramics, and the art of function. All these are referenced in my work, from the moment I start layering patterns throughout the piece, to the point when I fill the vase with water and flowers and make sure all my seams are leak proof!

Varied Vases

I make many variations of vases—wide, squat, fat, tall, slender, and dainty. I love to play with textures and patterns that work together within the forms and I normally make several versions of the pots and then tweak the rims and the feet to change them up a bit. Flipping a pot over to create a whole new form was an idea gleaned in graduate school from one of my instructors, Anne Currier.

I begin working on my vase forms, as with every form, considering the function of the pot. Will this vase be for a large centerpiece with a grouping of tall flowers, or will it hold just a wispy wildflower bouquet that I might put in a small niche of a room to cheer it up? When making anything with clay, even an open flower pot, the right proportions and weight are important. Height, balance, and shrinkage are all taken into consideration when designing vases. These thoughts are all in my head while cutting the clay away from the block and preparing my slab.

Spatial Illusions

I am interested not only in formal elements of the vase but also in creating illusions of space through

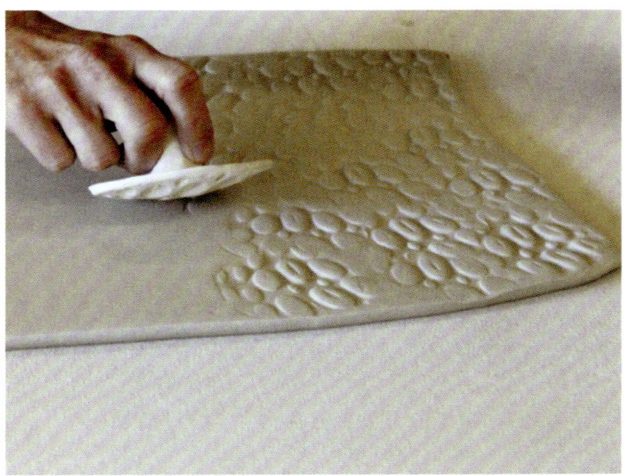

1. Throw a slab out onto a canvas-covered table, or a sheet of drywall, then imprint texture on the slab.

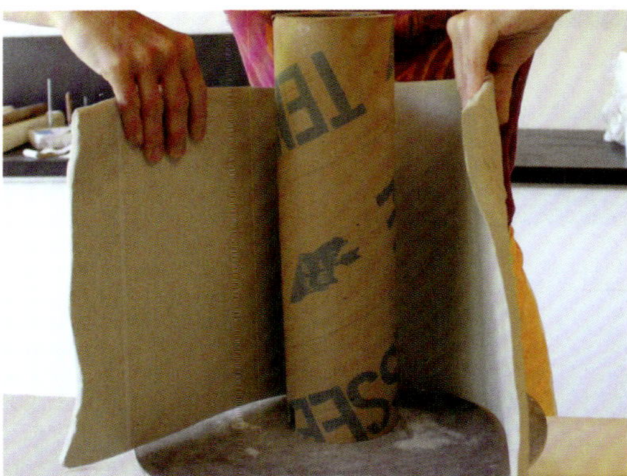

2. Set up a cardboarc cylinder on a banding wheel then stand the slab up so it's encircling the tube.

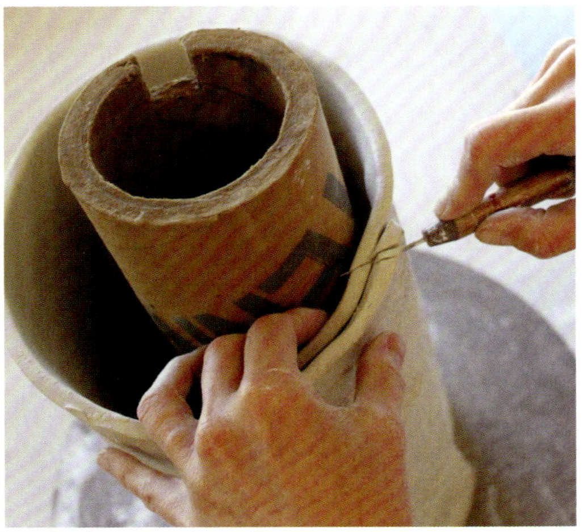

3. Overlap the slab then cut through both layers on an angle close to 45° to give the seam extra strength.

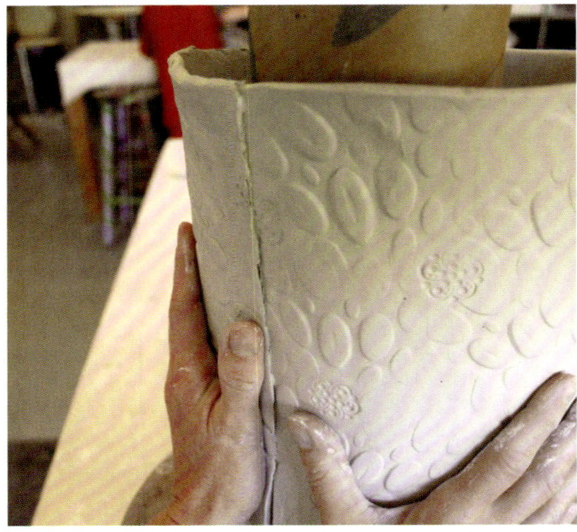

4. Score, apply slip, and push the seam together carefully so as to not disturb the texture.

a combination of layering patterns onto the wet clay surface, then using glazes that pool and flow to both accentuate and soften or distort the pattern and create a sense of depth to the surface of the pot. Most of my attention in the process is in the wet state when the surface design is being manipulated and stretched. My glazing is straightforward and entails hitting the texture with different accent glazes, then dunking the piece to cover it completely with a final glaze.

Layered Interests

By layering all of my interests together through structure, texture, pattern, and functionality, I am never bored with a form. I cut, alter, and tailor all of my vessels from a slab, sometimes using a hump or slump mold, or soft-filled pillow molds to create the form; however, the forms that are the most intriguing to me are ones that start as a straightforward, slab-built cylinder. I build the body of the pot free-hand and then integrate a foot to lift it off the table. The final step brings the form to life with a rim to tie the vessel to the foot and emphasize the volume in the form.

Texture, Shape, and Volume

My *Concord Flower Vase* has a full-bodied form with its scalloped edges and rounded feet. Like all of my pieces, this vase starts with a slab that I toss out onto my canvas-covered table. I don't use a slab

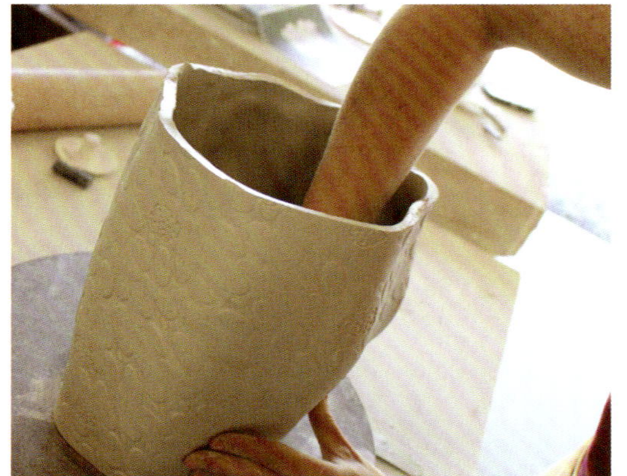

5. Create scallops: press out with one hand, while pressing in with your fingers on either side of the bulge.

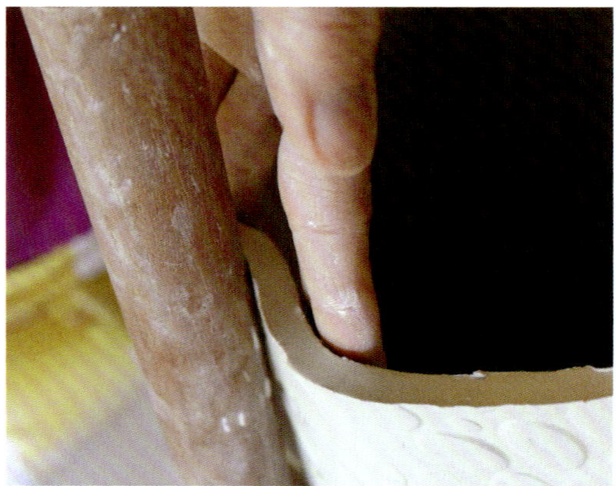

6. Use a 2½-inch dowel rod to support the outside and define the scallops without disrupting the textures.

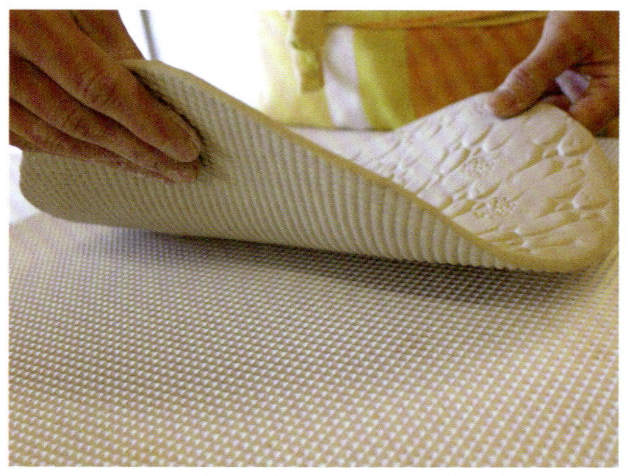

7. Throw out another slab for the base of the form, add texture to both sides.

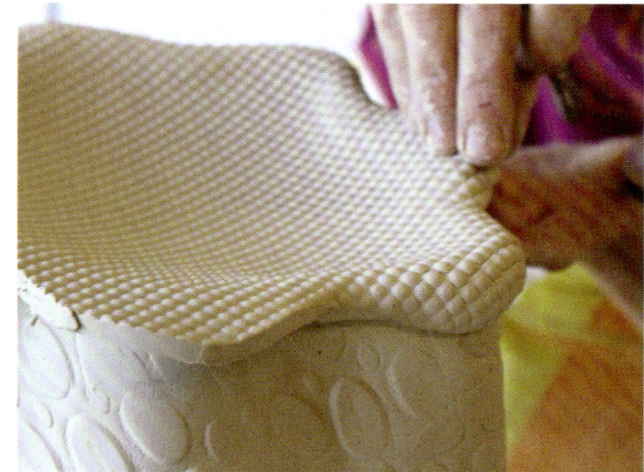

8. Place the bottom slab on the cylinder and fold the extra clay over to make a bellied foot for each scallop.

roller; it's quicker for me to stretch and flip the clay by hand, and I have more control of the thickness and width by tapping the ends and the top and bottom of the slab. I leave the slab a little thicker than the finished slab will be since it's stretched out later to give the piece more volume after texturing.

I have a tool box full of treasured textures, found objects, and sewing notions in my studio that I have found all over for my surface textures. I imprint the slab with a texture I took from the sole of a shoe and made into a bisque stamp (figure 1), then layer another pattern over it using a button that was glued to the end of a short dowel. After I make the textured slab foreground, I stretch out the slab a little more to distort the impressions by throwing it back out onto the canvas.

I set up a cardboard cylinder on a banding wheel as a support, and then stand the wet slab up against it. Depending on the height and wetness of the slab, I use this cylinder to help keep the clay upright (figure 2) at the beginning of the process.

To form vases, I always work on a bat on my banding wheel so that transferring the pot later is more manageable. I don't use the cardboard cylinder to shape the vase, just to brace and support it until I finish joining seams. Overlap the slab according to the desired diameter, then use a sharp knife to cut through both layers at a 45° angle at the same time to create the seam (figure 3). This type of cut maintains an exact seam that matches up perfectly. I need the seam to be strong because it will be stressed when I alter the form later.

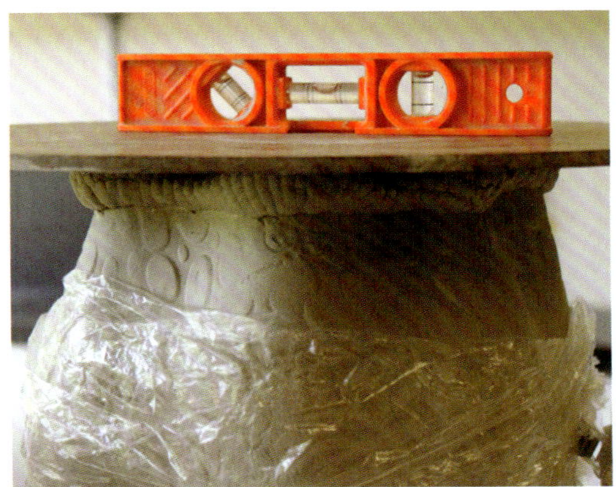

9. Place another bat on top of the piece and use a level to adjust alignment of the feet.

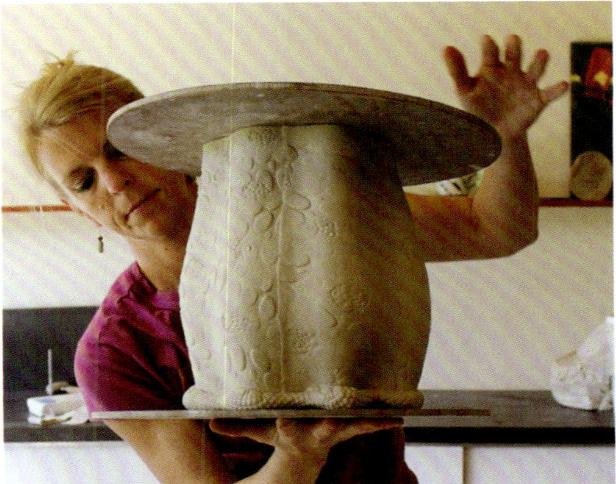

10. When the feet can support the weight, sandwich the cylinder between two bats and flip it over.

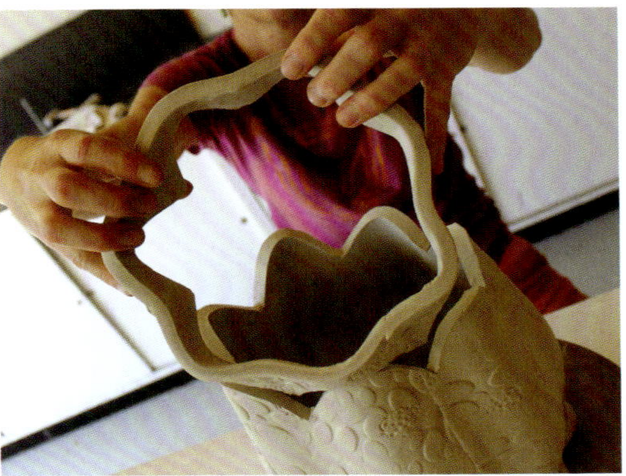

11. Cut the top with an X-Acto knife to create seven or eight scalloped shapes, then remove the excess.

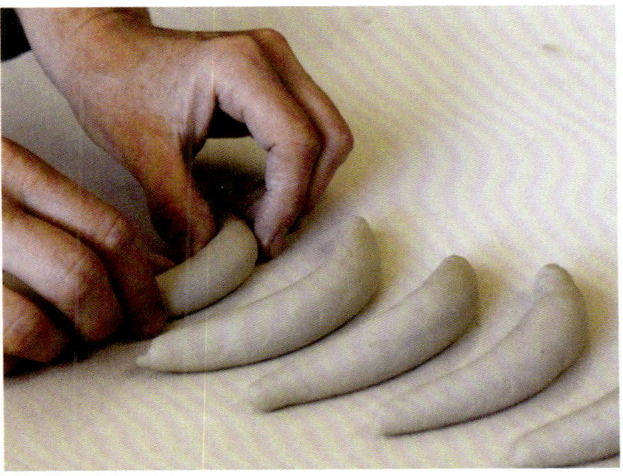

12. Roll a small tapered coil for each scallop then curve each coil into a gentle crescent-moon shape.

I score both edges, and use a deflocculated slip to adhere the seam. The deflocculated slip requires less water to stay fluid. It's made from bone dry clay slaked in a bucket with enough water to create a thick slurry then deflocculant is added before mixing to a honey consistency with a drill mixer. This deflocculated slip is helpful because its water content is closer to the water content of the slab, so the slip shrinks less as it dries and there's less stress overall on the seam. I join the ends together, pushing with my palms and thumbs carefully so as to not disturb the texture (figure 4). Pressing the clay against the cardboard cylinder on the inside gives the stability needed to apply some force on the outside without breaking open the seam on the inside.

Once the cylinder is complete, I start to define the scalloped shape. After removing the cardboard tube, I use my hands on the inside and outside at the same time to push out and up in a straight vertical line while using the fingers of my outside hand to press in on either side of the bulge (figure 5). It's important to press lightly so as not to disturb the texture while still accentuating the bulge in the form. To further define the scallop of the form without disrupting the textures, I use a 2½-inch-diameter dowel rod to provide support on the outside while I use my fingers to push out from the inside (figure 6).

Once the form is ready, I make a second slab for the base. I place it on a large, 3-inch-thick plaster texture mold that I made using the cover

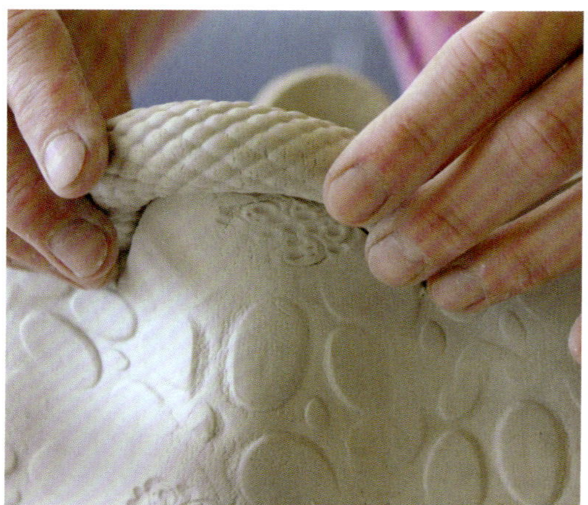

13. Shape and taper one curved coil around each scallop to ensure a tight fit and strong seam then attach.

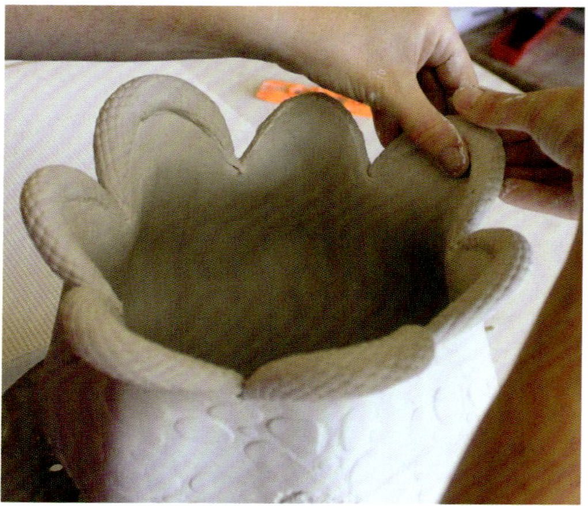

14. Squeeze each scallop up against the coil. Clean up any excess slip that squeezes out of the seam.

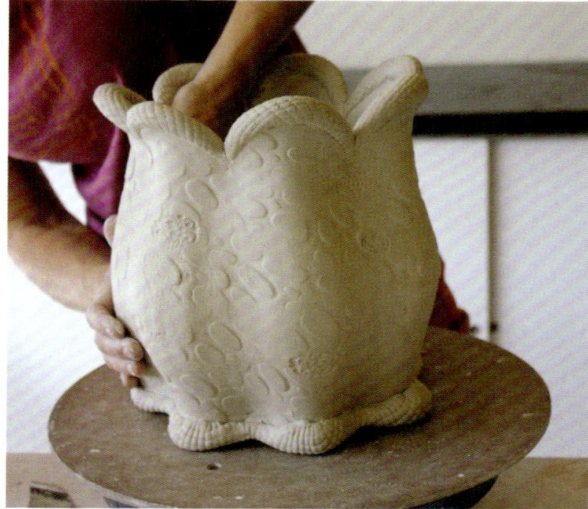

15. Smooth and compress all joints and make any final adjustments to the scallops and overall shape.

of a fluorescent light fixture. Then I texture the top of the slab with the same pattern that's on the body of the pot (figure 7) so the texture at the bottom mirrors what's on the outside.

I attach the slab to the cylinder, taking care not to disturb the texture. I'm working upside down, so what shows here as the top of the piece (see figure 8) will become the bottom of the finished piece. To make a foot, I cut around the edge leaving a wide margin. I fold the extra clay over and make a bellied foot for each scallop (figure 8). As I work the clay from the inside, I am also pillowing the foot out to create more volume.

After all the feet are finished, I cover two-thirds of the vessel with plastic so I can finish the rim and top of the pot once stiffened. I place another bat on top of the piece and use a small level to make slight adjustments to the alignment of the feet (figure 9). This ensures the vessel sits level.

When the foot can support its own weight, I flip the piece over and work on the top. I sandwich the leather-hard vase between two bats and flip the form over (figure 10), so I don't press on the sides of the pot and distort the form.

At this point, the top rim is cut with an X-Acto knife into seven or eight scalloped shapes, according to the overall form of the piece (figure 11). Then I slightly thin and push out the scallops to open the top of the pot to receive flowers. I roll a small, moon-shaped coil for each scallop, with the ends tapering and the center swelling (figure 12) and roll them onto the same textured slab used for the base.

Each coil gets carefully formed and tapered around each scallop of the rim (figure 13). The coil is then neatly attached by scoring the bottom of the coil and the edge of the rim, applying deflocculated slip, squeezing the rim up toward the base of the coil, and cleaning up any visible slip (figure 14). Final adjustments are made to accentuate the scallops and the overall shape (figure 15).

Advanced Techniques

LARGE NESTING BOWLS

by Courtney Murphy

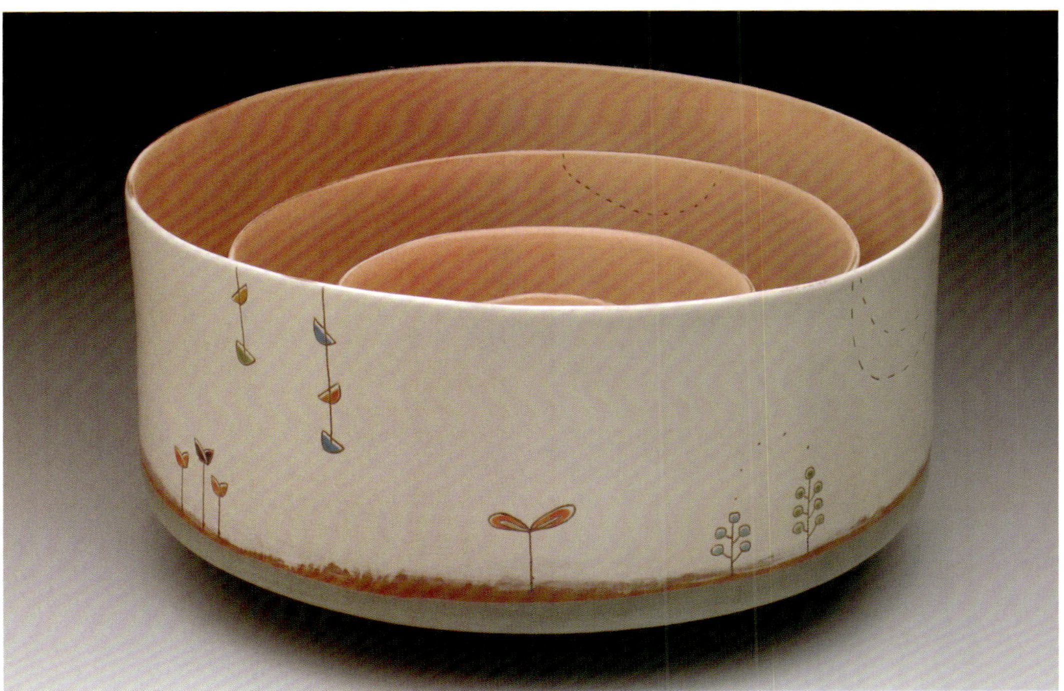

A few years ago, when I switched from cone 6 porcelain to low-fire earthenware, I was excited about the potential to work larger. I had come up with some ideas, and even made some sketches, but had never actually made anything very large.

I had been searching home improvement and salvage stores for years, looking mostly at lighting fixtures, but really any object with a relatively shallow continuous curve to make a mold from. Finally, a little over a year ago, I borrowed a giant mold shaped like a satellite dish from a friend. I was attracted to the gradual uninterrupted curve of this simple form, and the flexibility that it offered. It could be the basis for a large platter, a round-bottomed bowl or a rocking, boat-shaped vessel. Using his mold, I created both a hump mold and a slump mold out of plaster.

After making the plaster mold, I created a series of bisque molds off of the hump mold to fit the larger bowls. I bisque all of my pieces nesting inside of one another inside the largest bisque mold. I also add a small amount of fine grog between each layer. The structure of the bisque mold prevents the rounded bottoms from warping or slumping in the kiln. Because I leave the pieces unglazed on the bottom, I can still fire my larger pieces inside of these molds for the glaze firings.

The larger pieces really benefit from having the extra support of the bisque mold, and firing them in the mold enables me to retain that continuous curve that I like so much. The smaller pieces in the set don't need to be fired in molds because they weigh less and have a shallower curve. They do well glaze fired in a pile of fine grog.

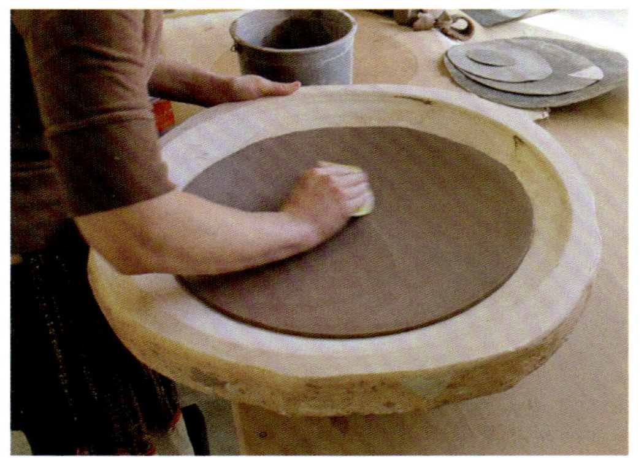
1. Cut bowl bottoms using templates. Smooth and compress the largest slab into the plaster slump mold.

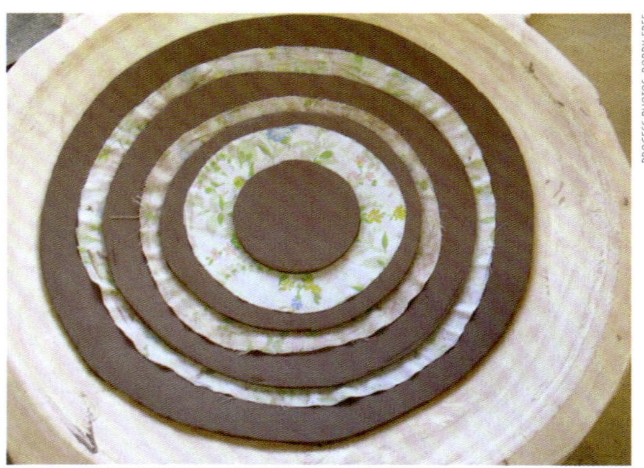
PROCESS PHOTOS: BOBBY FREE

2. Each slab bottom is added, separated by a thin cloth, then ribbed to conform to the curve of the one below it.

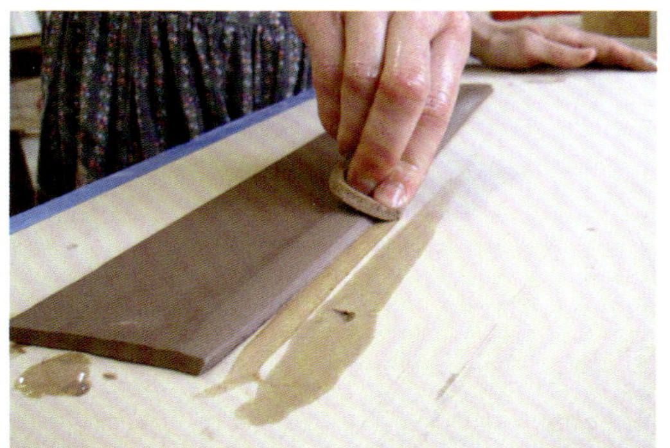
3. Cut slabs for the walls of the bowls, then taper and soften the rim edge with a rubber rib and sponge.

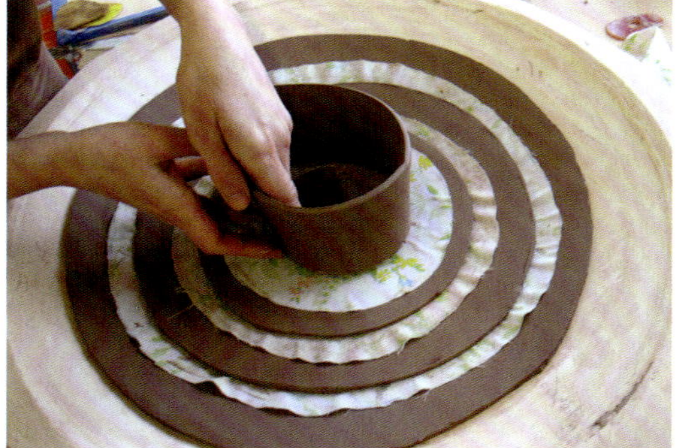
4. With smallest bowl in place, score the bottom edge of the wall and the edge of its base, Apply slip and join.

Having several bisque molds also allows for separating the pieces out to work on the inside of one, or to allow for more even drying without the danger of the bottoms slumping or deforming in the greenware stage.

Now that I had this very large mold as a starting point, it was time to go ahead and try to create more significant pieces. I like the idea of things that nest or fit together, with each thing having its own particular place.

Forming the Bases

To create the bottom of each bowl in a nesting set, I start with circular templates cut from tarpaper. This material is durable and impervious to water, which makes it great to use over and over as a template for clay. Tarpaper can be found at home improvement stores, often in giant rolls, which are cumbersome, but will last forever. Using a compass, I trace four concentric circles, each about two inches smaller than the next in diameter. Cut four circles out of a thin cotton bed sheet, each just slightly larger than the tarpaper circles. Since the bottoms are stacked during forming, so that each one conforms to the one below it, these fabric circles keep the stacked clay slabs from sticking together.

When rolling out slabs, rotate the slab so that it doesn't get stretched out in just one direction repeatedly, which can weaken the clay. I roll out my clay between ¼- to ⅛- inch thick, compressing it with a rib. I then use the template to trace the largest (bottom) circle of the nesting set and to move it into the plaster slump mold, smoothing it into the curve of the mold with a rubber rib (figure 1).

Working from the largest to the smallest, place one of the fabric circles down, then lay the next slab circle on top. Use the rib to conform each slab to the one below it and repeat the process until all slabs are placed and rounded (figure 2).

Building the Walls

After making the bases, roll out slabs for the walls of each piece of the set. Figure out the circumference for each bowl by wrapping a reinforced cloth tape measure (the kind you find in fabric stores) around each of the stacked bottoms, then roll out slabs, trying to conform roughly to those dimensions. In the case of my large nesting set, the wall of the largest bowl is 6 inches tall with a circumference of 52 inches. My second largest wall stands 5 inches tall, the third is 4 inches, while the smallest bowl has a height of 3 inches and measures 14 inches in circumference.

Once the walls have reached soft leather hard, taper the top edge or rim first with a stiff rubber rib then with an elephant ear sponge (figure 3). Tapering the edges creates a visual lightness and sense of delicacy to the bowls.

After thinning out the rims, stand the slabs on edge to shape them into circles. The slabs should be stiff enough so they can stand this way without collapsing, yet soft enough that they are not in danger of cracking when curved. Keeping the slabs on the slightly softer side is also an enormous help when you're blending the seams together.

After forming a slab into a circle, flip it over, placing the tapered top end down, and score the bottom as well as the attachment area on the corresponding base, then apply slip to both scored areas. When attaching walls to each base, work from the inside smallest piece outward to the largest so your hands have space to move around (figure 4). Use a fine-toothed flexible serrated rib to smooth the edges of the wall together. Join the two sides together at a 45° angle to enable the largest surface area point of contact (see figure 6). After the seam sets up slightly, add a thin coil to reinforce it (figure 5), then smooth the seam repeatedly with

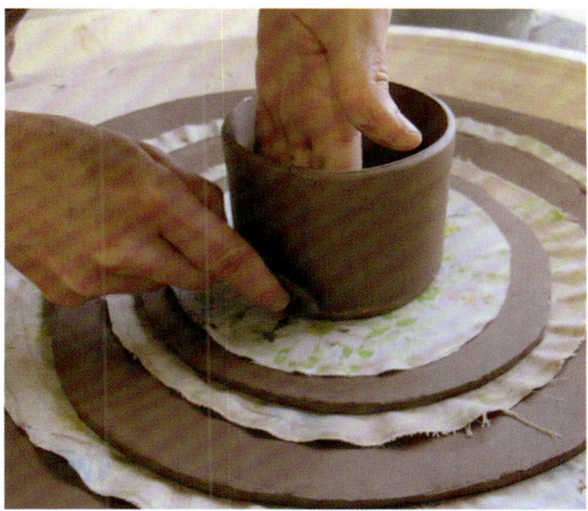

5. Add a thin coil, then compress and blend the seam together with a fine serrated rib and a soft rubber rib.

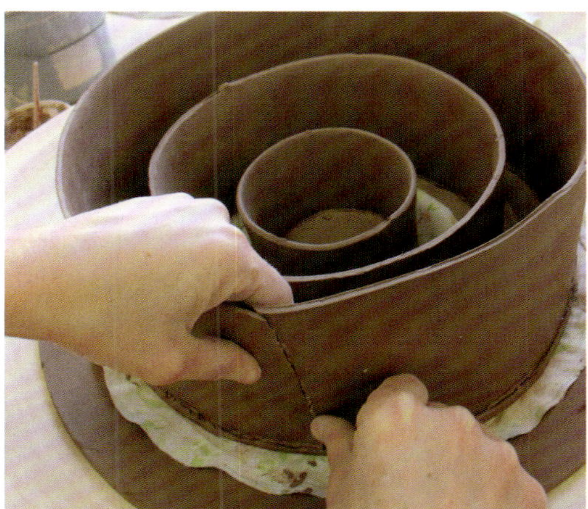

6. Work from the smallest to the largest bowl. Bevel, then attach the ends of the wall slabs.

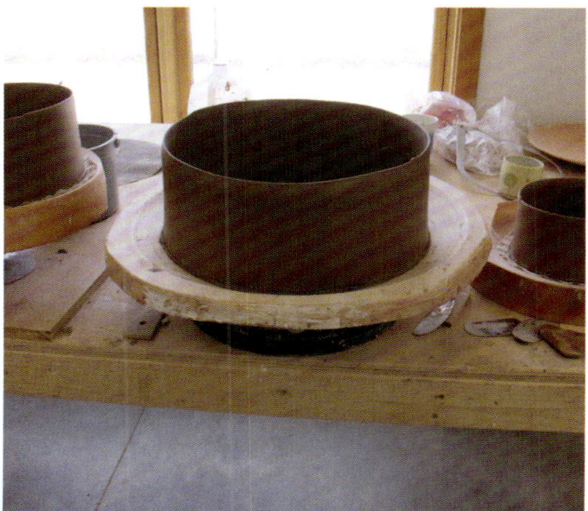

7. Using bisque molds made from the hump mold, separate the pieces to allow for more even drying.

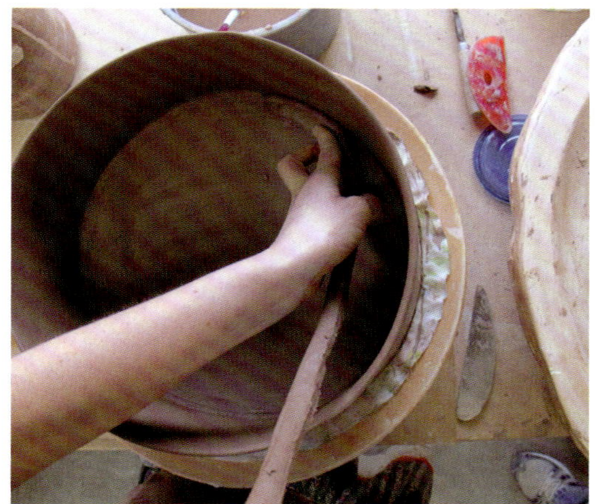

8. Add a wide, soft coil to reinforce and soften the seam then smooth with a rubber rib.

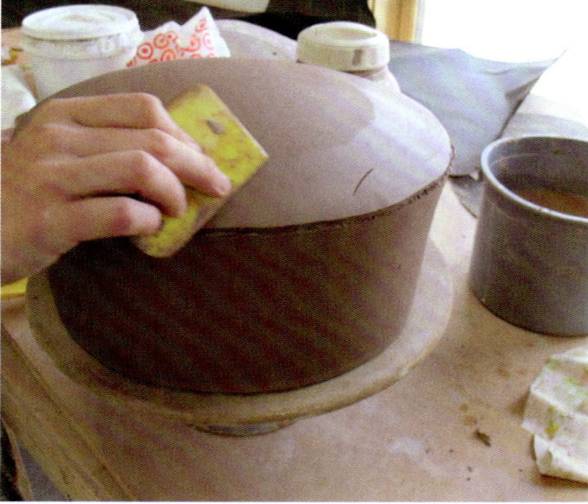

9. Turn the leather-hard bowl upside down and clean up the bottom using a medium soft rib.

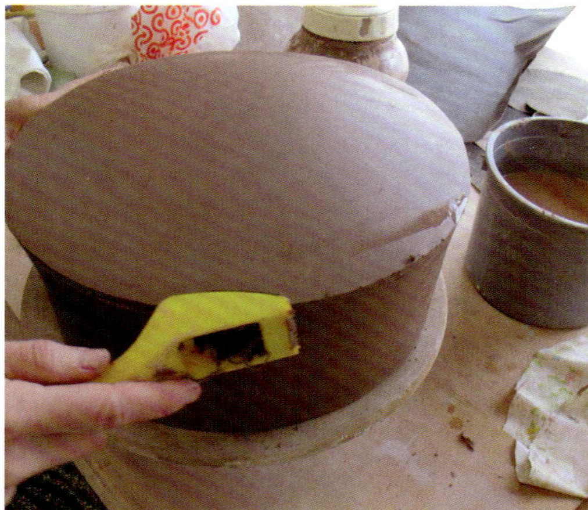

10. Clean the outside seam where the base meets the wall with a Surform rasp, then smooth with a rib.

a series of stiffer to softer rubber ribs. This helps both to smooth the seam as well as to compress it and prevent cracks while drying.

Continue to work from the inside out, attaching walls to each of the concentric circular bases. Since the largest bowl calls for a 52-inch long slab, which would be very challenging and awkward to work with, I piece together two or three shorter slabs to create the wall of the outermost pieces (figure 6).

After all walls have been attached to all bases, allow the piece time to set up. The entire process start to finish takes several days.

Once the pieces have stiffened to leather hard, place the bowls into separate bisque molds (figure 7) and add a fairly thick coil on the inside to reinforce the seam as well as to create a softer and smoother transition from the walls to the base of the piece (figure 8). Smooth the coil into the seam, first with a serrated metal rib to remove some of the excess clay, then a slightly stiff rubber rib. I'm a huge fan of the Mudtools ribs. The yellow rib number Y2 has the perfect curve to create a nice transition in the bowl where the base meets the wall (see figure 9).

At this point, the bowls should be stiff enough to pick up and place upside down to work on cleaning up the bottom. Placing the upside down bowl on foam (to protect the rim) on a turntable, very gently smooth the bottom of the piece with a rib (figure 9), filling in any indentations with very small coils of clay. Use a Surform rasp to clean up the outer edge where the wall meets the base (figure 10). After using the rasp, go back and smooth this area over with a rib. The pressure from this clean-up work sometimes creates a bit of a bulge on the inside of the pot. It's important to keep flipping the piece over to a minimum, but if necessary, fix this bulge by adding coils or removing excess clay from the inside.

Once all pieces have been cleaned up on both the inside and outside, place them all back together, leaving them this way overnight under plastic to equalize in moisture. Allow to dry then bisque and glaze in the style of your choice.

TEXTURED FLOWER BASKET

by Marion Peters Angelica

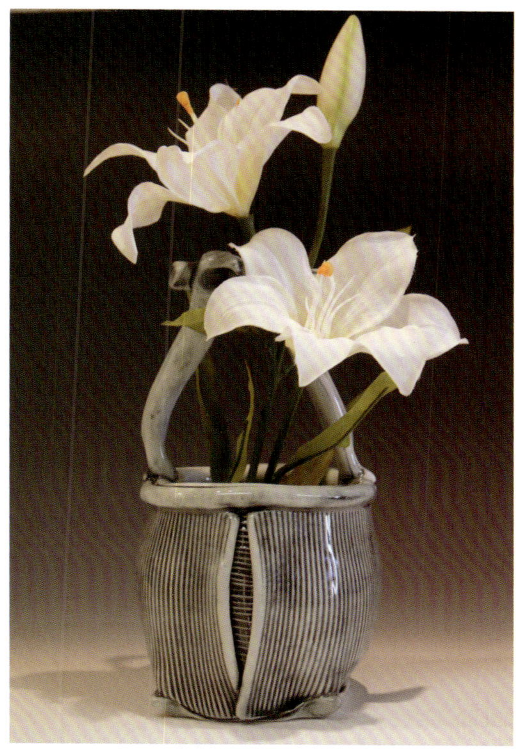

The handle on this flower basket supports blooms for vertical flower arrangements, and adds character and movement to the piece when the basket is not in use.

Ceramic baskets are fun to make and have around the home. They are useful in all seasons, whether they are filled with gourds in the fall, dried flowers or holiday ornaments in the winter, or flowers or fruit in the summer. Even though their versatility means they might not be empty very often, ceramic baskets need to be interesting forms on their own, too. This flower basket was designed with that in mind, and with the idea that its handle can support and enhance a flower arrangement.

I work with soft slabs because they enable me to give my work a sense of fluidity and attitude. While I start off with precisely measured pieces, I allow the soft, fabric-like nature of soft slabs to give the work a casual and lyrical feel. Soft slabs also accept texture readily and offer a great canvas for those who love to apply texture to embellish their work. I confess to being a texture addict. In making your own basket, please use whichever textures you enjoy.

Working with soft slabs requires that you handle the clay as little as possible to keep it fresh looking. It also requires a firm touch when you want the clay to move or attach. For example, when creating the handle for this basket, attaching the handle pieces should be done with a simple, firm pressure, just once, in order to retain the fresh look and sense of movement in the clay. The same is true when turning up the basket base corners—do it quickly, firmly, and just once.

Preparation

Roll out a ¼-inch thick slab that is large enough to fit all the pattern pieces (figure 1). (Remember that the side panel and inset pieces are cut twice creating a total of five clay pieces, see figure 4.) Compress the slab with a rubber rib, first horizontally, then vertically, and then diagonally. Do this on both sides of the slab. Compressing the clay is essential to reduce cracking and warping. Lay your templates onto the compressed slab, and cut them out. Once the pieces have been cut, slide your fingers firmly along all the cut edges to compress and smooth them.

1. Cut 2 side panels, 2 insets, and 1 base using the flower basket templates.

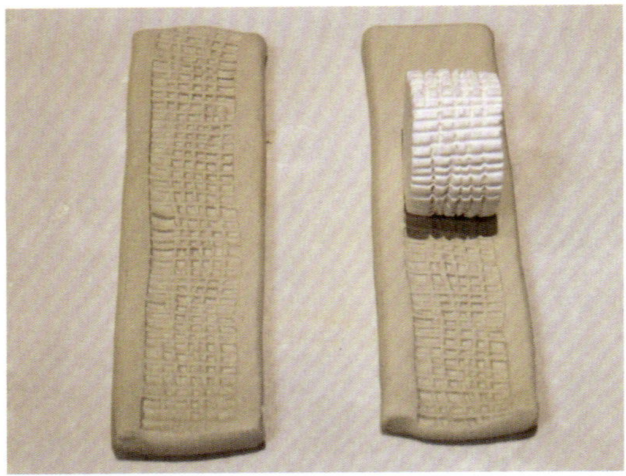

2. Apply a contrasting texture to the inset pieces using a roller.

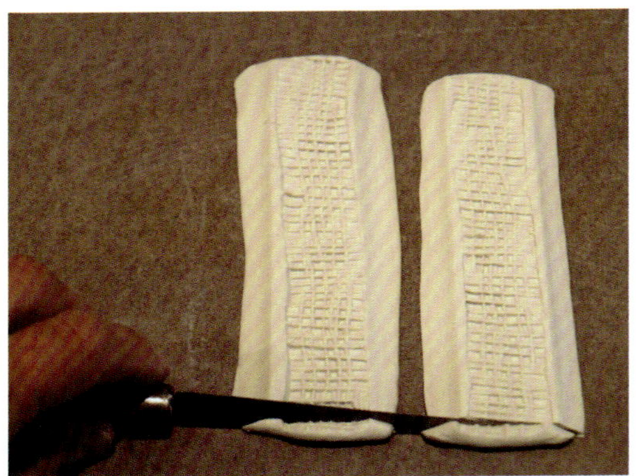

3. Square the ends of the inset pieces so the base will be level.

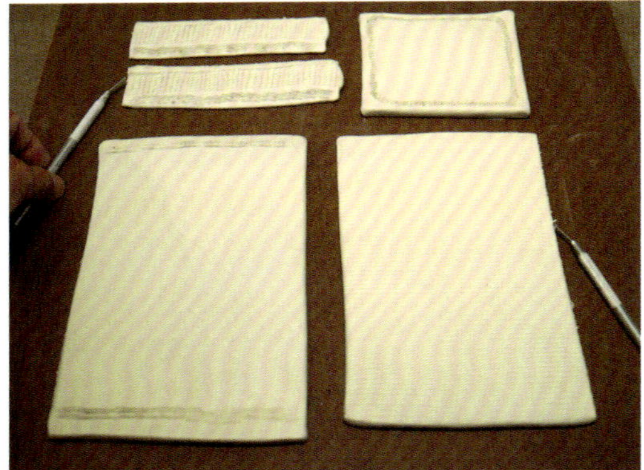

4. Score each piece prior to handling it to avoid marring the texture or warping the slab.

You can add interest to the basket by applying contrasting textures to the side and inset panels. On this basket, I used corrugated paper for the side panels and a bisque roller to make a cross hatch texture on the insets (figure 2), but stamps, rollers, and fabrics all make wonderful textures to personalize your basket. After impressing the texture on the side panels and insets, bevel the sides of the inset pieces and even out their bottom edges (figure 3). Score all the pieces in advance of assembly (figure 4). Score the interior (non-textured side) of each side panel ¼ inch from the edge, as well as the bottom edge (the long side) of each side panel. Score the beveled edges of the two inset pieces and the bottom edge of each. Score ¼ inch from the edge of all four sides of the base piece, going around its corners in a slight curve. Note that on the interior of the side panels and on the base, you do not score right at the edge of the pieces.

Assembling the Basket

Put slip on the scored area of the base piece and the bottom edge of one side panel. Center the side panel on the scored area of one side of the base and gently wiggle it to assure a tight fit. Then curve the portions of the side panel that overhang the side of the base so they contact the scored areas on the bottom slab. The panel should end at about the middle of the opposite side of the base (figure 5). Repeat this same step with the second side panel, so that the panels are attached to the base, but are not attached to one another (figure 6). The two panels may overlap slightly or have a small gap

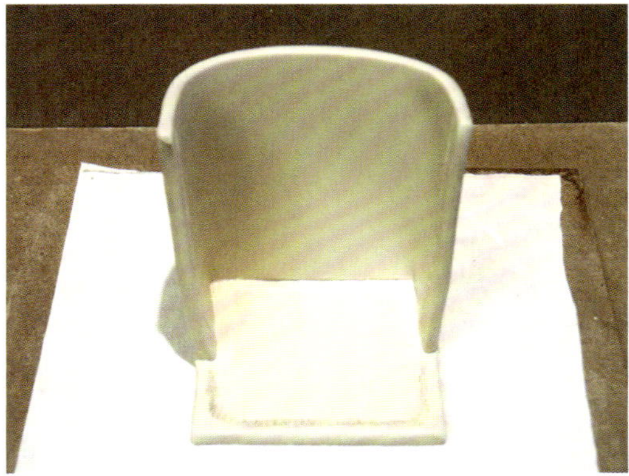

5. Put slip on the scored area of the base and the bottom edge of one side pane. Attach it to the base slab.

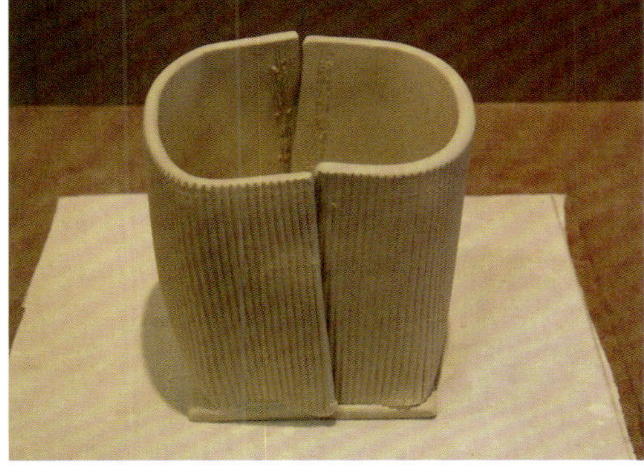

6. Repeat with the second side panel. Do not put slip on the scored edges of the side panels yet.

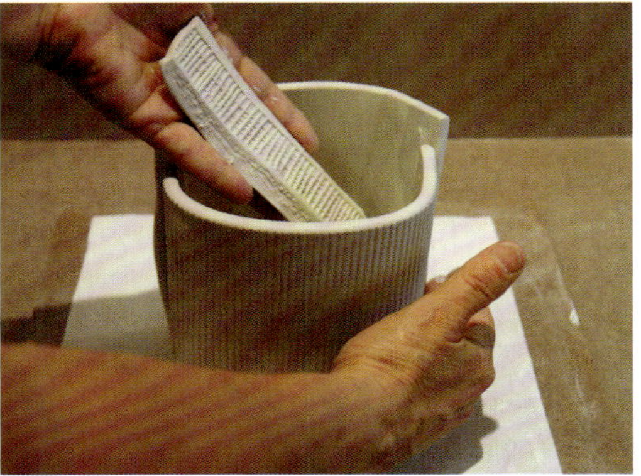

7. Apply slip to the inset and side panels and insert the inset piece between the two side panels.

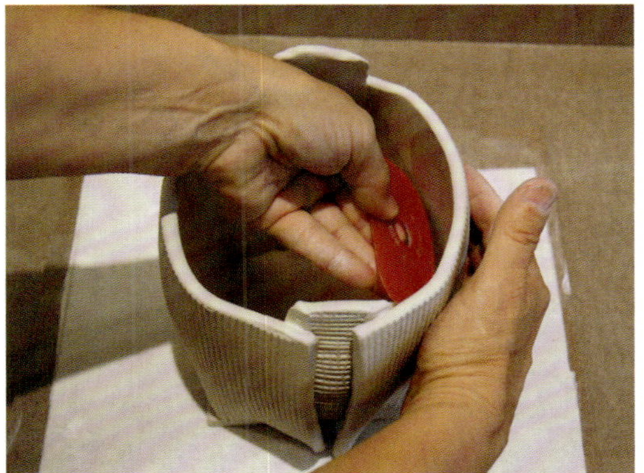

8. Using a soft rib inside the form, and gently supporting the exterior, add volume to the basket.

between them based upon how precisely you cut them. Either way is fine.

Next put slip on the scored bevels and scored bottom of one of the inset pieces and put slip on the scored areas on side panels that are next to one another. Holding the inset in the palm of your hand (figure 7), place it firmly on the scored areas of base between the two side panels. Gently join each side of the insert to the side panel where they are scored. As you join these seams, support the side panels with your other hand, but allow the side panels to move out slightly and move apart as you insert and attach the inset piece. Repeat this with the second inset piece. Smooth and firmly seal all seams to assure they are tight.

Using a soft rib on the interior of the form, and supporting the exterior with your other hand, add volume and shape to the piece (figure 8). Don't be afraid to use the rib to really belly-out the form, if you wish. The insets will become more visible as you add volume to the form. Once you have the degree of volume you desire, trim off any excess clay from the tops of the inset pieces to make them even with the top edges of the side panels (figure 9).

To give the basket a sense of lift, pinch up the base at each corner (figure 10). To do this, put one hand into the interior of the body of the basket, hooking your thumb over the top edge. By gently closing your interior hand's thumb and pointer finger on both the inside and the outside, you can lift and tip up one corner of the basket. Pinch the base up at the corner with your exterior hand while keeping a finger of your interior hand in the corner of the base and side panel to counterbal-

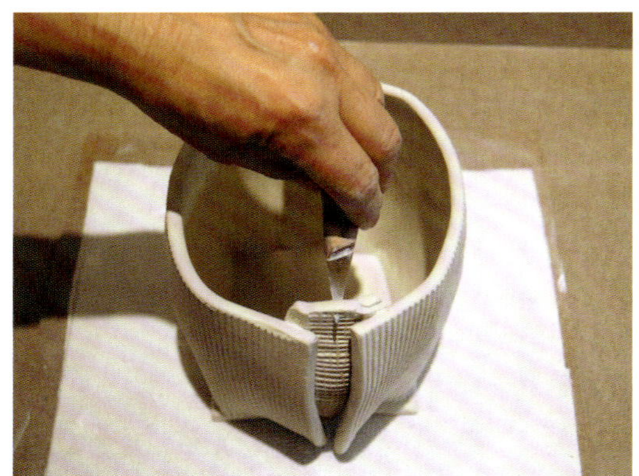

9. Trim off excess clay on the insets to level them with the side panels.

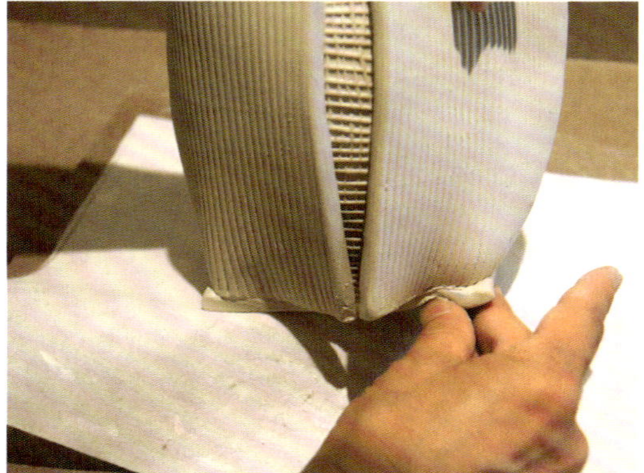

10. Pinch the base upward while supporting the area from the inside.

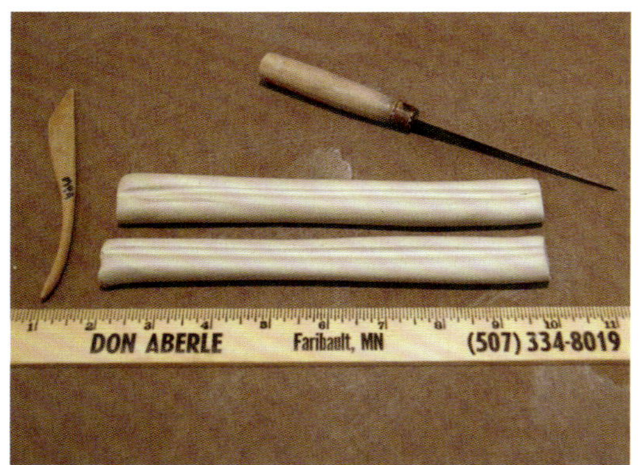

11. For a vase this size, roll a coil for the rim and cut it into two 8-inch sections.

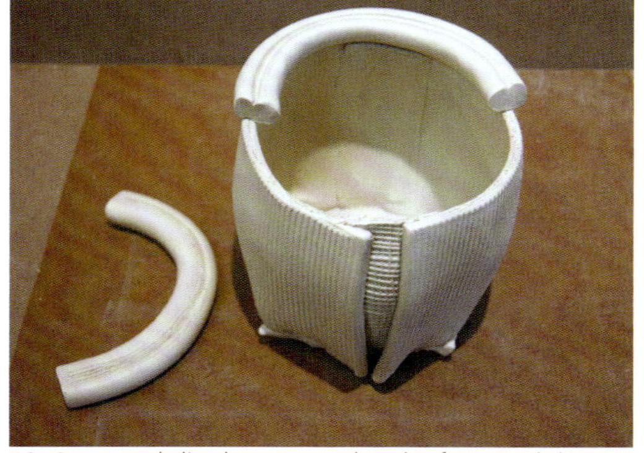

12. Score and slip the upper edge the form and the underside of each rim coil then set them in place.

ance the force from the pinch. Repeat this at all four corners. Remember to use simple and firm pressure on the clay.

Adding the Rim

The basket rim and handle can give your basket a great deal of personality, so consider carefully how thick or wide you would like them to be. Make sure they coordinate with one another and don't create a visually or physically unbalanced form. To make the rim, roll a coil to the thickness you would like. I like to press a groove into the rim to catch glaze and add interest (figure 11). Cut the coil into two 8-inch lengths, soften the cut ends of each coil where cut by tapping or smoothing them, and bend these to match the curve of the top of the basket body. Score and slip the top edge of the basket body and the underside of the rim coil. Add the two rim coils having them meet in the center of the side panels, not over the insets (figure 12). Creating this joint over the side panels adds strength and sets up the handle to show off the contrasting textures of the insets. With both coils in place, gently press or paddle the rim to assure a tight fit and pinch the joint between the two parts of the rim adding strength and interest (figure 13). Again, use the soft rib to adjust the volume and shape of the basket to its final form.

Making the Handle

Roll a coil approximately the same thickness as the rim coil and cut it into two equal sections that will form the vertical sections of the handle and a shorter one for the cross bar. With a sharp knife,

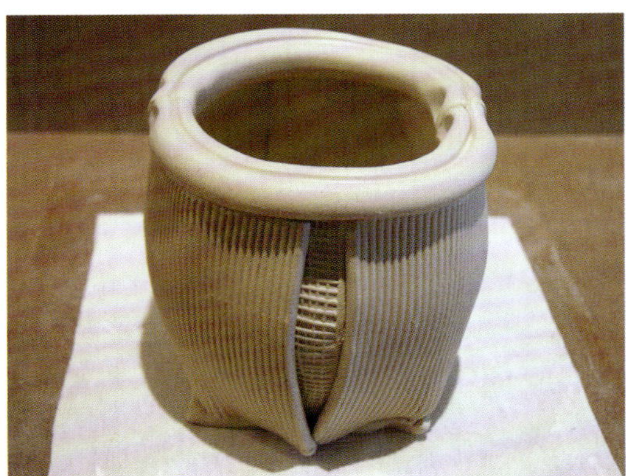

13. Pinch the rim pieces together to create a solid connection between the coils and the wall slabs.

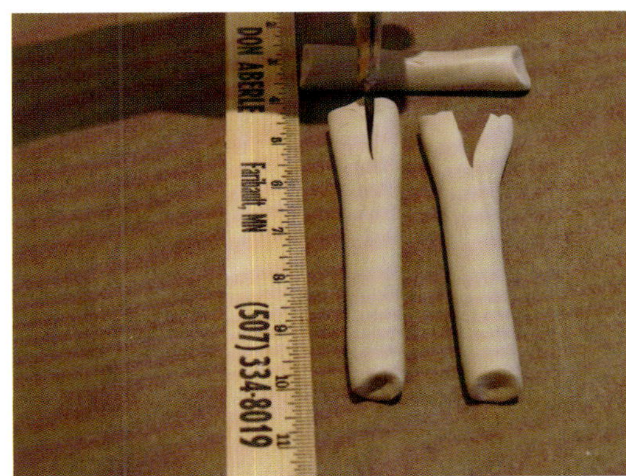

14. Cut a long coil into three sections. Cut 1½-inch-long slits into the top of each upright.

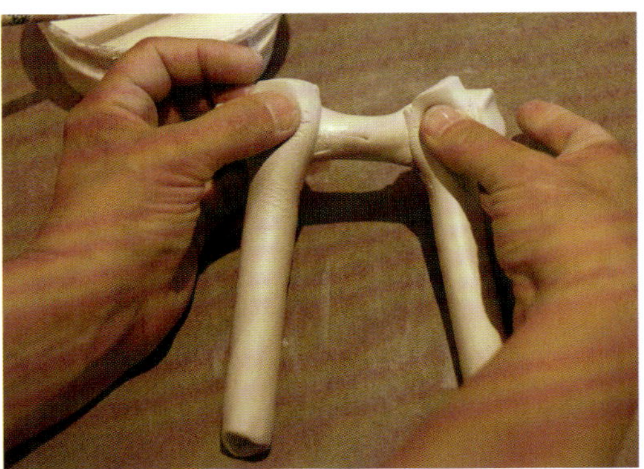

15. Insert the crossbar piece into the slits and pinch together the cuts pieces of each upright to grasp it.

cut 1½-inch slits in the top section of each upright (figure 14). Score and slip the insides of the slit and place the cross bar piece inside the cuts as though they are biting it. Firmly pinch the cuts closed over the crossbar (figure 15). Do this firmly and only once to keep it looking fresh. Let the handle set up to a soft leather-hard state. It should be firm enough to carry its own weight, but still pliable. If necessary, wrap a plastic bag or thin plastic sheeting around the bottom ½ inch of the uprights to keep them soft. If you choose to leave the handle as one sweeping curve, make sure the coil is long enough, and that it is thicker on the ends than in the middle for support.

Deeply score the rim where the two rim coils meet one another and score the bottoms of the handle uprights. Add slip to both scored areas. Firmly press

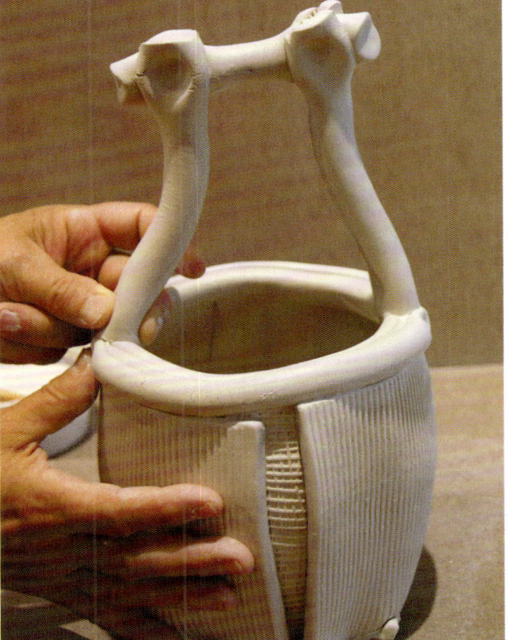

16. Add slip to both the scored rim and handle, then attach the leather-hard handle to the rim.

and pinch the uprights into the rim while supporting the rim with your other hand (figure 16). Adjust the handle to give it the "attitude" you desire, then allow the piece to dry slowly under plastic.

Test out your flower basket with a variety of blooms to see what works best, and when there aren't any flowers in the house, try out fruits, veggies, ornaments or anything else you think might work well to create a personal statement.

Advanced Techniques
CALLA LILY WINE STEMS

by Marion Peters Angelica

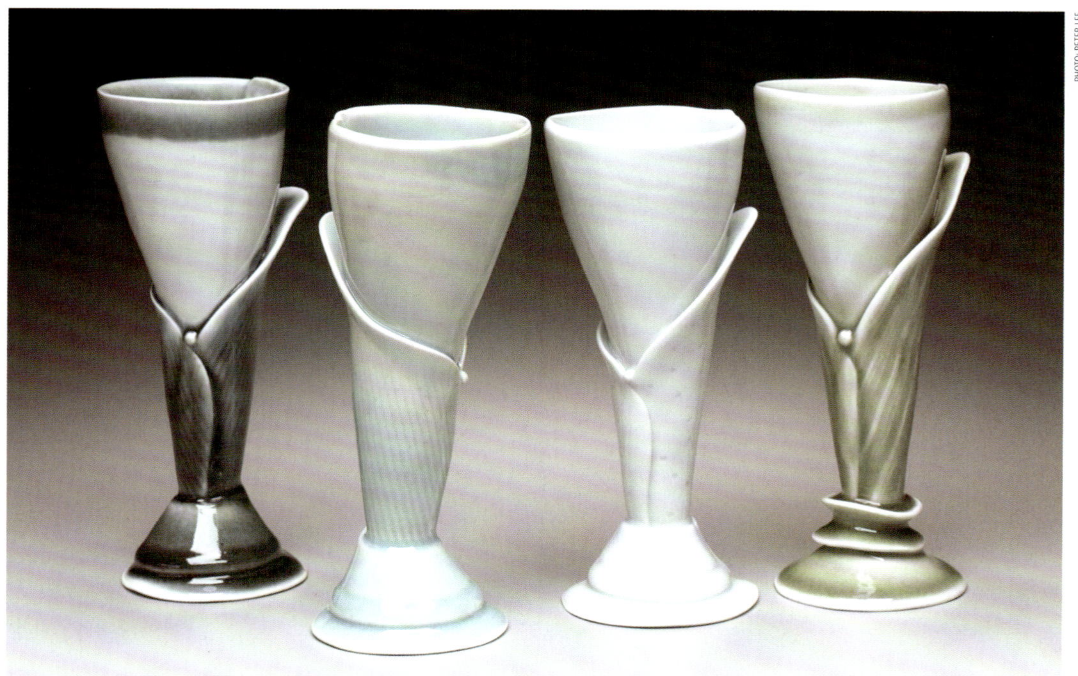
PHOTO: PETER LEE

Working with soft slabs allows handbuilt forms to have a sense of movement and to retain a feeling of softness even after they're fired. Using a soft slab to make a stemmed wine cup may seem a little intimidating, but it doesn't need to be. The design is up to you, but it's best to make a few prototypes first to get the balance and proportions worked out.

Prepping the Soft Slab

When making a slab for this project, compression is an essential step in preparation. Both the design of the cup form and the stem require curving the clay significantly. The better compressed your slab is, the less likely it is that it will crack. Roll your slab to between 3⁄16–1⁄4 inch thick and, using a medium-hard plastic rib, compress the slab in all directions on both sides (vertically, horizontally, and diagonally in both directions). Hold the rib at a 30° angle to the clay and draw it across the surface with moderate downward pressure. If the rib is leaving heavy marks as you work, you are pressing too hard. Cover the prepared slab with plastic and protect it from drafts so the edges don't dry unevenly.

Timing

There are three components of the wine stem that are made before assembling the piece. The order in which these are made is important. Make the base first, the stem second, and the cup last. This order gives the most set-up time to the support components that need to be firmer when you assemble the wine stem. Place each component under plastic as it is finished to keep the moisture content as similar as possible so that cracks don't form.

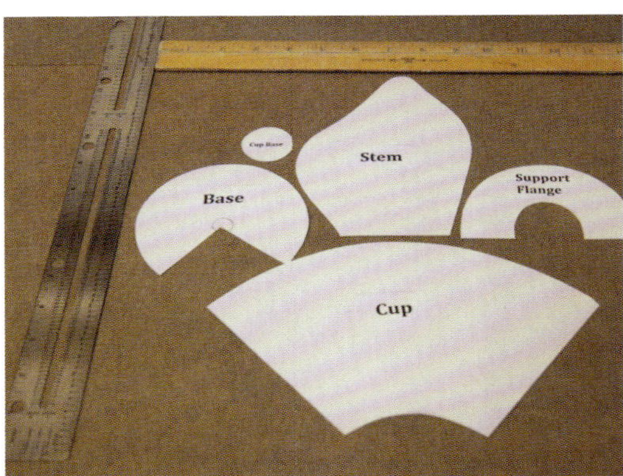

1. Make patterns using tag board or old file folders, then cut the shapes from a slab.

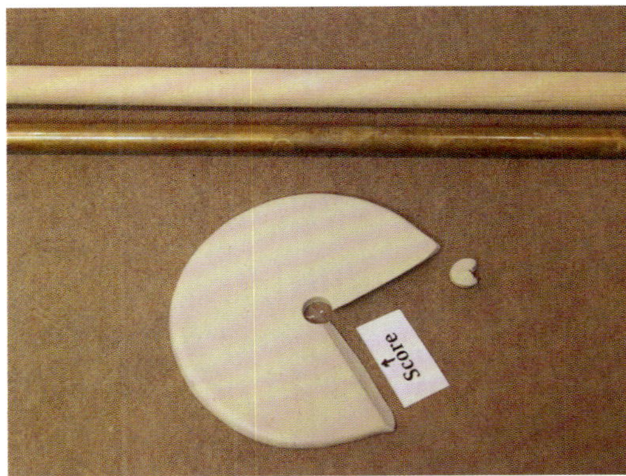

2. Cut a hole in the base where the two edges will meet as a seam using the metal tubing. Bevel each edge.

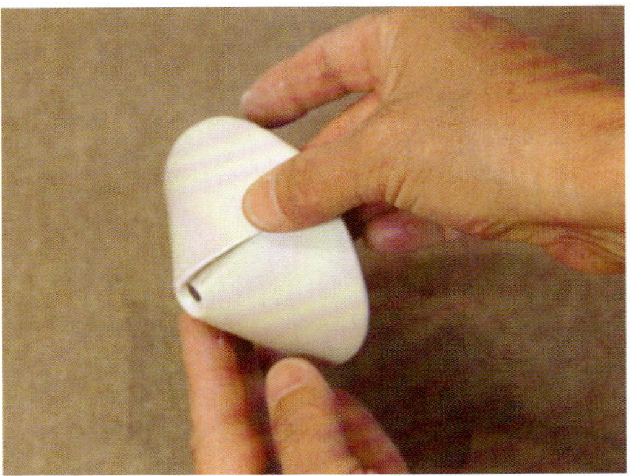

3. Score and slip the beveled edges, curve the cone, and press along the seam to tighten it securely.

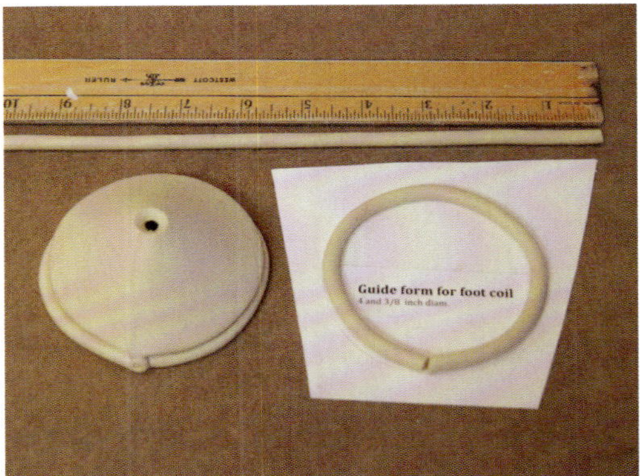

4. Make a coil, shape it around the template, score and slip the base, and set it onto the coil.

Using Paper Patterns

The pattern pieces I use for this form are made of tag board or old file folders (figure 1). This thicker paper allows the knife to cut smoothly and cleanly around the pattern. This material is inexpensive and easily replaced if it wears out. The cup is made using a curved, fan-shaped template designed so that the bottom opening is $1\frac{3}{8}$ inches in diameter. A separate, circular template of the same diameter covers the hole and creates the bottom of the cup. I use a semi-circular pattern to create the conical base, and it's designed so that the finished diameter of the flared bottom is $4\frac{1}{4}$ inches. The stem comes from a free-form leaf or petal-shaped pattern. Finally, a half-circle or rainbow-shaped pattern gives me a support flange that strengthens the joint between the stem and the conical base.

Once the patterns are ready to use, place them on your slab, and use a fettling knife to cut them out. As you work with each clay piece, compress all cut edges with your finger before you do anything else with the piece. This is important because cracks start on edges of pieces and compression heals any micro-cracks that may have formed as you made the initial cuts.

Assembling the Parts

Once you have all of the parts cut out, assemble the base cone. Start by beveling the seams. Beveled seams work particularly well for this project because they create a lot of contact area for a strong seam and they have enough "give" so that when you stretch or belly out pieces, they still hold well. To create a bevel on a soft-slab piece, I position a

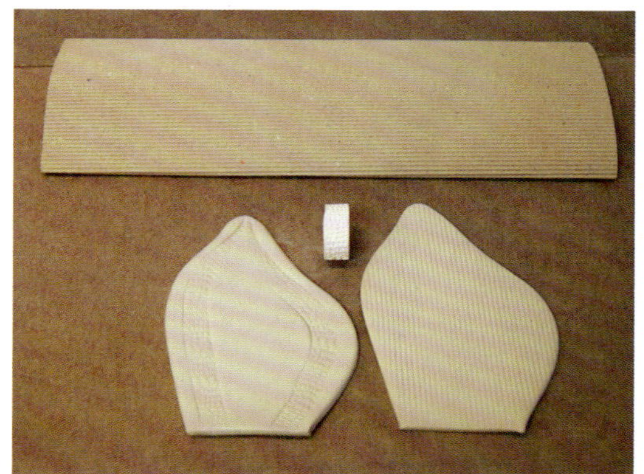

5. Create texture on the exterior of the stem with texture rollers, corrugated paper or fabric.

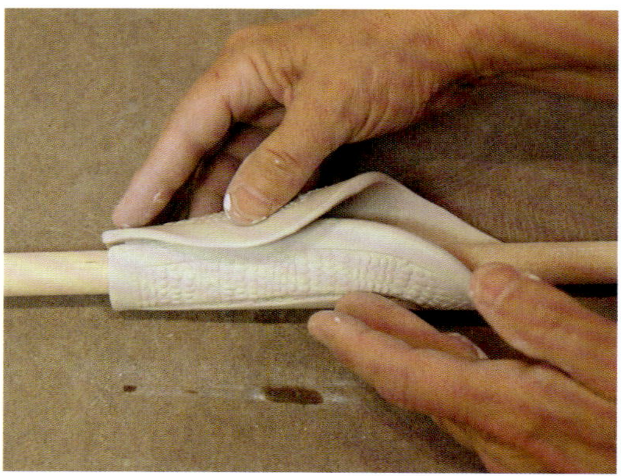

6. Wrap the rounded side of the stem over the straight side until the bevels overlap, add slip, and tack together.

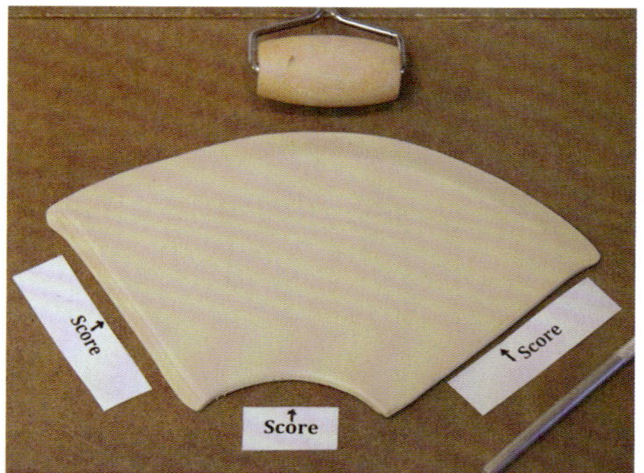

7. Thin the large curve in the cup pattern with a pony roller, then bevel the seam edges with a 1-inch dowel.

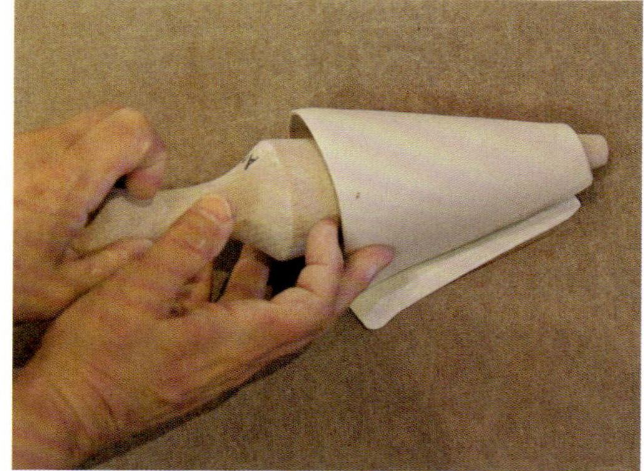

8. Score and slip the bevels on the slab and gently roll it around the chinois to form a cone. Tack the seam.

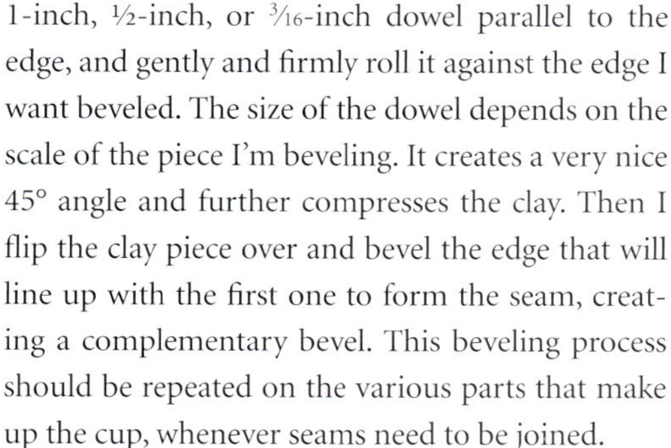

1-inch, ½-inch, or 3/16-inch dowel parallel to the edge, and gently and firmly roll it against the edge I want beveled. The size of the dowel depends on the scale of the piece I'm beveling. It creates a very nice 45° angle and further compresses the clay. Then I flip the clay piece over and bevel the edge that will line up with the first one to form the seam, creating a complementary bevel. This beveling process should be repeated on the various parts that make up the cup, whenever seams need to be joined.

Use a length of ½-inch diameter metal tubing to cut a hole in the base where the two edges will meet as a seam (figure 2). Bevel each edge of the seam with the ½-inch dowel. Remember to flip the piece over to make the second bevel. Score and slip the beveled edges, curve the slab into a cone, and tighten the seam securely (figure 3).

To create a more finished look to the bottom of the base and add a foot, make a 10-inch-long, 3/16-inch diameter coil. Either use a hand extruder with a die that size, or roll it out to around that diameter by hand. Shape the coil into a circle on a paper guide (4 3/16 inch in diameter) and join the two ends. Score and slip the underside of the cone, then set it firmly on the coil (figure 4). Set the completed base aside under plastic.

Assemble the stem next. Create texture on the exterior of the stem with texture rollers, corrugated paper, or fabric (figure 5). Bevel the lower half of the straight side of the stem with your finger on the textured side of the piece and bevel the lower third of the rounded side on the non-textured side this same way. Score both bevels. Using the ½-inch diameter dowel as shown, gently curve the rounded side of the stem piece over the straight side until the bevels overlap, add slip, and tack together (figure 6).

Keeping the ½-inch dowel in place, turn the stem upright and tighten the seam with your finger using the dowel for resistance. Gently stretch and curve the stem to take the shape of a calla lily or leaf. When done, place the stem on foam so it does not get misshapen and wrap it all in plastic.

Now you're ready to form the cup. The large curve in the cup pattern is the lip. In order to make this a nice, thin, tapered edge that's comfortable to drink from, press the rounded end of a pony roller into the lip as you roll it, following the contour of the slab. Bevel the straight sides (seam edges) with the 1-inch dowel (figure 7).

The side of the cup lip that has been thinned goes on the interior of the cup. Score and slip the beveled edges and gently roll the slab around a chinois pestle (a conical cooking tool with a bulbous handle) to form a cone (figure 8). Tack the seam together. With the chinois pestle still inside the cone form to support the shape, stand it up on the tapered end and hold the pestle against the inside of the seam. Press the seam together with your finger from the outside, ensuring a good join.

Remove the pestle from the cup and, using the bulbous end, work and stretch the interior until it is softly bellied out (figure 9). As you push out with the pestle, support the other side of the clay with your hand. Don't go all the way to the lip of the cup when bellying it. Score, slip, and attach the small circular slab to the bottom of the cup to seal it. Gently round the edge of the lip and set the cup aside, wrapped in plastic.

Assemble the stem and base next. Score the top of the base and the interior surface at the bottom of the stem. Slip both surfaces. Gently but firmly wiggle the base and stem together until there is a tight joint. Orient the base so that the seam is at the back of the stem piece (figure 10). Bevel the ends of the support flange (figure 11) then add it to the base and stem (figure 12). The support flange hides the joint and gives extra support to the stem. Don't wrap the flange too tightly as it's likely to be wetter than the

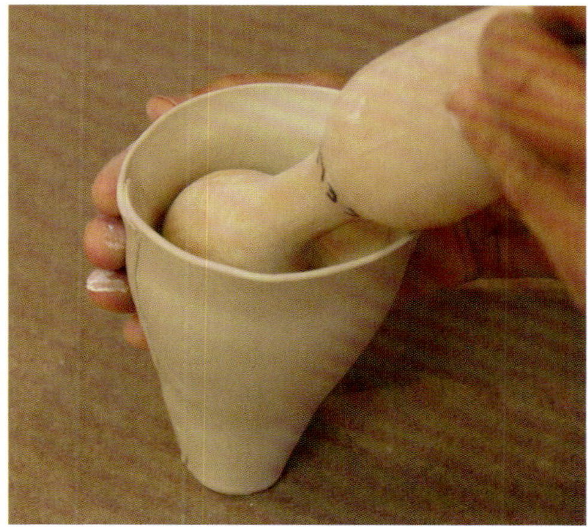

9. Using the bulbous end of the chinois, belly out the interior of the cup form.

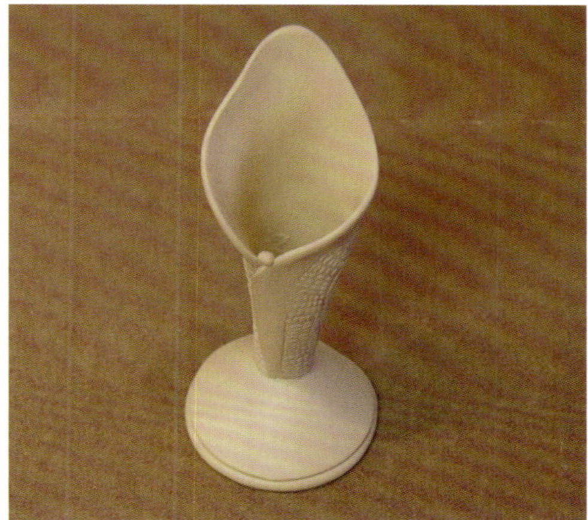

10. Score, slip, then wiggle the base and stem together until there is a tight joint.

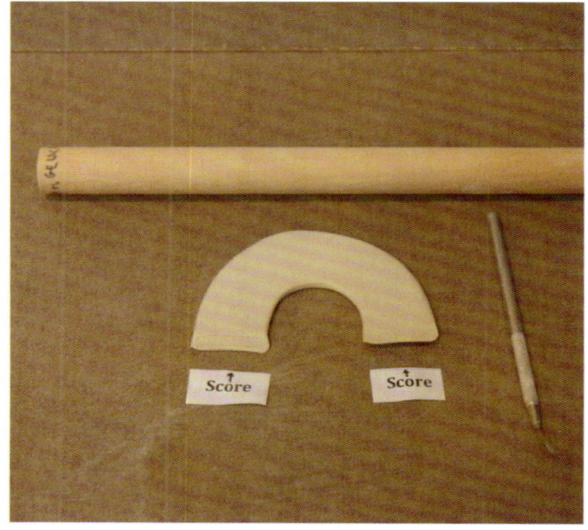

11. Bevel, score, and slip the ends of the flange.

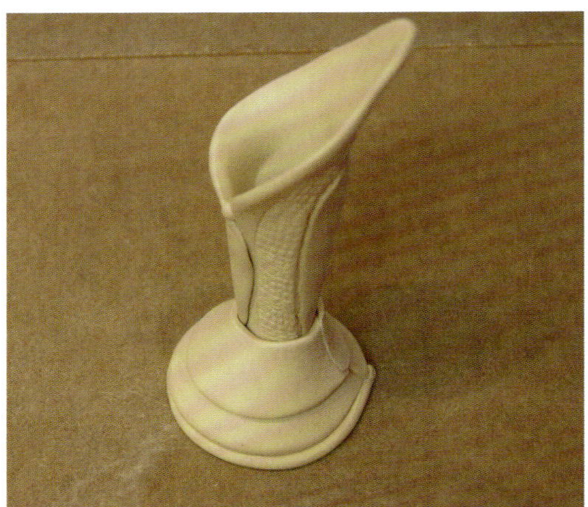

12. Wrap the flange around the stem in a conical shape. Line up the flange seam with the seam on the base.

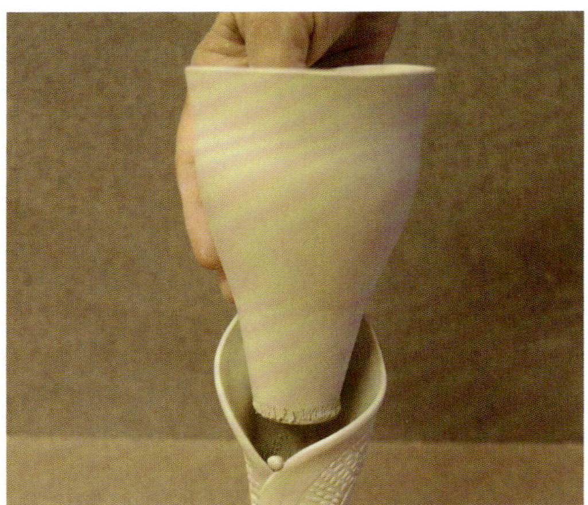

13. Score the cup and stem, add slip and gently but firmly push the cup into the opening in the stem.

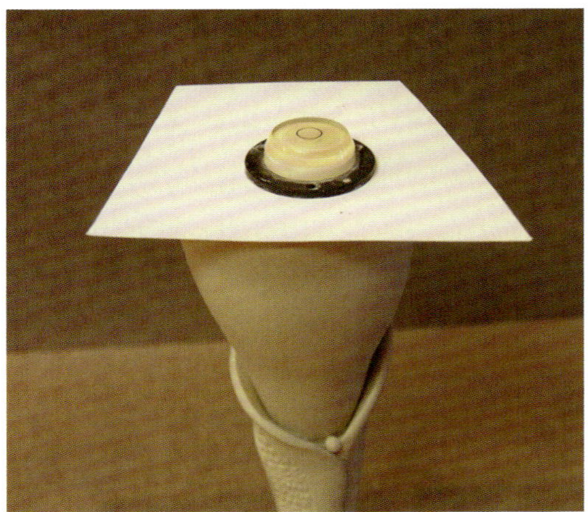

14. Place a piece of cardboard on top of the rim, then place a round level on top to make sure the cup is level.

stem. If it's too tight, it may crack as it dries and shrinks. Set the assembly aside to firm up.

Let this structure set up to soft leather hard. It should be firm enough so that it can hold the weight of the cup, but don't let it get so hard that it can't be moved or bent a little. Test how the cup and stem fit before beginning to score them. Score around the base of the cup and around the interior of the stem where the base will touch it (figure 13). Add the cup and then adjust the entire piece to assure that the cup is level. Place a round level on top of a light piece of tag board that covers the lip of the cup and adjust the cup/stem to be sure the cup is level (figure 14). This can also be done by eye by placing the piece on a banding wheel and gently adjusting the wine stem so it looks level from all angles. Wrap the piece tightly with slightly moist newspaper under the piece or put it in a damp box to let the components' moisture content even out. Dry slowly and avoid drafts.

I often make this work in a series so I don't get impatient and rush things. When I work on multiple pieces at once, by the time I have made the third set of components for the wine stems, the first base/stem is set up enough to add the cup.

Drying

Put the fully assembled wine stem into a damp box (with no drafts) for a few days. This will help even out the moisture in all the parts of the piece. If you don't have a damp box available, place the piece on slightly moist newspaper sheets and wrap well with plastic. Let the wine stem sit in either of these environments for a few days before taking it out of the damp box or removing the moist newspaper. Again rewrap the wine stem in plastic. Dry the piece slowly and away from drafts.

Glazing

Because the form itself is complex, the glazing need not be. These wine stems look elegant in a single glaze. If you want to make them reminiscent of the plant on which they are based, you can dip the stem in one color and the cup in another. I suggest a bit of the stem color be used on the rim of the cup to tie the piece together.

Advanced Techniques

UTENSIL HANDLES

by Kristin Pavelka

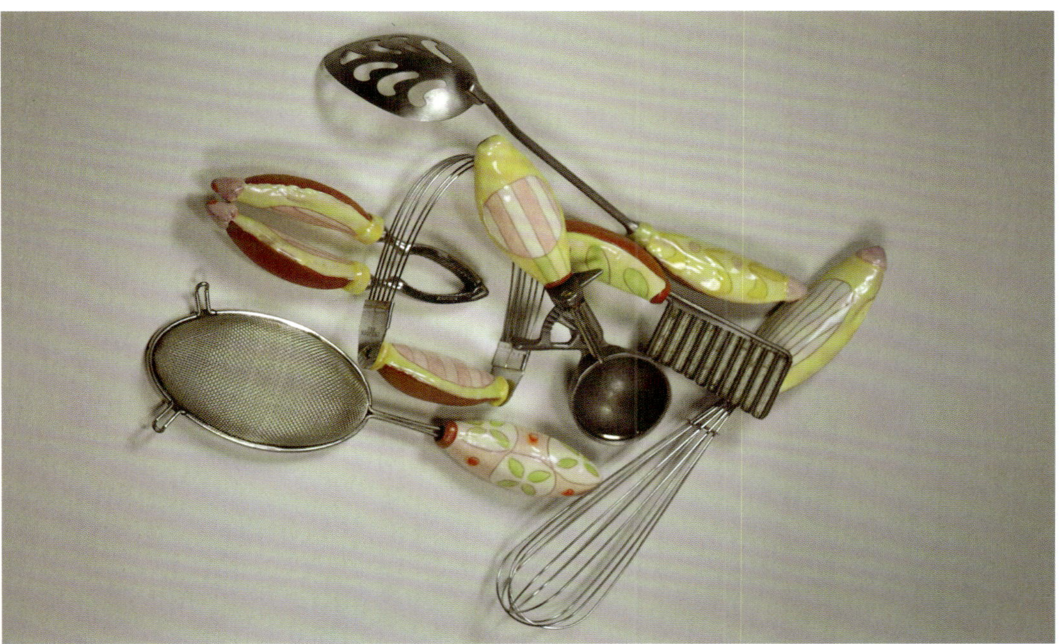

In an effort to produce a functional ceramic object that was more "earth friendly," I started tinkering around with combining vintage kitchen tools with my earthenware handles. This project combined my love of thrifting, vintage objects, and ceramics while being a little more "green." As a bonus, the kitchen tools are a fun addition to the daily cooking routine and make for wonderful conversation starters!

Sourcing and Cleaning

All the metal components of the kitchen tools are upcycled from mainly vintage kitchen utensils and gadgets that I've happened upon in my treasure hunts. I pick up spatulas, whisks, spoons, meat forks, pastry blenders, beaters, scoops, ladles, you name it, I probably have it in my stash. I am especially drawn to the old pieces from the 1930s–1950s, the ones with the painted wooden handles and interesting patterned blades. I like the quality of the metal more than that of new utensils, and I like the rich patina that has developed on the pieces over the years with use, much like a well-loved pot. If I stumble upon a utensil with a handle in nice condition, I won't replace the handle. I use only pieces with cracked, damaged or hideously ugly handles, therefore staying true to the spirit of upcycling—if it isn't broken, don't fix it.

Garage sales, estate sales, and thrift stores are the best places to score utensils at a reasonable price. Vintage shops are more expensive as are eBay and Etsy, but worth searching if you like the aesthetic of an earlier time. With some digging, you may still come across inexpensive pieces.

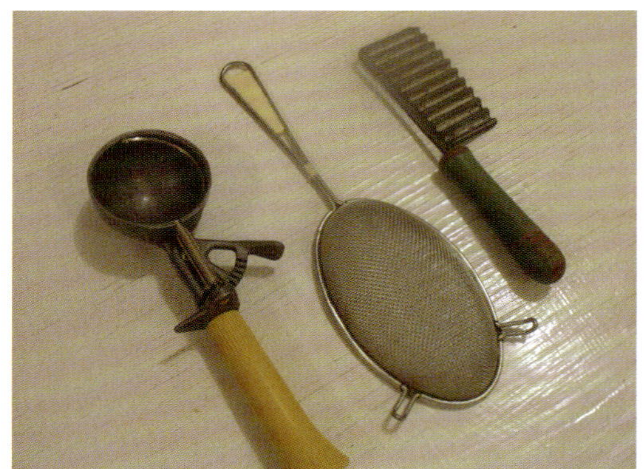

1. Choose a few of your collected utensils to design new handles for.

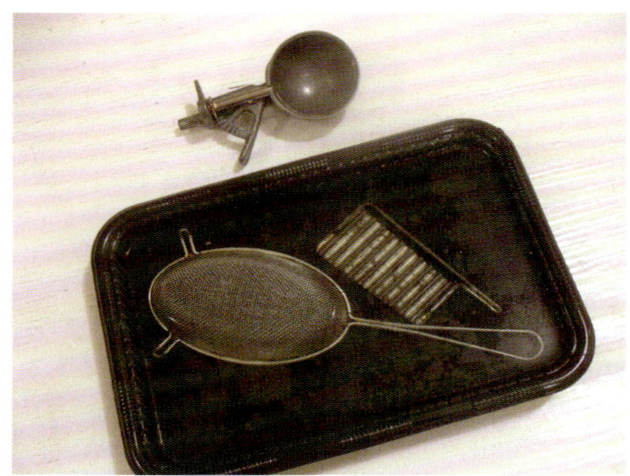

2. Remove the handles and soak the metal parts in white vinegar for ½ hour.

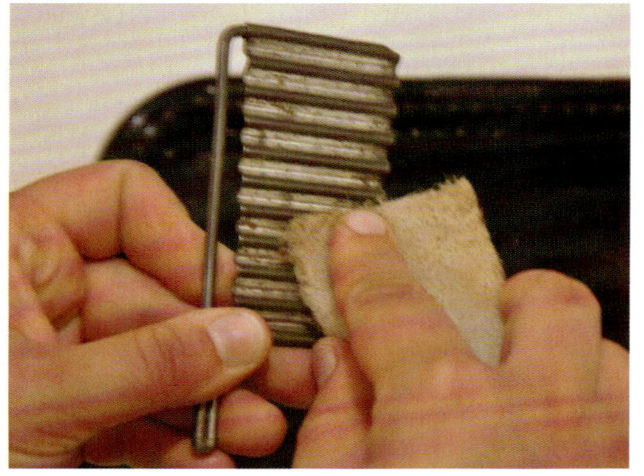

3. Scrub the surfaces with synthetic steel wool to remove stubborn residue.

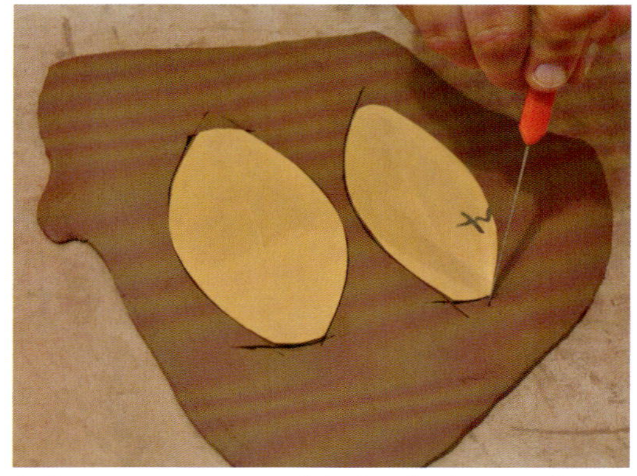

4. Create paper patterns of the handle shape, and cut them out of a clay slab.

Once you've accumulated a collection of utensils, choose a few to start with (figure 1), and detach the handle so that the entire metal piece can easily be cleaned. Some handles come off readily, others take a bit of muscle. For a plastic handle, try freezing the tool and then, wearing eye protection, crack the handle off with pliers or a hammer. If the shaft is long, sometimes I cut the metal piece off at the handle rather than struggle with removing it. If I'm lucky, the handles are wooden or already cracked and easily pulled off with a pair of pliers, broken down with a hammer, or cut off with a saw. A hacksaw is useful for cutting thick gauge metal and tin snips or a wire cutter works well for thick wire.

Next you'll want to clean the metal parts. Yes, patina can be nice, but lots of rust or gunked-on grease and food is not. To remove rust and residue, soak the metal parts in white vinegar for a half hour (figure 2) and then scrub with a bit of steel wool (figure 3). The synthetic steel wool I use doesn't mar the surface and removes only the grunge and rust. If the residue doesn't release after the first scrub, soak a bit longer and scrub again.

Design Work

Once the metal is clean, design a new handle. I think about the length that I want the tool to be and the size of the handle in relationship to the size of the blade. As you design, think about whether there is a design element from the metal component that could be brought into the handle. Slotted spoons and spatulas demand some patterning on the handle that either echoes or contrasts the pierced designs, or balances the larger, metal component end visually. The surface design must be considered in the physical handle design to help

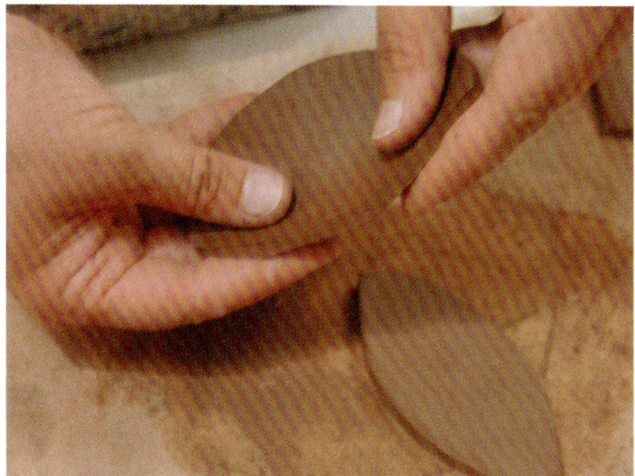

5. Push out on the inside of each pod-shaped slab to create volume.

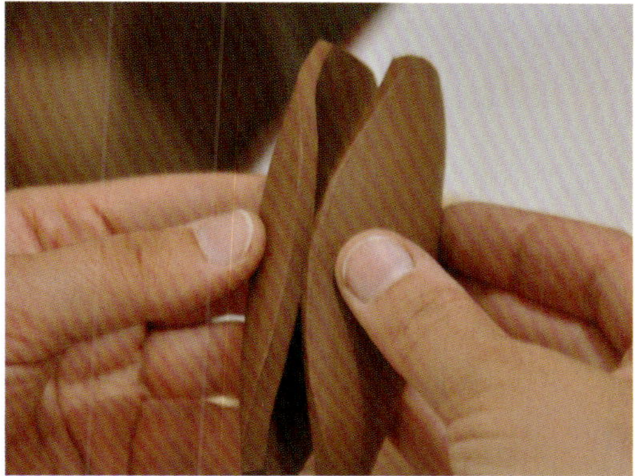

6. Press the two halves together around the curved edges.

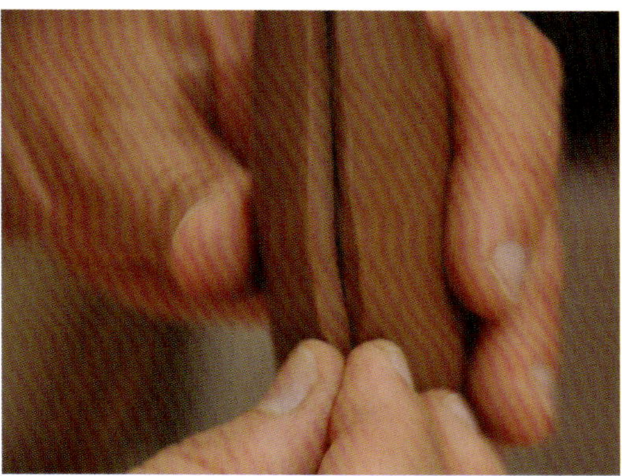

7. Pinch the edges together with your fingertips, trapping air within.

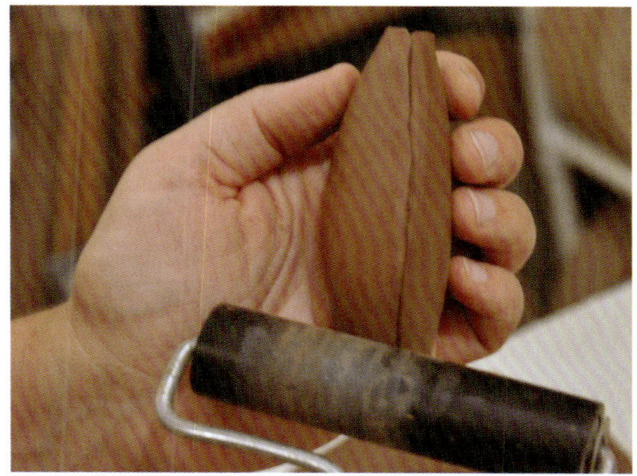

8. Use a small brayer to compress the seams while leaving the join visible.

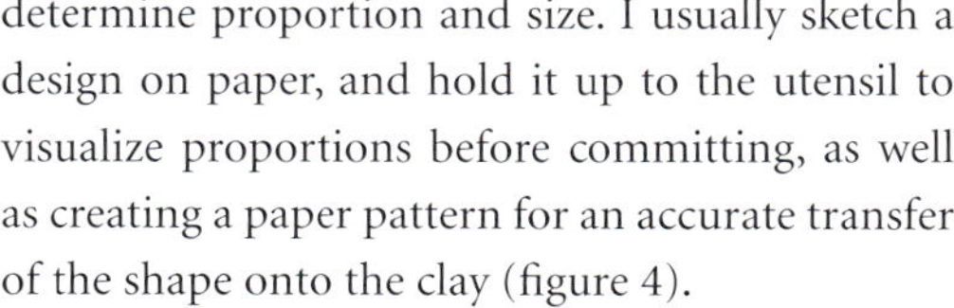

determine proportion and size. I usually sketch a design on paper, and hold it up to the utensil to visualize proportions before committing, as well as creating a paper pattern for an accurate transfer of the shape onto the clay (figure 4).

Forming Handles

I enjoy the hollow pod shape as a handle because it feels nice in the hand, it's symmetrical, there's an animal quality to it, like that of a turtle shell, lending itself to some fun decorating decisions. The pods are comprised of two slabs, about ¼ inch in thickness, that are pushed out from the inside to create a curved volume (figure 5), pressed together around the curved edges (figure 6), then pinched together with my fingertips, trapping air within (figure 7). As the clay is very soft, no slip is needed for the joint. I use a small printing brayer to compress the seams (figure 8), but leave the evidence of the joint visible to create a nice dividing line. A small disc is joined to the end of the handle where the metal element will be attached after firing (figure 9). Using a wooden kidney rib, I press along the seam to create a more uniform and defined line (figure 10). The handle is curved by pulling down on the ends with one hand and up on the middle with the other hand (figure 11). Then it is left to set up to leather hard.

With an appropriately-sized drill bit (I used a ⅜-inch bit), create an opening for the connection to the metal piece (allowing for shrinkage), that will accommodate the metal shaft of the tool (figure 12). I compress and taper the edge of the hole with a soft rubber-tipped cleanup tool (figure 13). This opening is checked throughout the drying process and tweaked as necessary.

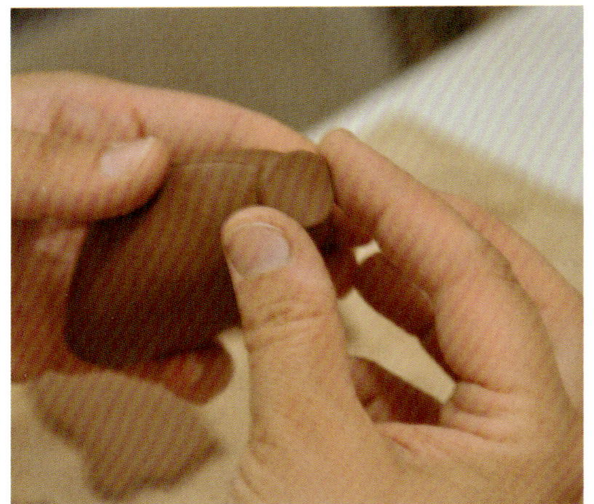

9. Attach a disk to the end of the handle where the metal utensil will connect.

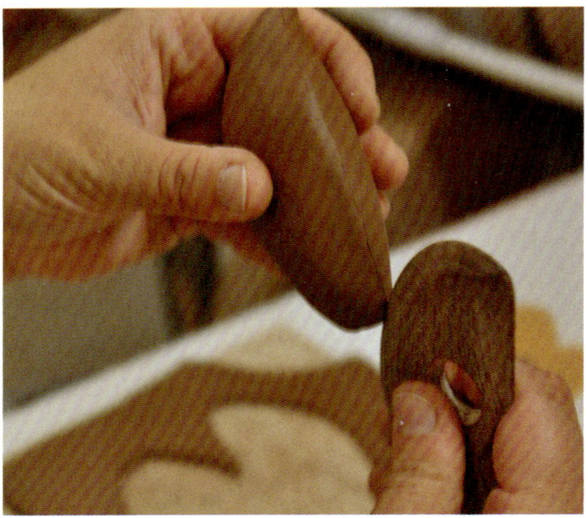

10. Press along the seam where the two halves were joined using a wooden kidney rib to define the line.

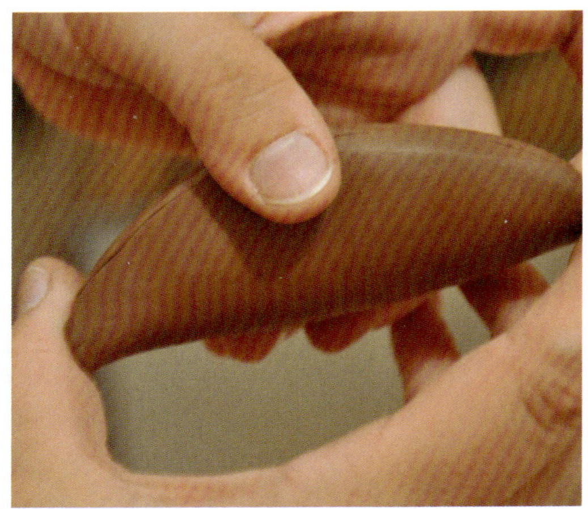

11. Curve the handle by pulling down on the ends with one hand and up on the top middle with the other.

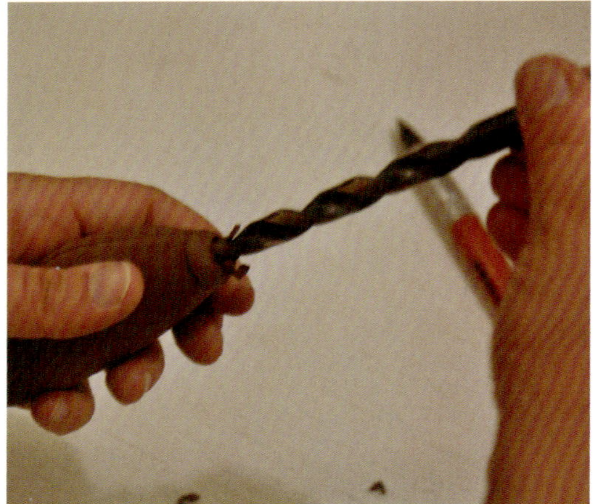

12. With a drill bit, create an opening in the leather-hard handle through the circular disc of clay on the end.

Finishing and Firing

Once the handle is dry, I dip my handles in red terra sigillata then apply slip with a soft brush on the underside (figure 14), but handles can be decorated and glazed just like any functional piece. Check the hole once more to make sure the shaft of the tool fits while also leaving some wiggle room for shrinkage. Bisque and glaze fire to your liking. I always leave one area of the utensil unglazed so that the handle can be positioned on the kiln shelf without the need for stilts. As the forms are long and slender, an internal firing prop may be required for your form, so plan ahead as you design, and build a custom prop or stilt to fire along with your handle in the bisque and glaze firing.

Uniting the Old and the New

Once the completed handle is out of the glaze firing, check to make sure the metal component still fits (figure 15). Fine tuning with a Dremel grinding bit on the hole may help the fit, otherwise the metal can also be filed to fit. If necessary, shorten the stem or shaft of the utensil to maintain the right balance and proportions (figure 16). I look for a sense of proportion that is pleasing to my eye that creates a good feel in the hand. Filling the ce-

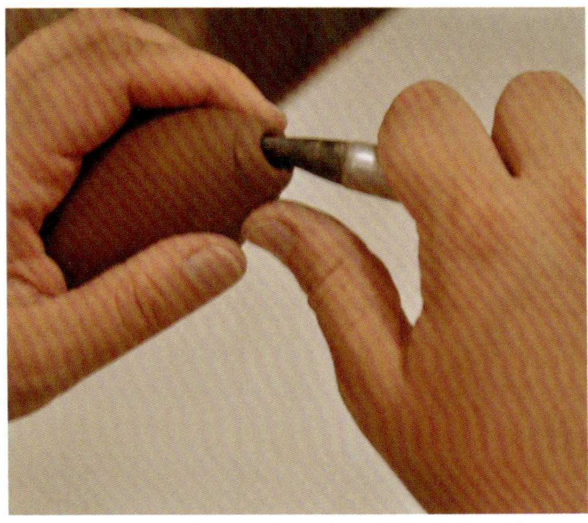

13. Compress and taper the edge of the hole with a soft rubber-tipped tool.

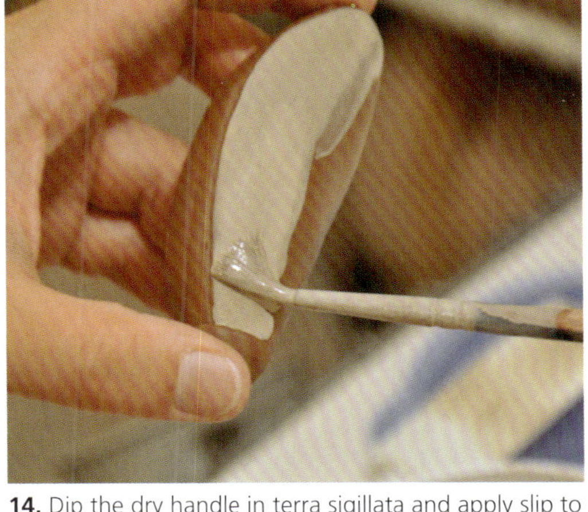

14. Dip the dry handle in terra sigillata and apply slip to the underside with a soft brush.

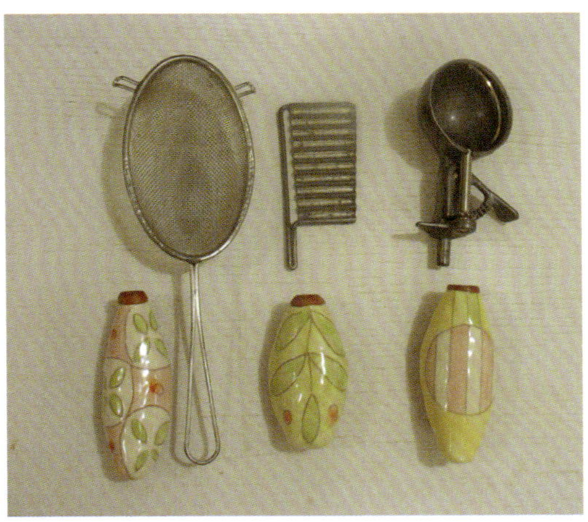

15. Check the fit and proportions of the metal component end after the glaze firing.

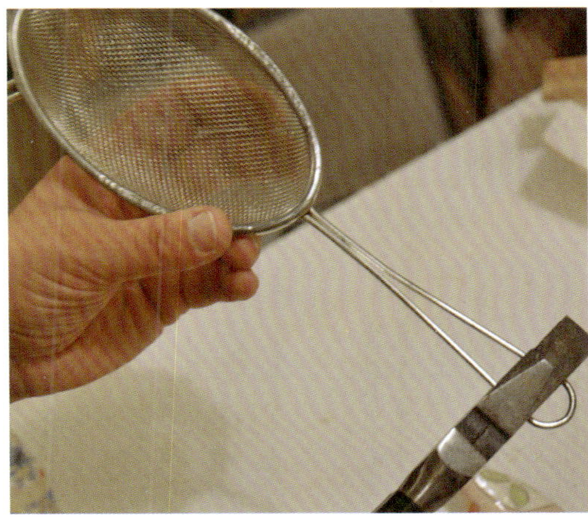

16. Shorten the stem or shaft of the utensil to maintain the right balance or proportion using pliers if necessary.

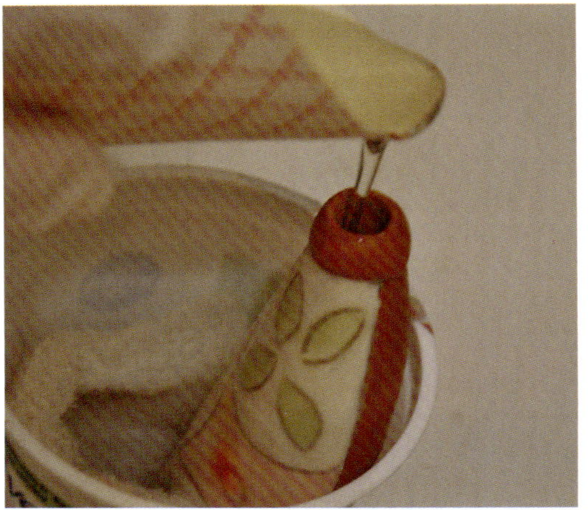

17. Prop up the handle and pour in casting resin until the handle is about ¾ full.

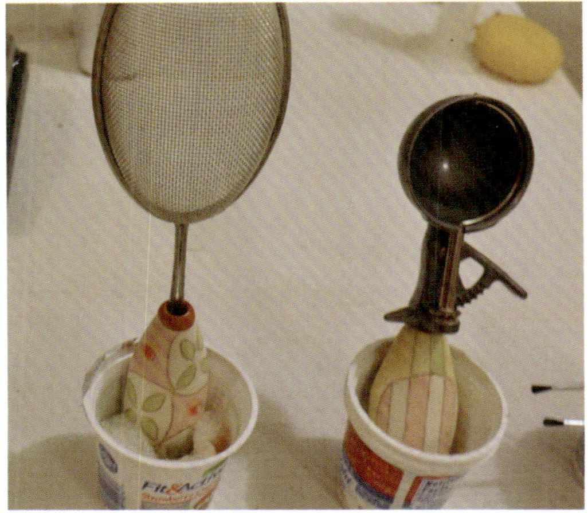

18. Insert the utensil shaft into the handle, and prop it up so the handle and implement are in alignment.

ramic handle with resin gives the piece a nice heft and weight in the handle, almost like the user is giving the utensil a handshake. If you find that a lot of tweaking is necessary to get the utensil end into the handle, it might be easier to make another handle with the appropriate hole-sizing revisions. Save the first handle for a future utensil.

To secure the metal in place, I use a casting resin inside the handle (Castin' Craft Clear Liquid Plastic Casting Resin). I've also used silicone aquarium sealant, but when visible, it's a little too cloudy and a little too flexible. The casting resin is labeled as being food safe. Handmade objects require a little more care, so I would opt to hand wash these utensils over using a dishwasher.

Prepare the resin according to the directions, and be sure to follow safety tips listed on the package. Mixing in a well-ventilated area, I fill my hollow handle about ¾ full using a disposable paper container (figure 17) and then insert the metal shaft. I prop it so both the handle and implement are in alignment and facing the appropriate direction (figure 18). Once the resin has cured, I do a final fill in with a bit more resin. Allow the final pour to cure, and enjoy your upcycled kitchen tool at the next potluck!

Sources for Utensils *by Jessica Knapp*

If you have a handle design and want to order new utensil heads/attachments instead of sourcing and retrofitting older ones, you have a couple of options for purchasing manufactured components.

Ceramic supplier Aftosa (www.aftosa.com) in Richmond, California offers several stainless steel utensils that can be purchased and used along with handles of your own design. Once on the site, click on the utensils link in the accessories section. The handle end of each utensil consists of a tang that you can affix into a handmade handle using epoxy (Aftosa recommends E-6000 adhesive for solid handles. Pavelka recommends Castin' Craft Clear Liquid Plastic Casting Resin for hollow handles).

- George Luxner & Sons (www.luxnerblades.com), located in Merrick, New York offers Sheffield stainless knife blades and other utensils (including cake servers, carving sets, letter openers and cheese blades) for use with custom handles.
- Woodcraft (www.woodcraft.com) has knife sets, flatware, and ceramic knife blades that can be mounted into custom handles. Search the website for knife making kits.
- Rowecraft (www.rowecraft.com) links to Woodcraft's offerings but also has garden tool components. Search the Project Supplies section for woodturning kits.
- Craft Supplies USA (woodturnerscatalog.com) has serving utensils and other items on the kitchenware project kits section of the website.

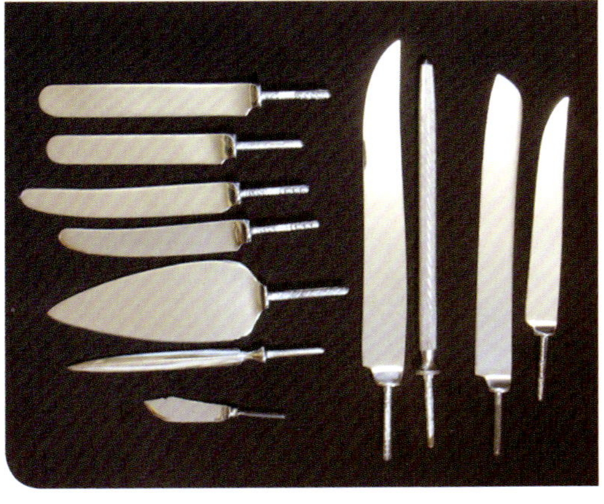

Sheffield stainless knife blades and utensil blanks from George Luxner and Sons. Photo courtesy of George Luxner & Sons (www.luxnerblades.com).